SPONTANEOUS REVOLUTIONS

SEEING AMERICA ONE PEDAL AT A TIME

LIZA MCQUADE

BALBOA.PRESS
A DIVISION OF HAY HOUSE

Copyright © 2022 Liza McQuade.

All rights reserved. No part of this book may be used or reproduced by any means, graphic, electronic, or mechanical, including photocopying, recording, taping or by any information storage retrieval system without the written permission of the author except in the case of brief quotations embodied in critical articles and reviews.

Balboa Press books may be ordered through booksellers or by contacting:

Balboa Press
A Division of Hay House
1663 Liberty Drive
Bloomington, IN 47403
www.balboapress.com
844-682-1282

Because of the dynamic nature of the Internet, any web addresses or links contained in this book may have changed since publication and may no longer be valid. The views expressed in this work are solely those of the author and do not necessarily reflect the views of the publisher, and the publisher hereby disclaims any responsibility for them.

The author of this book does not dispense medical advice or prescribe the use of any technique as a form of treatment for physical, emotional, or medical problems without the advice of a physician, either directly or indirectly. The intent of the author is only to offer information of a general nature to help you in your quest for emotional and spiritual well-being. In the event you use any of the information in this book for yourself, which is your constitutional right, the author and the publisher assume no responsibility for your actions.

Any people depicted in stock imagery provided by Getty Images are models, and such images are being used for illustrative purposes only. Certain stock imagery © Getty Images.

Print information available on the last page.

ISBN: 978-1-9822-5681-4 (sc)
ISBN: 978-1-9822-5683-8 (hc)
ISBN: 978-1-9822-5682-1 (e)

Library of Congress Control Number: 2022904580

Balboa Press rev. date: 06/09/2022

This book is dedicated to my biking partner,
husband, friend, lover, and soulmate.
Robert "Clark" Campbell
January 9, 1948–December 29, 2010
I will always love you.
Liza

CONTENTS

Foreword xi
About Bud Clark xiii
Acknowledgments xv
The Spark That Never Died xix

Week 1 1
   And So It Begins 1
   A Day of Firsts 6
   Should We Quit Now? 10
   Oranges, Dogs, and More Self-Doubt 13
Week 2 20
   Never Wallpaper a Room Together 20
   Backroads & Camping 22
   America the Beautiful 26
   Eavesdropping 29
   Ocean Lullaby 33
   Eyes Up Here, Mister 37
   Busted 41
Week 3 43
   Goodbye, Pacific Ocean 43
   It's the Journey, Not the Destination 45
   The Helpful Hippie 47
   Old Goats, New Tricks 52
   Entering Cowboy Country 57
   Mistaken for Drainbows 61

Week 4 67
  Chuckles 67
  The Rude Awakening 75
  Where's Wally? 78
  In Search of Happiness and the Two-Pass Day 81
  Day 23 and Still in Oregon 83
  Interstate Madness 85
  Tan Fat Is Prettier Than Marshmallow Flab 88
Week 5 90
  Water Shortage & Attack of the Mosquitoes 90
  Snake Country 97
  Who Knew? Hayden Hates Mushrooms 99
  Oh, Hail 101
  Nothing Hurt 105
  Humpty Dumpty Joins the Parade 106
  Good Friends and Fresh Trout 111
Week 6 112
  Twirlwind Vacation Shoes 112
  Is That a Bear Outside Our Tent? 114
  Elk Dung Fire and Other Camping Tips 121
  Foiling the She-Devil 125
  The Spirit Grows Even Though the Wallet Diminishes 129
  The Pork Chop Incident 131
  Layers of Time 137
Week 7 142
  Tackling the 9,000-Foot Mountain 142
  Horsing Around 150
  Crop-Destroying Devils 151
  Leiterville Country Club 153
  Clark Saves the Day 156
  Naked Rain Dance 160
Week 8 165
  Biting Flies on the Rise 165
  Killer Cowboy 168
  I Got Me One of Them 173
  Hill City Hell 175

- Steve..178
- Floating on Water...183
- Mosquito Merengue...188

Week 9...192
- Free Camping...192
- Hospital Breakfast 194
- The Kindness of Others..199
- Huron In 206
- Magnet Lady 208
- Liza Takes Another Header 212
- Beige Edna...215

Week 10...223
- Iron Horse Connection...223
- Son of Monster Face..225
- Psycho Killer?..228
- Speckled Hands 232
- Darts with the Boy Next Door...235

Week 11...238
- Synchronized Mowers 238
- Hysterical Markers...241
- Haunted House...243
- Duped by a Dalmatian..247
- Town Scandals 250
- We're Not Leavin' Till We're Heavin' 252
- Look at the Legs on That Girl!..255

Week 12...261
- How to Dislodge a Cockroach from a Human Ear 261
- You Can Go PP If You Want...263
- The Green, Green Grass of Home.......................................265
- Memory Lane and Butter Burgers.......................................273
- Turtle Woman...275

Week 13...279
- At a Crossroads with No Clue 279
- One Pedal at a Time...281
- Snap, Snap, Snap 284
- Meeting the Postals..290

    Fairy Houses and the Land of Million Dollar Sunsets................294
    "Hey, Lady! Nice Equipment!"..299
    Hypnotized Zombies and the Toilet Team 302
Week 14..313
    Nothing Works Better for a Tummy Ache than Donuts............313
    A Leisurely Labor Day 316
    Loonies and Toonies, Eh?..317
    The Ride-and-Dive Method...321
    Babble … Chew … Babble … Chew … Tilt............................325
    Clark's Nose Knows 328
    Sometimes Food is Funny...331
Week 15..336
    The Ketchup and Mustard Map 336
    Rottie Man...339
    Lunatics Outside the Door..344
    A Few Miles, a New World...350
    The Way to a Man's Heart..354
    Bartering Gone Bad 355
    Celebrity Status and Then the Fall from Grace.......................361
Week 16..368
    It's Hard to Argue with Sore Buns 368
    Three Dog Day...370
    "Another Full Moon and I'm Still in Love with You"..................373
    The Butterfly Whisperer...377
    Olympic Dreams..383
    Misconceptions and Liars 384
    The Plastic Tempest and Cyclone Woman 388
Week 17..393
    Humpty Dumpty Falls Again...393
    The Grim Reaper..397
    Hello, Neighbor 402
    Twin Lobsters..404
    An Unexpected Invitation...407
    An Unfortunate Accident and Über Peepers 412

Week 18..418
    Hard to Leave, But Time to Go..418
    Off Again, On Again..422
    Laughing Fever 423
    Glam Girl and the Chorus 430
    The Trip-and-Fall Café..435
    Portland to Portland in 122 Days..438

Epilogue...441
The Return...443
Our Route - Portland, OR to Portland, ME 447
The Author...449

FOREWORD

"WOW," was my first reaction when Liza McQuade wrote to me about her book, *Spontaneous Revolutions: Seeing America One Pedal at a Time*. A spontaneous trip across America on a bike. Liza and her husband Clark had a huge idea, but to follow through and carry it out was an even bigger endeavor, a challenge, especially on bicycles.

Liza kept an audio journal of the 122-day trip from Portland, Oregon to Portland, Maine. They pedaled across America together -- over 3,000 miles -- a longer distance than Lewis and Clark traveled in 1805. With a keen eye, Liza gives the reader delightful descriptions of the interesting characters they meet across the continent, their dips in the Pacific and Atlantic Oceans, their ups and downs, determination, the process of getting in shape, bicycle woes, where to stay (camp or motel) -- all the things they did not plan for because ... they did not plan.

Liza also offers observations and sidebars of interesting historical descriptions of the geography, points of interest and towns they travel through. Hers is a travel book like no other since it is at the level and speed of bicycles that keeps you looking forward to "what's next?"

I think most of us have thoughts of adventures we would like to have. I know I do. I don't have a Bucket List, but if I did, a bike ride adventure across the United States would be on it. I am too old to do it now, but low and behold; I did it vicariously via Liza's wonderfully written book.

If I had taken Liza's advice in 1948, when I was 18 years old, I might have made it over the Blue Mountains east of Pendleton to visit my Grandmother Edna. The plan was to bike from Portland, OR to see my grandmother in Boise, ID, but no, I gave up my trek at 200 miles from Portland and put my bike, a pre-WWII, two-speed bike, and myself, on a Greyhound in Pendleton to ride the last 200 miles to Boise by bus! So, I sort of know what it is like to bike across this beautiful country.

The course of the trip across the continent roughly follows the 45th parallel with north and south deviations, even a short northern visit into Canada. Too bad I did not get all the exercise and physical training that Liza and Clark did, but I enjoyed every minute of their trip from my comfortable chair. When the pair put their bike wheels into the waters of the Atlantic Ocean, as they had put those same wheels in the Pacific waters, and hugged, it brought tears to my eyes.

Liza's book is a gift to carry me on from 1948 and travel the 3,200 miles across America to Portland, Maine from my home in Portland, Oregon -- one page at a time. Thanks, Liza.

I hope you enjoy the book as much as I did.

Whoop! Whoop!!
Bud Clark

ABOUT BUD CLARK

John Elwood "Bud" Clark, Jr. was born in Nampa, Idaho, December 19, 1931. Bud became an icon in Portland, Oregon. He was Mayor of the city for two terms, owned and operated Goose Hollow Inn with his family, was co-founder of the Neighbor newspaper, now the Northwest Examiner, and was the raincoat-wearing model for the classic poster "Expose Yourself to Art."

Bud ran for Mayor with almost no political experience, but helmed Portland with resounding success, earning an award as the best managed city of its size in the United States. Bud always maintained a wonderful spirit of adventure and can-do attitude. His colorful style and popular appeal even gained him a spot on the Johnny Carson show in October 1994. The eccentric Mayor commuted to work on his bicycle and was known for his vociferous "Whoop, Whoop!"

Bud bought the now-famous restaurant, Goose Hollow Inn in 1967. Budweiser recognized "The Goose" for selling more of their beer per square foot than any other tavern in the U.S. Sadly, Bud passed away February 1, 2022 but his spirit lives on at the pub and all-around Portland.

ACKNOWLEDGMENTS

I would like to start by thanking the two key people who made this journey and, resulting book, possible. First, love and gratitude to my late husband, Clark Campbell, whose spontaneous nature and willingness to risk the unknown for a shared adventure made this incredible bicycle trip possible.

The greatest measure of gratitude for helping me finish this book goes to one of my oldest and dearest friends, Ann Sprague. I could never have completed this project without her encouragement, patience, brilliance, sense of humor, kindness, love, understanding and support. It was healing for me to relive this journey alongside someone who knows and understands me. I can never adequately thank her for all she did to make this possible.

A million thanks to Dale Sprague at Canyon Creative for being the inspiration for all the design elements including the book cover, map, and photos. And for all the creative ideas, enthusiasm and support over the years. As well as allowing me to monopolize so much of Ann's time and energy.

Thank you to my mom, Marjory Panetti, who never tired of hearing me read sections of the book and website over and over. She helped make numerous small changes that added up to a big difference in the final copy.

Much appreciation to my dad and stepmother, Al and Mary Grube, who hosted us in their home during the trip and never doubted for a moment we could do this ride successfully.

A heartfelt thanks to my sister, Lauren Grube, who took care of matters at home, while we travelled unplugged. She was an ardent supporter of both the ride and writing process and never seemed to lose enthusiasm no matter how many times I stopped and started this project.

Deepest gratitude goes out to my stepkids, Ryan and Taea Campbell, and my daughter in-law, Allison Campbell. They never stopped getting excited about this book and continued to believe in me, even when I didn't believe in myself.

Hats off to the late, great Larry Hinds, who house-sat our 150-pound dog, Mozart and spitfire cat, Phil. He kept his good humor despite the fact that the animals outsmarted him on a regular basis. The stories still bring me joy!

Many thanks to my dear friends who let us stay with them for three or four days along the route, while we healed our sore muscles, fixed our bikes and procrastinated our return to the road. In each case, they allowed us free reign of their homes, automobiles and refrigerators. They include: Carol and Drew Barney, Sue and Chuck Cooper, Carla and David Marshall, Joanna and Kelly Redfearn and Carol and Keith Waller.

Reams of gratitude goes to Lubosh Chech who stepped in mid stream to design my book cover. His creativity and open communication made this important step so much easier.

Appreciation to Sarah Fortener from Nicely Creative Services for doing the final edit and displaying ultimate patience both with my slowness in getting her the required pages and continually making a mess of them.

Thank you to Gale Bonnell, who did an early read of Spontaneous Revolutions and offered her wise advice for how to make it better. Kim Hefty and Chris Fowler who lent us their tent and bicycling wisdom despite the fact they barely knew us. Sarah Vandervoort for scanning all my pictures into readable computer files. The fine folks at Balboa Press. And to my many instructors at Marylhurst University who helped build my writing confidence.

Cheers to my two computer gurus, Sherri Curley and Jonathan Hecht who always make themselves available and remain patient despite my continuous computer frustrations and issues. Never once have they laughed at my stupid questions.

A credit to photographer Sarah Eastlund who took my author photo and put me at ease by teaching me to stick my neck out and look like a chicken.

Thanks to the many members of Willamette Writers who made concrete suggestions for improving the direction of this book and website. I am especially appreciative for the advice and encouragement to stay with my own vision of the story.

A monster credit goes out to all the kind and wonderful people who supported us along the way: offering shelter, roadside assistance, buying us meals or honking and cheering as we struggled uphill or through inclement weather. You will never know how much you added to our journey!

And finally, a special note to my grandkids, Arwen Campbell and Ari and Avery Jackson, as well as any kiddos who may come along later. I hope as you grow you'll get a chance to know your grandfather, Clark, and find inspiration for your own journey through the pages of this book.

THE SPARK THAT NEVER DIED

Thank you ... you're amazing ... I love you ...

Those were my husband's final words before he slipped out of my reach and crossed to the other side.

~

A few weeks earlier, I came home and found Clark sitting in a chair, ashen faced.

"You don't look good," I told him when I walked in the door that December afternoon.

"I don't feel so good," he answered.

"Hospital?" I asked.

"Probably," he said.

This was unusual for him. Clark wasn't one to run to the doctor easily. So, if he was saying yes to that, I knew it was bad.

I got a nurse on the phone and gave her a brief rundown. "Get him to the hospital now," she said.

I jumped into action.

Moments later, we were in the car and on the way. Clark was in so much pain, he could barely speak. I got him inside with the help of a wheelchair and waited. Then waited, and waited some more.

"Can you do anything for his pain?" I asked the woman behind the admitting desk.

"We'll call you when the doctor can take him," she said brusquely, smacking her gum as she talked.

"Can I speak with a nurse?" I asked, annoyed.

"I am a nurse," she told me.

I walked back to Clark, who was in such pain, he had to hold onto me to sit up. I fixed a steady gaze on another nurse. It worked!

"Let me see what I can do to get him checked in faster," nurse number two said.

Soon he was taken to a private room and admitted to the hospital.

~

It took several days to discover that Clark had a blood clot in his intestinal vein. The plan was to attack it with drugs. Surgery was a consideration, but that would be an option down the road. They started the therapy immediately.

Later that evening, alert but in pain, Clark suggested I go home to rest. He was in good hands and needed to sleep himself, so I agreed and left.

I barely slept.

The phone rang at midnight.

"Well, he made it through surgery," said the voice on the other end of the line.

I didn't know he was in surgery. It had been an emergency decision. And, as it turned out, a good one. The doctor saved his life and brought Clark back to me.

"He's in intensive care, resting," the doctor told me. "You don't have to come right now. Wait until morning."

Of course I returned to the hospital immediately.

Clark was unconscious. They told me he didn't know I was there. He was restless and breathing erratically.

I whispered in his ear, "Fight, Clark, fight!"

He tossed and turned, pulling at the straps that pinned him down for his own protection.

"You're going to get through this," I encouraged. "But you need to fight with everything you've got!"

My words seemed to agitate him more.

~

Over the next week, I popped in and out of intensive care to visit Clark. His medical team advised letting him rest. One senior nurse explained, when loved ones are in the room continuously, many patients—even if unconscious—try to stay awake. That made sense, so I went back and forth, visiting him in short spurts at all hours.

In his moments of lucidity, I asked if he wanted visitors. He shook his head no. I imagined he didn't want people to worry.

I changed my language from "fight" to "you're healing." I talked about friends and family, giving him messages from all of them. The kids are sending love. Your sister is sending big hugs. I told stories. And praised him for doing a good job getting better. He was still in and out of consciousness.

I also requested that no one discuss anything negative over his bed. I stopped doctors from talking about him in the room. I believed somewhere inside he could hear and understand. I only wanted positivity around him.

At one point, a young doctor said, "Most people who have this surgery die."

I'm sure he was trying to prepare me and be helpful but …

"He's NOT going to die," I said firmly. "Please don't say that in front of him again!"

I surprised myself, and probably everyone else, during this time in the hospital. Although I was running on empty, I made fast, wise decisions and managed to stay present with what was going on. Clark didn't need me melting down.

~

Clark said some rambling things.

"I'm one fightin' dude!"

Not exactly his lingo, but it made me believe he heard me tell him to fight.

One time, after I spent a long day at the hospital, he asked the nurse to call me at home. It was 3:00 a.m. She apologized, saying he insisted. Clark wanted to tell me, "I love you."

He was awake when I came in one morning and seemed more coherent. I said, "Hiiiiiiii" and gave him a kiss.

The on-duty nurse said, "Clark, do you know who that is?"

"Yes," he answered. "The love of my life!"

Even drugged up and in pain, he could take my breath away!

~

After 10 days, Clark came home. What a happy day. My long-time friend Joanna was there to help. She opened the door to greet us as he walked up the stairs. The look on his face was a mix of exhaustion, pride, and willpower. "I beat death twice," Clark said with satisfaction, as he settled into the recliner.

It was going to be a long, slow recovery—at least a year, maybe two. But we tried to stay positive. Clark and Joanna taught me how to care for someone so sick. I learned how to help lift Clark, get him up and down steps, watch for scary medical signs, give shots and medications, and cook what little he would and could eat.

I stayed realistic, yet positive. My patience, never a strength, improved tremendously.

I worried constantly and was afraid to leave Clark for even a minute. I found myself rushing to the store or pharmacy, running up and down the aisles grabbing what I needed off the shelves, hardly noticing what was in my basket. I was always anxious. Even spending time in the laundry room felt too far away.

"I don't want to leave you," I told Clark one afternoon.

"I don't want you to leave me either," he confided. "Everything is so much better when you're close."

~

Friends and family were a huge support during this time—phone calls, short visits, and food deliveries. Plus, supportive cards and thoughts were sent from all over the country. I was so grateful for their support.

But, most importantly, Clark and I had the chance to talk in depth about our lives and relationship—our mistakes, dreams, disappointments, passions, fears, and visions for the future. His admiration for my strength increased. He thanked me time and time again. We realized what we had in each other. Our love grew stronger and deeper. And, through it all, I learned a powerful lesson: Human beings are resilient. We step up and do what needs to be done, in terms of both healing and helping. And, from a personal standpoint, I surprised myself by discovering that I'm smarter than I thought and stronger than I ever dreamed.

~

Time slowed and stretched as if an elastic band were running the clock. One evening, about a week after Clark came home, his pain amped up. I called the doctor for suggestions. He offered a few, in the form of medication. We tried. It didn't work. I called again. More medication … still didn't work. I called a third time.

"I don't know what to tell you. Take him back to the hospital!"

The doctor seemed irritated.

When I told Clark I was going to call the ambulance, he said, "I don't want to go."

"Why?" I asked.

"Because if I go, I won't come home."

He knew something serious was happening.

While we waited for the paramedics, he took my hand and whispered, "I've always loved you!"

"I've always loved you, too," I answered, barely taking a breath. "You're going to be okay. This is just a small setback. They'll help you at the hospital. It's going to take a little while, but it's going to be fine."

He squeezed my hand and stayed silent.

~

The paramedics arrived. They were a team of strong, bright young men who took charge and had him down two flights of stairs and into the ambulance in no time.

"Should I ride with you?" I asked Clark.

"Take your own car," he advised. "That way you can come home when you want."

I sped behind the ambulance, racing through red lights along with them and parking as close as I could get. I jumped out of the car and dashed frantically into the hospital.

"I'm here, Babe. I'm with you," I told Clark as they wheeled him into emergency.

He was admitted quickly and hooked up with fluids. Medical staff surrounded his bed. I sat at the back of the room feeling helpless. This was the only time during the entire process that I cried in front of him. Watching someone you love in pain and not being able to do a damn thing was awful. He didn't notice my tears, but a nurse did and gave me a supportive hug.

"What's your pain level?" the doctor asked Clark.

"10!" he said.

She administered morphine, waited a few minutes and asked again. "What's your pain level?"

"10!" he repeated.

She studied his face and then the monitor back and forth, back and forth, with a concerned and kind expression. Then called for more morphine.

I heard her down the hall quietly consulting other doctors.

Even though Clark had barely eaten for 3 weeks, he had gained 25 pounds. Acidosis … severe water retention, the doctor explained.

"I think we should drain his belly," she told us. "It's a dangerous procedure, but it's the next best step. And it should help ease the pain." Clark and I agreed the risk was worth it, and they started the process.

From my chair I watched his belly deflate as they drained the liquid away. Clark felt instantly better.

By then it was 7:30 a.m. We'd been up all night, so Clark was ready for some rest. The doctor moved him to intensive care and I left the hospital feeling exhausted, but positive.

~

A little over an hour after I got home, I received a call asking me to come back to the hospital.

"The doctor wants to talk with you," said the voice on the other end of the line.

That was a strange request. They'd called numerous times since this nightmare began, but always to say we need you to sign this form or that or the doctor needs to talk to you about something specific. The mystery in the person's voice sent a chill down my spine.

I rushed to the hospital. Honestly, I don't know who drove there. I did, of course, but I was on autopilot. Somehow, I was dressed … strangely, even put earrings on.

I was relieved to see Clark was alive. He was weakened by the ordeal but awake and coherent. I smiled widely and kissed him hello. We talked for a moment before the doctor came in. He matter-of-factly started discussing Clark's status over the bed. I stopped him.

"We're not talking here," I said authoritatively. "And I need to sit down."

Before leaving the room, I kissed Clark another time and said, "I know you're tired, but can you fight? Can you fight one more time?"

"I'll try," he told me with an exhausted smile.

Once I was sitting the doctor told me Clark had developed an infection. They were doing everything they could. The plan was to try one more medication, but if that didn't work they would put him on comfort care.

Comfort care?

"What are you saying?" I asked. "Is he going to die?"

"Probably," the doctor answered.

Oddly, I felt strong, connected, present. I didn't even cry. It was weird. I instinctively knew what to do.

I went back into Clark's room and changed my language from "fight" to only words of appreciation and love. I held his hand. I thanked him for choosing me as his partner and for all I learned and all he gave me during our time together. I recited a poem we'd heard years ago that made us laugh.

I knew when I first met you,
that you'd someday break my heart,
but since it wasn't going to happen right away I thought
... so what!

Clark smiled, squeezed my hand, said his final words, and was gone.

~

In the blurry days that followed, I learned Clark died of an infection only five people in recorded history have had. The doctor told me even if they'd known exactly what it was, they didn't have the right drugs to stop it.

Although no one knows for sure where he got the infection, I'm guessing it laid low since his time in the jungles of Vietnam when he was drafted as a combat medic for the Army's 9th infantry. Long before I knew him.

Helicopters dropped Clark's unit off in the Mei Cong Delta on his 21st birthday, January 9, 1969. It was a complicated, bloody war, killing and injuring hundreds of thousands on both sides. Much of the fighting occurred in the jungle and involved civilians supporting the armies and surprising the enemy on every front. It was a new way of fighting and the U.S. military was tactically unprepared.

The country was polarized, but concern spread as the war dragged on. Worldwide uneasiness mounted and mistrust escalated. Pressure from the American public eventually helped turn the tide. Still, the conflict raged for 20 years. It bitterly divided Americans. And the financial and human costs on both sides was staggering!

~

Clark was on the front lines and, like all the brave men and women who were there, saw horrifying, disturbing, terrible things. As a medic, his job was to patch guys up and keep them alive until a helicopter could take them from the battlefield to a hospital outpost. He crawled under intense gunfire to stop bleeding, administer morphine, bandage and stabilize victims in an effort to save lives.

During one particularly bloody battle, Clark made his way to an injured soldier – his hands hurriedly attempting to stop the bleeding. In the process, a bullet shot through both of Clark's arms, right at the elbow. He fell back in the mud. His best friend saw what happened and crawled out to help. Clark was still coherent and gave him directions for administering aid. In the process, another bomb went off, severely injuring his comrade. Without the use of his arms, Clark could only lay there, his life ebbing away—and those of the two young men next to him. Meanwhile, the shouts of other injured soldiers asking for a medic went unanswered.

Clark had no sense of time or even reality, but somehow the blood coagulated and he was "dusted off" to a medical facility in-country. He remembers looking at the doctor before surgery, telling him, "Don't take my arms. Look, I can move my fingers. Please don't take my arms."

The doctor did not respond.

~

When Clark awoke from surgery, he laid there, afraid to open his eyes. Would he have arms? What happened to the men in his platoon? Where were they now? What would their lives be like after all that had happened? Was any of this worth the price paid?

Clark spent 9 months recovering in the hospital, followed by a year of traveling, trying to forget.

~

I was attending junior high school. My simple world revolved around age-specific things: giggling with good friends, boys, cheerleading, student government, learning about cloud formations in science and

20th century novels in literature. Growing up in an idyllic small city in Wisconsin, I had a comfortable, relatively carefree family life. It was a "Leave it to Beaver" kind of place, along the shores of Lake Michigan. After finishing high school and attending college, I backpacked the Appalachian Trail, then went on to ski bumming in Jackson Hole, Wyoming. My life was good.

Exciting as it was, after a few years, I wanted more, so went back to broadcasting school and started my career. I was in my mid-20s by then. One of my first jobs was as a news anchor at KPAY in Chico, California.

And it was in Chico that I met Clark.

He was enjoying a beer in a downtown restaurant after completing a marathon, and I was in there with friends. It was love at first sight ... fireworks exploded around us. We couldn't take our eyes off each other. The energy was palpable. An attraction so powerful there was nothing to do but go with it. We coupled up that night and never parted.

That spark never died, even during arguments or when we didn't like each other much. I'm not pretending our relationship was perfect. It wasn't. Like most relationships, there were moments we weren't happy and almost gave up ... except we didn't. We loved each other too much for that. Our connection, perseverance, and communication helped us through the hard times.

~

One thing I loved most about "us" was that we were both adventurous and spontaneous. Almost to a fault. It was fun. And it led to the adventure of a lifetime ... an unrealistic, unplanned, unorganized bicycle ride across America.

WEEK 1

PORTLAND, OREGON, TO NEHALEM BAY, OREGON

And So It Begins

    Day 1:   Wednesday, June 4
    Weather: Rain
    Distance: About 40 miles
    Route: Portland, Oregon, to Rainier, Oregon

What made us think we could ride bikes from Portland, Oregon, to Portland, Maine? Why didn't we train? We were over 50, overweight, and out of shape. Were we insane? That was a distinct possibility. Clark and I were filled with anticipation, trepidation, excitement, and slight hysteria. The proverbial wheels were in motion. We'd told everyone about our cross-country bicycle trip. Hasty arrangements had been made, the kids were with their mother for the summer, and the pets had a housesitter.

My mind was racing. Should we have planned a route, like normal people? Would we be safe? What if we got hurt? And, the most critical concern, would I look like I was jammed into sausage casings when I squeezed into my skin-tight, black cycling shorts?

We made a conscious choice to ride "unplugged." No cellphones and definitely no laptops. We wanted to be independent, two-wheeled adventurers, fending for ourselves, living in the moment, and taking on whatever came our way. No turning back now.

~

It was 4:30 a.m. on Wednesday morning; the idea was to leave at 6:30. We thought getting up so early would give us plenty of time to pack up and hit the road, but we weren't even close to being ready. By first morning light, we were still trying to get organized, which mostly involved stumbling around the basement looking through musty boxes for camping gear. Right after deciding to take off on the Big Journey, we shopped for everything we thought we'd need ... bicycle tubes, tires, spokes, gloves, shoes ... most still in bags with sales tags on.

As we randomly dug around the basement, I thought about the notes I wrote to let friends and family know what general part of the country to search in case of emergency. The only thing close to planning we did was plot out guesstimates of where we'd be and who we hoped to visit along the way. We only got as far as Wisconsin because we couldn't figure out the best route around the Great Lakes. In typical Liza–Clark fashion, we decided to deal with this task "later," which meant "when we got there." Flying by the seat of our pants was our favorite method of solving problems.

We were still trying to handle the last bits of personal business, such as paying bills and trying to get the house ready for our friend and pet sitter, Larry, who would arrive any moment to move in for the summer. Yeah, procrastination is one of our special skills.

Before long, the rain started. Then it rained harder. And harder. Were the weather gods trying to send us a warning? My sister, Lauren, called to check in around 10 a.m., long past our planned hour of departure. Being an ace photographer, her job was to drive us to the outskirts of the city and take our picture at the "Leaving Portland" sign.

"Are you ready to go?" she asked cheerfully.

"Of course not," I answered. "Can we call you in a few hours?"

There was a moment of silence. She was surprised we weren't packed and waiting in the driveway. You'd think my sister, of all people, would know our *modus operandi*.

I offered a lame excuse for our tardiness, but my voice trailed off. Lauren seized the opportunity to point out the ongoing deluge and suggested we leave the next day.

"Well, let's see how it goes," I said.

Clark and I busied ourselves choosing clothes to pack and trying to lighten the load. I selected a few t-shirts; my tight-fitting, Lycra biking shorts; cycling shoes; a pair of jeans; and a skirt, tennis shoes, and sandals for times we'd be off the bikes. (I reasoned a skirt could cover a variety of lumps and bulges.) I also tucked in a few sundries we could replace on the road, as well as undies, earrings, small camera, tape recorder, notebook, pens, stamps, and a first-aid kit. We'd each carry our own sleeping bags, food, and water, but Clark would carry the borrowed tent, camp stove, and cooking supplies.

We spent the next couple hours trying different ways to fit all our stuff in the back-wheel bike bags (*panniers*). We packed and repacked at least a dozen times before realizing we'd never practiced attaching the panniers to our bikes. Neither of us could figure out how they worked, so we called friends for instructions. They were far too nice to comment or criticize, but we knew they must have been amazed by our disorganization.

Then, it dawned on us we'd never ridden our bikes with the gear strapped on. Each bike weighed an extra 60 to 70 pounds. After the storm passed, we went out on a practice ride, which we thought would involve a quick spin around the driveway, but what a difference the added weight made! We ended up wobbling around the neighborhood on full display, trying our best to steer. If we'd known how hard it was to pedal our burdened bikes, we might have bought plane tickets to Mexico instead.

Lauren arrived mid-afternoon, when we were sufficiently ready and able to steer our bikes without fear of falling. So innocent and naïve. We loaded the bags into her car and strapped our bikes onto the bike rack, then headed for the sign at the outskirts of Portland. We smiled big as Lauren snapped the photo, hugged good-bye, mounted up, and pedaled off toward adventure.

~

The only planning we did, a day before leaving, was to do a "shakedown" ride along the Columbia River heading west to the Oregon coast then south along the Pacific, before turning east toward Portland, Maine. There were two reasons for this: (1) to perform a test ride, and (2) to put our wheels in both oceans—Pacific and Atlantic. (A secret, third reason was that we could wuss out if we needed to.) After that, it seemed logical to basically follow the 45th parallel across the country.

~

Sometimes going downhill is a good thing. Germantown Road, a few miles from home, is steep, windy, and narrow with no shoulder, which isn't ideal for bike riders with wide loads. Fortunately, we whizzed along safely, feeling free and in high spirits.

When we hit level ground at Highway 30, which led us to the coast, the rain returned. Wiping our glasses constantly made little improvement in our vision. We were shaky on our bikes, and heavy traffic made the ride more challenging. Irritable drivers hunched over steering wheels mouthing swear words to each other as they stopped and started along a stretch of road construction. But, nothing could diminish our enthusiasm. We were too oblivious to realize we were in no way, shape, or form ready for this trip, imagining ourselves instead as invincible 20-year-old athletes.

The road skirted the Columbia River, which borders Oregon and Washington. Both river and road snake though small, picturesque towns surrounded by dense greenery—beautiful on a sunny day, but we saw only gray skies and the outline of towns and hillsides as we remained focused on the pavement in front of us. In spite of this, we let go of our daily workaday rut and relaxed into what would become a new routine.

The extended daylight hours of summer worked to our advantage, especially after our late start. The rain let up just as rush hour kicked in and Portland commuters headed home. We barely noticed our body parts starting to ache and soaked clothing melding to our skin. The rough ride only made our resolve that much stronger … at least until the next morning, when sore muscles announced themselves.

As we neared our Day 1 destination, the town of Rainier, a double rainbow appeared on the horizon. Maybe the weather gods were taking pity on us? "You can almost see that pot of gold," I said, with rapturous sincerity. "It's a good omen!" Clark grinned in agreement, and we rode on, completely unaware that our muscles would soon be screaming bloody murder.

Darkness shrouded Rainier as we wheeled in. Fortunately, I had the good sense to make a last-minute reservation at a motel earlier that morning. It was the only reservation we made during the entire trip. After covering 40 long miles, we were happy to get off the bikes. No doubt this would be an easy ride for an experienced cyclist, but our "training" consisted of talking about riding over beer and spaghetti. My legs felt like gelatin, but my spirit was giddy: We really were going to spend the summer on the road. We were doing it!

As we removed our helmets and gloves, a new reality set in. Exhaustion took over. We looked like zombies walking through mud as we slowly trudged toward the check-in desk. The chipper receptionist couldn't knock us back into present time as she merrily extolled the virtues of our accommodations.

Her simple questions seemed complicated to our muddled minds. What is your license plate number? Huh. Good one. Address? Um, The Road? After we completed the interrogation, she rewarded us with a key and we trundled off to our room.

We mustered just enough energy to hang our damp bike wear around the room to dry. We would have enjoyed an intravenous feeding but instead went out in search of something more substantial than the fruits and nuts stashed in our bags. Still road-dirt grungy, we made a slow beeline to a restaurant 50 feet from the motel. When the waitress mentioned something about a special, we stared at her blankly, scarcely comprehending her words.

"Sure, we'll take two," Clark mumbled, "and we'll need a carafe of house wine to go with that. I don't care what color." That was completely out of character for a culinary expert chef like Clark. Dinner was a blur, and I could hardly keep my head up, but we practically licked our plates clean before shuffling back to the room.

"Want to go first?" I asked, bobbing my head toward the shower, unable to raise my arm to point. Clark stared at the bathroom door, then at the bed, then at me, then at the bed again, and made the obvious choice. So did I.

A Day of Firsts

Day 2: Thursday, June 5
Weather: Sunny and warm
Distance: 27 miles
Route: Rainier, Oregon, to Westport, Oregon

Did I get hit by a car? That was my first thought. Bright sun streaming down on my face made me blink and squint. Even that was painful. I looked around the room. Oh, yeah. We're on the adventure of a lifetime. So far, it hurt.

It was 6 a.m. When I turned to hug Clark good morning, I realized every part of my body was sore. Even my jaw muscles ached from clenching my teeth through yesterday's busy traffic. One look at Clark's face told me he was in the same condition. "Don't … touch … me," he said in semi-mock jest.

I was the first to tackle taking a shower. Raising my legs up and over the tub was a huge effort; even washing my hair posed a challenge. The warm water soothed, though, and being clean again helped bring me back to life. Clark was still in bed, motionless, gazing at the ceiling. I finally convinced him a shower would feel good.

We dressed slowly, finding it hard to bend even slightly. Our 50-something-year-old bodies were presenting aches and pains in muscles we didn't know we had. I secretly wondered if our chubby frames could take several months of this.

When a now-squeaky-clean Clark suggested grabbing breakfast, we poked our heads out of the room and spied a mom-and-pop diner down the block. Walking gingerly, we hobbled in that direction. The wooden chairs reminded me what an important role butt muscles play in bike riding, but there was nothing wrong with our appetites. Fresh-baked muffins, scrambled eggs, toast with jam, crisp bacon, hash browns, fruit cup, orange juice, and plenty of hot coffee … all memorably delicious.

~

We spent over an hour loading gear into our packs and securing the bags to the bikes. (Fortunately, within weeks, we became seasoned at this chore and shortened the time to under 10 minutes.) Just outside the city limits, we encountered our first uphill climb. Three-quarters of a mile long and so steep we stopped many times to rest. The bikes suddenly weighed hundreds of pounds. Every turn of the pedals was agonizing. Our legs shook from the strain, and I was close to tears. Cars and trucks zoomed past at nerve-wracking speed. Again, I wondered if the trip was a good idea.

Clark moved ahead of me quickly. The macho thing kicked in, pushing him onward. I knew he was sore and tired and admired his stamina and refusal to give up. His determination spurred me on. I kept my eyes focused on his back, trying to push my pedals in unison.

At a steep part of the hill, his bike chain slipped off the track and jammed his gears. He took a terrible tumble, falling toward traffic and coming down so hard I could almost feel the earth shake. I heard myself scream. A car came within inches of crushing his head, but the driver didn't slow down. Somehow I mustered the energy to pedal up to him at full speed. Amazingly, Clark hopped up unhurt, seemingly unaware of his brush with a skull-crushing death. He moved his bike to the shoulder and calmly went about fixing the chain. I couldn't stop shaking. Clark glanced up from his task, probably wondering about my unusual silence. One look at my face held the answer. He set the bike down and held me close.

"It's OK," he said, soothingly. "I'm alright," he repeated over and over. I couldn't hug him tight enough. When my heart stopped pounding, he went back to un-wedging his bike chain from the gears and checking the pedals' movement. A break in traffic gave him the perfect opportunity to perform a road test, and all seemed to work fine.

Clark looked over his shoulder, gave me a winning smile, and waved me forward. Leftover fear and adrenaline got me the rest of the way up that hill. We stopped at the summit and slapped the first of many high fives we'd share along the way. It was a small, yet very big, victory.

Then came the payoff—a fast downhill run. The only energy I exerted was shouting a loud "woohoo" as the wind whipped across my face and cooled my body. Worry to carefree in a matter of minutes. As the road flattened out and the exhilaration of our effortless dash wore off, we heard a train whistle blow plaintively in the distance. That melancholy sound was always magical for us. Without saying a word, we slowed, then stopped along the roadside to kiss.

"I love you," Clark said tenderly, "I'll always love you."

"You're the love of my life," I whispered back.

Our aches, pains, and Clark's horrifying spill forgotten.

~

In Clatskanie, we stopped in a park to admire the forested foothills of the coastal range around us. We lunched on Melba toast, cheese, and apples as wild geese waddled around our table and honked for handouts. We spread our map on the picnic table and pinpointed the day's stopping point—just 12 short miles away.

As we pushed off, I heard a strange hissing coming from somewhere close. We couldn't find the source and were baffled. I blamed the birds, but when the sound followed us that ruled out their guilt. Half a block later, my bike felt "off." I had a flat tire. Of course, neither of us had ever changed a flat and didn't even have the necessary tools for the job. Surprise, surprise.

Rather than panic, we shifted to reconnaissance mode, walking our bikes to the center of town where, as luck would have it, we found a bike shop. The mechanic on duty didn't scoff at our ignorance. Instead, he offered to give us a lesson on how to change a flat. We took him up on that and left with the tools and new-found confidence to make future repairs on the road.

> Clark became quite a pro at fixing flats. I did the math: In the beginning of the trip, it took 1.5 hours to change a tire, but by the end Clark could change a flat in 15 minutes. He became 83% more efficient. I never felt comfortable with the bike maintenance—too many levers, knobs, and small bits to tweak and adjust.

By the time we started riding again we were refreshed and made it quickly to Westport. Too sore to camp, we negotiated a good price on a spacious and tidy motel suite. Close options for dinner were limited, so a hot dog and salad bar at a convenience store had to do. Hunger is the best cook.

Should We Quit Now?

>Day 3: Friday, June 6
>Weather: Gray, cold, and windy
>Distance: 40 miles
>Route: Westport, Oregon, to Gearhart, Oregon

We woke up tired and crabby. I'd like to blame it on the nitrates in the hot dogs, but realistically it was because we were so out of shape. The exertion of the last two days was catching up with us. We packed slowly, getting in each other's way, despite the size of the suite. I repacked my belongings several times, sighing with frustration pathetically. Clark zipped and unzipped his bags loudly, muttering under his breath about how nothing fit properly. We downed breakfast bars and fruit and swigged motel coffee, stirring in packaged cream and sugar with a vengeance. Sore and hurting, we hit the road by 9 a.m. without discussing our physical agony.

The first order of business was to face a 5½-mile climb. Not the best way to start our day. Breathing heavily after only a few minutes and swearing unapologetically, I counted each pedal stroke to stay in the groove. Clark concentrated silently as we made our way. The top never seemed to get closer, but we kept going—up, up, push, breathe, swear a little, grunt, breathe a little harder, swear a little louder, and pant. It seemed endless.

We took frequent breaks to catch our breath, take in the view, guzzle water, and stare at each other in exhaustion. Each time, we forced ourselves to ride again before losing momentum. Over an hour later, we reached the summit and mustered the energy to high five. For a brief moment we were completely full of ourselves—that is, until we spotted the elevation sign.

"Shit. We only climbed a little over 600 feet!" I groaned. It felt like 6000.

"Better quit bragging because you ain't seen nothin' yet," Clark said in a Three Stooges voice.

We burst out laughing—so hard it hurt our smarting muscles. Laughing, groaning from pain and laughing some more. We needed the release.

~

The temperature dropped, and our muscles were cold and stiff. We were exhausted, in pain, and had already ridden beyond our athletic ability. We struggled to push forward and would have stopped for the night if we had the time, but there was a small party planned in our honor at a friend's place in two days. Pride and commitment would not let us miss this celebration. How could we explain our absence after only a few days on the road? So we pushed onward, our egos helping us find the strength.

When we finally made it to Astoria, our first official coastal town, we were too tired to celebrate. Instead, we found a tiny park and laid down for a rest. Actually, it was more like passing out. We laid there for nearly an hour, flat on the grass, rubbing our muscles and moaning. People commented on our slothfulness, probably thinking we were transients. But we couldn't move—no matter how hard passersby gawked. At one point, two uniformed men stopped to question us.

"Need a nap?" one asked sarcastically.

"Yeah," I told him from my comfy position, "It's been a long day on the road. We're just taking a break."

"Probably not the best place to sleep," he said snidely, studying our round bodies.

"Yeah, there are unsavory characters in the area—you could get *rolled*," the other one added, nudging his buddy and snickering.

"Thanks," Clark responded flatly, standing up, brushing himself off, and stepping protectively in front of me.

As the guys walked away, I realized they were not police, just nosy utility workers. The thought was both funny and annoying, but I was too tired to care. We staggered to our bikes and mounted up. I was afraid if we didn't get moving soon we might never, *ever* get up again.

Before long, we came upon our first significant bridge. The Youngs Bay Bridge spans 4200 feet across Youngs Bay, where the Columbia River meets the Pacific Ocean. The middle section of this vertical-lift bridge raises straight up to allow water traffic to pass safely underneath. We paused to watch the mechanics of this maneuver, impressed by the engineering genius.

Wouldn't Lewis and Clark have been amazed? Those brave explorers reached Astoria in November 1805 after a long westward expedition of about two years. In their journal, they observed, "Great joy in camp, we are in view of the ocean, this great Pacific Ocean which we have been so long anxious to see." I hoped it wouldn't take us two years to reach the East Coast.

We nervously started our bridge crossing. The wind was gusty, shoving us around as we pedaled like mad. Cars, trucks, and RVs flew past so quickly they were just a noisy blur, whizzing by, leaving only inches to spare between them and us. Our knees screamed but the adrenaline kicked in as we tried not to think about what would happen if we lost control. The water below looked turbulent, dark, and ominous. It was far from a relaxing ride.

Bridges often have bumpy, wide gratings that are sometimes the perfect width to trap a tire and stop you in your tracks. This is especially scary when you have good forward momentum and are carrying a heavy load. Also, bridges can ice up quickly, adding another element of risk.

Clark hated bridges. He felt trapped, with nowhere to go if something unexpected or dangerous happened. Some of those feelings were no doubt residual effects from his traumatic experience serving as a combat medic in the Vietnam War. He didn't like situations where there wasn't more than one way to escape from potential threats.

> Much of the 1985 movie *"The Goonies"* was filmed in and around Astoria, Oregon. The family comedy-adventure follows a gang of kids who set off in search of treasure after finding legendary pirate One-Eyed Willy's map. To this day, movie buffs flock to locations where the film was shot. June 7 is celebrated as official Goonies Day each year.

Although our plan was to camp in Gearhart, we were too exhausted to shop for groceries, set up the tent, and cook over a camp stove. Again, we splurged on a motel. Robotically, we paid for our room, took showers, ate dinner, and collapsed into bed.

Oranges, Dogs, and More Self-Doubt

> Day 4: Saturday, June 7
> Weather: Cloudy and windy, with occasional sun breaks
> Distance: 25 miles
> Route: Gearhart, Oregon, to Nehalem Bay, Oregon

We popped out of bed early after a sound night's sleep. Still sore, yet bolstered by the promise of a party with friends and a day off. We only had 25 miles to ride but three coastal headlands to scale before day's end. Tillamook Head is just over 500 feet in elevation, but rises cruelly. We were sweating and cursing in no time. Struggling along, I realized the road was much steeper and more daunting than it ever seemed from the car. We had driven this road many times and barely noticed there was a hill. How different it was on two wheels.

We reached the crest and talked about taking a break in artists' haven Cannon Beach, then realized it was all downhill, which meant it would be all uphill to get back to Highway 101. We quickly re-evaluated. There was NO WAY we were going to add another mile—especially uphill. Instead, we stopped at a wide spot along the shoulder and pulled an orange from our pack. Oranges became the victory fruit on our cross-country trek. We peeled one every time we reached a summit. Nothing tasted better!

As we plodded up the second climb of the day, we had our first run-in with a dog. A big hound shot out across a busy section of road and headed straight for us, baring his yellowed teeth. Clark was ahead of me, as he often was going up hills. Instinctively, he pedaled as fast as he could while waving his arms and shouting at the beast. I knew I could never out-pedal it, so instead I slowed to a crawl—a challenging feat considering I was already going at a snail's pace. The dog continued his aggressive gallop toward me. I could hear deep panting as he neared, and felt myself starting to sweat.

"It's OK. It's all right," I said softly to the dog, trying to convince myself as much as him. "Good dog. You're a good boy. I won't hurt you."

I forced myself to smile and sound cheerful and in control, but inside I was terrified. Though we'd picked up cans of mace at the bike shop in Clatskanie (at the mechanic's suggestion), they were buried deep in our packs. Fortunately, when I started talking, the animal stopped. Maybe he realized I was human—a dog person—or maybe it was pure luck. Whatever, he lost interest and wandered away. I was glad to escape his beady black eyes and sharp fangs unharmed.

When I looked up I saw Clark coasting back down the hill toward me. I gave him the "I'm-OK-stop-where-you-are" wave and pedaled up to meet him. We debated about the best dog-bite aversion techniques: ride like hell or try to talk yourself out of danger? Coming to no solid conclusion, we moved the mace cans up from the depths of our bags to easy-access locations—just in case.

~

It occurred to us that a road trip on bikes isn't exactly the safest way to travel. Thoughtless drivers rush past without noticing bike riders sharing the road, crazy dogs appear out of nowhere, weather turns dangerous on a dime, and hitting a rock or pothole could send a rider flying into the traffic or over a mountain's edge. It was a sobering realization, and we wondered again if our adventure was a good idea. Yet, there we were, so we put it out of our minds and made a promise to look for smaller, less-traveled roads, even if it meant adding a few miles.

~

The next two peaks were higher, steeper, and closer together. At the top of the second summit we were dog-tired and crabby —whose idea was this anyway?

"We could've been sipping margaritas on a Mexican beach right now," Clark goaded.

"With salsa and chips," I added longingly. Snapping back to reality, I said, "Let's just get over these hills. We have a party waiting."

Thankfully, a little downhill action gave us some relief and a bit of a lift. We even cycled part way up the final incline before resuming our whining, swearing, and sweating. Completely beat and struggling, we finally gave up and walked, pushing our bikes to the summit. We got up and over those coastal killers, but it was the worst ride of our lives. So far.

Comparing notes later, we'd individually contemplated quitting. Maybe we couldn't do it after all. Could we really get in shape on the road? We're physically unfit and overweight—what were we thinking? Holy crap, what were we doing?

Truthfully, though, I was most worried about friends on their way to the party passing us on the road and seeing our bedraggled state.

~

We stopped in Manzanita, one of our favorite places, for a bite to eat. The beautiful coastal town is the source of many happy memories. Weekend getaways, smooching all over town, and holding hands like schoolkids. It's just that kind of place. A gorgeous white sand beach stretches for seven pristine miles; Neahkahnie Mountain tumbles into the ocean at one end, and Nehalem Bay Jetty holds fort at the other. Manzanita is smack in the middle between two of Oregon's many state parks—Oswald West and Nehalem Bay. The section of road that travels along the water is so ridiculously picturesque that ad agencies clamor to film commercials there.

We sat down in the soft sand to appreciate the view, catch our breath, and reminisce. Soon, exhaustion sucked us into a black hole. Clark fell fast asleep. I curled up next to him, snuggling in close. We didn't move for a long time.

A pair of young kite flyers reeling around on the beach roused us from our slumber. I stretched and shook the sand out of my hair. Clark rolled over and fell back asleep. A couple college-aged kids wandered by and took an interest in our gear. I answered a few of their questions but was so tired I had trouble forming complete sentences. Clark snored on next to me. They stared down at us, unapologetically peering at our rotundness.

"You two are biking across the country?" one of them asked incredulously. Thought I already answered that question. "Yup," I confirmed through sleepy eyelids. Without responding, they abruptly strolled off down the beach glancing back at us three or four times.

~

Clark's friend Ray owned a winery in Nehalem, where we would spend the night and celebrate with friends. Seeing everyone, meeting new people, and indulging in some good wine would no doubt dull our aches and pains. The winery, famous for blackberry wine, perches on a small hill and resembles a Swiss chalet. The place was built in 1909 and originally housed an old creamery, part of the Tillamook

Creamery Co-op. The building was abandoned in 1959, and it wasn't until the mid-1970s that the property was turned into a winery by a man named Patrick McCoy. In 1991, Ray met Mr. McCoy, and the two hit it off instantly. They remained good friends and business partners until McCoy's death in 1993.

Ray greeted us with a big smile and open arms. My first impression was that he looked like a fit and healthy Santa. He radiated happiness. The two guys bear hugged, pounding backs with open palms like guys do and laughing with hearty gusto. Ray's focus shifted and he warmly enveloped me in a hug. Clark grinned and said, "Ray, meet Liza."

Self-conscious fears about my weight melted away instantly. There was no judging evident in Ray's kind eyes. Dressed in a flannel shirt and well-worn jeans, he exuded an unpretentious, easy-going style. His long, white hair and beard flowed seamlessly together, creating a soft blanket on his chest.

Ray showed us to a quaint room upstairs where we could get some rest before the night's festivities. The second we shut the door we fell in bed and were out cold for two hours, so tired we could have slept on railroad tracks. When I awoke, I dragged myself up and into the hallway bathroom. I was aghast at the reflection in the mirror, feeling fat and ridiculous in my tight cycling shorts. There was a black smear of grease on my right calf, where the bicycle chain had rubbed against my thick leg. It was a mortifying sight.

Clark knocked and poked his head in the door. "Mind if I shower first? I'd like to catch up with Ray before everyone gets here." As Vietnam veterans, Clark and Ray had a deep connection; the wounds of war had turned into a tight bond of friendship.

This gave me the opportunity to go back and check the sheets. Whew. They were grease free. I dug into my pack to retrieve my one and only "nice" outfit—my baggy/stretchy skirt and matching top, both wrinkled from being stowed away. I rooted around for make-up and earrings. And by make-up I mean "mascara." Somehow, I reasoned, by disguising myself with girlie trappings no one would notice my chubby body.

~

I joined the boys on the deck, where they were preparing food for the barbeque while wisecracking and ribbing each other, like guys do. Ray spends a lot of time traveling the world and has been described as the "Indiana Jones of the North Coast." He has amassed an impressive hat collection from his travels abroad, including formal top hats, alpaca wool stocking caps with long earflaps, and tight-fitting Asian skull caps. He was wearing a stylish fedora for the party.

Just as the coals achieved ashy-red perfection, our friend John, an attractive, smart, and mild-mannered ladies' man, showed up with his latest girlfriend. His women never seemed to last more than a few dates. This one was relatively young by comparison and said she was a dancer. She seemed nice. Too bad I'd never see her again.

Soon, the rest of the party-goers arrived and were greeted by a hearty round of hellos and hugs from Ray and Clark. I'd never met any of them before, but after a couple glasses of wine we were all good friends. Ray served up a feast: barbecued pork ribs, baked potatoes, sweet corn, salad made from local lettuce, and grilled veggies, complemented by an array of the winery's finest vintages. Dessert appeared in the form of rich dark chocolate and generous pours of the blackberry wine. The women giggled about how they really shouldn't as they reached for seconds and thirds from the confection platter.

Talk turned toward our trip. We confessed to being out of shape (as if they couldn't tell) and freely admitted to not planning much of anything before our departure. Some were impressed by our carefree attitude toward travel but others clearly thought we were nuts.

We fessed up that the first few days had been a struggle. Somehow, expressing this aloud resulted in a spontaneous round of applause. We were way out of our athletic league, but still standing and even laughing.

Proud and feeling the warmth of admiration, Clark squeezed my hand and smiled like the Cheshire Cat.

It was a long, boisterous night with no problem finding reasons to open "one more" bottle. There were toasts to everything from our trip to Ray's hat collection to the cows across the way. We hit a crescendo at 1 a.m. that morphed into quieter conversations and finally to everyone saying their sleepy goodnights.

WEEK 2

NEHALEM BAY, OREGON, TO FLORENCE, OREGON

Never Wallpaper a Room Together

    Day 5:   Sunday, June 8
    Weather: Sunny
    Distance: Rest day
    Route: From the winery to the restaurant next door and back

We woke up happy. Dressing quickly, we joined Ray who had parked himself on the deck in a cushioned chair. We sipped strong coffee and rehashed the party highlights. Good times. The horizon stretched for miles—farmland in the foreground, the coastal range and ocean in the distance. Brilliant-green hills, pastureland where cows grazed lazily, and a sky dotted with billowy white clouds. The fresh morning air carried a hint of salt as it wafted past. Our senses alive as the sun warmed our faces.

    Ray amused us with stories. My favorite took place next door. It involved some jealous cows. During a harsh winter, hungry elk moved into the pasture and attempted to steal the cows' food. Finding nourishment during the coldest months is difficult for wildlife. The elk were unusually bold and encroached on the dairy herd's turf, but the cows would have none of that. As Ray recollected, they banded together, standing shoulder to shoulder, and glared threateningly at the intruders. After a long stare-down, the cows emerged victorious. Dejected, the elk moved on, never to return. And from this brave group of bovines comes Oregon's famous Tillamook Cheese.

~

The only chore of the day? Laundry. Our clothes were rank. I cleared my nasal passages of their odor by taking a big whiff of organic detergent. We soon learned that finding a place to wash clothes could be an onerous task. Cyclists don't carry many changes, and riding gear gets dirty (and stinky) quickly. So laundry day, and putting on a fresh ensemble, was always a happy experience.

~

In mid-afternoon, Ray left for a trip, which allowed us time for idle relaxation. We accomplished a much-deserved nothing. When hunger set in we walked to a nearby bistro. It was a slow Sunday evening, and we were the only customers in the four-table restaurant. The owners were happy to see us. We ordered five appetizers and a couple glasses of red wine. The couple took turns delivering our food, lingering each time to hear more about our cycling adventure. After reaffirming our membership in the Clean-Plate Club, we invited them to share some of the wine. Spontaneous fun.

The restaurateurs had left high-paying jobs on the East Coast in search of a simpler life. They bought a place that "needed work" and ended up having to redo everything. It was more expensive than planned, so they did the renovation themselves. All went well until the job of hanging wallpaper, when, they confessed, they almost killed each other. If you want your relationship to last, they advised, hire someone else for that job!

Summer was in the air. We walked back to Ray's hand-in-hand under a bright night sky.

"Another full moon and I'm still in love with you," Clark whispered and hugged me tightly. We kissed and lingered, savoring the universe above. He professed his "full moon" affection every month since he'd declared his love—which was pretty much the moment we met.

~

We were enveloped by pitch-black darkness as we unlocked the door to the deserted winery. Fumbling around, Clark found the light switch and a note from Ray: "Enjoy any bottle you like." We selected a nice red and one glass into it got giggly and frisky. Who knew a darkened, silent winery could be so much fun?

Backroads & Camping

Day 6: Monday, June 9
Weather: Sunny
Distance: 50 miles
Route: Nehalem, Oregon, to Pacific City, Oregon

The sun danced across the bedspread, waking us gently. The day of recovery made a big difference. Our muscle aches fading, we were looking forward to getting back on the road. Ray continued to play gracious host even in his absence. We found another note in the kitchen pointing us toward coffee, eggs, bacon, toast, juice, and cookies. The coastal mountains staged a breathtaking backdrop for our breakfast. Ocean breezes and the sweet scent of summer flowers hung in the air. My heart skipped a beat as I thought about the odyssey ahead of us. Every day a new, unknown adventure. Whatever, wherever, whenever …

I wrote a thank you note to Ray and tucked it into the computer keyboard so he wouldn't miss it. Clark went out to load up his bike while I started throwing things into the bike pack. My sunny mood dampened when I caught a glimpse of myself in the full-length mirror. I hadn't dropped a single ounce and tried to convince my reflection I should have lost at least 10 pounds by now. Maybe the winery's scale was off?

I trudged down the stairs with my stuff, the faulty scale still in my thoughts.

"Hey, my gear weighs 82 pounds," Clark bragged, as if reading my mind in some way.

"I think that scale is broken. It claims I haven't lost a pound," I answered dejectedly.

"It worked fine for me. I'm down six pounds."

Damn it.

> A quick check of our finances sobered our mood. We started with $500 in cash, which was supposed to last us a couple weeks. Of course, we had credit cards stashed away, but we wanted to be careful with our spending. We'd already blown through most of the cash in the first five days. The trip was going to be more expensive than planned. Oh, wait—we didn't plan.

Click, click, ..., click, click. It was good to be back on our bikes. The satisfying sound of snapping into our clipless pedals was a motivational exclamation point. We were rested, well fed, and ready to ride. Crystal-clear sky framed a landscape of verdant greens and rich blues, punctuated by hits of color here and there. The first 12-mile stretch was a quiet back road bordered by Tillamook State Forest on one side and open pasture on the other. We sang *a capella* with the birds, hitting perfectly timed crescendos as we glided along.

By the time we reached the city of Tillamook we'd forgotten our vague promise to eat lighter. We picked up a big bag of cheese curds (protein, we convinced ourselves) and downed some ice cream (dairy, for strong bones) from the Tillamook Cheese Factory.

From Tillamook, we veered off Highway 101 onto a side road that brought us closer to the ocean. As we rolled along, my thoughts focused on Clark as I watched him ride with carefree abandon ahead of me.

Clark was an "über foodie," always willing to deviate from the path for a chance to eat something special. The culinary arts were his passion. He was an extraordinary, well-trained chef with a food science background and possessed a wealth of knowledge on everything related to food. He was also an artist. His plates were perfectly presented. I never figured out how he did it because I don't have the same eye for detail and composition. One time, while hosting a dinner party, he gave me the simple task of putting cookies atop ice cream we were serving for dessert.

Clark scooped and topped an example and asked nonchalantly, "Do you think you can do that?" Of course, I thought—how hard could it be? I was wrong. For the life of me, I couldn't get my cookie arrangement to look like his work of art. One of our guests giggled at my attempts and offered to eat the bad one to hide it from view, but Clark spotted my disaster and took over the job, letting out an exasperated sigh.

This passion wasn't always easy to be around. Some evenings, when the kids and I were waiting for Clark to put the finishing touches on dinner, we would get crabby-hungry, wanting to just sit down and eat. Though we appreciated his efforts, we sometimes didn't care if the asparagus landed the wrong way on the plate. But Clark did. He would pick the vegetables back up and arrange them differently if the layout didn't match his artistic sensibility. Despite our occasional impatience, Clark was right: Food that looks beautiful always tastes better. In fact, we never had a problem getting the kids to eat their veggies.

In the middle of my daydreaming, Clark turned back toward me and smiled. I melted immediately. Did he know I was thinking of him? He pedaled on and I continued with random memories flitting through my mind.

Clark's perfectionism spilled into the party planning phase, too. He often sketched out ideas for food arrangement while planning a special meal. His cooking was so good, he could turn die-hard vegetarians into carnivores for a day.

Clark's love for food started when he was a child. He spent summers with his grandmother in Germany. He adored her and helped every day in the kitchen. They would talk (in German, of course), and he would learn her techniques and taste-test everything. She was an excellent cook. In those days, people shopped daily—first the bakery, then the produce stand, and finally the meat market. The butcher gave Clark a sausage sample wrapped in stiff white paper every time they visited.

He told me another story about waiting patiently for Easter dinner when he was eight years old. While his mother was busy with preparations, he climbed a big tree in the backyard and carved "Ham for Dinner" inside a heart on the bark.

~

By the time we arrived in Pacific City we'd forgotten about camping and instead bartered for a motel room. This was one of our favorite games—to see if we could get (whatever) for a better price. We were bartering pros, skilled players, and strong competitors. Our skills failed us at the first place we tried. The stodgy manager wouldn't budge, not even a penny. He wasn't any fun so we decided to try our luck elsewhere.

I fell in the driveway of the next hotel. When the bike leaned toward the left, I couldn't stop fast enough and tipped over. I released my foot from the right-hand pedal, but couldn't snap out of the left in time to avoid a tumble. Naturally, there was a crowd to witness this spectacle. They rushed to my aid, asking if I was all right. But all of them, especially Clark, tried not to laugh when they realized I was unhurt. This was the first of many falls, soon dubbed "Pulling a Humpty-Dumpty," which I always executed in front of an audience.

The humiliating fall had its benefits. The front desk woman offered to let us spend the night for free at the small campground. Soft grass blanketed the campsite, and a creek protected us from the noise of sporadic traffic. No one else was set up nearby, which meant we'd have private use of the communal bathroom. A perfect way to ease into camping mode.

The money we saved went toward dinner. And copious amounts of wine.

~

As fate would have it, I had to get up to pee three times. This meant unzipping my sleeping bag, wiggling out, cramming into clothes and shoes, then crawling over Clark to get to the tent entrance. My big bum would invariably throw me off balance, especially in my half-asleep/half-tipsy state. I'd knock into a bag or tent pole, then overcorrect and fall in the other direction—usually on top of Clark—who was jolted fully awake. Another zipping procedure at the door slowed the process even further. Eventually, I'd escape, usually with a little push from Clark. I worried my floundering would collapse the tent.

I made my way to the dark bathroom, using a penlight to safely negotiate a pebble-strewn path. Moths scattered as I flipped the light switch. A single bulb dangled from a black cord rigged to the ceiling. The glare cast sharp shadows and a chemical smell permeated the air.

I inspected the surroundings during my visits. Cobwebs fluttered as spiders skittered into corners. Graffiti informed me that "Julian was here." I wondered when. "Loren loves Zachary" was scrawled in flourishy letters, followed by the crudely written, "But he doesn't love YOU!" My personal favorite: "Question everything." Answered by, "Why?"

After finishing my reading, I performed a reverse series of actions until I was snuggled back into my sleeping bag. So much for our first night of camping.

America the Beautiful

Day 7: Tuesday, June 10
Weather: **Sunny and nice, a great day to ride**
Distance: **27½ miles**
Route: **Pacific City, Oregon, to Lincoln City, Oregon**

Morning came too soon. We dragged ourselves out of the tent, hungry, dry-mouthed, and disheveled. I gave my hair and teeth a quick brush to make myself more presentable. Fortunately, a nearby café was open. The interior was spotless and cheery. Colorful artwork hung on every wall, and a vase of fresh flowers graced each table alongside kitschy salt and pepper shakers.

Our waitress bustled toward us in a ruffled apron that matched the patterned tablecloths. She was artsy-cool and had crafted black tights and several large brooches into a magnificent, gypsy-like head accessory. Tufts of copper-colored hair framed her face in soft waves. Costume jewelry jangled from her wrists, and a wide belt cinched her tiny waist. In a sweet, almost-magical voice, she recommended the house special, homemade biscuits and gravy. Clark looked captivated. His voice softened as he readily agreed to her suggestion.

"May I have a side of fruit with that?" he added, almost whispering.

I was amused, but kept it to myself.

~

The weather was sunny and warm. A slight breeze carried that distinct ocean smell—not fishy, more briny and wild. Tempting as it was to lie on the beach and relax, we couldn't justify another day off. Most times, one or the other of us felt self-imposed pressure to keep moving. Usually, it was me. On this day, Clark was ready to ride. He felt confident and energized from seeing our friends and basking in the glory of their compliments.

In general, I was the one more concerned about reaching Portland, Maine. Clark, on the other hand, was relaxed about the whole affair. He got into the day-to-day Zen faster and didn't seem to worry if or when we made our final destination.

I'm usually the first one to go with the flow, but there was an underlying motivation that propelled me to stay on track and move forward. It was a personal challenge because there were some people (who shall remain nameless) who didn't think we could do it. I was determined to prove them wrong. Having an end goal made it easier to stay positive and keep going when days were tough.

We consciously did a few things to make the enormity of the journey more palatable. By focusing on the next town or next meal or next whatever, the trip became mentally more manageable. But, we didn't look ahead too far. Going from micro to macro, in a sense, our next bigger goal was to get to an upcoming stop or a "friendly outpost." We called any place where we could stay with family or friends—old or new—a friendly outpost.

That next bite-sized piece was to scale a mountain, reach a state line, cross a time zone, or anything else that might mark our advancement. Rather than lamenting about how far we had to go, we'd reflect on how far we had come since the day, week, or month before.

~

Preferring to avoid busy Highway 101, we found a side road just outside Neskowin. This took us along a beautiful 10-mile stretch through the Siuslaw National Forest, thick with old-growth trees. Ancient Douglas fir, cedar, and spruce lined the road. Long branches reached out as if to welcome us and guide the way. Something small rustled leaves and scurried into hiding as we approached. Down the road, a husky coyote peeked around a tree warily. A bird cawed and swooped close to our heads. Caw-caw, we called out in return.

The serenity soothed the pain of an uphill climb. We hit the crest and coasted down the other side, belting out "America the Beautiful." It was off key, but who cared? As the ride downhill leveled off, we shouted, "We loooooove to bicycle!" and "Life is gooooooood!" We were a pair of crazy old kids.

Eventually, we hit Otis, a tiny town consisting primarily of the Otis Café. A sign, straight out of the '50s, featured a swooshy arrow pointing to the word "CAFÉ." Many boast this is where you'll find the best homemade pies around. We couldn't pass that up, ordering marionberry and strawberry rhubarb. The warm, fruity fillings oozed from under the crispy crusts. We closed our eyes while eating to enjoy the full sensory experience.

~

Highway 101 was a stark contrast to the calm we'd experienced earlier. Roaring motorcycles, logging trucks, motorhomes, and cars of all sizes came out of nowhere. It was time to stop—at a motel. No camping that night. We checked in, cleaned up, and padded barefoot along the beach heading toward a seafood restaurant. We waded across the narrow D River, the shortest river in the world, measuring 440 feet in length during low tide and only 120 feet at high tide. An oceanview table awaited. People played on the beach and in the surf while the sun made its final appearance for the day. Caesar salad, crab cakes, a cup of chowder, and salmon linguini satisfied our hunger. We ordered a carafe of wine to toast our first week on the road. A major milestone notched into our belts.

Eavesdropping

   Day 8: **Wednesday, June 11**
   Weather: **Varied from misting to heavy rain**
   Distance: **27 miles**
   Route: **Lincoln City, Oregon, to Newport, Oregon**

We stopped by the motel restaurant for breakfast at 7 a.m. and discovered it didn't open until 8. Therein lies a long-distance cyclist's dilemma. Do you keep your bikes safe in the room and wait for food to be available nearby? Or, do you ride on with an edge of hunger and have breakfast farther down the road? The philosophical difference is whether you're in a hurry to get to the next destination or content to move at a slower pace, live in the present, and go with the flow.

We decided to delay. When we circled back to the restaurant, right on the hour, a busload of seniors pulled up. We hurried in ahead of them as they shuffled along with canes and walkers. We were seated right away but didn't beat the rush. While waiting for breakfast, it was all but impossible to miss the conversations swirling around us. Even with their hearing aids turned up, most of the bus troop spoke loudly over each other. They had no social filter, much like when kids blurt things out at random.

The hot topic: crime and lack of parenting. We heard snippets about gang violence and their disappointment with the criminal justice system and uninvolved parents.

"The Cripes and Hoods ... they're scary gangs," an older lady shuddered with fear.

We stared at each other silently, a small smile cracking on my face when I realized she meant "Crips and Bloods."

> We captured bits and pieces of what Americans think by spending time in cafés, bars, city parks, grocery stores, and post offices—anywhere people gathered. The economy, crime, education, societal values, housing, corporate corruption, the environment, terrorism, and waste in government. Discussions were the same all across the country.

Liza - Ready for Rain - Pacific Ocean - Lincoln City, OR

It was 10 a.m. before we started riding. No matter how early we got up or how motivated we were, we still couldn't manage to get on the road before late o'clock.

A soft mist bathed the landscape, creating the illusion of an impressionistic painting. There was a definite change in the air as clouds gathered. We donned our rain gear in anticipation. Good call. Moments later, the tap-tap of raindrops began pelting our helmets. The drops increased in size and speed, and, despite our plastic protection, we got wet. Really wet. And dirty. Mud kicked up from our tires, splattering our legs and backs in thick blobs. The sludge dripped down in unique patterns, like a Jackson Pollock painting coming to life. Clark's bike had a plastic fender on the rear wheel that offered him more defense against the mud. As I pedaled along, a black stripe formed down the middle of my back, reminiscent of a skunk stripe.

At Cape Foulweather the weather was—not surprisingly—foul. The rugged promontory is 500 feet above sea level and has a breathtaking view of the Pacific Ocean. It was discovered and named in 1778 by the renowned British navigator Captain James Cook. This is where he spotted the North American mainland for the first time. On the expedition, he encountered a fierce storm along the coast that almost ended his historic journey. "Cape Foulweather" was the apropos name bequeathed by Captain Cook. On clear days you can see fishing boats, cruise ships, sea lions, and sometimes whales from the lofty vantage point. We couldn't see a thing. Cape Foulweather was living up to its name.

By the time we hit Newport, we were cold, wet, and worn out. We'd hit the wall and decided to call it a day as soon as we saw the city limits sign. The weather gods won.

~

The motel looked old and rundown, but we didn't care. The small, dank reception area was littered with old brochures and used coffee cups. An ashtray overflowed on a rickety table that sat next to a filthy chair. The manager greeted us skeptically (in all our muddy glory), oddly asking, "What do YOU want?" The troll-like man had a long, scraggly beard that looked out of balance with his short stature. Beady black eyes sank into his hollow cheeks, the gray pallor of his skin not enhanced by the dim lighting. I wondered if he ever ventured out into the light of day. A pseudo-German accent popped up every other sentence, as if he was practicing a new persona.

The guy appeared agitated by our presence. Were we taking him away from a secret project in the back room? His eyes darted back and forth from us then toward a small curtained door and back again, like he was worried we'd push past him and steal it—whatever *it* was.

He didn't seem dangerous, in a psycho killer sense, just crazy-weird, but not exuding enough strangeness to make us fear for our safety. After a bit of bartering, he begrudgingly gave us a small room at a good price. The room was dark and dingy, but the bathroom was clean and the bed comfortable. Didn't expect that. A boxy, monster-sized TV loomed over half the room. This in striking contrast to a dinky refrigerator that did double-duty as a table top.

~

An extra-large pizza, loaded with meat, mushrooms, black olives, onions, and extra cheese, satiated us. We scarfed it down like ravenous beasts. We tucked two leftover slices into our tiny fridge.

The rain stopped by early evening and left everything shiny and new. It was one of those balmy nights where everyone wanted to be outside. We explored a nearby neighborhood and watched as rookie firefighters practiced their skills on a controlled burn of a dilapidated house. They worked intensely, determined expressions spreading across their young faces as they battled the blaze. It was a tough fight. Just when it looked as if the fire was out, another part of the building went up in flames. Thick, black smoke darkened the sky.

A curious crowd gathered, hypnotized by the dancing flames. A guy standing next to Clark engaged in small talk about the fire. He looked like a musician—long hair, beret, tats, and a vintage rock t-shirt—and he was. Jason was a bass player who had just moved to Oregon to break into the music scene. He asked us, in all sincerity, "How can you guys be so clean?" Maybe it didn't dawn on him that it was possible to shower, even on the road.

Ocean Lullaby

Day 9: Thursday, June 12
Weather: Rain, rain, and more rain, then a beautiful evening
Distance: 23 miles
Route: Newport, Oregon, to Yachats, Oregon

Sometime in the wee hours, Clark made a clandestine pizza raid, devouring every last crumb of our leftover pizza. He tried to blame it on a fridge mouse, but I didn't buy it.

As a diversionary tactic (to draw attention away from his dastardly deed), Clark flicked on the TV. We mounded pillows, pulled the covers up, and settled in to watch "Mutiny on the Bounty" with Marlon Brando.

After the movie, we felt motivated to ride, so we packed quickly and checked out. The troll was still at the front desk. Or maybe it was his twin brother. He scurried to whip the secret room's curtains shut before we could see what was back there, then wordlessly took his position behind the counter. His eyes flitted toward us but never rested. Clark dangled the room key in mid-air. The troll made eye contact with the shiny object and snatched it away with shocking speed, immediately disappearing behind the curtain again. What inner angst tormented this wretched soul?

~

We cycled a few busy miles through town, then crossed Yaquina Bay traveling on the most recognized bridge along the Oregon coast. The Yaquina Bay Bridge is over 3200 feet long and hangs 133 feet above the water. The architect was influenced by Art Deco, Art Moderne, and Gothic styles. The most striking feature is the arch that spans 600 feet.

Just on the other side of the bridge, we stopped at one of our favorite oyster places. We ordered in bits and pieces—oysters, crab, clam chowder, and then another round of oysters, more crab, …. We were biding our time for two reasons: the great food and the rain.

We shared a small table with three older women. They seemed interested but skeptical about people "like us" doing a trip "like this." The disbelief flashing in their eyes was a dead giveaway for their underlying cynicism. I imagined one sourpuss thinking, "Sure you're biking cross country. Are you doing that by gorging on massive quantities of seafood?!" I glanced at Clark. He had a shiny stream of butter dripping down his chin. Oh, God. He looked at me and smiled, innocent and unaware, oblivious to his chin butter and the sarcasm dripping from the old biddies' mouths.

When the rain let up, we ventured out again, but Mother Nature fooled us. It wasn't long until it was pouring again. We dove for cover, nestled together under an awning. The skies soon cleared, so we left our refuge from the storm.

~

In Waldport, we stopped at a burger joint. We parked our bikes and peeled off our gloves, taking our helmets and front bags inside with us. The handwritten menu board offered five kinds of burgers, fries, hand-dipped shakes, and other all-American favorites. Often, a burger is just a burger, but this one was especially good. Juicy beef topped with thick bacon, Tillamook cheese, and tomatoes bursting with flavor packed onto a hard roll. Clark complimented the chef. It turns out the man was also the owner. The place was quiet so he grabbed a seat at the adjacent table.

"Glad you like my food," he said appreciatively.

"Love it," I assured him. "*Killer* burger!"

"What do you guys do?" the man asked.

We told him about the trip and a little about our background—Clark being a chef and food scientist and me in the television world. These facts seemed to keenly spark his attention.

"I've been doing this a long time and getting ready to retire. The restaurant's for sale," he told us matter of factly. "You two should buy it."

We stopped chewing and looked at each other, mind-melding the possibility.

"You'd be the perfect pair to take over: knowledgeable, friendly, and outgoing. The right mix to run a restaurant," he added.

These accolades piqued our interest.

"I'd help you get started," he reeled us in further.

Keep talking.

"It's a nice town, too. No place like the Oregon Coast."

Agreed.

He didn't miss a beat, and from that point on, we listened intently. Yeah, he'd wait until we finished our trip. Yep, he'd train us, introduce us to the community, and make us feel at home. We were ready for something new, loved the coast, and the deal sounded appealing. Adventure is our middle name. We gave it serious thought. We didn't have jobs lined up at the end of the trip. That was the beauty of a long journey like this. It allows time to think about what else is out there. You develop a free-spirit attitude. Take the road less traveled or roam the beaten path?

~

We started an uphill climb toward Yachats. At the crest, about four miles into the ride, we pulled into Beachside State Park Campground. The Oregon coast is almost completely designated as state park land, making the beaches open to the public up and down Highway 101.

The camp host told us there were no showers, but insisted this was the nicest campground around. The rain was long gone, and predictions were for a warm, clear night. We were sold. We could hear the ocean from our campsite but were protected from the wind. We pitched the tent and set about discussing the next order of business—dinner.

Clark's choice was to pedal a short distance to Yachats, where restaurants would be abundant. I wanted to keep it simple: walk to the store and eat dinner on the beach. We settled on going into town, but we hitchhiked because I didn't feel like getting back on my bike. I worried no one would pick us up, especially after dark. But Clark insisted he was an old hand at thumbing a ride.

So, off we went confidently to the side of the road. We were there, thumbs in the air, for 20 minutes. Although many cars passed, no one stopped. Drivers looked at us skeptically or not at all. Just when we were about to give up, a 30-something guy pulled out of a driveway across the street and signaled us to come over. We climbed in the cab of his pickup and introduced ourselves. His name was Luke and he taught auto mechanics to troubled teens. Luke told us the kids had been working on the old truck all afternoon. The jalopy bounced and rattled down the road loudly, but we were happy for a lift.

"Still more work to do," he said.

Luke had kind, intelligent eyes and a shy smile. I could feel his sense of commitment and authority. He dropped us at the front door of his favorite restaurant, a place renowned for fish and chips. We ordered up and were in seafood heaven, until it was time to hitchhike back to the campground. It was getting late, and cars passed without slowing. One after another after another. Clark put me out front, reasoning a woman would seem less threatening. It worked. Two young guys stopped and motioned us to hop in their rusty truck bed. We hoisted ourselves up and sat amidst old tires and loose beer bottles. The truck rumbled off and we slammed around helplessly for four miles. Ah well, beggars can't be choosers.

The driver stopped at the campground entrance and motioned us to jump out. Clark awkwardly spilled over the back gate, bouncing the cab heavily before he landed alongside it. I was nearly catapulted into the air. My unladylike dismount consisted of falling over the side and flailing about to stay upright. The two young men burst into fits of laughter but didn't offer to help. Why should they? It was more fun to watch.

Eyes Up Here, Mister

Day 10: Friday, June 13
Weather: Sunny and warm
Distance: 30 miles
Route: Yachats, Oregon, to Florence, Oregon

We slept like babies. The soothing sound of the ocean lulled us into dreamland and we woke feeling peaceful and ready for the day. We broke camp quickly and rode into Yachats for a tasty blueberry pancake breakfast. It was a gorgeous morning. We attacked the steep hill outside town with renewed vigor, both of us pumping along without complaint. We stopped to take in the ocean expanse at a scenic overlook. The breeze cooled our warm bodies. My eyes panned from where we were standing to a hill of colorful wildflowers and then to the churning water below. The rugged, rocky coastline caused waves to hit hard and spray high into the air, creating a brief misty haze.

A policeman approached us. He pointed toward a car in the rest area. An ashen-faced woman sat behind the wheel. We hadn't noticed her or the car. The cop asked lots of questions about that vehicle: When did we arrive? How long had the car been there? Did the vehicle pass us on the road? He pumped us for answers we didn't have.

The officer moved in closer to the car, with us trailing behind. The driver was slumped over the steering wheel. At first glimpse, I thought the woman was dead. As it turned out, she was very much alive. Just drunk. Really drunk. And, judging from the bottle still in her hand, the culprit was lemon-flavored Absolut Vodka.

Clark helped the cop pull the lady out of her old Lincoln, and they struggled to put her into the back of the squad car. The inebriated woman kept insisting she wasn't the one driving, but her belligerent protests didn't unnerve the policeman. He remained calm and kind, even when the wasted woman tried to get out of the squad car and took a few crazy, off-balance swings for good measure. The officer cuffed her, stuffed her back in the car, read her her rights, and drove away with a curt nod in our direction.

This situation was an eye opener. Here was a drunk driver, who sometime earlier that day had shared the road with us. She could easily have hit one or both of us as we headed up the hill. The reality of impaired drivers being on the road sunk in deep. It's one thing to be relatively protected inside a car, but yet another when you're on a bike, exposed and vulnerable. So, with a bit more sobriety, we pedaled on.

~

We met a muscular German cyclist at Heceta Head who was also traveling cross-country. He spoke almost no English and was delighted to meet Clark. The two of them were instant pals, chattering away in German. I stood by politely, grinning and making believe I was part of the animated conversation, nonchalantly drifting away when they were fully engrossed in their exchange. I was happy seeing Clark so engaged, knowing how much he enjoyed the intellectual exchange.

I gazed at Heceta Head Lighthouse from the scenic viewpoint—a place I'd visited many times before. The idyllic setting high above the ocean and fairy-tale architecture were a beacon in so many ways. Since 1894, the lighthouse has guided sailors to safe harbor, beaming 21 miles out to sea with the brightest light on the Oregon coast. No wonder this place is said to be the most photographed lighthouse in the United States. Rumor has it, the lightkeeper's house is haunted by an elderly woman nicknamed Rue. She purportedly moves things around, does some light housekeeping, and has even appeared on several occasions.

A loud guffaw startled me out of my daydream. Hans and Clark were cracking jokes that of course were a mystery to me, but their hilarity was contagious. As I walked toward them, I couldn't help giggling. Laughter—the universal language of happiness. Clark drew me into the conversation by sharing the highlights. Hans was 59 years old and had just arrived on the Oregon Coast from New York City. Amazingly, his ride only took two months. He rode a lightweight racing bike, carried minimal gear, and traveled over 125 miles a day. That seemed crazy to us, but I was pleased to learn he'd lost 20 pounds off his already fit frame.

I wondered if Hans enjoyed the ride as much as we did. How could he stop and take in the life and character of a place when flying through so quickly? When did he feel the heartbeat of America? Or meet the people and smell the roses? I couldn't help thinking our slower pace had myriad benefits. At least for us. Ultimately, everyone chooses the journey that suits them best, whether a life path or bike path.

~

The wind picked up and brought a chill. It was time to get moving. Last stop for Hans was San Francisco, where he'd rendezvous with his wife and daughter. He shared some final bicycling wisdom. First, get mirrors. A smart cyclist, I realized, would never leave home without this safety feature. And his parting advice, "Keep your ears stiff," which basically means "Listen for cars!" We waved good-bye and pedaled off as Hans finished adjusting something on his bike. A couple minutes later, he blew past us, shouted *"auf wiedersehen"* and was out of sight, before I could bat an eye.

~

We made good time to Florence and treated ourselves to a motel with a pool, hot tub, and sauna. As we lollygagged by the pool, an older man sat down next to us. It was obvious he wanted to talk. He started off by telling us his age (77) and where he was from (Hungary) and then launched into his life story. It was interesting, but disconcerting, as he spent the entire time talking directly to my breasts.

"I love this country," he said, while gawking at my bosom. "Anything is possible here."

Not quite.

He talked of his wife and marriage and how lucky he was to find a woman who allowed him such freedom. Was this some kind of vague come-on? The guy waxed poetic about his love for his wife, but not even for a moment did he take his eyes off my boobs. Clark finally had enough of the Hungarian's lecherous downward glances at my cleavage and suggested we get out of the sun.

Busted

Day 11:   **Saturday, June 14**
Weather: **Sunny**
Distance: **Never touched our bikes**
Route: **Walked to meals and back**

It was five days since we'd had a day off. We didn't feel like leaving the ocean yet and called the desk to reserve our room for another day. Lolling in bed, we dreamed up our ideal breakfast. If it could be anything, Clark would go for bagels and lox, while I catered to my insatiable sweet tooth, and fantasized about savoring a sinful cinnamon roll.

As luck would have it, cinnamon rolls were prominently displayed on the menu at the restaurant next door. I ordered one without a second thought. It was huge. As big as a pillow. I was shocked by its size. The caramel glistened seductively. Chopped nuts dripped off its plump loveliness. It was delicious but so big even I couldn't finish the whole thing.

As we walked toward the door, I heard someone ask, "Wow! What is that? I wonder how many calories are in that thing." Everyone at that table and several others, including a family of six and two groups of thin, attractive couples, turned to stare. They looked me up and down, checking out every body part. A rush of embarrassment came over me. My face reddened. I felt like running, but tried to act casual as we exited.

I could have stopped to talk about our action-packed journey and the likely number of calories burned in a day, but I'm not sure they would have believed me if I had. In retrospect, I should have smiled and said, "It was good, but recommend splitting it." Sometimes humor is best.

> People can be rude, always cluck-clucking about what others are doing, what they're wearing, and how they look and judging them for it. You never know what a person has been through. Did they lose a job? Have a fight with their best friend? Did their car break down? Are they silently suffering from chronic pain or is their house being foreclosed on? We all need to be more empathetic toward others.

With our bellies full and accommodations set, we spent the day exploring historic Old Town Florence. A lively folk band was jamming on a street corner surrounded by a circle of people dancing and clapping along with the beat. A giggling baby in a stroller rocked out next to a woman wearing a jester's hat. Just another summer day along the Oregon coast.

We wandered in and out of art galleries, shops and checked out the marina. It was bustling with boats. We played a game of "Which Would You Want If You Could Have Any?" It was a tough choice, so we narrowed the field by picking our favorite names: *CostaLotta, Fishful Thinking, The Old Goat's Boat, Breakin' Wind, Yes Dear, Aquaholics, Loon-a-Sea,* and *Yachta-Yachta*. For obvious reasons, we had to go with *Campbell's Sloop.*

WEEK 3

FLORENCE, OREGON, TO MITCHELL, OREGON

Goodbye, Pacific Ocean

    Day 12: Sunday, June 15
    Weather: Overcast
    Distance: 70 miles
    Route: Florence, Oregon, to Eugene, Oregon

It was Father's Day. We were both a little homesick, so I called my Dad, then contacted the kids. Ryan and Taea were living in Europe with their mother for a while. Clark missed the children, especially on this day. So did I. A forlorn look, then a smile, drifted across his face when he heard their voices.

I missed my father, too, and Clark had lost his less than a year earlier. Happily, we'd be with old friends later that night.

To help kick our melancholia, we set out to find a scenic place to take pictures of our rear wheels in the Pacific Ocean. Many people don't realize Portland, Oregon, is not a coastal town. It's actually 70 to 80 miles inland. Riding west and dipping our wheels in the water commemorated the start of our eastward passage toward the Atlantic Ocean.

We found the perfect spot in the sand, flat and firm, and backed our bikes into the water. A jogger volunteered to snap our photo. Mission accomplished.

~

Our turn toward the Atlantic reinvigorated us. We harnessed that energy and, despite the hilly terrain, kicked out a number of miles quickly, traveling east along the Siuslaw River toward Eugene.

A case of jittery nerves set in just outside the mouth of a deep, narrow tunnel. Cars and trucks whizzed through without slowing. The 1,430-foot tube unassumingly named "Petersen Tunnel" had no shoulder and offered no room to avoid an oncoming vehicle. We watched with trepidation for a long while.

A big button, located at bike level, generated blinking lights and drew attention to a sign warning drivers of "Bikes in Tunnel." Clark executed a test push. Caution lights sprang to life, but the cars continued shooting in and out of the tunnel one after another.

No other cyclists in sight while we waited it out, hoping for safety in numbers. I peered into the hole and saw only headlights and taillights blurring together like a time-lapse photo. When the frustration of waiting overtook the fear of moving forward, Clark pressed the button for real and we took off, riding on adrenaline. We stayed close together, pedaling like crazy.

Halfway through, we heard (or maybe *felt*) a car race up from behind. I nervously glanced over my left shoulder, just as the obnoxious driver angrily laid on his horn. The sound reverberated through the tunnel. My heart skipped a beat, and Clark, startled, accidently veered further into the road. This caused the jerk in the car to scream incomprehensible obscenities and blast the horn for 30 seconds straight. There was nowhere for us to go. No escape. We pushed our legs to their limits, with laser focus on the "light at the end of the tunnel."

Our efforts weren't good enough for the lunatic behind the wheel. He took the opportunity to screech around us as traffic on the left slowed, just a hair's breadth from grazing our bikes. We made it through the tunnel unscathed but had to pull over to regain our wits. "Fear energy" propelled us onward. We were almost to Eugene before it wore off.

~

Five miles from the house of our friends Joanna and Kelly, Clark felt his bike starting to wobble. I dropped behind to see if I could spot the trouble. Flat #2.

Instead of stopping to fix the tire, we called our friends for personal roadside assistance. They arrived within minutes and threw Clark's disabled bike and our gear in the back of their truck. Clark climbed into the vehicle, and one of our friends' twin boys jumped out. He pulled his own bike out of the truck bed and guided me to their house on a tree-lined bike path. I listened to his happy chatter and enjoyed the freedom of sailing along without the heavy bags bogging me down. The sensation of lightness and unbridled preteen vitality leading the way made for an unforgettable ride.

When I walked in the door, Clark was enjoying a beer—the day's troubles behind him. Joanna whipped up a big salad and Kelly fired up the barbecue. A few laughs and a few adult beverages later, we forgot we owned bikes at all.

It's the Journey, Not the Destination

Day 13 & 14:	Monday and Tuesday, June 16 and 17
Weather:	Rain, but it didn't matter
Distance:	Not very far
Route:	To the refrigerator and back

We spent the day vegetating, running errands, and hanging out. Clark fixed his flat tire. I did laundry and stocked our food supply for the upcoming trip over the mountains.

We called our housesitter and learned that Mozart, our 150-pound husky–wolf mix, missed us terribly. He was moping around the house, emitting pitiful doggy sighs, looking at his babysitter with big, sad puppy eyes. No amount of petting or even dog bones lifted his spirits.

Mozart was 4 years old. We'd picked him from a litter of eight ridiculously cute puppies. They all looked like miniature wolves. One little furball tippy-trotted over to us, scrambled onto my lap, and leaned into me. I guess Mozart chose us.

We put him in an open box with snuggly blankets for the trip home. I sat in the back seat and stroked his thick fur to comfort him. Eventually, he drifted off to sleep. A few minutes later, he popped up and let out the sweetest wolf howl we'd ever heard. Oww-oooooooh…. I couldn't resist picking him up and tucking him into my coat.

As Mozart grew into his enormous adulthood, he didn't realize how big he was. Even when full grown, he wanted to be on my lap. He was my boy. Once in a while, the two boys would "spoon" on the floor: Mozart in the front position and Clark with his arm wrapped lovingly over him.

The day before leaving on the trip, we put our car in the garage and removed the battery since the vehicle would sit idle for months. Mozart monitored our every move closely. As we finished up, he jumped into the backseat and refused to move. It took a lot of coaxing to get him out. How did he know we were leaving?

I told Mozart and our orange tabby, Phil, that we'd be back soon and everything would be fine. I guess the message didn't get through to our dog. That made me sad. Fortunately, Phil was fine and seemed unaffected by our departure. He was such a character—loving and funny, sometimes playfully naughty. He'd scratch the furniture, get sprayed with water, race to another chair, scratch, spray, repeat. Phil was also adaptable to change and didn't care who fed him or who he slept with, as long as he was full and warm.

~

Clark awoke with flu symptoms on the day we were to leave. He was achy, tired, and crabby. Our friends encouraged us to stay so he could sleep it off. A wise choice. Clark rested and I enjoyed some quality time with Joanna, just the two of us. She was with me when Clark and I met and was the first to spot the connection between us, insisting he noticed me the moment I walked in the restaurant. Clark corroborated that later.

Joanna is one of my closest, long-time friends. People seem to gravitate toward her like planets around the sun. She's that person you can tell anything to and not feel judged. Even if I do something extraordinarily stupid, she has a way of making it seem funny and comes up with great ways to fix any missteps.

Joanna also routinely shares wise advice. This day was no exception. In a philosophical moment, she reminded me, "It's the journey not the destination. Enjoy every day, every minute. Make it your own, play by your own rules, not the expectations of others."

The Helpful Hippie

Day 15:   Wednesday, June 18
Weather: Sunny and warm
Distance: 50 miles
Route: Eugene, Oregon, to Blue River, Oregon

Clark still felt a bit peaked, but it was a beautiful day and time to ride. Plus, we didn't want to overstay our welcome. We set aside a bag of things to leave behind. Clark took out a radio that never worked very well, a big camera case, a pair of jeans, and an extra pair of riding gloves. I only had one roll of film to contribute. It didn't change the weight of my pack, but helped psychologically to see the big pile of stuff we wouldn't have to carry anymore. Joanna tucked the bag away on a closet shelf for safekeeping. We'd pick it up after the trip.

The family gathered for our send-off, and the twins volunteered to guide us to the bike path. They were serious about this job and didn't ride too fast for fear of losing us old farts.

The plan was to take the path to Springfield, then pick up Highway 126 toward the mountains. Any well-maintained bike path is a joy to ride. Easy-breezy until we needed to connect with the main road. At that point, we got confused and cycled in circles for nearly 45 minutes trying to find our way. We asked directions from three people, inadvertently getting misdirected each time—or maybe we were in an alternate, looping universe?

At a high point of exasperation we were rescued by a white knight in a beat-up blue VW bus. Our hero? An old hippie, complete with long gray hair, peace-sign tattoo, tie-dyed t-shirt, and love beads strung loosely around his neck. He leaned out the flower-stickered window and asked, "Hey, man, where ya goin'?"

Eugene is hippie heaven. A gathering place of those who still happily live in the '60s. Peace, love, and Birkenstocks.

Our white knight's mouth formed a perfect "O" when we told him Portland to Portland. And, with a look of equal parts admiration and disbelief, he stammered, "Whooooooa. That's heavy. Cool."

~

We traveled lazily along Highway 126, feeling mellow, following the McKenzie River and enjoying the warmth of the sun. Two pseudo-hippies on the path of life.

A man in a sports car beeped and waved, then pulled onto the shoulder and waited for us to pedal up.

"I noticed 'Portland to Portland' painted on your tent bag," he said. "That sounds like fun!"

He took a few minutes to make sure we saw the area from the best perspective.

"There's a nicer road that bypasses the highway. Less traffic and fantastic scenery. But, it's a little longer and hilly."

I pondered the idea of "longer" and "hilly" with my best poker face.

One glance at Clark told me he was doing some pondering of his own. We thanked the man and waved until he was out of sight. In the middle of a "do-we-or-don't-we" conversation, a young woman pulled up, jumped out of a pick up, and ran toward us with infectious gusto.

Now what?

"My husband just called and told me you're riding across country. Can I come along?" she teased.

Before we could get a word in edgewise, she continued bubbling with genuine excitement. "Where are you staying tonight? We live a few miles up the road. Why don't you stay with us? We'd love it!"

The woman was so energetic and positive, it took everything in us not to quit for the day and head for their house. But we were in the mood to ride and had hours of daylight ahead.

Despite the extra legwork, we decided to take the hilly, scenic route and keep moving. I was also a little worried the couple might drive back and be offended if we didn't.

Clark said, "You're sweet, but are too concerned about what other people might think."

He was right. What a happy thing to know that total strangers would go out of their way to help. No ulterior motives or expectations from them. They just wanted to share in our adventure.

Kindness was a theme that prevailed throughout the trip. There are not psycho killers around every corner. Most people truly want to reach out and connect. This is the real America.

~

The day's goal was to get as close to the base of Santiam Pass as possible so the ride would be shorter and less stressful in the morning. We churned out 15 miles with relative ease, then turned off the main road toward a campground we'd heard about in Blue River. After riding a while, all we saw were three older homes and wondered if that's all there was to the community. Each house was stone quiet, not a living soul in sight, not even a dog or cat. We pedaled a few more blocks looking for signs of civilization.

"I don't think Blue River exists. Let's go back to the highway," Clark said.

We turned around and headed back. It was only seven or eight blocks, but felt like miles.

We finally saw two kids skateboarding down the road and asked how to get to Blue River.

"It's a mile up that way," one young man said as he pointed in the direction we'd just explored.

We spun our heads around, then back to the boys.

Amused by our exasperation (and probably used to giving directions to out-of-towners) they said in unison, "You didn't go far enough."

"Thanks," we answered, trying not to sound too frustrated. This time we found Blue River without mishap. A tiny main street is situated perpendicular to an imposing mountain peak, giving a postcard-perfect view. The pine-covered highland watches over the town like a benevolent guardian.

We rolled up to a woman sitting on a bench in front of a store to ask directions to the campground. She was eccentric in appearance, wearing a 1940s-style halter dress and ankle-strap shoes and lips adorned with exaggerated red lipstick; her gray hair was perfectly coiffed into Betty Grable waves.

"Hi," she said, smiling broadly, shielding her eyes from the afternoon sun, her slender hand tipped with long, red fingernails.

"Hi," we responded. "Can you tell us where the campground is?"

Confusion crossed her face.

"I don't know," she said. "I'm new in town. Only been here a few years."

We stared at her, creating an awkward silence.

"O-oh," Clark stuttered, giving me a sidelong glance.

"Yeah, sorry. I'm new," she repeated vacantly.

We were stunned.

Fortunately, a lady walking into the store heard the conversation and pointed us in the right direction—a couple blocks away.

We looked back toward "Betty." She shrugged indifferently, slipped on oversized black sunglasses and tilted her face toward the sun.

~

The campground was predominantly filled with older folks in motorhomes. We were the only tent campers that night. The "residents" were inquisitive as we rode up. They surrounded us, eyeing our faces and belongings closely, asking lots of questions.

What are your names? Where are you from? Where are you going? Do you work? Do you have kids?

After we passed their scrutiny, they accepted us into the fold and were welcoming and friendly, wandering back and forth for casual conversation until late in the evening.

For years, most of these RV-ers spent summers in this same spot and knew each other well. The continuity of seasonal friendships was appealing. You could feel camaraderie in the air.

~

Dinner would have been day-old burritos from the general store. But, instead, we were invited to a BBQ at an RV owned by a retired couple from Colorado. Our hosts welcomed us with wine, cheese, and crackers. Then we feasted on charbroiled burgers, a big salad, corn-on-the-cob, and homemade baked beans. Another neighbor dropped by with a family-recipe chocolate cake. Clark tried to weasel the secret ingredient out of the baker, but no luck.

There was good-natured bantering all night long under a sky filled with millions of twinkling stars. Other campers joined the party, as the moon rose high in the sky, pulling their lawn chairs up for the best view. For them it was a nightly ritual. For us, a special treat.

Old Goats, New Tricks

>Day 16: Thursday, June 19
>Weather: Sunny, but cool and windy
>Distance: 67 miles
>Route: Blue River, Oregon, to Sisters, Oregon

Despite the wine and soft grass, the night was long and uncomfortable. We tossed and turned, waking up often, worrying about the mountainous ride ahead—our biggest challenge yet. We'd have to climb up and over the steep 4,817-foot Santiam Pass. Dread hung over us like morning fog on the ocean.

We gave up on sleep uncharacteristically early and walked the few blocks into Blue River for breakfast. Oatmeal with crisp bacon on the side. We chose something that would stick to our ribs, fortifying us for the formidable mountain pass ahead.

Back at camp, we packed for the long day's ride. Our neighbors, still curious, came over one by one with more questions.

Tell us again … why are you doing this? Aren't you afraid? What do you do when it rains? Have you had any trouble? Is a friend following you in their car? Are you packing a piece? How do you charge your cell phone? Do you lose the signal in the mountains?

They were shocked when they heard our answers. We're doing it for fun, just because we want to. The only things that scare us are mountains, bridges, tunnels, and traffic. When it rains, we get wet! Most people reach out with kindness and support. No one is following us in a car. We aren't carrying a gun and didn't bring a cell phone, so there's no chance of it going dead in the mountains.

"Strange people out there … like hippies who take baths in outdoor hot springs … *with nothing on!*" one octogenarian exclaimed in all seriousness.

"They even do *IT* in broad daylight," a prim-looking woman whispered confidentially.

It seemed our unusual adventure, or maybe our physical vulnerability, made people feel they could speak more openly and honestly. Often, perfect strangers let their guard down and shared their wildest dreams and deepest, darkest fears. Maybe they were inspired by two chunky monkeys—two unlikely folks—pedaling cross-country. Maybe we motivated them to follow their dreams.

~

The climb was gradual at first. I wasn't in the lowest gear but could feel the consistent strain of pedaling. We stopped every couple miles, resting briefly, then started again slowly. For me, stopping frequently made the ride harder. Just as I warmed up, we stopped again. I was psychologically ready to confront the mountain and wanted to keep moving.

Chug-a-lugging along, with no bursts of great speed, I didn't want or need to rest as often as Clark. He pedaled ahead like mad, grunting and panting, preferring to stop frequently (the proverbial tortoise and the hare).

We agreed to stay within shouting distance, in case one of us needed help. We inched along like caterpillars, but even at our slow crawl made progress.

Clark was leaning toward making a stop at a campground a third of the way up, complaining about not feeling well. We had 10 grueling miles before reaching the summit. I wanted to go on, but didn't want to be insensitive to his malaise.

As we weighed the pros and cons of stopping, two young men pulled over to ask if we were OK. They gave us fresh water, a candy bar and listened to our tale. Clark and the guys compared notes on cycling equipment and strutted around the bikes like peacocks, outdoing each other with their technical expertise. Fascinating. I suspect every woman has seen men do this dance.

"Hey, let's plan a trip!" one of the young men suddenly blurted to the other.

"Yeah, how 'bout next summer?" the other responded like an eager puppy.

Their enthusiasm renewed Clark's inspiration to tackle Santiam Pass. A fresh determination set on his face. He remounted his bike with revived energy.

Our discussion of stopping clearly over. Those two young men will never know how much they helped us.

~

Hours went by. The climb got steeper and steeper and steeper. We struggled, sweated, played mind games to keep going, and rested often. We even walked our bikes part of the way. It was far from easy, but we kept moving forward pedal by pedal, inch by inch, and eventually reached the summit.

There was no fanfare when we reached the top—no crowd waiting with balloons, cheers, and beers. We felt cheated. Where was everybody?

> Clark liked the "stop-and-walk" method. Walking worked different muscles and gave our butts, knees, and hands a break. For me, though, it was more work. Once I stopped, it was hard to start again. Getting my feet snapped into the clipless pedals while sliding backwards on a steep slope wasn't easy. Plus, getting all that fat moving in the same direction took a lot of energy, even on a flat road, but it was much worse when you had to do it going uphill.

Dark clouds gathered, and the night air turned cold. We piled on extra clothes, then started down the other side of Santiam Pass. The road was steep and long and we used our brakes to stay in control on the curves, stopping often to cool the brakes down avoiding extra wear. Night was fully upon us as we coasted into Sisters.

Setting up camp put Clark in an unpleasant mood. Maybe it was not the night to give up any comforts. Unfortunately, there were no showers or even warm water at the park. The wind picked up, making it a challenge to pitch the tent. We argued about everything.

I wanted to take off my sweaty clothes and get into something warmer before fighting with the tent. Clark wanted to get the tent situated and warm up in town over a beer. I wanted to lock up the bikes; he thought I was paranoid. He wanted to lay out the sleeping bags; I didn't.

~

We stopped at the first bar we saw, Bronco Billy's Ranch Grill & Saloon (a.k.a. Hotel Sisters), mostly to avoid being alone together. Screw beer. A big pitcher of margaritas was what the doctor ordered for big ol' bickering babies. We started being civil after downing just one, admitting exhaustion had possessed our bodies.

While eating dinner, we amused ourselves by watching a boxing match on TV. Country music drowned out the sound. Through dog-tired, margarita-world eyes, it looked like the boxers were punching along with the music and that made us laugh.

Our eyelids were drooping. While sitting there our muscles had turned to rubber. Walking the mile back to the campground seemed like an endless, cold treadmill of pain.

~

We zipped our sleeping bags together to share warmth, but it was challenging with our round bodies bursting from under the covers in various ways. The fleshy bits froze quickly and we'd readjust to compensate. As the night wore on and margaritas wore off, the temperature dropped further. Our battle for optimum warmth raged on.

Entering Cowboy Country

Day 17:   Friday, June 20
Weather: Sunny and hot
Distance: 43 miles
Route: Sisters, Oregon, to Prineville, Oregon

We woke up just after 5 a.m., the temperature already warming. Thankfully, we had an easy ride ahead—40 miles of flat terrain—giving us plenty of time for a nice breakfast and a slow wake-up for sore muscles.

~

The mile walk back to Sisters went smoother than last night. A small café, nestled between two historic buildings, called our names. After breakfast, we strolled back to the campground to pack up.

A couple dressed in black spandex sauntered over to inspect our gear and criticize our habits. They were riders, too, and "appalled" we were still in camp when it was nearly 10 a.m. They mentioned several times they would always be on the road by 6 a.m. and done with their ride by noon.

"So … you're still here …?" I asked ever so innocently.

"We're on a layover day," the skinnier of the skinny two replied.

They bragged about camping every night and going for days without showers. For a final dig, they sarcastically mentioned seeing us struggle up Santiam Pass and commented on how long it took. *They* had ridden to the summit just last year in record time.

Clark and I were annoyed by the passive–aggressive behavior. We communicated telepathically and with subtle eye contact, using that "secret language" couples who've been together a long time develop. Fortunately, the obnoxious pair seemed oblivious to our code, got bored with us, and left.

Our favorite visitor that morning was a 67-year-old cyclist named Bill, on his second foray across the country. He traveled solo, had top-notch equipment, and the body of a god.

"I did this trip 10 years ago. It's harder this time," he said. "I really notice the difference. But in a way it's a better trip."

He rode with his grandson last time. The young man wanted to ride fast and never stop to enjoy the moment.

"I like riding alone. I go as far as I want and stop often."

"Aren't you lonely?" I asked.

"It's funny ... when you're alone and old, people are curious. They can't believe I'm still rolling along. Strangers invite me into their homes to vicariously experience my ride. No one's afraid of a decrepit guy like me," Bill said with a laugh.

The way Bill traveled was validating. He agreed about 50 miles a day was a good distance—far enough to cover ground but not so straining and fast that you miss a chance to meet people and "smell the roses."

We learned he ate in restaurants twice a day and only carried snacks for lunch and power boosts. That made us feel better psychologically, because we'd been eating out regularly and sometimes felt guilty about doing so.

Bill didn't carry a cook stove. After his first trip he realized it was too much of a hassle, took up too much room, and weighed the packs down. That caught Clark's attention. He already wanted to send our stove home.

Bill was our confirmation there really are a 1,000 ways to undertake an extensive bicycling vacation. No rules; no right or wrong—only what works best for you. We were encouraged to see a more experienced cyclist riding our way: taking time to enjoy the moments.

After Bill rode off, we felt inspired to follow suit, heading out of the campground to cheery "good lucks" and "safe travels" coming from all directions.

The day was sunny and warm, birds were singing, and our muscles, although still sore from the trauma of Santiam Pass, felt ready to move again.

Redmond was 20 smooth miles away. In a few hours we were seated in a Mexican restaurant. My eyes followed a string of Christmas lights looped along the ceiling. The place was awash in their color. Clark's grin spread from ear to ear as he bit into a corn chip piled high with guacamole and spicy salsa.

"Mmmmmm…" is all he said.

After lunch our pace slowed. The afternoon sun blazed. The 20-mile trip to Prineville was torturous. Without shade, my freckled nose, ears, and forehead turned beat red. I lathered on sunscreen, but the powerful rays found a way through.

As we plodded along, the vegetation changed from thick pine forest to the muted colors of high-desert sage brush. The variation marked a substantial milestone and moved us into an environment completely different than the familiar lush green of Portland.

~

Prineville was bigger than I remembered. Either the city had grown in the last few years or perspective changes when you switch your mode of transportation from car to bike.

High-school rodeo weekend filled the town. Hotels, restaurants, and coffee shops were packed. The streets teemed with rowdy teens ready for a night out. A little persistence on our part paid off and we managed to finagle the last motel room in the area.

We hauled the bikes and gear up a long, steep flight of stairs to our room. No small feat. I called my Mom and heard great relief in her voice when she learned that we were safe and sound; we hadn't realized the depth of her worry. We put her on speaker and tag-teamed the storytelling. Soon she was laughing, her concerns alleviated. We promised to check in more often.

After the call, we took long showers and laid down for a rest, taking turns rubbing each other's sore muscles. The air conditioning and soft bed felt heavenly after the hot ride and two nights of restless sleep.

"How does a 67-year-old make a trip like this?" Clark wondered aloud.

"Bill probably trained," I reasoned, "I'm sure he gets tired. What hurts on you?"

"Everything," Clark responded, "Pick a spot. How 'bout you?"

"Same."

That's the last thing I remember saying. We fell asleep and didn't stir again until dusk.

~

I woke up from our nap thinking I should be thinner by now. We did the math, realizing we were only 16 days into the trip and had pushed pedals for just 11 of those. Clark brightened at that revelation.

"It takes three to six weeks of exercise before the effort starts to make a difference," he rationalized.

"So, you're saying we have to actually PEDAL for a minimum of 21 days before we can even begin to see a difference?" I asked, trying to avert my eyes from the reflection in the mirror.

We agreed not to be so hard on ourselves. Yet, part of me felt disappointed. All that pain and suffering and I still looked exactly the same. In my next life, I'll push my way into the "Skinny Line!" Tall, thin, no tits, no ass. With my luck, though, I'll be a giraffe.

Then we realized it was time for dinner.

~

We couldn't pass up a restaurant featuring a big metal sign reading, "If you start a fight in here you're 86'd for life!" We were in cowboy country now.

Our seats offered ring-side views of the activity outside. A parade of youthful cowboys and girls, dressed in their finest, traipsed up and down the street eyeballing each other—the boys in cowboy hats, boots, and tight jeans with gigantic belt buckles, and the girls decked out in head-to-toe denim, their feet stuffed into high-heeled boots and hair fluffed and sprayed to amazing heights.

The food was good, but our waitress was better. She wore tight clothes designed for a teenage girl and was missing three front teeth. Her dyed jet-black hair hung to her waist, pulled up on the sides with baby barrettes adorned with frilly pink and blue bows. She was full of stories about young cowboys, fights and nights at the local bar.

"Yup, that's Prineville," she told us proudly. "Gotta love 'er for that!"

After dinner, we strolled the main street taking in the hormone-/testosterone-loaded action, invigorated by the lust in the air.

Mistaken for Drainbows

    Day 18:   Saturday, June 21, the longest day of the year
    Weather: Sun to hail to sun to rain to sun to wind
    Distance: 54 miles

Route: Prineville, Oregon, to Mitchell, Oregon, over the Ochoco Pass (4,720 feet)

Over a breakfast of French toast, sausages, and applesauce, we considered spending another night in Prineville to enjoy the rodeo and experience other cowboy activities. When in Rome ..., we figured.

Unfortunately, our hotel was fully booked, as was every room for miles around. This left us with only two choices: ride to the Ochoco Lake campground 8 miles away or take on a 54-mile ride up and over the Ochoco Pass into the small town of Mitchell. Neither of these options sounded good, so we dragged our feet getting started.

Our plan: Go with the flow and see what happens. We packed the bikes, pushed them down the narrow staircase, and pedaled out of town.

The campground looked tempting. Clark held down a prime picnic table while I went to a nearby store for snacks. I cruised all the aisles first to check out the options.

A female clerk came rushing toward me.

"Can I help you?" she asked in an unacceptably snotty tone.

"No, thank you," I said, trying to be friendly, "I'm just deciding what I want."

She didn't smile or offer a suggestion, just stood frozen, staring me down. I was confused by the cold reception and felt uncomfortable, so grabbed some salty chips and a couple sodas, paid, and left.

Meanwhile, Clark had a similarly negative experience. As he waited at the picnic table, a group of children hiked past with a camp counselor in tow. They were on the hunt for a good spot to eat lunch. A couple of kids wandered toward Clark, who offered to share our table. As soon as the counselor saw this, she raced over and pulled them away in a panic.

She continued glancing back to make sure Clark stayed where he was. He could feel her hostility.

We traded stories, mystified by our icy reception. When I returned to the store to recycle the soda cans, the place was filled with people talking and laughing. Suddenly, they fell silent and stared. It wasn't friendly. I was unwelcome but not sure why.

Did they not like strangers? Did my thighs scare them? Did we look like serial killers? Was there trouble recently with a marauding, lookalike couple in town? It was baffling. We didn't discover the reason until later. The decision to move on was obvious.

~

The slow ride took us 30 miles up a long hill that included steep shots three or four blocks long. The surrounding vegetation changed again, this time from high desert to alpine. The area was greener than we expected, probably due to late-season rains. We'd heard the weather had its own rhythm. And so it did.

Out of the blue it started hailing—so fast and strong we jumped off our bikes, dropped them on the roadside, and ran for cover. The marble-sized ice balls stung our skin. We huddled together, hiding under a pine tree with thick branches, thankful for our helmets, which provided excellent head protection.

The onslaught stopped just as quickly as it started. The temperature dropped significantly, and we were anxious to get rolling again. The weather pattern continued throughout the day. One minute raining, sun beaming the next, with short bursts of hail mixed in with calm skies and high wind. Mother Nature couldn't make a decision.

When the wind started to howl, we donned more clothes and prepped for a chilly ride down the mountain. A strong gust hit Clark and I watched him wobble from the impact. Without warning, a second blast hit me squarely on the side, throwing my heavy bike off balance. I teetered on the brink of tipping for a moment but caught myself before falling. Periodic gusts swept up the mountainside, taking away the fun of riding downhill. For the first time ever, I was glad for my extra bulk. I believe the weight (my own plus the heavy gear) prevented me from getting blown off the road, into traffic, or off the mountainside. What a relief when the winds calmed and the road flattened out.

~

I hit the proverbial wall about 5 miles from town and struggled to go on. Hunger pangs and loss of energy were winning the battle. Clark was tired, too, but anxious to finish the ride and quit for the day. Trying to keep the same pace is a downside of riding as a couple. It's a test of patience for whoever has to wait. Sometimes we supported each other well, but other times our differing speed and energy levels created problems.

I wolfed a granola bar and chugged water, while the wind blew fiercely around us. Clark nibbled on some pecans but restlessly waited to move on. The brief stop gave us needed fortification, as it took over an hour to go those last 5 miles. We fought low energy, frustration, and strong wind all the way into town.

The town of Mitchell was charming in its simplicity. It could pass as a stage set for an old Western movie—a true step back in time. Downtown Mitchell is only two blocks long and 1.2 square miles total. Population 130.

We parked our bikes in front of the historic Oregon Hotel and checked in. A small lobby offered a gathering place for morning coffee and evening wine. The owner, born and raised in Mitchell, shared pictures from years gone by. He pointed to a group of men in a faded brown photograph: "That's my father there and this is my uncle Ben, and there's Joe down at the feed store … ."

He told us his dad was known for cutting down the biggest tree in the county.

"When it fell, that thing filled five trucks with lumber," he said proudly.

Our travel plans were the next topic of conversation and he warned about the road ahead.

"You know we're in a valley here and there's a HECK of a climb to get out of it. Steep and long," he said. "Which way did you say you were heading? East, right? Oh, east is a bad one—the worst, in fact. Too bad you're not going west. That's MUCH easier!"

We wished he had left that part of the conversation out.

He showed us to our room, a comfy place with no TV or phone but a nice bed with fluffy pillows. The highlight was a claw-foot bathtub, a nod to the building's origins in the late 1800s.

After a relaxing bubble bath and dinner, we found our way to a local fiddle fest. The players were mostly older men who played with abandon. Their joy for music was infectious. People cheered wildly for their rock stars.

Eventually, an ancient guy on a respirator got up and walked toward the stage.

Clark pondered, "Do you think that guy is gonna play?"

"Yeah," I answered, "I think so."

Play indeed he did. For an hour.

> One reason we wanted to make the trip was to re-experience small-town life. The fiddle fest gave us a glimpse into a place where families and friends were interwoven through the generations. The impression? A community bonded by loyalty and history.

The scent of homemade pies and baked goods filled the air. We sniffed our way over to them and showed our appreciation by ordering gigantic molasses cookies. The bakers, who recognized we were out-of-towners, gave us their two cents before we left.

"You have a nasty climb tomorrow," one warned.

"No way out of it. It's a bad one for sure," another chimed in.

"I wouldn't want to go up that on a bike," a third one said, looking worried.

"Hope you're feeling strong!" said a fourth.

~

The evening took a strange turn near our hotel. A busload of unruly teens and 20-something guys pulled into town. They spilled onto the streets with angry energy. We watched in horror as one kid picked up a woman's dog by the ears. The puppy yelped in pain, and the owner rushed in. Clark yelled "Hey!" and was on the verge of intervening, but held back when the dog was safely in the owner's arms.

Other jackasses drank beer, crushed the cans, and threw them deliberately into the street. They demanded to use the hotel bathroom and hurled obscenities when the owner refused. The horde seemed universally proud of this obnoxious behavior and cheered like a rebel cry for whoever was the loudest, rudest, and raunchiest.

There was a palpable feeling more trouble was ahead. I was glad we'd spent the money to stay inside that night. We breathed a sigh of relief when they stumbled back onto the bus and headed east, taking trouble with them.

WEEK 4

Chuckles

Day 19: Sunday, June 22
Weather: Sunny and warm
Distance: 35 miles
Route: Mitchell, Oregon, to Dayville, Oregon

Over an early breakfast, we bumped into Bill, the cyclist we'd met at the Sisters campground. He'd spent the night at the same hotel, but we managed to miss each other. We shared a table and learned more about Bill. He was a professor from Chico, California, where Clark and I met and fell in love.

We compared notes on the day's ride. He'd been hearing the same disheartening stories about the difficulty of the climb. Bill's plan was to tackle it early, while our method was to procrastinate as long as possible, in the hopes of finding a way around it.

Bill pushed his chair back and said, "Well, better hit the road."

We ordered another cup of coffee and split a doughnut.

All the dire warnings about the "impossible pass" weighed on our minds, psyching us out. Our concern about making it to the top had turned to fear—which slowed us down more. When we thought we'd done all we could do to waste time, we readied ourselves to ride, packing our gear in worried silence.

Just as we were about to push off, Clark noticed I had a flat tire. Number three, on the front. A pain in the neck under most circumstances, but a good excuse to procrastinate further.

I took off my bags, while Clark got the toolkit. He had learned his lessons well and had my bike ready to ride quickly. He also tried to patch the old tube, in case we had more trouble down the road, but discovered the patch kit was out of glue. No problem, we thought, we're well prepared. We had a second patch kit. Little did we know, the glue in that kit was old and dried up. And, unfortunately, the only stores that carried the kits were fresh out and the new shipment wasn't expected to arrive for "a week or maybe two."

There was nothing left to do but ride. We could search for glue in the next town and hope we didn't get another flat before then.

Standard procedure is that long-distance cyclists should carry two spare tire tubes instead of only one, as well as a complete patch kit per person, and everything should be thoroughly checked before riding. Of course, we hadn't done that.

~

It was time to face the mountain. Back in the saddle again, we soon found another convenient distraction a few doors down from the hotel. Beautifully crafted picnic tables and chairs. The woodworker looked up and smiled curiously as we approached. We were only too happy to stop and chat about our trip when he hailed us over.

"What kind of wood is that?" Clark asked.

"The best western red cedar you can buy," the man responded.

"Nice," I added.

"Thank you," he said as he stroked the smooth table top.

We talked for a long time. I sensed he was lonely. This meant I worked harder to be nice, which meant he talked to us longer, which meant we couldn't start riding. It was a symbiotic relationship.

Not surprisingly, Picnic Table Guy couldn't say good-bye without adding his take on the hill.

"It's thousands of miles long and has a 6% grade, too!"

~

We rode a couple hundred feet from the main street to Highway 26—the start of the climb—and promptly freaked out. Essentially in full view of everyone in town.

"We can do this," I said nervously, gazing at the steep incline.

Clark responded by sticking out his thumb.

"What are you doing?" I asked incredulously.

"Trying to get a ride," he said, in all seriousness. "This thing is way too long and steep. I don't want to do it."

He'd already made up his mind.

I didn't want to hitchhike. I wanted to prove all the naysayers wrong but didn't want to ride without him, either. Cars and trucks passed by for 20 minutes.

We stood a bit longer—Clark hopeful, me humiliated. But fate was on my side. Thankfully, no one stopped to pick us up.

A few vehicles later, I finally found my strength.

"Maybe the ride *will* be too hard. But we should at least TRY," I said. "If we can't make it, we'll hitchhike."

Clark countered with, "Let me try a few more cars."

"I'm going to ride," I said with newfound determination. I was not going to let the climb beat me.

Not long after, Clark gave up hitching and settled on brute strength. A few minutes later he pedaled past me. In no time, we were both breathing hard and sweating heavily, but on our way up, under our own steam, and that felt good.

~

We learned an important lesson about success and determination that day. The challenge was primarily between our ears—a psychological game—to keep a positive mindset. You can't let yourself get psyched out or let other people's fears overwhelm you. We had worked ourselves into such a state of self-doubt that we weren't sure we could reach the summit. Getting beyond the negative helped us overcome our fears and conquer the mountain.

I'm not pretending it was an easy ride. It wasn't. We struggled. The ascent nearly broke our spirits. We pedaled at a tilt, our calves and thighs constantly tensed against the pressure of hauling our bodies, bikes, and gear up the cruel incline. The pessimists were right; it was SOME hill. Six miles long and 4,372 feet high at the peak.

Clark beat me to the summit and stood, arms crossed, chest pumped, watching my progress. As I neared the top, he ran down and pushed my bike up the last few feet. I laughed so hard I lost what little breath I had left.

And then came the payoff: We glided down the other side! And what a ride it was. Probably the most fun I've ever had on a bicycle. A nice, slow, easy downhill roll. Not so fast and curvy that it was dangerous, just enough to keep us going without pedaling.

We laughed all the way down. You couldn't pay for a carnival ride this much fun. To add pleasure upon pleasure, the air smelled like heaven. White wildflowers dotted the roadside, scenting our path with an invisible gauntlet of sweet fragrance.

The delights continued at the bottom of the pass. We followed the John Day River, which meanders south–southeast for 281 miles across Oregon. It's a tributary of the Columbia River and one of the nation's longest free-flowing rivers.

The road wound along the steep canyon walls of the John Day Fossil Beds. The national monument covers 20 square miles and dates to nearly 40 million years ago. Fossil remains include skeletons of early horses, rhinoceroses, camels, and other mammals. Heavily eroded layers of ancient volcanic ash created the distinct bands of red, orange, black, and tan.

The natural beauty of the landscape humbled us to the point of silence. I felt insignificant amidst the magnificence of the Painted Hills. It was hard to believe we stood in a place where rhinos roamed with camels. We were just a tiny speck in time.

~

We were only 8 miles outside the little town of Dayville when our energy levels plummeted. We stopped to eat energy bars three times, rested often, walked part of way, and tried to sing. It took all we had to keep going.

Heavy road construction started 2 miles from town. Solid pavement changed to gravel and dirt, which meant tougher riding conditions. The wheels slid around, with no stability, and we pushed hard to move at all. We tried walking the bikes, but that was more difficult than riding. So, we went back to pedaling—only to dismount a few yards farther on to walk again. The process seemed endless.

~

We pulled into a café on the main street, too tired to find a place to sleep until after dinner. The waitress tipped us off to a church that let cyclists spend the night for free. The safe haven included showers, too.

Knowing we had a place to stay later allowed us to relax and soak in the atmosphere. Dayville, a town of less than 200, had a light, easy ambiance that made it comfortable to spend a couple hours hanging out in the café people watching. And we did plenty of that. Of course, visitors are subject to being watched right back.

In walked an older guy with a face full of character and experience, weathered by the sun, wind, and perhaps an occasional beating. He was dressed in worn jeans and a flannel shirt and had a red scarf hanging loosely around his neck. A gaping hole in the brim of his cowboy hat looked as if someone had taken a bite out of it. His boots were cracked and breaking along the tops and clunked heavily with every step.

"Hey, Chuckles!" a chorus of patrons greeted the man enthusiastically.

What a perfect name. Clark and I grinned at each while sipping our sixth glass of iced tea.

Everyone liked him. He spoke in a drawl I couldn't quite place.

~

We walked our bikes through town, heading toward the church, when Clark spotted a familiar face and shouted, "Hey, Chuckles!"

The cowboy stopped and said, "Do I know you?" in that mysterious twang.

"No," we admitted, confessing we'd seen him at the diner.

He pushed his oversized hat back and flashed us a smile. "You headin' to church for the night?"

We nodded.

Without a pause, he invited us to bunk at his place.

"I got plenty of room."

Clark tried to decline the generous offer, but Chuckles wouldn't take no for an answer.

"I got cold beer in the fridge, darlin'," he said, winking my way.

That was too hard to resist.

~

We walked alongside Chuckles through a modest neighborhood of small, identical homes. All a non-descript tan color, well maintained, and simply landscaped. A little kid whizzed by on a bike with training wheels, giving us a big thumbs-up. Neighbors waved from porches, calling greetings to Chuckles, who tipped his hat in their direction.

He turned up a short walkway and opened an unlocked door. "We're home."

The tiny living room had a couch, two wooden chairs, boxy TV, and dusty VHS machine. A stack of unopened mail sat on a shelf. I noticed several trophies and lots of pictures of a rodeo clown.

"That's me," Chuckles said. "Retired now, but it was one heck of a life."

Chuckle's photos hung haphazardly throughout the home, mixed in with pictures of his kids. He told us some of his sons had also chosen a rodeo life.

We dropped our stuff in a dinky back bedroom and joined Chuckles in the kitchen. He was busy popping caps off three beers and started in on rodeo stories before we could sit down. He loved a new audience.

His real name was Chuck, and during the '70s he won best rodeo clown in the nation two years in a row. He'd broken his legs nine times, his arms seven, and every rib in his body at one time or another, showing us scars as he talked. He recounted stories of getting hooked by bulls, stepped on, kicked, and butted. Sometimes he was lucky enough to walk away with bruises; other times he was rushed away by ambulance with serious injuries.

"If it didn't hospitalize you for more than a week it wasn't worth mentioning," Chuckles said matter of factly.

He motioned us to sit on the couch and pulled up a chair for himself, digging out a gigantic scrapbook full of newspaper clippings, photos, rodeo ribbons, and other memorabilia.

"I've been in jail too many times to count, mostly from drinking too much," he said. Chuckles looked off to nowhere in particular and added, "I'm an outlaw, but don't worry, I'd never steal from you."

Somehow, I knew that was true.

Stories flowed long into the night. Chuckles chain-smoked and drank Hamm's beer while telling wild tales about drunken parties, gambling raids, getting shot, and the time he drove his car over a cliff and managed to walk away without a scratch.

He talked about his kids with great affection and his multiple marriages and relationships with bittersweet comedy. When one of his kids asked where he'd like to be buried, Chuckles answered (with a great cowboy drawl), "Well, shi-i-i-it. Wherever I fall down-n-n-n!"

In the wee hours, Chuckles broke out his guitar and sang country ballads he'd penned.

"I love being a cowboy. I could fight bulls till the day I die!"

The Rude Awakening

    Day 20:   Monday, June 23
    Weather: Sunny and warm, but not too hot. A perfect day!
    Distance: 30 miles, but actually rode 40 (I'll explain)
    Route: Dayville to John Day, Oregon

Chuckles' "accommodations for two" turned out to be a double mattress hanging over a single box-spring. Clark started out on the side away from the wall and rolled out of bed when he moved too far from center. After he tumbled to the floor three times, we took turns sleeping on that side. Three tumbles. Switch. It was a challenge akin to staying atop a bucking bull. Ultimately, we pulled the mattress to the floor, but the room was so small the double-wide curved up, squishing us into a not-so-comfy snuggle position.

We woke to a warm, muggy room, so opened the window for fresh air. We heard Chuckles rummaging around in the kitchen. He told us he had to leave early, but we could stay as long as we liked. We said our goodbyes the night before, so we rearranged ourselves in the wedge bed for a few more winks.

A loud "voomph-voomph-voomph" and water pelting into the room jolted us from dreamland. Chuckles had turned the sprinkler on before he left, unaware of our open window. The icy-cold spray shocked our grogginess away. We flopped about like fish trying to escape the wedge and shut the window.

Giggling giddily, we gave up on sleep, packed up, left a thank you note, and closed the door behind us.

~

We went back to the café for breakfast, and perhaps not so surprisingly the customers already knew we spent the night with Chuckles. News travels fast in a small town.

"Hey, bikers. How'd you sleep?" someone called out. "Did Chuckles keep you up all night with stories?"

Even the waitress had a big grin on her face when she said, "It must have been an interesting night for you two!"

> I wrote to Chuckles during and following the trip, and we talked several times a year by phone. He always started the conversation with, "Well, hello darlin'."
>
> He was often in some sort of trouble.
>
> "Oh, hell. I'm not worried," he'd say. "They don't want me in jail. I'm not a criminal. Just get in trouble with the car is all."
>
> He told me he saved our thank you note in his scrapbook and always "threatened" to visit. Sadly, Chuckles passed away before he could do that. I miss him and our conversations. He was one special guy.

Thirty miles was the day's goal. Seemed manageable. Imagine that. Only a few weeks ago we would have considered it a long haul. What a difference a short time made.

We sailed along for 25 miles on a beautiful, curvy road, despite our lack of sleep. The pavement was smooth and nearly traffic free. It was bicycling bliss until—BANG! My bike swerved sharply sideways. A blowout on the front tire. What a scare. And a hassle. We'd forgotten to restock the repair glue and fix the spare tube. We were out of luck. My heart sank as I gained control of the bike and steered off the road.

Clark contemplated creative ways to fix the problem while I waited by the road with my thumb stuck out. To my great surprise, a driver stopped at once.

"What seems to be the trouble?" he asked kindly.

We explained the circumstances, and without a second thought he threw our bikes into the back of his shiny, blue pick-up. He knew of a good bicycle shop in the town of John Day and we were on our way.

Our Good Samaritan was a handsome man in his early '40s, with a crooked grin that stretched from ear to ear. There was a rugged simplicity about him. He was witty and laughed easily.

As Clark helped unload the bikes, he mentioned our stay at Chuckles' place the night before.

The wide grin reappeared, "Oh, I know Chuck. Everybody knows him. Can't think of a better man from here to the border."

~

We fixed my tire and stocked up on supplies, including a new repair kit and a super-thick bike tube the clerk claimed would outlast any other. Then, we secured a room for the night, removed our bike bags, and did something completely out of character. With plenty of daylight still on the clock, we went back to pedal the section of road missed earlier. Our bikes felt light and easy to maneuver without the extra weight.

I watched Clark as he effortlessly pumped his pedals, breathing easily, not a care in the world. We were in a new rhythm, finally found our groove. The exuberant expression on his face said it all.

Strong and proud, now able to "live on the road." With a little help from others, we'd do just fine.

~

Still on our mental and physical high, and with more energy to burn, we walked several miles to the laundromat, carrying 12 pounds of dirty clothes. Yes, we weighed it. Laundry, not an enjoyable chore, was fun and fast when we did it as a team. I stuffed the clean clothes back in our sleeping bag sacks, and we started the hike back.

We crossed paths with a family from India drying *papadums* on clean bedsheets spread out in a quiet apartment parking lot. I'd eaten the flat, deep-fried cracker bread in Indian restaurants many times.

One of the women told us they were drying the freshly made papadums naturally, in the sun. She explained restaurants dry them in an oven, but families traditionally spread them out in an open space to take advantage of the warm rays.

"It's important to dry them first so they don't spoil. Plus, they'll stack without sticking together," she said.

Clark asked if there were any family secrets for the recipe. She avoided specifics but divulged the simple ingredients: home-ground lentil flour, salt, pepper, cumin, and water. The woman handed each of us a sample. The salty-crispness woke our taste buds—which were never dormant for long—and started us dreaming of dinner.

Where's Wally?

Day 21: Tuesday, June 24
Weather: Hot and dry
Distance: 15 miles
Route: John Day, Oregon, to Prairie City, Oregon

We ran into a cyclist after breakfast. The 20-something woman immediately grabbed Clark's attention. She was attractive and in great shape, but it was her magnetic energy that was particularly appealing. Clark was mesmerized.

I felt a pang of jealousy.

Not only was this young woman physically beautiful, but she was also a genuinely caring person: riding cross-country raising funds for a non-profit. Radio station listeners followed her whereabouts, getting daily progress reports.

Clark listened intently as she described her cause. His eyes never left her face. While he was entranced in the conversation, I finally noticed a young man standing nearby and struck up a conversation.

Although he met the charitable rider only a day prior, he told me they'd hit it off and made plans to cycle together for the trip. This comment caught the woman's attention. She smiled, a bit awkwardly at first, then flashed her bright whites back at Clark.

The pair asked if we wanted to ride with them. Clark jumped on that idea. I had no desire to spend any more time feeling old and fat, so made excuses of needing supplies and said we'd see them down the road.

"Where are you planning to camp?" I asked with a Cheshire smile.

The little voice in my head was shouting, "No way will I ever ride with you, and not only that I'll do what it takes to make sure we're miles away from your campground tonight."

They rode on. We didn't.

"I didn't want to ride with them because we'd slow them down," I said innocently, trying to make my case. "We'd never be able to keep their pace."

Silence.

So, I tried another tactic to ease Clark's crushed hopes by suggesting we enjoy a relaxing day.

"How 'bout we ride 15 miles to Prairie City, then have a nice, leisurely lunch?" I asked, with a special emphasis on *lunch*!

He looked interested.

"I'm in the mood for a good bottle of red," I added.

His eyes brightened.

"Don't forget," I continued, "We have to scale two summits tomorrow. We should take it easy today and prepare."

I had him at "leisurely lunch" but wanted to be sure.

~

We fell in love with Prairie City instantly. It was all good things small-town America encompasses in one quaint setting. The little town is nestled on a prairie at the edge of the Strawberry Mountains, where the John Day River headwaters start. Prairie City is also on the "Journey Through Time" Scenic Byway. The Byway spans 286 miles through Oregon, passing through places that "tell stories of fortunes made and lost, of Chinese laborers, of towns boomed and busted, of timber, agriculture, and pioneer settlers." Beautifully restored historic buildings grace the short main street, reflecting a time gone by.

We made our way to the campground, a mile from the town's center, pitching our tent near a small creek that murmured beyond the trees. We set up quickly and walked back to town for our special lunch.

The fare was simple, but outstanding. Beef barley soup, crusty French bread still warm from the oven, spinach salad, and a bottle of

Oregon Pinot. I let Clark crack the caramel topping of the crème brûlée dessert. He loved being the first to do it—something about the sound.

> The Strawberry Mountains are a well-known hotspot for harvesting mushrooms. Some locals make a living gathering and selling them to tourists, restaurants, and grocery stores. In fact, a "mushroomer" came in to sell morels to the chef during our lunch. The 'shroomer intrigued Clark with stories of his hunts and the Humongous Fungus located in a nearby forest. The giant mushroom is documented as the largest living organism in the world. Scientists estimate it covers 3.4 square miles and has been growing for 2,400 to 8,650 years! The fungus grows mostly underground, so autumn is the only time you'll see it—when the "honey mushrooms" come into bloom.

The disappearing light at sunset brought out the red and purple hues of the mountains. As stars filled the pitch-black sky, we romanticized about moving to Prairie City until long after nightfall.

In Search of Happiness and the Two-Pass Day

Day 22: Wednesday, June 25
Weather: Hot
Distance: 50 miles
Route: Prairie City, Oregon, to Unity, Oregon

We pointed our bikes eastward, toward the first climb of the day—Dixie Pass. It topped out at 5,280 feet (1 mile). On the way up, we stopped at a turnout to rest and admire the view. A couple around our age pulled up in a motorhome, hopped out, and strolled over to us. Our bikes and gear were often a magnet.

After introductions, the newlyweds shared they were on a mission to find the best location to start their lives together. They'd sold everything:

businesses, homes, furniture, and most of their belongings. Their one car was hitched to the back of the motorhome and everything else that remained was piled inside. The pair was vagabonding around the country in search of their personal utopia.

People of a certain age, like us, often start to question what to do with the rest of their lives. Most go down this path one way or another. How much money, stuff, and commitments are needed to make us happy for our remaining time on Earth?

~

We were surprised and happy to find the lonesome valley had a restaurant. Over a BLT, we met an adventurous, overweight couple crisscrossing the countryside on a Harley. Kindred spirits, for sure.

They were dressed in full leathers. He had tattoos traveling up and down his arms, a silver tooth that flashed when he smiled, and the confidence of a politician. His wife, dressed in similar style, managed to camouflage her middle-aged spread and even look sexy in her gear.

The guy was on the mend from a motorcycle accident, one that nearly cost him his life. He didn't seem fazed by that scare and had a devil-may-care attitude about the misfortune. Biker Mama's dry sense of humor kept us entertained with a long stream of jokes. She was outgoing and probably the life of the party. I wanted to be her. She was that cool.

~

The day was getting hotter, so we forced ourselves to move on. We tackled Blue Mountain Pass, all 5,098 feet of it, ever so slowly. We saw more wildlife than people: deer, antelope, pheasant, grouse, and a young fox that paralleled us. We heard him hopping through the brush and spotted the curious animal sneaking an occasional peek in our direction.

We heard a low rumble coming up behind us. Our motorcycle friends zoomed past, performed a few zigzag maneuvers, and laid on the horn until they were out of sight, the sound echoing long after they disappeared. No other cars passed us on the desolate road until a cop slowed alongside us, asking if we were OK.

Laughing, Clark told him we'd be better after reaching the summit.

"Hey, maybe this'll help," he said, grabbing a couple bottled waters from an ice chest. A call squawked in on his radio. "Gotta go. Stay safe!"

~

We cheered at the sign marking the second summit. Managing a "two-pass" day and still feeling strong, we zipped down the other side of the mountain. But, things can change quickly on the road. A strong headwind slapped us in the face outside of Unity, making the next 8 miles seem endless. The work of pumping uphill with heavy loads in hot weather, combined with intense wind, caught up with us. We pushed as hard as humanly possible, yet felt like we were standing still and, at times, going backwards. We rested often and didn't talk, only nodding when we were ready to move on again.

It was a supreme relief to see the outskirts of Unity—just a tiny dot on the map. The Cat Stevens' song "Miles from Nowhere" could have been written about this isolated place. As we pedaled in, brown dust and gnarly tumbleweeds drifted across our path. There was a ghost-town feel, with little activity in the streets. We heard the voices of children floating on the air, but never saw them.

The town's motel had seen better days. Camping was an option, but the thought of pitching a tent exhausted us. Food was all we cared about.

Day 23 and Still in Oregon

Day 23:   Thursday, June 26

Weather: Sunny and hot
Distance: 87 miles
Route: Unity, Oregon, to Ontario, Oregon

The enticing aroma of bacon wafted out the café door. The waiter smiled and head-bobbed our way as he took an order and hurried back toward the kitchen. Moments later, he emerged with an armload of perfectly balanced plates and set them down in front of a table of four, then turned to us. The man had his routine down and seemed to enjoy the ebb and flow of the job.

In no time, plates laden with three eggs, bacon, toast, and hash browns arrived. It was the kind of meal meant to keep you going all day. And it did.

~

Eldorado Pass was a "mere" 4,623 feet, and we climbed it quickly. The landscape was beautiful in its barren glory. We watched antelope springing lightly across a field. They stopped to study us intently, determining if we were friend or foe. The smell of sagebrush was thick in the air. Morning sun traveled across our bodies, warming weary bones. I was struck by the quiet, the sound of silence almost deafening. We glided along, taking in the far-off expanses and the close-up views of fat, furry marmots running to and fro, skittering across the rocks.

At the summit, we crossed into Mountain Time Zone, left Baker County, and entered Malheur County, all at the same time. We kissed and congratulated each other.

The ride down the backside was fast and easy. We maintained a solid 29 mph for a long while, then let loose and reached speeds of 40+ mph as we sailed into Ironside.

This teeny town consisted of a post office and a handful of houses. We stopped to rest, grab some shade, and search for water. Everything needed was at the post office. The postmistress welcomed us into the little building, filled our water bottles, and then sent us on our way with fresh fruit and a bag of nuts. Small-town hospitality at its finest.

Clark - The Road Ahead - Ironside, OR

The rugged desert landscape unfolded for another 45 miles. You could look out into the vast panorama in any direction and see nothing—yet everything. It's the same land where Native Americans roamed and cowboys, Japanese farmers, Basque sheepherders, and European pioneers set down roots.

Last stop for the day was Ontario, 15 miles away. It was our 23rd day on the road, and we still hadn't left our very wide home state. Tomorrow, we'd cross the border into Idaho, come what may.

Interstate Madness

Day 24: Friday, June 27
Weather: Sunny and warm
Distance: 60 miles
Route: Ontario, Oregon, to Boise, Idaho

Big decisions to make. It was time to choose the best route to Sun Valley, Idaho. This was our next "friendly outpost," where we looked forward to several days of rest and relaxation. There were two main route options: the first was to go up and over Banner Summit at 7,056 feet toward Cape Horn, drop into the Sawtooth National Recreation Area, tackle the 11,170-foot Galena Peak, and then ride into Sun Valley.

Plan B was to travel the Interstate until Mountain Home, then take Highway 20 and head north on Highway 75 to Sun Valley. You can ride bicycles on Idaho interstates, so this would be a faster and flatter route.

The first plan would be more beautiful; however, several cyclists had warned us not to attempt it, citing no shoulders, lots of switchbacks, and inattentive drivers who watched the scenery and not the road.

Plan B it was.

~

We took the next on-ramp to the interstate, and in a matter of seconds we were in bicycle hell. The 75-mph speed limit meant everyone drove 85 to 90. The traffic raced by at break-neck speed—going so fast I doubt drivers even saw us. Certainly, no one slowed to indicate they did. It was petrifying.

We were suddenly afraid of a lot of things: something flying out of a truck bed, being hit by a speeding vehicle, crashing and rolling into busy lanes of traffic, a bike tire blowout, and cars kicking up road debris, knocking out our teeth (or worse). The morbid scenarios in our heads increased as the traffic continued to fly past.

We took advantage of the wide shoulder by riding *way* over on the right-hand side. I gripped the handlebars so tightly my fingers ached. Clark was behind me, and I had no idea how he was holding up. We covered 10 miles, breathing a sigh of relief when an exit for a rest stop appeared.

Our bodies were tensed and contorted into a shape that matched what we looked like while riding, even though we'd dismounted our bikes. It took a few minutes to unkink and breathe normally again. My hands felt severely arthritic. I couldn't open them or hold anything, not even my water bottle. We were both scared, although Clark was faring better than me. It must have been all those years he spent riding a motorcycle to and from work that prepped him for the fast traffic. I wondered if my strength, mobility, and guts would ever come back.

"Maybe we should take a bus from here," I said, still shaking.

"Sounds good on paper," Clark answered, "But I doubt any buses stop at an interstate rest area."

So, there was our answer. It was time to simply shut up and ride.

We tightened our helmets, shared a hug, and hit the road.

~

When we finally made it to Boise, I was ready to call it quits for the night. A campground just off the freeway beckoned. It was actually a small, depressing RV park next to an airport. The park didn't seem relaxing for "tenters," plus we'd be subject to a steady stream of traffic and jet engine noise all night long. Sweet dreams would not come from a spot like this. We got back on our bikes and looked for a motel we saw from the road.

The hotel clerk agreed to let us stay for a discounted rate. Once inside, the modest room felt luxurious. A laundry room down the hall was the icing on the cake. We walked across the street for some basic highway food. As we were eating, an older couple approached our table.

"I recognize you," the husband said, "I saw you riding on the interstate today and said to my wife, 'They must be nuts!'"

Tan Fat Is Prettier Than Marshmallow Flab

Day 25: Saturday, June 28
Weather: Sunny and hot
Distance: 35 miles
Route: Boise, Idaho, to Mountain Home, Idaho

The shock of noisy, fast traffic hit us hard, and our fears returned immediately. My knuckles turned white from gripping the handlebars, and the stress from the previous day came back before we were a mile down the road.

"Interstate travel is out of the question from now on!" I screamed.

Clark nodded in agreement. Then we put our heads down and pedaled as fast as we could, barely resting until we saw the turn-off to Mountain Home. No one has ever appreciated a road sign more than us.

Our energy shifted to "calm" as we cycled around town looking for a place to stay. We selected a motel with an outdoor pool and a steakhouse next door. We knew we'd stay no matter what, but couldn't resist trying to get a deal on the room rate.

The clerk stated a price; I came back with a much lower figure.

He looked at me in disbelief.

I laughed and said, "Feel like bartering?"

"Not really," he complained, then laughed in spite of himself and added, "How 'bout we split the difference?"

~

We enjoyed a few quiet hours swimming and sunning, when a group of rowdy young boys ruined our peace. It was a good excuse to head to the room for a romantic nap.

As it turned out, we were lucky the kids interrupted us. If we hadn't gone inside, our bodies may have burned to a crisp. We thought tanning our white blobs of marshmallow flab would help camouflage the lumpy-bumpies. Although our faces and arms were brown and used to the sun, our swimming suits exposed body parts that weren't accustomed to seeing the light of day.

WEEK 5

Water Shortage & Attack of the Mosquitoes

    Day 26:   Sunday, June 29
    Weather: Hot and dry
    Distance: 68 miles
    Route: Mountain Home, Idaho, to Fairfield, Idaho

The afternoon by the pool and a good night's sleep reinforced us for the long, dry, deserted road and 7,000-foot pass ahead. We packed and rode slowly through town, looking for an interesting spot for breakfast. Found it! A turn-of-the century building with an "Open for Breakfast" sign in the window.

    The old place still had some glamour left. A chandelier dripping with crystal prisms hung in the center of the room, and the furniture, although faded, showed signs of its former glory. History permeated the walls.

    Two elderly employees glanced up as we entered. The pair shuffled into a ready position. I assumed they were smiling at us, but it was hard to tell with the Shar-Pei wrinkles lining their faces.

    They moved in slow motion with an occasional freeze frame, as though to regroup their thoughts. The pair seemed to communicate with each other telepathically.

The ancient waitress took our order with minimal discussion and shuffled across the floor to hand it to the old cook. He checked the order, trundled into the kitchen and quietly prepared our meal. Oddly, we heard no pots or pans or any other sound that proved he was still alive back there.

Although it was a bit of a wait, the food was fabulous. The cook, as old and tired as he seemed, still had a flair.

~

The day was heating up. It was going to be a scorcher. There was also some serious elevation gain ahead. Concerned there might not be a place to refuel along the way, we stocked up on supplies before leaving town. We were getting better at thinking ahead.

In a short 10 miles we caught a glimpse of Cat Creek Summit, weighing in at an overwhelming 5,528 feet. More than a mile. Shit.

Why couldn't the highway department cut a big old tunnel through the mountain? Why did it have to be so hot? When would the ride get easier? Where was an air-conditioned car when you needed it?

For a moment, we considered turning around and taking another day to rest. We felt defeated. And then something serendipitous happened. Two men on bikes skidded to a stop in front of us.

They were seasoned cyclists out for a morning ride, brimming with such enthusiasm and energy it lifted our spirits. Our dread drifted away as they gave us the low-down on the road ahead: exactly how many minutes the uphill lasted (for them), how the grade changed, where to stop for water and see the best views, and how to avoid the hot pavement via a side path through the woods.

All this positivity and good information prevented us from turning back. Instead, we created a game that kept us pedaling.

We shouted to the mountain, "You're no big deal! You're nothin' but a little molehill."

"I've thrown bigger balls of dirt than you!"

"I've stacked marshmallows higher than this."

"Yeah, MINI marshmallows."

~

The sophomoric smack talk dwindled as the day grew hotter and the elevation steepened. I dripped sweat from every pore. It plopped into my eyes and blocked my vision. Then I made the mistake of applying sunscreen to my eyelids thinking it would protect me from dangerous UV rays.

The sweat/sunscreen combo circled down my lids and trickled to my eyes, creating a sting so powerful I had to wash it out with precious water. When I resumed riding, seconds later the sweat pooled and dripped again. It slithered down my back and soaked the waistband of my shorts. Perspiration oozed from my scalp, forming rivulets along the length of my hair. The sweaty drops fell to my legs, where they dried quickly, leaving an itchy presence.

I looked ahead toward Clark to see how he was faring in the heat. His thick, dark hair matted damply in clumps and hung limply from under his helmet. Sweat changed his light-gray shirt to a moist charcoal color. I noticed his arms were getting more toned, the musculature more defined by the sunlight hitting his glistening skin.

The cottonmouth was so bad I could hardly breathe. I tried spitting out the "cotton," but my mouth was too dry. I couldn't muster any saliva. No matter how much water I drank, it didn't quench the unbearable thirst.

Then, the biting flies moved in. They buzzed around, attacking every exposed body part. I'd swat at them, almost losing my balance, but they managed to avoid the hit and zip around to the opposite side to dive in for another bite. They were impossible to ward off and made the climb even more miserable.

So, there we were, slapping flies, dripping sweat, dying of thirst, trying to pump our way up the mountain. It was almost more than we could stand. Then, Clark's water ran out.

I split what was left of mine with him as the temperature and terrain continued to climb. The eternal optimist in me was left by the roadside with all the other pleasant thoughts. Negativity took over and continued up the hill with us.

Clark stopped unexpectedly and threw down his bike in frustration.

"Oh, shit, I have to take my shoes off," he said gruffly, with no explanation.

I stood staring blankly at him.

"My socks are bunched up," he said, looking up at me with the eyes of a 5-year-old.

It was hard not to smile as he sat cross-legged on the ground tugging his socks back into position. Moments later, a pick-up packed with two young couples in the front seat pulled over. The driver asked if Clark needed help.

"Nope, I'm OK. Thanks," he said, hopping up on his feet.

"We could use some water," I croaked out pathetically.

"How 'bout a lemonade?" the man said, looking cool and refreshed from the air-conditioned comfort he'd been enjoying.

"I'm Tommy," he told us as he exited the truck, walked to the back and pulled two icy beverages from a mega-cooler. We guzzled lemonade while he talked about their plans—a trip to his family's lakeside cabin.

"Hey! If you're out of water, I could take you to the store. It's just 10 miles up the road."

Of course we accepted this Good Samaritan's offer, as our bottles were on empty. We threw our bikes and ourselves in the back of the pickup. His friends knocked on the window, waved, and turned up the music.

The young man was such a fast, wild driver we had to hang onto the sides of the truck for dear life—it was like being on a roller coaster without a seatbelt. We sat, wide eyed, across from each other. I wanted to get out, but couldn't let go of the truck to signal my desire.

The driver barreled by cars in no-passing zones and flew down the winding mountain road at breakneck speed. He took the curves on two wheels. I'm sure of it. More than once I thought we might fly out of the truck from sheer gravitational force. We were white from fear when our feet hit solid ground and could barely mumble words of thanks.

On the verge of vertigo, we wobbled into the store and focused on getting something cold to drink. After drenching our insides, finally felt refreshed.

"Want a lift back to the main road?" our reckless friend asked.

We hadn't noticed him in the store and assumed they were long gone. Of course we wanted a lift back, but not badly enough to undergo another ride of terror. There was an awkward moment of silence.

"We don't want to hold you up. We'll be alright," I answered.

"OK. See ya."

He was fishtailing out of the parking lot in a minute flat.

An old ranch hand one aisle over had seen and heard the whole thing.

"I know *them* kids. How was your ride?"

He didn't wait for an answer.

"I'm headed to the main road. I'll take you if you want to ride with me."

Bingo!

We crawled into the front seat of the cowboy's truck and were happy for a peaceful ride back to where this whole adventure began.

"I was behind you on the way up. Wasn't sure you'd stay in that truck."

I wanted to hug him, but decided a smile would suffice.

~

It was miserably sweltering, and we still had 30 miles to go. As time dragged on, we had to start rationing water again, which only made us want more. Incredibly, the temperature continued to rise.

I flagged down passing cars and asked if they could spare something to drink. Two cars stopped but weren't carrying fluids. Thankfully, the third one had a juicy orange, which helped quench thirst, raise our spirits and blood sugar.

After all those uphill miles, the road magically transformed; it flattened out and provided a couple downhill stretches. We scanned the horizon for anywhere we could refuel our bodies.

Soon, the small village of Hill City lay before us. With only a smattering of houses, our chances of finding someone home were limited. No luck with house #1. We heard the radio playing in house #2, but no one answered. Next try, I walked through a modest home's white gate, crossed my fingers, and knocked on the door. Clark stood outside the gate, not wanting to appear threatening. After some time, an elderly woman nervously answered. Door #3 was a winner.

I explained what we needed as sweetly as possible, apologizing for our intrusion.

"I'm not used to strangers coming to the door, but you look all right," she said, tightening the belt of her light housecoat and smoothing her hair.

"You have a lot of bottles there, why don't you come in and fill them up," she offered, opening the screen door for me to enter. "*He* can stay right there," she added, pointing to Clark.

As I followed her through a long, dim hallway to the bright kitchen, I noticed her slippers; pink feather pompons sprouted from both satin toes. A flashback to the 1940s.

The "kitsch-en" was neat as pin but hadn't been updated in decades. Rooster salt and pepper shakers perched on a windowsill. Old-fashioned, windowed cabinets showed off a collection of dinnerware and cut glass. A cuckoo clock beat time loudly next to an aquamarine refrigerator.

I admired the yellowed needlework hanging on the wall. The intricate, perfect handwork told of days when craftsmanship mattered in even the simplest tasks. She told me her mother had sewn them as a wedding gift 63 years before.

Something delicious smelling bubbled on the stove. The woman caught me sniffing in the direction of the pot.

"It's beef barley soup. Would you like a little taste?" she asked, while grabbing a clean spoon and handing it to me.

"Mmmmmm ... it's delicious!" I cooed.

She filled a cup and gave me another spoon.

"Here, share this with your husband. I'll be out in a couple minutes."

Clark and I shared the savory soup, wishing for more.

The creaky porch door swung open and the little lady trotted down the stairs with something in her hands.

"I thought you might get hungry later, so I made you some cheese sandwiches," she said, giving the "now-approved" Clark a friendly wink.

Her generosity was touching. Neatly wrapped in waxed paper and bow-tied with string, the sandwiches looked like little presents.

"Oh!" she blurted, "We almost forgot ... the water bottles need to be filled!"

~

It felt like many days had passed since we started the ride that morning. So much had happened—mini adventures all day long. Even though our bones and butts were tired, our spirits soared when we rolled the last 14 miles into Fairfield.

Our intentions to camp were sincere, but a horde of buzzing mosquitoes sent us charging toward the protection of the nearest motel.

Snake Country

Day 27: Monday, June 30
Weather: Sunny and windy
Distance: 57 miles
Route: Fairfield, Idaho, to Sun Valley, Idaho

By morning our sore muscles felt restored. We rode the first 25 miles in just over an hour, even though the wind gusted ferociously.

"There it is," Clark shouted, "That's my dream home!"

"OK," I said, "Let's move in tomorrow!"

There it was—beautiful, impressive, and inviting. The multi-story log cabin was crafted of massive timbers hewn from pine. Expansive windows graced all sides and three wide decks allowed spectacular views of the idyllic landscape. I imagined us riding together, bareback on a black stallion, galloping through the countryside, not a care in the world.

A girl can always dream.

~

The rhythm of the morning unfolded flawlessly until we nearly ran over a rattlesnake slithering across the road. Fortunately, we saw it first and caught the reptile by surprise. There was no time for the snake to strike. Its triangular head turned toward us, beady eyes sizing us up. We skidded to a stop. The patterned creature took flight, quickly undulating into the brush.

A few miles later, we saw a second snake. This rattler wasn't so lucky—a victim of hit-and-run. Tire tracks marked its poor twisted body. Man vs. nature. Despite the gruesome display, the head and scales remained intact. This descendent of ancient serpents still looked beautiful, even in death.

~

At Highway 75, we turned north, picking up the Wood River bike trail. The path would take us all the way to Sun Valley. Interpretive signs scattered along the way educated us about the valley's history, geology, and local flora and fauna. One interesting fact we learned was the steel truss bridge along the route originally came from Oregon. In the late

1800s, it was used to cross over the Snake River into the city of Ontario, but was moved in 1917 for use on the Oregon Short Line railroad.

In the 1880s, long before the 32-mile path was a bike trail, Wood River Valley was known for its mining heritage. Sheep ranchers drove their herds through the area in the 1930s, and Union Pacific Railroad seasonal ski trains trundled through in the '50s and '60s. Fortunately for us, the rails-to-trails conversion started in the 1970s.

~

We arrived in Sun Valley at the home of our friends Carol and Keith and their two kids. Carol and I met during our ski-bum days in Jackson Hole, Wyoming. She was an inspiration to me, because she believed in herself so confidently—never letting fear get in the way. Carol didn't know how to ski when I met her. She just pointed her skis in the direction she wanted to go and went for it. On the slopes and in life.

Who Knew? Hayden Hates Mushrooms

Day 28: Tuesday, July 1
Rest Day: We played tourist!

Our morning started in front of the TV with the two kids. "Sesame Street" taught us all we needed to know: Forward, Backward, Left, Right, Up, Down, Please, and Thank You.

~

Carol and Keith loaned us a car so we could explore. First stop, Sun Valley Lodge, a luxury hotel built in 1936. The spectacular location, with its skier-friendly amenities, has long been a playground for the rich and famous. We studied photographs hanging in the long halls; the impressive line-up of celebrity guests included silent movie star Mary Pickford, Ginger Rogers, Gary Cooper, Clark Gable, President Harry S. Truman, Lucille Ball, Louis Armstrong, Marilyn Monroe, some of the Kennedys, Ricky Nelson, Clint Eastwood, and Bruce Springsteen. In fact, Ernest Hemingway penned much of the classic *For Whom the Bell Tolls* in room 206.

We left the lodge and continued up and over the 11,170-foot Galena Peak in the Sawtooth National Recreation area to the mountain town of Stanley. The drive took our breath away. We drove slowly, craning our necks and stopping often to take in views of the 50 peaks above 10,000 feet and four mountain ranges: Sawtooth, Smoky, Boulder, and White Cloud.

The weather turned when we reached the summit. It was cold and started hailing big icy droplets that hit the roof with loud pings as they landed one after the other. How nice to be warm and dry inside a car, although it felt strange to be behind the wheel again. It had been a month since either of us had driven.

Clark made dinner that evening. I helped and managed to contribute without seriously mucking up anything. We made lasagna. Everyone loves lasagna, especially kids. As Carol and Keith anticipated the first bites of their meal (we all looked forward to Clark's food), their 5-year-old son started screaming and crying when he spotted a mushroom in the lasagna. The parents, embarrassed by his actions, marched him upstairs for a talk about manners.

"Oh, God," Clark said, "I forgot little kids hate mushrooms. What was I thinking?"

"I didn't think about it either," I said, trying to make him feel better. "I guess hotdogs should have been our back-up plan."

"It's OK, he probably wasn't hungry. I like it. It's good!"

The sweet, little voice from the other side of the table reminded us we weren't alone. Little sister's words of wisdom made us laugh. Soon, the rest of the family was back at the table and all was well again. (Keith discreetly forked all the mushrooms out for his young son.)

Oh, Hail

Day 29: Wednesday, July 2
Weather: Rain, hail, dark clouds, and moments of scattered sunshine
Distance: 92 miles
Route: Sun Valley, Idaho, to Arco, Idaho

We savored morning coffee and a hearty breakfast with our friends. The conversation was groggy, but flowed easily. Clark pulled out a map, and as I traced a finger along our route we realized we'd covered a surprising amount of ground. Although I couldn't say we were in shape, we were getting stronger and feeling better.

While Carol and Keith prepped for work, we packed up, then sorted through a pile of mail that had been waiting for us at their house. Family and friends shared their latest news and offered words of encouragement and support.

After saying a heartfelt thank you and goodbye, we pushed our bikes to the nearest UPS store four blocks away, each balancing a huge box of supplies on our handlebars. Our plan: send one box to the next friendly outpost in Sheridan, Wyoming. Tucked inside, a fresh set of clothes and a bit of personal bling—jewelry, belts, make-up, and nice shoes. This would lighten the load and feel like Christmas when we opened the package later. The second box was headed home—things we wanted to keep but didn't want to carry, such as the metal cookstove and fuel containers.

Immediately, we noticed our packs were more spacious without the extra things inside, but neither of us could feel the difference in weight. That seemed odd when the weight of the box going home felt heavy. It was one of life's mysteries, like where the socks go when they disappear in the dryer.

> Many long-distance riders would never let go of their cookstove. For us, it made sense. We preferred to eat out. Clark refused to dine on standard camping meals, like chili mac and beanie weenies. That's part of what the trip was about—sampling the fare across America, enjoying local specialties and the people who prepared them.

The noon whistle blew, saluting our departure. We pushed off with a satisfied sigh and rolled out of town. This area, Stanley and the Sawtooth Mountains, in particular, lingered in our minds long after they were out of sight. We added it to our list of places to move.

A few miles out of town, the sky turned inky black, ominous clouds rolled in, and rain threatened. We picked up our pace, with me riding as fast as my thunder thighs could pedal. Out of nowhere, tiny hailstones pelted down, stinging sharply as they hit—this time without cover of a car.

Sunlight poked through the darkness ahead.

"Let's outrun the storm," Clark yelled.

"I'm in!" I shouted back.

Adrenaline flowed, energy surged; we put our heads down and kicked up speed, trying not to look back. Mother Nature challenged us further by sending heavy wind to battle. It was no match for our determination. We raced onward, never stopping until the barrage subsided. The clouds morphed and mutated, kaleidoscopic patterns in shades of gray and black.

When our legs grew tired, we ducked inside a small café in Belleview for a rest. All eyes were riveted on the Weather Channel. A small TV blared warnings about golf-ball-sized hailstones dropping in the Sun Valley area. Everyone was advised to take cover.

We stood outside, studying the sky, contemplating our next move. The dark mass appeared to be moving west, away from where we were headed.

As we looked skyward, a car pulled up. It was Keith. He had come to check on us.

"Massive hailstones pounded the house. We were worried about you," he said, suggesting we stay another night.

We paused to consider the offer. On one hand, we were feeling strong. On the other, it was another 30 miles into Carey. We looked up at the sky ... back to Keith ... then psychically connected with each other.

"Thanks, but let's bike it," Clark said confidently, looking in my direction for agreement.

"Funny how everyone advises us to do one thing and we do the opposite," I laughed.

"That's why we love you," Keith smiled. "Have a great ride!"

~

The challenge of staying ahead of unpredictable weather kept us moving for miles. We pedaled fast and furious, stopping off and on to grab a snack from the pack and survey the ever-changing sky. Rain–sun–clouds–rain–sun–clouds. The pattern repeated itself for hours. If we slacked off, Mother Nature was at our heels, so we didn't stay long in any one spot.

We made it to Carey by mid-afternoon, finally allowing ourselves to rest longer than a few minutes. As we pulled up to a small restaurant, Clark spotted an elderly woman struggling to get out of her car. He leaned his bike against a tree and offered to help.

She accepted his hand, saying, "Oh, how nice to see young people with good manners. You can join me at my table."

It wasn't so much an invitation as an order. (I especially liked the part about being "young.")

We ate a hearty lunch and listened to her childhood tales. My favorite story involved her then-teenaged, mischief-making brothers. One Halloween night, they tried their hand at pushing over neighborhood outhouses, toppling a few without mishap. But, unfortunately for the farmer inside, the third outhouse fell to pieces when they gave it a push. The burly man, overalls around his ankles, chased them off his property screaming, "I'll get you God-damned kids! I know where you live!" Their troublemaking days came to a screeching halt after this incident. The rambunctious teens were forced to spend the next few weeks building the disgruntled farmer a new, *two-seater* outhouse.

The woman had friends of all ages who stopped by the table to share a hug and inquire about her news and health. There was a sincere, comforting familiarity in these small-town exchanges, where families know and watch out for each other through the generations. A slice of life repeated every day across America.

> We met two young riders traveling cross-country east to west. They'd been speeding along for weeks, only taking four days off. The men were youthful, strong and had abundant energy to ride hard every day and camp every night. What worked for them wouldn't have worked for us. Everyone chooses a traveling style and pace that suit them best. That's the beauty of adventure travel.

Luck was on our side: The big storm never touched us, we had energy to spare, and long summer days meant hours of light ahead. It was late afternoon, and we had 45 miles to go, so off we went. The day turned to a perfect temperature of cool, creating an ideal environment for riding. Oppressive heat wasn't sapping our energy, allowing us to enjoy the terrain. The landscape was dry and desolate, but beautiful in its starkness.

We were in Craters of the Moon National Monument country where a vast, ancient landscape of lava flows was frozen in time. Islands of cinder cones stuck up here and there. Scattered patches of sagebrush and wildflowers softened the hard, volcanic panorama.

It's amazing to imagine so much wildlife exists there. Our animal count included songbirds, ground squirrels, lizards, jackrabbits, a hawk, two ravens, several mule deer, plus some beetles and a flattened porcupine that must have crossed the road too slowly.

We would have spent more time exploring, but nightfall was around the corner. It was best to keep moving, especially since we knew bobcats, coyotes, and mountain lions combed the area after dark.

Deep twilight engulfed us by the time we reached Arco. We pitched our tent in darkness, bragging about our strength and youthfulness as we devoured all the food left in our packs.

We had covered substantial ground and were on top of the world. The rest of the trip would be a cinch. Right? The conversation ended there. We slept straight through the night without moving a muscle.

Nothing Hurt

Day 30: Thursday, July 3
Weather: Overcast and cool with a bit of light rain
Distance: 81 miles
Route: Arco, Idaho, to Rexburg, Idaho

I woke up first and took a tally of my body parts, stretching and shifting to gauge any pain. Shockingly, nothing ached, even after our longest day. That was so exciting I shook Clark awake to make the announcement. He smiled, took a moment, and said he felt the same.

We sprung out of bed, motivated by this revelation and ravenous hunger. Breakfast was first on our list. On the way, we noticed a sign: *Welcome to Arco First City in the World Lighted by Atomic Power.*

Posters for the mid-July "Atomic Days" celebration were plastered everywhere. Parade! Rodeo! Car Show! Carnival! Arts & Crafts! And our personal favorite, the Ping Pong Ball Drop, where a plane flies over the parade route and drops balls onto the crowd. People grab them and turn them in for prizes! Too bad we'd be in Wyoming by then.

Today's destination: Rexburg, via Howe, Mud Lake, and Terreton. A map check affirmed the route's desolation offered few options for food, water, or shelter. As more seasoned cyclists, we knew we'd have to prep well for the journey to ensure safe passage. We filled water bottles and camelbacks to the brim and purchased extra bottled water, fruit, cheese, and protein bars. Feeling sufficiently prepared, we set out.

Surprising, even to us, we felt strong and confident for the second day in a row. Plus, motivation to reach West Yellowstone by the 4th of July propelled us forward. Mostly flat road and minimal traffic made the pedaling easy to the campground. The elements even threw us a bone—the temperature was cool with a light blanket of misty rain. An invigorating mix of circumstances.

Humpty Dumpty Joins the Parade

>Day 31: Friday, July 4
>Weather: Sunny and warm
>Distance: 65 miles
>Route: Rexburg, Idaho, to West Yellowstone, Montana

It was Independence Day. I realized we'd traveled over 1,000 miles. Another reason to celebrate!

We packed up and headed downtown for breakfast. People waiting for the big parade lined the streets, sitting on blankets and folding chairs—everyone in great spirits. Kids frolicked, dressed in red, white, and blue, waving tiny flags. They chased each other, squealing and laughing; jumped rope; and drew colorful pictures on the sidewalk with chalk. Adults sat curbside, drinking coffee and enjoying the company of friends and neighbors.

We rode along the parade route looking for a place to eat. Everyone watched as we rolled by and, at one point, the crowd clapped and fluttered their little flags high in the air. Maybe they thought we were the parade kickoff?

We were often the center of attention when we arrived in a new town, but cycling down a street lined with people felt extra strange. To make matters worse, I accidentally discovered a new way to be in the spotlight.

Clark, cycling a few feet ahead, spotted a place to eat. He made a sharp turn into the driveway, hitting a bump, which knocked off his front pack. I swerved hard to the right, trying to avoid it. No luck. Contact. I performed an acrobatic header (think *Humpty Dumpty*). Whereas Humpty tumbled vertically off the wall, I flew horizontally, accomplishing a spectacular crash-and-slide in front of the whole town. How humiliating.

Everyone turned to look. I scanned the crowd from my uncomfortable position on the pavement, noting their expressions. Some stood frozen with mouths agape and faces full of concern, while others stifled laughter with various levels of success. Clark fell into that category— barely controlling himself.

Thanks for the support, buddy.

No one came to my rescue. I landed in a strange position and had to fight to escape the clipless pedals by contorting my body back and forth. I'm sure there were "beached whale" comments on the lips of many. I struggled and flailed, finally getting myself loose and upright again. I wasn't hurt—only suffered minor scrapes and bruises and a massive ego blow.

I limped over to the restaurant, only then noticing the big bay windows with dozens of noses pressed tightly against the glass. All eyes on me. I walked toward our table, past the intense stares, trying to pretend nothing had happened. But my beet-red face surely gave me away. I slumped into a chair and tried not to make eye contact. It was my most embarrassing moment.

~

The next stretch of highway had bumpy ruts on the shoulder that couldn't be avoided, there to alert drivers if they drifted too far over. Every few feet we'd bounce over those little indentations and heard *Brrrt-Brrrrrtttt*. It was especially jarring on a bike. We both made the machine gun-like "a-a-a-a-a-a-ah" sound, laughing at the rattle in our chests. Funny at first, then not so much.

Clark started complaining about his bike "dragging." He stopped several times to take a look, but found nothing visibly wrong. I moved behind him and noticed his rear wheel wobbling but couldn't tell why. The vibrating worsened as the miles clicked by, with nowhere to stop for repairs. Plus, we were heading into Targhee National Forest. Losing control in mountainous terrain could be deadly.

I offered to flag down an oncoming truck and ask for help.

"Do you think cowboys carry bicycle tools in their pickups?" Clark asked.

Probably not. So we moved on.

As the terrain grew steeper, our pace slowed and Clark's frustration heightened. Whenever I started the "asking for help" conversation again, I ended up with the same answer. Men are strange that way—a woman would have asked for help miles back. We continued this routine for several more hours.

Clark adjusted the wobbly wheel often, but nothing seemed to reduce the annoying shake. The stopping and starting slowed us further. By this time, we were in the middle of the forest and weren't hopeful about finding a random bike shop along the way. We bantered back and forth about what to do.

A loud *spronggggg* broke up our discussion. A broken spoke. *Spronggggg! Spronggggg!* Another. And another. It wasn't looking good. We stopped on the roadside to assess the situation.

Just when we were fresh out of ideas and feeling completely disheartened, a ruggedly handsome soul in a cowboy hat pulled over.

"You alright?" he asked through the pickup window. I zeroed in on his sparkling blue eyes.

We explained our situation. Fortunately, he was on his way to West Yellowstone, and could take us there "no problem." After loading our bikes and gear into the truck bed, we were on our way.

Out of the corner of my eye, I nonchalantly studied the driver's square jawline and tanned skin as we talked. His strong hands rested comfortably on the steering wheel, eyes scanning the countryside and road ahead. He had the outdoorsy look of a hunky Marlboro Man. Oddly enough, we learned he *was* one of the manly men featured in the famous cigarette commercials.

Our rescuer also trained horses for a living. Actually, he re-trained them, after people trained their horses the *wrong* way. When a horse was considered more or less ruined, he'd step in, buy it, and turn the beast into a "good" horse, then sell it again.

As we approached West Yellowstone, we discovered he knew our friends Drew and Carol. In fact, he dropped us off at their driveway, no directions needed. Small world.

~

We caught up with Carol and Drew as we headed to the bike shop. The mechanic was surprised Clark was able to ride at all judging by the condition of his bike. We were quite happy to leave the whole mess in their hands and proceed with our holiday weekend.

The evening started with a BBQ on a beautiful ranch property outside West Yellowstone. An expanse of grass provided a lush meadow carpet for all the kids to play on. A circle of trees protected the bonfire from wind, if there'd been any, but fortunately it was one of those soft, still summer nights. We were soon comfortably folded into the group as if we'd lived there our whole lives.

"Let's move *here*," I whispered to Clark. His answer was a tight hug.

The moment was interrupted and our minds changed when a swarm of persistent mosquitoes moved in at twilight. The air was thick with them. Buzzing like an electrical transformer, their nasty bites immediately turning into itchy, red welts all over our bodies. The stealth attack dispersed the crowd in every direction. An abrupt end to the party.

The four of us headed home to watch fireworks from the rooftop. Drew built a tall ladder in minutes—literally, *built a ladder*. I was so impressed. Even the dog, old arthritic Pete, gingerly climbed up, with Drew behind offering butt support.

I also hiked up the ladder gingerly. I'm afraid of heights, so Clark offered me butt support, too. I didn't move around much and positioned myself firmly in the middle of the roof. Clark held me close the entire time. He knew how to make a gal feel safe, warm, and happy. We snuggled on the rooftop, whispering "I love you's" and watching the blasts of colorful explosions decorate the sky.

Good Friends and Fresh Trout

    Day 32:   Saturday, July 5
    Weather: Changed constantly
    Distance: Much-needed rest day

Clark and Drew rose early to go trout fishing, and Carol had to work, which meant I had a day to myself. Leisurely phone conversations with friends and family, napping, watching TV, and grazing filled my time. I took full advantage of Carol's offer to eat what I wanted. Sweet treats and salty chips for breakfast. Ice cream for a mid-morning snack. A meaty sandwich with all kinds of ingredients for lunch.

The fishermen returned home in good spirits, having bonded during their wilderness experience. Huge grins said it all as they held up two strings of fat trout.

Carol walked in the door clutching heavy bags of groceries. I helped unpack them, Drew popped open the wine, and we feasted.

WEEK 6

Twirlwind Vacation Shoes

>   Day 33:   Sunday, July 6
>   Weather: Changed constantly
>   Distance: Another much-needed rest day

The next day, we picked up our bikes. Mine was tightened, tuned, and ready to go. But, when Clark took his for a test ride, several spokes popped out, so back to the shop it went. Time for a whole new wheel.

While his bike was getting a re-do, Carol, Clark, and I drove into Yellowstone National Park's Norris Geyser Basin—the hottest and most unpredictable thermal area in the park. Norris is also home to "Steamboat," the world's tallest active geyser. We parked and set out to explore, marveling at the many roiling, bubbling pools of water and colorful, moving mud. We watched in awe as powerful eruptions sent spray heavenward. Hissing steam vents spewed vaporous loads. Pungent, sulfurous odors permeated the air.

It's amazing that microscopic life, or any life, is able to survive in this extreme, prehistoric-looking environment. Imagine what the first person to witness this topography thought? No wonder early travelers dubbed it "The Land of Fire and Brimstone."

A whiny child broke our thoughts.

"Mom, can we go home now? I'm bored."

"Yeah, I think we've seen everything here."

"Where's my video game?"

The mother dug through her purse and pulled out the object of his affection. The boy grabbed it and turned his focus to the inanimate device.

I'd encountered the same jaded, unimpressed attitude all over the world—The Great Wall of China, Niagara Falls, the tropical forests in Belize, the ancient pyramids in Central America, and at the mile-deep Grand Canyon.

The three of us rolled our eyes. Then, in a sarcastic entrepreneurial moment, we figured out a way to make money off this "I'm Bored" attitude—special ballet shoes that allowed the wearer to pirouette easily. After a brief gander at some natural or manmade wonder, the antsy tourist could quickly spin around on their toes and speed off. We named them "Twirlwind Vacation Shoes."

Our silly antics halted when we came upon a massive elk holding court in the middle of the trail. The animal wasn't bothered by our presence. Though we were close enough to pet him, knowing better the three of us kept our hands to ourselves and stood silently admiring his regal pose.

~

Back in West Yellowstone, our day continued with one of my favorite idle-time activities—exploring tacky souvenir stores. Clark went in search of jackalopes, the mythical animal that's half jackrabbit and half antelope. Instead, he found a flying pheasalope—half pheasant and half antelope.

Carol and I played my favorite game, "Who Can Find the Most Useless Item in the Fastest Time?" Every nook and shelf was filled with potential winners. Carol lost no time, dangling a hideous, hat-shaped macramé doorknob weaving in front of my face. It was so dreadful I fell into a laughing fit and couldn't stop. I wheezed and snorted so hard and long, Clark came from the back of the store to see if I was all right. Carol slinked several aisles away, pretending she didn't know me.

After my embarrassing outburst, we picked up our bikes, choked down the repair bill, and headed out for a night on the town.

Is That a Bear Outside Our Tent?

Day 34: Monday, July 7
Weather: Sunny and warm but heavy on the mosquitoes
Distance: 50 miles
Route: West Yellowstone, Montana, to Canyon in Yellowstone National Park, Wyoming

Back to business. We did a load of laundry and ate a breakfast of granola, tea, and fruit. I started to get melancholy and knew we probably wouldn't see our friends for a long time. It's never easy to say good-bye to people you love. Like many things in life, leaving Drew and Carol's happy home was a double-edged sword. We wanted to continue our grand adventure, yet the allure of staying put was powerful.

As we moved in slug-like fashion, our friends gave us signs that it was, indeed, time to go.

"We're so proud of you," Carol said. "Imagine how you'll feel when you reach the East Coast!"

"I know you're anxious to keep moving," Drew hinted. "It was great you could stay as long as you did."

"Where's your next stop?" Carol asked inquisitively.

"Noooooo, please don't make us leave," I wanted to shout.

Clark shot the breeze, looking longingly at the couch. My gaze turned toward the refrigerator, for one last look. When it was obvious we couldn't delay a minute longer, we hugged farewell. With hearts heavy, we rode away. It was almost noon.

~

We entered Yellowstone National Park again—this time on bikes. Within 10 minutes, something crashing in the bushes caught our attention. We stood motionless on the shoulder of the road, listening for the sound again. There it was! We moved a few feet ahead and peered down into a gully. To our surprise, we saw two bison rubbing their big wooly bodies on tree trunks.

We realized no one traveling by car could see them, but we had the perfect vantage point. As traffic rolled past, passengers craned their necks for wildlife but managed to miss what was right in front of them. We had the bison to ourselves.

Next, we spotted several elk playing in a stream. Tourists behind the wheel didn't miss this action. Cars stopped in the middle of the road. Families flung doors open, spilled from their vehicles, whipped out cameras, and snapped like mad. Surprisingly, the young elk didn't seem bothered by hoards of gawking people and continued to put on a show. They chased each other, bucked around, and played tag, splashing in the water like little kids.

~

Soon after, we crossed into Wyoming—another state under our belts. Clark whistled as we traveled along. Life was good again, real good.

Just past Madison, heading toward the Norris Geyser Basin, we hit a horrible stretch of curvy road. Deep potholes pitted the pavement, forcing us to slalom gingerly around them. Heavy traffic, combined with narrow lanes and no shoulders, kept our eyes focused downward. Unfortunately, distracted drivers weren't watching the road so carefully. They took in the scenery with their passengers, scanning the horizon for a glimpse of wildlife, weaving dangerously close to us. To make matters worse, there were dozens of barn-like RVs taking up more than their share of space.

Clark had a terrible scare. In truth, he almost got killed.

He was riding three car lengths ahead of me when an RV blew past us with barely an inch to spare, almost catching Clark's handlebars. Simultaneously, a fast car approached from the opposite direction. For some unknown reason, the bulky RV sped up, the driver oblivious to the danger he was creating.

I watched in horror and confusion as Clark kept crazy pace with the big vehicle. A mountainous wall of granite flanked our right side, the massive motorhome on the other, but he raced along—left shoulder nearly touching the side of the metal beast. Why didn't he slow down and let the RV pass? What was he thinking?! Was this some kind of macho display?

This went on for an uncomfortable amount of time. Finally, the road widened again, the vehicle won the race and left us behind. Clark stopped immediately and got off his bike.

When he turned around to check on me, his face was devoid of color. He was gulping in short, deep breaths and looked terrified.

"The draft sucked me in. I had a feeling something bad was about to happen. I thought I was a goner," Clark said, almost too quietly for me to hear.

"What?" I responded, now realizing this was not a case of machismo.

He explained the RV was creating its own wind, drawing him into the vortex. He didn't have the strength or speed to escape the wind tunnel. No one on a bike could.

"It was so tight. There was nowhere for me to go, even if I had the power to break free of that draft," he said, still shaking. "I haven't felt a premonition like that since the Vietnam War— right before I got shot."

I stayed quiet as he processed what just happened.

"The RV was so close I couldn't stop. Even if I could, it would have meant twisting out of my clipless pedals. I was afraid my foot would knock into the motorhome and propel me under the tires. It felt like someone else was driving my bike."

There was a long pause.

"I can't believe I'm standing here in one piece."

I could only hug him and be happy he was safe.

~

Next, we faced an unexpected steep hill. We'd heard this part of Yellowstone was flat. Wrong!

Clark raced up the mile-long steepness in record time, probably propelled by leftover adrenaline. I struggled much longer, moving in stop-motion before reaching the summit. How dare a hill have the audacity to place itself in our path like that!

We were famished by the time we reached Norris and pawed through our bags wildly for something to eat. We chowed granola bars, apples, and whatever else we could get our hands on.

A young mother, holding a toddler by one hand and a heavy thermos in the other, approached. She looked like a ray of sunshine, in a yellow sundress, long strawberry-blonde hair falling in tendrils around her fresh face.

"Want some lemonade?" she asked sweetly.

Without waiting for an answer, she fished around in the deep pocket of a bag strapped to her stroller, pulled out two clean glasses and poured. From another pocket, a little bag of Cheerios appeared. The daughter, a mini version of her mom, grabbed the bag. She grinned at us with unabashed curiosity while working on her cereal, dropping more of it on the ground than in her mouth.

"Where ya going?" the mother asked.

I could tell she wasn't just being polite but was genuinely interested. She continued asking questions, listening intently while pouring glass after glass of juice into our plastic cups.

"You're an inspiration," she said, eyes filled with admiration. "I so envy you athletic people!"

This was the first time someone called us "athletic." What an ego boost.

~

Nature perfumed the air with the sweet–earthy scent of wildflowers. Glistening streams painted the landscape with silver ribbons. Ancient, craggy peaks zigzagged on the horizon. A feeling of peace and connectedness reigned. Small and insignificant as we are, everyone and everything part of the planet's grand scheme.

As much as I wanted to capture this feeling in a photo, it was impossible. It's one of those experiences I'll carry as a magnificent image in my mind forever.

~

When we reached Canyon Campground, we made a beeline to the store, plunked down on the porch, and slugged back several waters. Then we got the news: every campground in the park was full and all hotels were booked. Not surprising, as it was the busiest week of the year in Yellowstone. A moment of panic passed between us.

But, here's the beauty of being on bikes—we could stay at any hiker/biker campground in the park, no matter what. If you travel under your own power you're never turned away. Why? Park policymakers understood; another 20-plus miles is easy for a motorist, but not for hikers or bikers using their own steam. Good thing because we were fresh out of steam.

We found a secluded spot without much searching. It was beautiful, except for … bzzzzzzzzzz. Mosquitoes! In seconds, they moved in with blood-thirsty vengeance. We had nowhere to hide from the siege of these small biting devils. This forced us to set up camp with the speed of maniacs and change into clothes with better bite-protection qualities.

We skipped taking a shower, not wanting to expose more skin.

"Not worth the trade off," Clark said. "I'd rather stink!"

Our campsite had metal locking "bear boxes" with chains to secure them. We were advised to put anything with a scent inside: food, toothpaste, lotions, gum, mints, etc.

"Those bears will rip open your bags for anything that smells tasty," the rangers warned. "They're smart. It's surprising how creative they are, getting into things you thought were safe."

We wondered if we should lock ourselves in the boxes, since without a shower we could smell pretty scrumptious to a bear.

With that warning, we ran for an indoor restaurant, swatting and slapping at mosquitoes along the way. Once safely inside, we focused on a buffalo steak dinner and drink specials while listening to live music—a quartet of violin, viola, viola de Gambia, and cello. Not a bad way to spend an evening in a national park.

~

We ran back to the campsite and dove into the tent without brushing our teeth—anything to escape the onslaught of mosquitoes that still plagued us. Clark smoked a cigar (inside the tent), which worked well as a repellent. I hunted down rogue mosquitoes that sneaked inside and squashed them one by one. After a brief recap of our exciting day, we fell asleep. But not for long.

Loud sounds of branches snapping in the bushes woke us with a start.

"What's that?" I asked, hoping Clark had a satisfying answer.

"It sounds like a big animal," he whispered back.

"Think it's a deer?" I asked hopefully.

The crashing got louder, as did the beating of my heart.

"It's closer," I said, barely breathing.

Clark didn't respond, but I could feel him tense up. We laid stone still, listening, when suddenly we felt the ground shake. The animal let out a juicy snort right next to our heads. The only thing protecting us from certain death was the thin fabric of the tent wall. We remained frozen, awaiting our fate.

I conjured disturbing visions of *The Night of the Grizzly*. The creature walked around our tent several times, grunting and snuffling and at one point stepped on the corner of our flimsy home. I held my breath. For the second time in a day Clark thought his life was over.

After what seemed like hours, we heard the bear's claws inspecting our metal box, trying to pry it open. Unsuccessful, he finally stomped away, making no effort to conceal his presence.

"Is he gone?" I asked in a voice just below a whisper.

"I think he's checking out our neighbors," Clark speculated.

We listened intently until the crashing sounds disappeared into the darkness. Neither of us slept the rest of the night. Our bodies tensed and ears perked up at every tiny sound.

Elk Dung Fire and Other Camping Tips

Day 35: Tuesday, July 8
Weather: Sunny and warm
Distance: 28 miles
Route: Canyon to Fishing Bridge, Yellowstone National Park, Wyoming

We were up and gone before anyone else in camp was moving. Though we were hyper-stimulated by our bear scare, exhaustion muddled our brains. Before long, though, the park's beauty and the serenity of the morning quieted our fears, helping us slow down, re-center, and appreciate our surroundings.

~

First stop, the Grand Canyon of Yellowstone. It's difficult to put its splendor into words. There are not enough adjectives to properly comment on this natural wonder. To describe some of its measurable attributes, the canyon is 20 miles long, up to 1,200 feet deep, and a half mile across. One of the waterfalls is double the height of Niagara Falls. You can hear its roar from afar as water cascades over steep canyon walls, into the rushing river below.

We stopped at every scenic vantage point as we meandered along. I was especially fascinated by a lonely, house-sized granite boulder that sits in the middle of a pine forest. Trees have literally grown around the massive rock left behind by a glacier 80,000 years ago.

The road twisted and turned, following the bends and curves of the Yellowstone River, which flows over 600 miles to North Dakota, where it eventually dumps into the Missouri River. The landscape softened as we approached Hayden Valley, my favorite part of the park. Grassy hills, bright green from the warmth of summer sun, surrounded a broad, marshy valley. Patches of yellow flowers sprouted parallel to a river. An idyllic setting for wildlife and people.

Flocks of ducks paddled in unison on this quiet part of the river, while pelicans lounged lazily on its grassy banks. Grizzly bears, bison, elk, wolves, foxes, and coyotes call this home, too. We glimpsed a wolf galloping through long grass and spotted six male elk with huge sets of antlers. They stood along the horizon, positioned at different angles, posing for tourists like proud body builders admiring their physiques in a mirror.

A baby moose and its mother wandered within yards of us. The little one stood quietly on her spindly legs, wobbling gently to and fro. She stayed close to mom, but watched us intently with big brown eyes, appearing more curious than afraid. The nostrils on the mother's soft brown muzzle flared in and out, protectively checking out our scents for potential danger.

We stood entranced for a long while, not noticing the vehicles piling up along the roadway, people scurrying to see the animal action. We were smack dab in the middle of a traffic jam. Those who parked at odd angles, blocking the road, seemed oblivious to other drivers beeping and shouting angry threats. RVs and tourist buses tried to pass in both directions, but no one was able to move. Gridlock.

Again, bicycle travel paid off. We hopped on our bikes, weaved our way in and around traffic, and were out of the snarl in minutes. Several jealous drivers honked and yelled frustrations our way. We smiled, waved, and headed off. Judging from the quiet roadway, it took a long time to untangle the motorized mess.

A huge herd of bison, maybe 200 or more, grazed nearby with their young calves. Only a small gully and stream separated us from the lumbering giants. It would have been dangerous if the bison wanted to stampede; we had nowhere to hide. They're surprisingly agile, can weigh more than a ton, and can sprint up to 30 mph. It's rare, but more people are hurt in Yellowstone by bison than bears. Good thing they seemed unfazed by our presence.

The fuzzy youngsters romped energetically, tails swinging back and forth as they played tag. Our favorite bison, the biggest of all, swung his massive head toward us, expressive eyes taking us in thoughtfully. A long, furry goatee hung from his chin, making him look old and wise, like an ancient prophet.

Some of the bison rolled on their backs, hooves in the air, taking a dust bath to ward off biting insects. Clark suggested we try the same bug-fighting technique to protect ourselves from the nightly onslaught of mosquitoes.

Suddenly, the same crowd from the moose pile-up was upon us, jockeying their vehicles for the best viewing position. Time to go.

~

Along a quiet part of the river, off the road, we discovered a peaceful setting where we listened to birdsongs and watched fish jump for bugs, splashing hard, rippling the water as they caught their lunch. A bald eagle perched in a treetop kept a keen eye over the water. All at once, the eagle swooped down and not 10 feet from us grabbed a fish with precise accuracy. A slew of smaller birds chased noisily behind, hoping for some of the spoils. The scene unfolded as if the director of a nature film gave an order, "Fish jump now – OK, cue the eagle!"

It was a "wow" moment, reaffirming our gratitude toward those who work tirelessly to preserve the environment and special places like Yellowstone.

~

Clark - Relaxing at Yellowstone Lake -
Yellowstone National Park, WY

We ended the day's ride at Fishing Bridge, the point where the Yellowstone River spills into Yellowstone Lake. Park literature said it covers 136 square miles, 20 miles long and 14 miles wide. It's also the largest natural freshwater lake above 7,000 feet and home to the wildest, most cutthroat trout in North America. Clark wished he'd carried his fly rod.

The campground was sold out, but our two-wheeled mode of transportation again enabled us to settle into a nice campsite without question. Once more, a barrage of mosquitoes found us as we pitched our tent. We hated putting on chemical-laden repellent but had little choice. Slather it on or get eaten alive! And, one more time, we chose to skip showers. Day #3. Gross, but neither of us cared.

~

Indoor dining was on our radar. We quickly hoofed the couple of miles into Lake Village for dinner. On the way back to camp, we got lazy and stuck our thumbs out. Luck was with us. A middle-aged man and a car-load of kids immediately pulled over to offer us a lift.

"We're heading up to the store, if you don't mind a small diversion," he told us.

Who? Us? What a perfect excuse to get a bottle of wine and some chocolate. The kids joined us in the candy aisle. I'm not sure who had more fun … us or them.

Back at the campground, Clark started a fire with dried dung he found in a handy pile near the tent. Elk manure was our guess, but, whatever it was, it burned well. We huddled inches from the fire, flames lapping at our kneecaps, in an effort to keep the bugs away. It worked and, happily, the dung smelled sweet—more like charcoal than poop. All was well.

> It struck me how quickly life renews. Wildfire had scarred the Yellowstone landscape, destroying wide swaths of forest in its path. Sticks of blackened poles, once great trees, stood like charred skeletons. But following that devastation, new plant life emerged from the ashes, the regeneration bringing balance back to nature.

Yellowstone has endured harsh weather, high winds, fires, floods, and extreme temperatures through the millennia, yet Mother Nature sustains herself. Life continues.

Foiling the She-Devil

Day 36:   Wednesday, July 9
Weather: Sunny and hot
Distance: 72 miles

Route: **Fishing Bridge in Yellowstone National Park to Cody, Wyoming**

I felt sick. Stomachache, headache, diarrhea, with alternating bouts of sweating and freezing. Didn't feel like getting up, but after several nights of camping in mosquito hell, the relentless itch drove me crazy. Red, bumpy bites dotted my body— legs, arms, face and neck. Those little bastards even found their way to my torso.

Scratch, scratch, scratch. I scratched myself raw. While Clark packed up, I dragged myself out of the sleeping bag and wore a trail back and forth to the bathroom, resting in between trips.

Even though I felt less than great, it was another gorgeous day in the park. Clark was happy to delay the ride until I felt better, one of the many traits I loved about him. He could flow with a day like no one I know. He busied himself making bicycle adjustments and breathing in the summer air, relaxing and appreciating the natural beauty before him. The sunshine warmed my skin like a comforting blanket and, after several hours, I was able to move.

~

We pedaled slowly toward the East Gate of the park but soon hit serious road construction. Loud, heavy equipment tore up the road, and jackhammers pummeled the ground. This left only one narrow lane of traffic crawling along. The dirt road was scattered with huge boulders, and sheer cliffs dropped off one side, with no barrier for protection. A tough-looking woman, with ruddy skin and no waist, directed traffic. She shouted at us harshly from a few yards away.

"What are you doing? This road is closed to bicyclists!" she bellowed in a repellent smoker's voice.

"No one told us," we shouted back.

"You can't go this way," she commanded, "It's not safe."

"But it's over 50 miles to the North Gate," I argued over the thumping and banging.

"That's not my problem. What's wrong with you? Do you want to get killed?" she replied brusquely, using her muscular arms to wave vehicles by.

"It'll take us an extra day to circle around," Clark countered.

"Tough shit. Those are the rules. Get out of my sight. You're pissing me off!"

We were dismissed but not defeated. Clark eyed the long line of vehicles waiting to pass and zeroed in on a 20-something gal in a black pick-up.

"Hell with the rules," he said, walking confidently over to the young woman with a big, friendly grin. He was going to sweet-talk her!

I stayed back, but noticed him pointing several times in my direction. She nodded sympathetically. I smiled and waved. My feminine, non-threatening presence was handy when asking for a ride.

Clark turned toward me and winked. His sexy smile finally did the trick. Even after all these years together, it still worked on me, too.

We threw our bikes in the back of her truck and climbed into the front seat. The three of us were friends by the time traffic started moving again.

Confession time: I loved seeing the shocked expression on the she-devil flagger's face as she saw us drive by. Her mouth agape, deep furrows creased her forehead as she realized we'd foiled her. I climbed over Clark and hung out the window to make sure she saw me. All of us waved cheerily as we passed.

When we saw the "Construction Zone Ends" sign, our kind chauffeur pulled over to let us out. It felt good to be back on solid ground.

~

Buffalo Bill Cody built Pahaska Tepee, just outside the East Gate, in the early 1900s as a mountain hunting lodge for himself, his wide circle of friends, and other notable visitors. It also served as a place for tourists to stay on their way to Yellowstone. The lodge is now on the National Historic Register and still offers accommodations today.

As we followed the Buffalo Bill Cody Scenic Byway, along the North Fork of the Shoshone River, we passed the town of Wapiti, halfway to our destination for the evening. We were floored by the natural beauty spanning in every direction. President Teddy Roosevelt was quoted as saying this drive, from the East Gate to Cody, is the "most scenic 50 miles in America."

~

The temperature had risen to the mid-90s by the time we arrived in Cody, hot, dusty, and ready for a soft bed and cool shower. We checked into a small motel and napped until the sun went down. Hunger pangs woke us up. I felt like myself again.

After a 2-mile hike into town, we chose a restaurant based on their sign: "Kick-Ass Cowboy Cuisine!" Mounted animal heads stared at us from every wall. Bison, elk, wildcat, pheasant, bear, deer, and even a big raccoon. Maybe all the carnivores watching us inspired Clark to order a monster T-bone steak. Still taking it easy, I went with a big bowl of chicken soup and saltine crackers. Clark raved on and on about his meat, popping a few tasty bites into my mouth.

Romance was in the air as we strolled home for the night. A warm, dry wind blew lightly at our backs, and the smell of wild sage wafted in the breeze. We held hands, stopping often to pick big bunches of the fragrant herb and steal sweet kisses.

~

Clark caught a glimpse of himself in the mirror.

"I'm thinner," he said, pleased.

"Yeah, you are," I agreed, surveying him intently. "That's not fair. How come I don't lose weight? I ride the same distance as you."

"You will," he assured, taking a minute to hug me. "Here, smell this sage," he said, holding it under my nose.

Clark's loving gesture drove the self-doubting demon away. I turned and looked into his eyes. I felt like the luckiest girl in the world.

The Spirit Grows Even Though the Wallet Diminishes

Day 37:   Thursday, July 10
Weather: Hot and humid with a side of wind and rain
Distance: Rest day in Cody
Route: Walked downtown several times
           (about 6 miles total)

Breakfast was a smorgasbord of disgusting fake food: warm, artificial OJ; rehydrated potatoes; puck-like biscuits; powdered, reconstituted eggs; rubbery bacon; canned fruit floating in a slurry of sugar water; something beige, mushy, and vaguely reminiscent of vomit; and bitter coffee. What a treat knowing we could eat as much as we wanted.

Although breakfast was a bomb, we scored free passes to a jackalope exhibit. These folkloric animals apparently exist across a wide range of the United States. Apparently, the tall tale started with sightings of rabbits infected with a virus, which caused horn-like tumors to grow on the unfortunate animals' heads.

~

In the late morning, while I napped, Clark visited a pub, wrote a few postcards, and ordered a plate of Rocky Mountain Oysters. Bull Balls, if you're not in the know. Calf testicles, if we want to be anatomically correct. Depending upon what part of the country you're in, they're also known as "Prairie Oysters," "Cowboy Caviar," "Dusted Nuts," "Montana Tendergroins," "Bull Fries," and "Swinging Beef." Clark's came deep-fried and tasted like chewy beef liver.

~

We spent the afternoon wandering the Buffalo Bill Historical Center, an affiliate of the Smithsonian Institution. It celebrates the spirit of the American West and is home to vast collections of historical memorabilia, art, and artifacts. It's a trip back in time to the Wild, Wild West. There are actually five separate museums: Buffalo Bill Museum, Draper Museum of Natural History, Plains Indian Museum, Whitney Gallery of Western Art, and Cody Firearms Museum. We spent 5 straight hours exploring.

~

I had a hankering for steak. The steak Clark had last night. Back at last night's restaurant, I ordered the largest slab of meat in these-here parts. Clark made it two. The steak was everything you hope for as a carnivore … thick, tender, and juicy. The seasoning was perfection, too. I ate the whole thing without a nod to the potatoes or salad that came with it. Even the glass of red wine took second shrift.

~

On the walk home, I told Clark I thought the motel owner, Bill, was a Vietnam vet.

"I think so, too. What makes you say that?" Clark asked with interest, surprised I might notice subtle signs.

"I'm not sure," I said. "It's just a feeling."

It wouldn't take long to find out we were right.

It was a quiet night. Bill was sitting on the porch steps, pondering the dark, starry sky, when we got back to the motel. He seemed open to talking.

We sat outside together for a long time. The conversation eventually wound around to the war and his life since then. He, like Clark, was angry and hurt about how soldiers were treated when they returned home from Vietnam. Military personnel, including Clark and Bill, were spit on, booed, and cursed at by anti-war protestors who unfairly blamed the soldiers for U.S. involvement in the war.

Young American men had been drafted in the 1960s. There was no choice. Go to war or go to jail. Clark and Bill were stationed "in the field" and saw the atrocities that occurred. Clark was working as a medic in the Mekong Delta when he was shot during a vicious fire fight. Nearly everyone in his Company was injured or killed. Clark spent 9 months in a military hospital recovering from his life-threatening injuries and lived with pain his entire life.

The two soldiers shared poignant memories of their times in Vietnam, silent for long moments after each deeply personal story.

The Pork Chop Incident

Day 38: Friday, July 11
Weather: Pouring rain and strong wind
Distance: 56 miles
Route: Cody, Wyoming, to Greybull, Wyoming

I was up and showered before Clark was awake. That hardly ever happened. As I sat on the end of the bed drying my hair, Clark stirred and smiled at me.

"I was dreaming about moving to Cody," he said.

"Should I add it to the list?" I asked.

"Yes ... I could live anywhere; as long as you're with me, I'm happy," Clark answered lovingly.

The trip had become a euphemism for life. The concept of "money can't buy happiness" was more relevant that morning. We felt filled up, content; living life in the moment; connecting with nature, people, and each other on a deeper level than ever before. At the risk of sounding trite, life was good.

~

In 1902, Buffalo Bill built the Irma Hotel and reserved a few suites and an office for himself, saying, "It's just the sweetest hotel that ever was." The setting is fancy enough to have pleased visiting royalty, simple enough for cowboy sensibility, and perfect for breakfast at the hotel saloon.

A massive, elegantly carved cherrywood bar dominates the space. The romance of the Old West permeates everything, from the beautiful pressed tin ceiling, to the crystal and antler chandeliers, to the ornate cash register. You can imagine cowboys mingling with gentry as they bellied up to the bar.

We overheard an octogenarian couple at the next table lamenting the disappearing life of cowboys. They talked of only small vestiges of cowhands still working in the state. My thoughts drifted off to the lyrics of a Paula Cole song: "Where is my John Wayne? Where is my prairie song? Where is my happy ending? Where have all the cowboys gone?"

People at the restaurant were engaging, most traveling on summer vacations of their own. Everyone talked back and forth across tables, laughing and sharing trip adventures. When they learned we were on bikes, they warned us about the Big Horn Mountains ahead. And, now that the towering giants loomed closer, our nerves started to jangle.

Comments ranged from "Those are bad ones!" to "Better plan to take a week and do a lot of walking."

I responded with a confident thumbs-up and a big smile, but secretly Clark and I had feared the Big Horns since we first pegged them on the map, two states back.

There were several choices of how to cross the mountains. We batted possibilities back and forth with a few folks and finally chose the Shell Canyon route. Though the road was steeper, it was definitely the most direct route to Sheridan, our next "friendly outpost."

~

It was time to ride. We packed up, tucking small stems of sage into our bike bags to neutralize the smell of dirty clothes. After a few chores—grocery shopping, filling our tires with air, and a bank stop—we rolled out at high noon.

~

We stopped to pay our respects at a Vietnam Veterans Memorial. I zeroed in on a bronze combat boot, overflowing with colorful flowers. The ideological contrast touched me deeply. Clark placed his palm onto the wall and bowed his head, connecting to his fallen brothers. We stood together, quietly, remembering those who were lost.

The wind picked up, carrying with it the sweet scent of clover. Clark breathed in deeply, eyes shut, chest expanding. I took his hand and, as we walked back toward our bikes, he turned and gave a final salute.

~

The skies darkened a few miles ahead and threatened rain. In open country, you can see storms rolling in from a distance, but it also means there's no place to hide from a deluge, wind, or lightning. We needed to pick up the pace, so dropped to single file, taking turns drafting one another.

Twenty miles into the ride, the storm rolled in. It wasn't bad at first. Cycling fast and sweating, we didn't mind the cooler temps and felt invigorated by the light rain. Soon the dark clouds intensified, and raindrops doubled in size and speed. We were drenched in minutes. The skies opened up, spilling out water as if a dam had broken. The wind gusted and swirled around us in tornado-like fashion. We almost expected to see the Wicked Witch of the West overtake us on her broom.

All at once, an "oh-no-not-now" sound added to the noise around us.

"I got a flat!" Clark yelled over the storm.

We stopped and stood in disbelief as he pulled a sharp piece of metal out of his front tire. The air escaped at warp speed, hissing like a snake as the tire pancaked.

After a moment of stunned silence, we burst into laughter at the absurd situation. Deserted highway. Torrential downpour. Screaming wind. And, flat #5.

"What's next?" Clark chuckled as he plopped down in the mud, whistling as he got to work. I hovered over him, trying to form a human umbrella with outstretched arms, giggling as rain poured down our already-soaked bodies.

Clark looked like a little boy blissfully playing in a mud puddle as he tinkered with the bike. With happy concentration, he fixed the tire in record time—just under 20 minutes.

I offered a hand to pull him up off the ground and used the moment as an excuse to steal a hug. As we embraced, two women in a sports car pulled over to ask if we needed help. It was interesting how, just when we needed it most, people magically appeared. Though there was nothing the women could do, we appreciated the kind gesture. Human nature at its finest.

~

Earlier that day at breakfast, I'd checked the map and noticed the town of Emblem. I asked the waitress if she knew of any restaurants there. I was already thinking about lunch.

She looked confused and said, "Emblem? I've never heard of it."

I figured she didn't get out much.

When we reached the tiny town, only a small sign acknowledged its existence. Emblem: Population 10. I guess that answered the question.

> We often started the day with little or no information about the road ahead. As the weeks passed, we realized the importance of always being prepared. Most general maps show state campgrounds, but there's not a lot of other useful information for cyclists. For example, a town may show up on a map but have a tiny population with no resources.
>
> Organized riders research these things ahead of time and often follow predetermined routes or ride with groups where everything is clearly defined before the first pedal turn. We preferred the adventure of "go with the flow," but began to understand the logic of knowing what lay beyond.

Greybull was a booming metropolis in comparison to Emblem. We were wet, cold, tired, and hungry and checked into the first motel we saw on the outskirts of town. The restaurant next door advertised "Good Home Cookin'."

Pork chops, one of Clark's favorites, were featured on the menu. He quizzed the waitress when she came to take our order.

"Now, are the pork chops good sized or that thin kind?"

"Oh no," she said with conviction, "They're good sized—big and thick. You'll love 'em!"

"Hmmm …," Clark pondered, digging a bit more, "But, there are different cuts, some are real thick and others very thin."

"I've seen them all," she said, knowingly. "These are *good!*"

We were sold.

Apparently, thickness is a relative concept.

Clark picked a chop up, studying it with disappointed amazement, and said, "If this was any thinner, you could read a newspaper through it."

The meal was rounded out with metallic-tasting canned peas, wilted iceberg lettuce topped with a blop of mayonnaise, and stale dinner rolls.

Poor Clark looked boyishly dejected as he slumped deep into his chair and went silent. All I could do was laugh, and laugh, and laugh. I lost complete control. The harder I tried to hold back, the more I laughed. This pulled Clark out of his depression and soon he was splitting a gut, too.

~

Sometime in the middle of the night, I woke up laughing. Clark's crestfallen expression was replaying over and over in my REM sleep and I lost control … again. I laughed so hard Clark woke up.

We often had 3 a.m. discussions—always honest and heartfelt, and sometimes what might have been troubling earlier was viewed through a different lens and became amusing. This was one of those times.

We went over the story—egging each other on, painting increasingly dismal images of the chops, ending with "meat so thin you can use it for skin grafts." We worked ourselves into a fit of hysteria, until neighbors in the room next door pounded on the walls.

We turned away from each other, covered our faces with pillows, and struggled to remain quiet. But, soon the bed shook from one of us laughing, and the mania started all over again. We were done sleeping for the night and I suspect the neighbors were, too.

Layers of Time

> Day 39: Saturday, July 12
> Weather: Overcast, then rain
> Distance: 22 miles
> Route: Greybull, Wyoming, to Shell, Wyoming

We weren't anxious to run into the neighbors we'd tormented, so stayed in the room until we heard them leave. I peeked through the curtains to make sure they drove away. With the coast clear, we headed to the center of Greybull for breakfast. The town was named after the Greybull River, which takes its name from the rare albino buffalo (or bison) many Native Americans hold sacred and spiritually significant.

Even with overcast skies, we had mountain views all around. The high-altitude beauty reminded us of the impending ride up Shell Canyon in the Big Horn Mountains.

While finishing our eggs, we played the game we now dubbed "Psych the Mountain" to ease some of the psychological stress of the impending climb and to help us mentally prepare. We smack-talked the dreaded peak to make it feel small.

"You're nothing but a tiny bump—we're not scared of you."

"Bring on the *real* mountains!"

"Yeah, you're just a whiny-baby hill."

"We can ride up over you in an hour!"

"And, the sooner we get it over with, the happier I'll be," Clark said. "But first, let's order a piece of pie."

~

It was early afternoon by the time we started riding. A storm threatened. White clouds streaked the darkened horizon with patches of blue teasing us in the distance. The landscape was oddly beautiful: a mixture of muted browns, grays, and greens. Earth-toned rainbows of rock exposed layers of prehistoric times and told of an age when dinosaurs walked the earth. We were getting close to the base of the Big Horn Mountains. So close, we couldn't see the cloud-shrouded peaks.

> Wyoming's Bighorn Basin contains an extensive amount of fossil deposits that date from as far back as the Cambrian Period, 550 million years ago. One of the world's largest meat-eating dinosaurs, the Allosaurus, was excavated in this area. Archeologists nicknamed him "Big Al 2."

The heavy winds and dark clouds caught up to us. It was a struggle battling against the gusts, so we ducked into a convenience store to take a break and avoid the oncoming downpour.

We needed to gather a few energy-sustaining foods for the trek up the mountain. There were minimal options and no fruit, so we stocked up on peanut butter, Ritz crackers, a bag of mixed nuts, and candy bars. The biggest worry was water. We refilled our four water bottles and a camel back, then grabbed a few extra bottled waters.

The rain came pelting down just as we stepped outside. We took a seat on the covered porch to watch the storm play out. Spectacular lightning flashes reached out of the sky, striking in every direction.

Crackling thunder rolled across the landscape, silencing the world around us. Torrents of rain poured steadily on the dry landscape. The storm's grand finale: sunlight streaming through the clouds, fanning across the panorama. The encore? Brilliantly colored double rainbows.

~

It was obvious we weren't going up the mountain that day. We found a place to stay near the foot of the climb—rustic cabin accommodations next door to a bar and restaurant. Our big bed was cloaked in a fluffy down comforter, and a rocking chair waited in one corner. Fresh mountain air flooded in from the windows, bringing with it that clean, after-rain smell. The modern conveniences of a phone, microwave, or TV were not missed and would have seemed out of place.

The room exemplified one of the things I loved most about the trip: You don't need to be constantly stimulated. The ultimate luxury was having the time to savor the little moments, without the distractions of technology or the noise and flurry of constant activity synonymous with everyday life.

I took my time getting dolled up for dinner, after Clark showered and went next door for a drink. While he was waiting for me, a pockmarked cowboy sauntered up to him and said, "Hey, pal. I left my wallet back at the ranch and need a drink real bad. How 'bout it?"

Clark was amused at first. The man was engaging and had some tales to tell. Not long after the cowboy finished his drink, he leaned in a bit too close and slurred, "I think you should buy me another!"

Obviously, he'd started the binge earlier. A little irritated, but going with the flow, Clark slapped more money down on the bar.

The cowboy's mood took an ugly turn a few minutes after he downed the drink. He got belligerent, spat on the floor, and loudly demanded, "You better buy me one more!"

Clark stayed calm while the drunkard staggered to his feet, looking like he was getting ready to pick a fight. A woman—the wife, Clark realized—glared angrily from a table across the room.

"That's it, buddy—go back to your wife now."

"Oh, *her*," the cowboy said, tilting his hat back, glancing in her direction. "She doesn't like it when I drink."

Gee, I wonder why?

~

Meanwhile, I'd slipped into my skirt and matching top and put on earrings and make-up. My face was tan and glowed with a radiance I'd not seen in a long while. I felt more feminine and confident.

As soon as I walked into the bar, and for the first time in ages, I noticed several men looking at me ... with approval. A handsome man tipped his hat and smiled as I took a seat next to Clark. Another gentleman motioned to join him for a drink, an odd request since Clark had his arm around me.

I wondered if women were scarce in this neck of the woods but enjoyed the attention nonetheless. And Clark, who tended toward possessiveness, watched the men making their not-so-subtle advances and seemed to enjoy it as much as me.

~

As we lingered over dinner, clouds settled low in the valley. An eerie light framed the silhouette of the mountain. The sky turned steel gray. Wind spun leaves around in a tiny vortex, blowing an ominous warning. Darkness cloaked the mountain's steep, brown walls and melted into the Big Horn River.

I looked at the mountain with trepidation. Clark instinctively knew what I was thinking.

"Let's not worry about that until tomorrow."

We tried to shove it out of our minds, but soon the conversation shifted to the next day's challenging ride. A diner sitting nearby told us to expect a 30-mile climb with a grade of 6% to 7% much of the way. We attempted to quell the building fear by ordering another round of drinks.

"Don't worry. It's not that bad," another patron told us.

"Really?" I said, "First time I've heard that."

"The climb is not bad—at least in a car," he said with a wink. "I'll bet your little buns will know when you reach the summit."

I laughed, but all I could think was did he say "little" when referring to *my* buns? Oh, God! I was feeling good!

WEEK 7

Tackling the 9,000-Foot Mountain

    Day 40:   Sunday, July 13
    Weather: Hot
    Distance: 33 miles
    Route: From the base to the summit of Shell Canyon, Wyoming

An odd sound woke me up. I shook off sleep and heard rain pelting the window. Clark stirred next to me. We'd managed to drink too much the night before, and I felt sluggish and hung over. Not the best way to feel when you have a grueling workout ahead.

"Should we shut up and ride?" I asked Clark, nestling closer.

"No. Sleep!" he said, hugging me tighter.

We dozed off again and woke an hour later, when the rain subsided and morning light streaked into the room. It was time to prepare—especially mentally.

First on the agenda: coffee.

We went next door for breakfast, the same place we'd imbibed the night before. The owner recognized us and asked how we were feeling.

We admitted to being a little shaky, but weren't sure if it was the alcohol or nerves.

"You like it here don't you?" he grinned. "The place is up for sale you know."

"Really?" Clark said. "How much are you asking?"

They bartered back and forth, then we came to our senses.

"It sounds like fun," I said, looking around, "But what would I do here?"

The man didn't think about it twice.

"You'd be the perfect hostess and front house manager. Clark would handle the back."

He had it all planned out for us.

"It's tempting," Clark said with stars in his eyes. "It'll give us something to think about as we grunt up the Big Horns."

"How 'bout I make you some sandwiches for the trip?"

"Sounds great," Clark said. "We'll pack up and come back."

~

We talked about what it would be like to live in Shell or any one of the small towns along the way. We loved the friendly atmosphere. People were welcoming and seemed interested in getting to know us. Would the warmth change if we actually made the move? Would we be seen as outsiders and not really accepted? Were we just an interesting oddity? An exciting one-night stand? We'd probably never know, but it was fun to dream about where life could take us.

~

Loaded and ready to go, we made one last stop at the restaurant to say goodbye and pick up lunch. Big thick sandwiches, piled high with ham and turkey, cheese, pickles, and plenty of butter awaited us. A small bag of chips, oranges, and a couple iced teas rounded out the picnic we'd enjoy later.

"This should hold you for a few miles at least," our new friend said, tempting us further with, "Last chance to get a lift up the mountain."

"Thanks, we can do it," I said, not giving myself a moment to reconsider. We exchanged hugs, Clark added a manly handshake, and we were off.

"Think about buying this place now," the man yelled after us.

"Will do," Clark promised with a final wave.

~

The first mile of the climb was easy—uphill, but only slightly. So, we started getting cocky.

"We can handle this," I said.

"Yeah, we'll be eating our victory oranges at the summit by noon." Clark agreed.

But as soon as those words left his mouth ... everything changed. The incline went up and up and up some more. The road got so steep we had to stand on our pedals for extra oomph. It felt like we were biking at a 90-degree angle and might tumble backward. Sweat poured off our bodies, dripping on the ground and collecting in little pools on our handlebar bags. Why did I turn down the ride?

After a few miles, a travel bus chugged by, then pulled over ahead of us at a turnout. A group of tourists spilled out onto the road. Instead of walking toward the scenic overlook, they aimed their cameras in our direction. One man followed me for an inordinately long time, recording my progress inch by inch. I tried to smile, or at least not grimace, as I passed him.

I kept riding, but Clark used the attention as an excuse to stop. He was engulfed by a crowd of 50 German visitors who wondered why we were doing this insane climb on bikes. Clark shared our story in their native language, able to paint a picture that made everyone roar with laughter. I stopped out of earshot, waved to the crowd and pretended to be patiently waiting, but secretly gasped for air.

When Clark caught up again, we continued the climb—moving slower than the last drop of ketchup in a bottle.

Clark - The Ride Up Shell Canyon - Shell, WY

Oddly, as we climbed, more tourists stopped to take pictures, and cars slowed while passengers cheered enthusiastically out the windows as they drove by. I think we were photographed more on this trip than the rest of our lives combined. We were happy for the unexpected attention and support, as it bolstered our energy.

However, not everyone was happy we were on the road. One man purposely drove behind us for what seemed like an eternity. When Clark tried to wave him around, the guy laid on his horn. The loud blare caused me to lose balance and swerve. The driver found that funny and laughed so loud I could hear him. He interspersed the rude guffawing with horn beeping and insulting comments as he slowly rode by.

~

When we finally made it to the visitor center, 9 miles up, we were almost out of energy and dangerously low on liquids. We stopped for a long rest, ate lunch, resupplied our water, and took in the views. Shell Falls plunged 120 feet over a sheer-walled canyon nearby. A nice distraction.

~

The break only sustained us another few miles. Our bodies shouted to quit. Knees, backs, butts, necks, and hands all hurt. We didn't talk, just dealt with the pain and continued the climb in silence. We stopped often for water and to stretch. The mountain never gave us a break.

Four hours from departing, we were only 10 miles into the ride, not even half way. This included two hours of riding and two hours of resting.

By the time we reached the 12-mile mark, I was pedaling, while Clark was walking his bike and outpacing me.

Up ahead at a turnout, a thin, tanned man stood near his truck, motioning us to pull over.

"Got some ice cold sodas for ya," he called out, "Pedal up this far and you get a reward."

We were too tired to laugh but managed to force a smile.

"That's a tough ride. You're doin' good," he said, probably sensing we needed some support.

We grabbed the drinks out of his hand, panting so hard, we had to pace our gulps to avoid choking.

"Thanks," I said, after satiating my thirst and catching my breath.

"Yeah, we really needed that," Clark added.

He offered us a lift to the summit, mentioning he'd driven several riders in the last month.

"It's too much for most people. I think they underestimate this old mountain—she's a steep one," he stated with the conviction of someone who knew this area well.

We wanted to say "yes," but changed the subject until finding the strength to say "no." He seemed in no hurry to be on his way, so we shot the breeze for half an hour giving him details of our ride. His generosity, the much-needed intermission, and the sugar infusion reinvigorated us to travel on.

Eight more uphill miles to the summit. *Eight.*

The burst of energy carried us only a short distance. Clark got crabby. I wanted to cry but didn't have the oomph to muster tears. We considered camping at a pullout along the road, but the thought of having to continue the ride in the morning was more than we could stand. We pushed past our limits and forced ourselves on, so miserable we hoped a car would fly around a corner and run us over, thus ending this terrible climb.

Rounding every switchback resulted in disappointment and frustration. Where was the top of the mountain? When would this torture stop?

"I can't ride anymore," I whined.

"Jesus, I hurt in places I didn't know existed," Clark complained.

Then silence.

After three more switchbacks, the whining started again.

"Why aren't we there yet?" Clark asked, sounding like an annoying 5-year-old.

More silence and one more switchback with no summit view.

"That's it. I'm camping right here," I declared.

Clark shot me a dog-tired look and was about to say something else when the road suddenly leveled off.

"We're here! We did it!"

Momentarily forgetting my exhaustion, I shouted, "There's the summit sign!"

We'd made it. We reached the summit of the Big Horn Mountains. Elevation: 9430 feet.

The victory celebration was short-lived. Diminishing light and dropping temperatures forced us to press on. Although we didn't know it, accommodations were still 13 miles away.

~

After painfully dismounting our bikes, we struggled to the check-in only a few feet away. I could feel my muscles freezing up and walked like Frankenstein toward the desk.

A rustic cabin was all they had left. Bunk beds, no bath. We'd have to walk a few hundred yards to reach the facilities. We wheeled our bikes into the room and lurched stiffly to the dining hall, powered by ravenous hunger. Food. Eat. Now. We slammed that dinner down.

A nightcap beckoned. A barrage of applause and whistles exploded as we walked into the bar. Our waitress had spread the word about our biking adventures, making us instant celebrities. The rowdy crowd encircled us.

"Wow! You came up the Big Horns?" someone exclaimed, "You deserve a drink now. Waitress!"

"I can't believe you did that. I'll buy the next round," another patron shouted.

"Man, you guys are amazing! What are you drinkin'?" the barkeep said.

This might have gone on all evening, but we couldn't keep our heads up – so bid goodnight after the second round.

"The beauty is, it's all downhill tomorrow," I responded, thanking the crowd and giving my finest Queen's wave. Elbow, elbow, wrist, wrist.

Everyone cheered.

We fell into bed, sound asleep in under a minute.

Horsing Around

Day 41:	Monday, July 14
Weather:	Hot
Distance:	54 miles
Route:	Shell Canyon Summit to Sheridan, Wyoming

An unnervingly close horse whinny woke us from a sound sleep. Startled, I sat up quickly and came face-to-face with big brown eyes. Was I dreaming? What was a horse's head doing in our room?

I came to my senses and realized our cabin adjoined a corral and the curious animal had put her head through our open window to check us out.

"Well, hello, girl," I said, stroking her long face.

Clark laid on his back, staring up the horse's nostrils, still slightly confused. Then, burst into laughter.

Sadie (I saw the name on her lead) whinnied and pranced around to show off for us, always coming back and poking her head in for more attention. We played hide-and-seek with her, concealing ourselves behind the curtains. She liked the game, ne-e-e-e-i-ghing her delight when she figured out where we were.

~

And the ride began. What a beautiful ride it was. Clear skies and smooth sailing. We could see for miles, all the way across the valley. A massive tumble of oblong rocks littered a mountainside, looking like an ancient civilization in ruins. "Fallen City," as it's known, is now a rock climber's paradise with its gigantic limestone boulders and precipices.

Tourists stopped to admire the formation. A few asked to take pictures of us and our loaded bikes. One shy couple tried to sneak up and snap some stealthy shots from behind. I happened to turn around and caught them in the act. Probably the fear of having my backside photographed made me sense danger and turn. Embarrassed, they sheepishly asked if they could get another photo. We agreed. Then they ran back to their car and disappeared from sight.

~

At the bottom of the mountain, we stopped for lunch and took a heat break. Temperatures had cranked up to uncomfortable by then. We were glad to find a side road lined with shade trees outside of Ranchester. It made for a pleasant ride the rest of the way to Sheridan.

We found our friend Melissa's place easily and were greeted by a big welcome sign on the front door: "I'm at work. Make yourselves at home! See you at 5." We hauled our things inside, met the cats, grabbed ice-cold drinks, took showers, and zombied-out.

Melissa lived on a quiet street; the house sat back from the road and had a large vegetable garden. Short-cropped grass tickled our toes as we explored. Clark was in heaven, eyeing the fat tomatoes and hearty zucchinis.

We were contentedly sitting on the front porch when Melissa got home from work. The celebrating commenced. Bacon-wrapped dates and a bottle of white. Then grilled steaks, potatoes, and a salad of veggies picked from her garden, served with a bottle of red. We caught up, sharing our lives since we'd last seen each other and laughed about the time Clark tried to blame his late-night refrigerator raid on a mouse. Melissa jokingly put out a trap to catch the rascal.

Crop-Destroying Devils

Day 42 & 43: Tuesday and Wednesday, July 15 and 16
Weather: Hot
Distance: Rest days
Route: Traveled around the area but mostly by car

Our next two days were filled with sightseeing, relaxing, and taking care of a few necessities: laundry, finances, airing out our gear, and finding Clark a pair of cowboy boots.

The sales clerk told us they were an excellent buy because, "They're in great shape with only a little shit on the soles."

Who could resist a sales pitch like that?

A trip to Sheridan wouldn't be complete without a stop at the world-famous King's Saddlery Western tack store. The store, internationally known for its ropes and saddles, was started by legendary cowboy and saddlemaker Don King in 1963. He revolutionized the business with his innovative tooling and stamping techniques, including his signature wild-rose motif, now known as the "Sheridan Style."

King made saddles and other tooled leather goods for many famous cowboys and notable people, including Queen Elizabeth II, Arab sheiks, and presidents Ronald Reagan and Bill Clinton. His saddles are displayed in the Cowboy Hall of Fame, the Museum of the American Cowboy, and the ProRodeo Hall of Champions.

The most important thing we learned—the wise words of fictional cowboy radio narrator Texas Bix Bender—"Don't squat with your spurs on."

We moseyed over to the historic Mint Bar, a popular hangout for over a century. It was hard to miss with its iconic neon sign of a rider on a bucking bronco. Inside, the walls of the classic watering hole are lined with taxidermied fish and animals, and thousands of brands burned onto wooden planks. At various times throughout its history, the Mint was a saloon, a cigar company/soda shop during prohibition (and also a speakeasy), and then once again a bar.

~

The next day, we were invited by *The Sheridan Press* for an interview about our cross-country journey. After years in the radio and TV industry, I could easily predict the questions and help focus the interview, since I knew what they needed for a story. It was interesting to be the interviewee instead of the interviewer.

As we left the building, Melissa saw a grasshopper bouncing along the sidewalk. It is important to note that she once worked at the Humane Society and is an ardent animal lover, as am I. I've seen her gingerly carry spiders out of the house and set them free. But, at that moment, a vicious look crossed her face and she lurched out of her way to stomp on the hopper. Oddly out of character for a critter lover like her.

"Melissa! What the …?!" I asked with surprise.

"I *hate* grasshoppers! Crop-destroying devils. You'll see what I mean," she answered cryptically.

In a few short days we'd find out exactly what she meant.

Leiterville Country Club

Day 44:   Thursday, July 17
Weather: Dark clouds and a little rain
Distance: 55 miles
Route: Sheridan, Wyoming, to Leiter, Wyoming

We didn't want to get out of bed and felt the same sad trepidation every time we had to leave our friends. Although we loved the journey, it was a challenge returning to the road after a couple days of rest and royal treatment.

It was time to travel on, so we bid *adieu* and many thanks to Melissa. Sheridan easily made the list of places we considered moving to.

Our plan was to head south toward Buffalo, then proceed east. At the outskirts of the city, a loud BANG! jolted us. Another blowout. It sounded like a car backfiring. Clark's tire went instantly flat. Fortunately, he was moving slowly so managed to stay on top of his bike. And more good luck—there was a tire store across the street. Although it was a car shop, we naively figured they'd carry tires of all sorts. We were wrong about that.

A blow out means the tire is ruined, not just the inside tubing, so both would need to be replaced. We carried an extra tube, but no tire. Clark took the wheel and hitched back to the center of town in search of a bike shop. He got a ride immediately by holding up the damaged gear. I stayed behind to watch our belongings.

Flat tire count: 6. Each of us had one on the back and two on the front. We were even at 3:3.

Clark was back in no time and we were off.

The terrain gave way to beautiful desert colors, blending rock and sky. Nature's stage play unfolded as we pedaled along. A deer appeared on the horizon. We watched its silhouette moving easily across the land, springing effortlessly over ranch fences. A young coyote warily peeked out from behind a rock, his soulful eyes monitoring our invasion on his turf. A quartet of horses bucked and galloped behind barbed wire in the distance, then moved in closer to get a better look at us.

Clark's knee started hurting at the 32-mile mark, just outside Ucross. We pulled over to rest and stretch under the boughs of a shade tree next to a dilapidated mailbox. An old man drove up from his long, dusty driveway in what seemed like an even older pick-up. He parked and shuffled slowly toward his mailbox, head down. He looked startled when he spotted us and uttered a grandpa-like "Huh?" Then his wizened face softened and a three-tooth smile appeared.

"Well, who are you?" he asked sweetly.

We struck up a conversation. He would talk, mostly about his memories growing up in the area, then randomly forget what he was saying and ask who we were again. He laughed loud and long when telling stories, giving us an excellent view into his gummy mouth.

"Do you know how old I am?" he asked several times. We guessed 65, to be nice. And he'd give us a bigger smile and again say, "I'm 93!"

"You must be thirsty. I got some water," he said, shuffling back toward the car. He returned with a handmade clay water jug. It was old and well used. I pulled out an empty water bottle from our pack. We didn't really need the refill, but he wanted to help, so we accepted. The man tipped the jug and water gushed out quickly, splashing over the bottle and down our legs.

"That'll do ya," he said, not noticing the spillage.

"It sure will," Clark laughed.

Just like that, he turned and trundled off.

~

The encounter gave Clark the break needed to rest his knee. We pushed ahead 9 more miles into Clearmont, only to learn it was another 9 to Leiter, the closest place with accommodations. We restocked provisions and took a long rest outside the general store. Parking our tired bodies on rickety crates alongside the building made us feel like hobos. But we didn't care and tore into our treasure trove of snacks.

~

It was almost 9 p.m. when we arrived in Leiter, population 28. The town consisted of a bar, restaurant, post office, and social club all under one roof. There were a few cabins and some horseshoe pits out back. Locals affectionately called this the "Leiterville Country Club." I'm proud to say we're now illustrious members.

We were shown to a tiny cabin, settled in, and left our bikes unlocked outside our door. No need to worry about your belongings in a little burgh like this.

Dinnertime! Martha, the Country Club owner, cook, accountant, waitress, housekeeper, entertainment, and hostess, fixed us burgers and fries. After she had served us and tidied up a bit, we invited her to join us at our table since the place was empty. She was blonde, solidly built, and attractive in a no-nonsense way. Martha's energy was magnetic, and the conversation unfolded easily.

We felt at home, Clark especially. The rapport between the two was uncanny. They were immediate friends. Not to say I wasn't, but they had a connection akin to old souls finding each other.

~

That night a big storm hit. Thunder boomed and echoed all along the valley, crashing so loudly shockwaves rocked our bodies. Lightning followed, sending out brilliant flashes that lit the landscape. We counted the time between the thunder and lightning to see how close the storm was. One second equals one mile. It was close. Large raindrops pounded at a constant tempo. We jumped out of bed and stood naked in the doorway watching the tempest run its course.

> Time felt different on our trip—it was distorted, moving slower somehow. So much, yet so little, happened every day. We learned to appreciate the small things in magnified detail.

Clark Saves the Day

Day 45:   Friday, July 18
Weather: Hot and raining a nasty surprise
Distance: 68 miles
Route: Leiter, Wyoming, to Gillette, Wyoming

Spontaneous Revolutions

We woke up refreshed. Clark's knee was feeling better and we looked forward to a relaxing breakfast with Martha. But that was not to be. A beloved, local rancher had passed away. It was his funeral day. People came to Martha's for breakfast before the service. She wasn't expecting such a big crowd and ran from table to kitchen to get the job done.

Martha took one panicked look at us, and Clark, recognizing kitchen stress, jumped in to help. He quickly took over cooking duties. Clark was an ace, flying solo in an unfamiliar kitchen with no time to learn the particular ropes. It wasn't long until perfectly cooked orders were heading out of the kitchen as fast as they came in. Hungry ranchers devoured the delicious food, and Martha breathed a sigh of relief.

I offered to help, but Clark said I wasn't "needed." Probably for the better; no one wants me around the kitchen when the pressure is on. Come to think of it, no one wants me in the kitchen at all, except when it's time to clean up.

After the rush was over, Clark and I ate breakfast. Martha tried to comp it, but Clark refused, paying full price and tipping her $10 instead.

We packed our things with a bit of melancholy and went to see Martha one last time.

"Love to have you stay," she said. "I could use the help if you want a summer job."

It was tempting, but time to go. Leaving Martha was like saying goodbye to an old friend.

~

Just outside of Leiter, we heard a flapping–buzzing–humming sound traveling on wind. We also noticed an odd change in the plant life. Everything was in sorry shape. Was it a plague? Upon closer inspection, we saw grasshoppers hanging on every spot of green—a carpet of insects as far as we could see. They were gnawing voraciously, destroying everything in sight. It was more than a little creepy.

Millions of grasshoppers had turned the beauty of the vast, open country into a pulsating nightmare. The creatures boinged off our arms, legs, and torsos and crunched beneath our wheels. One hopper rode with me for a couple miles, hanging onto the top of my bike bag. I looked closely at its face and was reminded of a horror flick I watched as a kid: *The Attack of the Giant Grasshopper,* or something along those lines. The script started to play out in my head and freaked me out. I tried to lose him by swerving and swaying in jerky motion, but he hung on and watched me with beady eyes.

Eventually, I lost sight of it but kept expecting him to reappear, growing larger and talking. Maybe he was making a nest in my bag and would show up in the tent later, angry that I crushed so many of his kind. I wondered if the movie writers experienced grasshopper invasions, gleaning story inspiration from the eerie phenomenon.

Riding further into the maelstrom, grasshoppers grew so thick they were spraying off both sides of our bike wheels, like the bow of a ship parting waves. I looked over at Clark and saw them crawling on his body, then glanced down and spotted the insects climbing up my legs. I kicked out both feet trying to dislodge the grasshoppers, but they were strong and clingy. I could feel their hairy legs on my bare flesh.

The grossest thing was the live hoppers seemed to be eating the dead ones. This was too much. We pedaled as fast as we could to escape.

Miles down the road, my bike started having problems. It would shift on its own and not allow me to change gears when I wanted to. Every time I tried to shift, the chain would come off and get snarled in the spokes. We'd stop, pry the chain loose, and put it back in place. The gears were embedded with slimy bug carcasses.

Spontaneous Revolutions

Grasshopper hell.

~

The tiny town of Spotted Horse, population 2, offered a much-needed respite from the nightmare we'd just encountered. As far as I could tell, the town was one building: a restaurant with a spotted horse sign outside. We stopped in for a break and a bite to eat and contemplated spending the night. But that meant camping with rattlesnakes and grasshoppers. No way.

~

The remainder of the day's ride was a long, dusty, stop-and-start struggle, but eventually we made it to Gillette. As we entered town, the feeling changed from cowboy country to coal mining, oil drilling, and rough necks. Branding irons were replaced with hard hats. Nothing typified the switch more than a sign on one of the local restaurants, "Welcome Propane Conference."

We headed straight for the bike shop, but it was already closed so we checked into a motel and planned an early morning return.

Clark followed his nose to a Mexican restaurant, the smell of fresh tortillas permeating the air. We drowned our grasshopper experience by ordering the special: all the top sirloin you could eat coupled with a pitcher of margaritas. OK, maybe it was two.

After dinner, we zigzagged through town to locate the source of live country music. A rowdy band cranked out twangy renditions of old-time hits on a blocked-off street. The thick crowd boot-scooted and rewarded the musicians with loud hoots and hollers at the end of each song. The men waved their cowboy hats high in the air. We held hands and swayed to the music.

Liza McQuade

Naked Rain Dance

> Day 46:   Saturday, July 19
> Weather: Horrid hot
> Distance: 31 miles
> Route: Gillette, Wyoming, to Moorcroft, Wyoming

We arrived at the bike shop as the doors opened and it didn't take the mechanic long to find the problem. As Clark suspected, I needed a new chain. It seemed a little soon to me, but we learned cyclists generally replace their chains every 1000 miles or so, especially when you ride as hard as we were. I hoped this new chain would take me to the finish line.

The benefit of having an expert look at your bike is that they know things. Imagine that. The mechanic recommended moving my handlebar ends up, which would take pressure off my hands and make for a more comfortable ride. Surprisingly, my hands—of all my body parts—hurt the most from the aggressive riding. I might have pinched a nerve from gripping the handlebars so tightly. (The numbness in my hands lasted nearly a year after we returned.)

~

Cheesy scrambled eggs and fresh-from-the-oven cinnamon rolls, dripping with caramel, butter, and sweet cinnamon, made for a filling breakfast. I had a craving for milk and ordered a big glass. My Dairy State roots were showing.

After browsing the local shops, we scored a jackalope pin—the prize of our state pin collection. Clark attached it to his bike bag, along with our Oregon, Idaho, and Montana pins.

Back in the hotel, we realized check-out time was at 10. It was a few minutes after. We hurriedly dragged our stuff outside, left the key in the room, closed the door, and finished organizing on a small patch of grass at the side of the parking lot. Just as the door shut behind us, we heard the phone ring. The caller hung up, paused a few seconds, then called again and again and again. It rang continuously for 20 minutes.

Clark took some time to adjust his brakes and gave our bikes a once-over. Meanwhile, the phone in our room rang on.

As we finished up, a motel clerk rushed at us like a freight train, huffing loudly.

"Aren't you out of the room yet?" she said in a snotty tone.

"We're out," I answered, ignoring her attitude, "Just doing a minor bike repair."

The clerk wheeled around on her heels, jangling a big wad of keys and unlocked the door. She let out a loud snort as she entered.

Seconds later, the woman rushed out of the room waving a single washcloth.

"Do you know what happened to the other one?" as if accusing us of a major crime, insinuating we must have stolen it.

I gave her a syrupy smile and said calmly, "I hung it over the tub to dry."

Clark didn't even look up.

She seemed surprised we weren't the criminals she imagined us to be and walked away, the limp rag in her hand.

~

Even with all the adjustments and paying a mechanic, neither of our bikes seemed to be working at top performance. We stopped often to readjust, frustration mounting. Clark's brakes rubbed on the wheels instead of the metal, and my bike reverted back to slipping, sliding, and shifting on its own. We entertained the idea of returning to the bike shop, but were miles away by then.

We found a side road to Rozet, happy to avoid the freeway. A small bar in town called our name, so we pulled over for a bite to eat. Another of our *modi operandi*: When we felt overwhelmed, frustrated, hot, cold, wet, tired, sleepy, achy, happy, celebratory—or almost any emotion at all—we stopped for something to eat or drink. This time it was a fortuitous choice. We met a gentleman who was a cyclist himself. He knew bikes like the back of his hand and happened to have a complete tool kit in his truck. He fixed us both up and we were back on the road in record time.

We made it to Moorcroft quickly, decided to call it a day, and started the motel bartering game. We divided the properties in close proximity and covered the town efficiently. Our system was to talk to the clerks, check the rooms, negotiate the best price, then come back together and compare notes.

One of Clark's motels had an especially sweet clerk. She apologized for not altering the room rate but offered to call another property and got a great price for us. Problem was, that motel was really run down, and the desk clerk so grouchy and vile, we changed our minds and went back to the place with the nice clerk.

Clark put on his charm, "Since you were exceptionally pleasant and THEY were ridiculously crabby, we decided to stay with you, no matter the price."

"Ohhhhhhh," she said, eating up the compliment. "Thanks! Hey, you know what? I'll give you that discount."

What goes around comes around.

~

Spontaneous Revolutions

The room was perfect, but dinner at a nearby restaurant was a disaster. The first tip-off of impending doom was sticky menus. I pried mine open and couldn't determine the substance that created the glue. Tired and hungry, we perused the menus hoping to find something that sounded good. Fried this and that, combined with lots of cheap, low-nutrition options ... but there was a salad bar.

I scanned the room and saw a five-foot set-up of iceberg lettuce, cucumbers floating in water, mushy tomatoes, flaccid pickles, processed cheese shreds, slimy coleslaw, graying hard-boiled eggs, and half a basket of rolls the size of a man's fist.

Clark looked up from his menu and caught my gaze, following it to the salad bar. We watched in horror as diners grabbed food with their bare hands, picking through the options, before plopping it onto their plates. One sampled a pickle and casually put the half-eaten item back into the bin. A child stood by, picking his nose and pilfering through the rolls.

Clark stood up. "We're outta here."

We hurried back to the room and ate what was left in our packs.

> Food was a big deal on our trip, not only because we expended so many calories and needed to replenish our energy stores, but also because we looked forward to trying foods from across the country. When presented with a culinary disappointment, it hit hard.

A big storm moved in sometime after midnight. Thunder rocked our room; lightning flashed, momentarily blinding us; and rain pelting cars created a metallic symphony.

When the lightning subsided, we got a crazy notion and ran naked into the field behind the motel. We stood in the pitch dark letting the water rush over our bodies, massaging our backs like a cool shower. Spontaneous moments like these kept our relationship fun. We laughed like children getting away with something wonderful. If anyone saw us, we never knew.

WEEK 8

Biting Flies on the Rise

    Day 47:   Sunday, July 20
    Weather: Hot, hot, hot
    Distance: 52 miles
    Route: Moorcroft, Wyoming, to Newcastle, Wyoming

Everything glistened from the heavy rain, and the air already felt muggy.

Devils Tower loomed 30 miles in the distance like a rocky sentinel protruding from the rolling hills. President Theodore Roosevelt established Devils Tower as our nation's first national monument in 1906. I recognized its rectangular shape from travel magazines and movies. Steven Spielberg shot a now-famous scene there for *Close Encounters of the Third Kind* in 1977.

Even from a great distance, we felt drawn to its mysterious presence, but our route took us south, away from Devils Tower. No matter how tempting it was to explore close up, the temperatures were soaring, so we rolled on.

In Upton, about 20 miles into the ride, nostalgia hit; an old-fashioned five-and-dime drew us in. Variety stores with malt shop counters were once the gathering place in many small towns. Clark and I sat on vinyl-topped stools that swiveled 360 degrees. I took a couple quick, dizzying spins just for fun. We ordered hot dogs, thick-cut fries, and two bottles of Coke. The aging décor was pure vintage, transporting us back to a time of innocence.

As a young teen, Clark had a date with a girl named Sally. His eyes twinkled as he recounted the experience. Sally had ocean-blue eyes and a light-brown beehive she adorned with a sparkly trinket. A yellow and blue pinafore dress accentuated her tiny waist. Sally must have been very alluring because she made Clark nervous as they shared a chocolate milkshake with two straws. He was so taken with this girl, he accidentally tipped the thick, sticky drink all over her dress.

My homespun memories involved small gaggles of best friends, huddled at the coffee shop counter, giggling and eating butter burgers. We pretended not to notice cute boys sitting across from us but flirted outlandishly. Funny how memories come whooshing back. For a moment, it seemed like yesterday.

~

As the day heated up, our energy waned. We felt blasé and sun-sapped. People seemed to empathize, and almost everyone waved, beeped, flipped us the peace sign, or rolled down their windows to cheer us on. The woo-hooing and outpouring of support were just what we needed to keep going.

Fifteen miles later, we stopped again in Osage. There wasn't much there but an empty bar. We went inside and were served pink lemonade from a nearly toothless gal. There was a certain loneliness about her that bothered us. We felt sad in her presence. Maybe it was just us projecting how we'd feel living there. Sometimes emotions get confused. We didn't stay long.

We called it a day in Newcastle and started our search for a place to say. The first opportunity was a slightly rundown motel with a pool, so we stopped to ask about room rates. The clerk quoted an out-of-line price and showed us a dark, dingy, room with a wobbly, three-legged table and a dresser that tilted to one side. The pool was out of order, but the clerk refused to budge on the rate.

"We'll look around," Clark said.

"You better come back quickly," he warned, "Those rooms fill up fast."

We exchanged glances that said it all.

We cycled away confidently knowing we would not return. Camping was always the ace up our sleeve, if all else failed. We continued the search for a place to stay. Eventually, we asked a shop owner who pointed up in the hills, "Nice B&B on top," he said, "If you want to ride that far."

Of course we didn't want to ride at all, but liked the idea, so pumped up three sets of steep hills to get our lodging reward. The B&B was nestled in a tree-lined neighborhood, looking warm and welcoming. We opened the door to a spotlessly clean, two-room suite decorated in a modern flower motif. A ceiling fan whirled above a pillow-decked king-sized bed, and fresh-baked cookies and a pitcher of iced tea waited on a table with a welcome note. The accommodations were made even sweeter by the fact that we'd bartered the price down $15. First thing on our list—stretch out for a long nap. Take *that*, wobbly table guy.

A pizzeria, a mile down the hill, was the closest place for dinner. Clark was hungry, so we ordered a large. He ate fast, which kicked me into crazy fears he might eat all the pizza, so I ate faster. Then Clark noticed me wolfing down slices and picked up his pace. Faster and faster we shoveled pizza into our gullets. The result of this animal-like behavior? We were so stuffed it was difficult to walk, especially uphill.

We burst into laughter realizing how ridiculous we acted, which made our bloated stomachs ache more. We dubbed ourselves "The Jealous Fatsos."

Killer Cowboy

Day 48:   Monday, July 21
Weather: Very, very hot
Distance: 40 miles
Route: Newcastle, Wyoming, to Custer, South Dakota

We woke to birds singing outside the window and felt a melancholy touch of homesickness with Ryan and Taea being so far away. We missed them and yearned to be on our sunny deck enjoying a quiet morning together. Deck time was always special for our family, and still is.

"Too bad we're away from the kids and Portland during the nicest time of year," Clark said wistfully.

"Yeah ...," I answered, drifting off in my own thoughts about family, friends, and home.

We had to set our sadness aside. Ryan and Taea were having a fun adventure in Europe, our pets were in good hands, and we had more adventures ahead.

~

The day was going to be a scorcher. I was antsy to leave. Clark dragged his feet, not anxious to leave our beautiful room, studying the map while I paced the floor. We finally left at 10:30, both a bit tired and blue. To make matters worse, my bike reverted back to changing gears on its own—the problem had returned.

When shifting, nothing happened or the bike responded to the command four or five minutes later, usually on an uphill section. The gears didn't move incrementally, but jarringly jumped three to five notches at once. Then the chain would come off or get stuck. I'd have to stop, pry it loose, and get it back into position. Sweat dripped from my head onto my black, greasy fingers. I was rapidly losing patience.

The temperature continued to spike for 20 empty miles or what seemed like eternity surrounded by nothingness. No shade, no water, no towns, nowhere to catch a break from the sun. We pedaled silently. There was nothing to say.

Frustration mounted as we started the climb up the Black Hills, slowly, very slowly. Heat rose off the cement road, shimmering in mirage-like waves. We were parched. Trying to work up saliva was impossible; the imaginary cotton balls were back and packed our throats. No amount of water could quench this thirst.

An old cowboy in a beat-up blue truck drove past, then slowed considerably. We could see him squinting at us, deep wrinkles creating an angry scowl. He spit some chew out the window after he cleared our path. We imagined him thinking, "What the hell are they doing on *my* road?"

He studied us in the rearview mirror while driving only 10 feet ahead, his expression frozen in place. I watched the pick-up inch forward, making note of a gun rack in the back window. Several long hunting rifles perched in place, silently warning us to stay away.

The brake lights blinked on. Then off again. Twice.

Perhaps it was the heat, but we figured this was it. We'd had it, we were dead. Trapped, with nowhere to turn, nowhere to hide. The cowboy could catch us, no matter how fast we rode. So, we nervously pedaled on.

When the summit came into view, the man pulled over and got out of his truck. Propped on the back of his rig, he watched us intently, one boot on the fender. Squinting and never cracking a smile, he chewed and spit, chewed and spit, chewed and spit.

We were goners. Although, I held out hope we could talk our way out of trouble. Just in case we couldn't, though, I told Clark I loved him.

He said the same and added, "Whatever happens, at least we're together."

"He could have shot us at the *bottom* of the hill instead of making us do all this work first," I said, trying to lighten the mood.

We continued on, sweat pouring off our bodies, for more reasons than the heat. When we were almost to the cowboy, he made his move, opening the passenger door. We were sure he was reaching for a gun. We exchanged another round of I love you's and held hands momentarily.

I winced as the cowboy ducked back out of the cab, but fear turned to relief when we saw two Cokes in his hands.

"Y'all looked like you needed theeeese!" he said in a perfect cowboy drawl, baring his teeth in a friendly smile.

I took a moment to thank him for not killing us before swilling the drink.

The man laughed heartily, saying, "I'd never hurt a fly, much less two heat-stroked folks on bikes."

Clark polished his Coke off so fast, the old man said, "Well, boy, you look like you need another!" and handed him a second can.

Clark took it appreciatively, popped the top and guzzled it down.

"I waited for you to reach the summit because Cokes taste better that way."

How right he was.

> Our encounter with the cowboy left us with renewed faith in humanity. He was the perfect example of the many incredible people we met along the way. A stranger, with no particular reason to be nice, took the time and energy to make our day. This simple act reminded us again that most people are essentially good.

~

After riding uphill only a few hundred feet, I shifted into first. My chain came off and got stuck. I wasn't fast enough to get free of my clipless pedals and down I went, making a dramatic, slow-motion crash. Another Humpty Dumpty for the record. It was a hard fall, and a fair amount of elbow and knee skin was left on the pavement. I might have cried if I wasn't so frustrated and angry. I limped alongside the bike to the top of the hill.

Clark gave me a sympathetic hug, then took my bike and worked on unjamming the gears and tweaking various bits and pieces to make it possible to finish the day's ride. I was ready to quit riding, so, as Clark worked, I tried to hitch a ride for us. I put on my best desperate face as one car after another passed by, not giving me a second look. The humiliation of standing there was overwhelming, so I put my thumb away.

The 10 miles to Custer took 4 long hours. I had a system: coast on the downhill and avoid shifting gears on the flats. During uphill portions, I waited until it was too difficult to pedal, then took my chances moving to a lower gear. Usually the chain would stick within minutes, so I'd walk up the rest of the hill, unjam the chain, and start the process all over again. And that's how it went until we arrived in Custer.

The bike troubles were so maddening we didn't realize until hours later we'd crossed into a new state and the heart of South Dakota's famous Black Hills.

> We noticed a change in accents as we headed away from howdy ma'ams in cowboy country to the flat, rhythmic speech pattern of the Midwest.

We found our way to a campground in the center of town, selected a grassy spot under a tree, and pitched the tent. Soon after, Judy, the campground owner, welcomed us with big glasses of lemonade. She filled us in on the city's tourist attractions, including best restaurants and directions to the bike shop.

Most other campers were in motorhomes situated away from us. The one other tent camper was a young French man, on an adventure walking across the United States. He spoke a little English, and we learned he was taking a few days to recoup.

As night fell, we headed straight to the steak restaurant Judy recommended and ordered two prime cuts. Mine got a gold-star ranking. Even though Clark ordered the same thing, his luck wasn't as good. The steak was too well done, so he sent it back to the kitchen. And to make matters worse, my petite cut appeared bigger than his large cut.

The replacement arrived underdone and stringy. A boyish disappointment appeared in Clark's eyes as he stared longingly at my steak. I couldn't help laughing. I gave him half of mine, but when he finished, he still stared at what remained on my plate, his expression screaming, "I got gypped!"

"Let me guess," I said, teasing him as we walked out of the restaurant. "You were tortured because my steak was so much better?"

With that, he jumped up and down in the parking lot shouting, "It's not fair, it's not fair!" The exaggerated melodrama was made more hilarious by his flailing arms. We laughed so hard it was difficult to walk.

~

Judy invited us to join her family around the campfire. She handed each of us a glass of red wine and two s'mores. The chocolate and marshmallow oozed seductively from in between the graham crackers. I was in heaven.

The French camper was sitting by the fire. He explained his trip was not only to explore America on foot but also to improve his English. In short sentences he shared some wisdom, saying traveling slowly allows you to see and experience so much more. Those who travel quickly miss too much. *"Zay see everysing, but zay see nusing."* I couldn't have said it better myself.

I Got Me One of Them

>Day 49: Tuesday, July 22
>Weather: Stifling hot!
>Distance: Rest day
>Route: Custer, South Dakota

A sweltering, hot day was in the cards. The kind where you don't need a meteorologist to tell you about it. A rest day was in order.

We dropped my bike at the shop to get the gear-shifting problem fixed ... at least that was our hope. Then we picked up chilled wine, fruit, cheese, and a baguette and lunched at our shady campsite. Dessert was a bag of sweet cherries. We ate them slowly, then practiced spitting seeds, banking them off a nearby tree. This simple pleasure was followed by a long, leisurely nap.

In late afternoon, we picked up my bike. I gave it a test ride and it appeared to be working, although neither of us was confident the problem was permanently solved. This was the third mechanic we'd paid. I guess that's the cost of not knowing how to fix the bikes ourselves. We walked my bike back to the campsite to drop it off as the intense heat continued, then sidetracked into an air-conditioned saloon and parked on barstools. Everyone was talking about the weather. One gentleman, visiting from Montana, offered to buy us a round. We accepted and shot the breeze for an hour.

When I excused myself to use the restroom, the man told Clark, "I'll wait for the little lady."

Clark realized he was waiting to leave and said, "She'll be right back."

The man didn't miss a beat. "Never mi-i-i-ind. I know how it is ... I got me one of *them*."

I had no idea why they were both laughing so hard when I returned.

~

As dusk fell and the temperature dropped, we took a tourist bus to Mt. Rushmore to see the famous monument. Strategic lighting illuminated the distinguished faces of our forefathers: George Washington, Thomas Jefferson, Theodore Roosevelt, and Abraham Lincoln. The 60-foot sculpture is carved from the mountains and surprisingly never completed.

The colossal project was started in 1927, the location selected because it's the area's highest peak and gets good light for most of the day. The artist, Guzon Borglum, and over 400 workers carved out 450,000 tons of granite to create the faces. Unfortunately, Borglum passed away during the project, but his son, Lincoln, continued the work. In 1941, funding ran out, leaving the monument as it stands today. Gazing up at the presidents, I couldn't help but feel an amazing respect for the dedicated artists who risked life and limb to create the monument.

On our way out of the staging area, a thunderstorm rolled in. We never felt a drop of rain, but had a bird's-eye view as lightning struck the valley below. We witnessed spectacular firebolts frozen in the sky, hanging for several seconds before disappearing into darkness.

Hill City Hell

Day 50: Wednesday, July 23
Weather: Hot, muggy, and rain, rain, rain
Distance: 48 miles
Route: Custer, South Dakota, to Rapid City, South Dakota

There was a long line for the only campground bathroom. Someone was taking their time in the shower, apparently oblivious to anyone else. No problem for Clark, he found a discreet spot behind a group of trees, but I stood there anxiously gritting my teeth, crossing my legs, and feeling frustrated that men had it so easy. It was a very long 20 minutes.

~

The day was already hot and muggy. We packed up the tent and headed back up toward Mt. Rushmore. It was interesting to see the area from two points of view—faster in a car, prettier on a bike.

Not far into the ride, we got on the George S. Mickelson biking, hiking, and riding trail. The 109-mile path was created in 1998 in honor of a former South Dakota governor. The gravel path has 15 trailheads, 100+ railroad bridges, and four rock tunnels. Its forests provide cooling shade, and the jutting rock formations are interspersed with panoramic views of the Black Hills. Purple prairie clover and wildflowers blanketed the landscape, complementing expanses of long, green grass. The trail was all but deserted; we only saw a few hikers and one small group of horseback riders. Not having to contend with motor vehicle traffic was cycling nirvana.

We arrived in Hill City and ducked into a restaurant just before a deluge unleashed itself. It poured while we studied the menu, increased while we ordered, and rained even harder when our lunch arrived. The rain continued, splashing onto the covered deck so fiercely we had to move the table closer to the door to stay clear of the storm's path. Diners paused, mid-forkful, awed by nature's display.

And when the rain subsided, big balls of hail plummeted toward earth. For a moment, I was mesmerized and leaned out a little too far to get a better view. A hailstone bounced off the brim of my cap and plunked solidly into my water glass. The resonating ring jolted me out of my daze and made everyone on the porch laugh.

~

Setting out after the storm lifted, we straddled our wet bicycle seats, heading toward Rockerville. Bad timing. In 5 miles, the clouds opened again, dumping buckets of water on our heads. It's unpleasant and dangerous to ride when rain is coming down so hard. The pavement is slippery, and motorists have trouble seeing the road, or anything else, including bike riders. We hurried to get out of the way and practically threw our bikes against the wall under an awning of an antique store, then ran inside for cover.

The dim, dusty shop was a warren's nest of crooked aisles crammed with old furniture, lamps, dishes, what-nots, and knick-knacks. I recognized some of it from my grandmother's home. The sight of a Singer sewing machine, complete with a foot pedal, set off a trip down memory lane. I remembered her long, thin fingers working the cloth under the needle as the machine hummed along. Another memory suddenly sprang forth: the peanut game. The object was to slightly crack a peanut's shell and pinch it onto your face. The player with the most peanuts dangling from their skin was declared the winner. Grandma was hard to beat.

The shop owner shivered aloud when lights flickered and cringed as rainwater dripped from the old metal ceiling. She'd never seen a storm of this magnitude, and wanted to close up and get home as soon as possible. When the torrent subsided a bit, we headed toward our bikes while she locked up and ran for her car.

We stood under the awning until the sky cleared – then rode on, making it 6 miles to Rockerville before heavy rain reappeared. Again, we found cover, this time under a motel overhang. Water gushed off the roof and formed miniature lakes in the parking lot. We were bound and determined to get to Rapid City, so when the rain let up, rode on again. Another cascade stopped us 2 miles later. We found safe haven at the gates of Reptile Gardens.

The attraction, opened in 1937, houses the world's largest reptile collection and has "more species and subspecies of venomous reptiles than any other zoo or park." A crocodile from the jungle-themed complex was featured in the 1973 James Bond movie, *Live and Let Die*, starring Roger Moore. Despite the enticing advertising, we chose not to go in. We were too wet and anxious to reach our destination.

We pushed the last 5 miles toward Rapid City, rain free. One last ascent took us to a summit. The prairie was laid out before us. A brilliant rainbow highlighted the grassland in hues of reds, yellows, and purples, suggesting the end of the storm at last. We gazed over the flatlands and imagined herds of buffalo lumbering through the Great Plains. As shafts of sunlight touched the earth, we realized how far we'd come. The road ahead would be different; we were out of the mountains and into the prairie.

~

We found a suitable motel quickly and started the process of drying out. Everything was sopping wet. Even the clothes stuffed inside our packs, protected by plastic bags and pack covers, had to be wrung out and hung to dry. We blanketed the place, dangling things in every available spot: windowsills, doorknobs, TV stand, radiator, light fixtures, and ceiling fan. Our wallets and the money inside were drenched, too. We spread the wet bills and paperwork across the dresser to dry.

Though super-pruney from being out in the elements, we needed showers to get the caked-on mud off our bodies. We put on our driest wet clothes and found a Chinese restaurant nearby. Four pots of hot tea brought back some balance. In spite of the horrible weather, we felt good about traveling nearly 50 miles.

I reflected back on the day—the beauty of the bike path, laughing at the hailstones, experiencing the storm, reminiscing about Grandma, and seeing the rainbow light up the prairie. I looked at Clark and felt radiantly happy. His expression mirrored mine.

Steve

> Day 51: Thursday, July 24
> Weather: Unbearably hot, 100°+ with 68% humidity
> Distance: 43 miles
> Route: Rapid City, South Dakota, to New Underwood, South Dakota

Everything was nearly dry, except for a solitary pair of undies that had fallen from the door jam. I re-situated the panties, flipped a few other items over, and decided to check the drying process after breakfast.

We ordered a light meal, then asked for directions to a frontage road that paralleled I-90. Everyone chimed in. It was fun at first (even funny) as diners and wait staff put in their two cents.

"This is the best way to go," someone stated with a confident air, describing the roads to take.

"No, it's shorter if you go this way," another person contradicted, indicating an alternate route.

"I couldn't help overhearing your discussion," added a well-meaning waitress, as she described a different course.

"*This* is the best way," an older gentleman offered, providing opposing directions.

"Check with the Chamber people," someone else shouted from across the restaurant.

This went on for 30 minutes. People tried to be helpful, but we ended up completely confused. During a lull in the conversation, we stood up, expressed our appreciation, and dashed for the door before anyone else came up with a new suggestion.

~

A pair of jeans and the underwear were still damp. Clark strapped the pants on the back of his bike and I fixed the panties to my left handlebar so they could flap in the breeze and finish drying.

An hour later, we were still within the city limits. The frontage road was hard to find. No wonder the directions were all over the place. State maps don't include the small details city maps do. We kept getting lost and confused, eventually flagging down a UPS driver who directed us to the right road.

It was unusual for Clark to get so disoriented. He had an amazing sense of direction, rarely getting lost. Finding his way to obscure locations, a tiny road with a great view, or an office building he'd been to once, in a city across the country, was no challenge. This sixth sense worked for restaurants, too. Clark could find good food by smell. When we first moved to Portland, he sniffed out something tasty blocks away and found his way there in no time. My sister affectionately calls this talent "Zen Driving," finding your way by feel or smell, instinctively.

> Making the decision not to carry a cell phone on the trip was a conscious choice. Not having one made us more resourceful. You have to rely on yourself or trust in the kindness of others who step forward to help.

The temperature soared past 100° by the time we reached the little town of Box Elder. One outdoor sign flashed 106°, another 108°. It didn't matter which number was right; the sun's intensity scalded everything in its path. We lathered on sunblock and stopped often to rehydrate.

The terrain consisted of long, rolling hills. If it hadn't been so hot, we would have enjoyed the ride more. After 13 scalding miles, we reached New Underwood and stopped for a rest under a massive shade tree. When we ran out of water, I made the one-block trek to a store for ice-cold lemonade. We downed two apiece, then Clark found the energy to "true the wheel" (adjust the spokes) on his bike. He was proud as a peacock that he could do this without help. He'd learned a lot since the day we left.

As Clark tinkered, I fought the urge to take a nap and mustered the energy to walk the half block to the post office for stamps. My full bicycling regalia gave me away, and it wasn't long until a crowd gathered and questions started rolling in.

"Where are you going?"

"Where did you come from?"

"How long did you train?"

"How many miles a day do you ride?"

"Are you packing a piece?"

I was there a half an hour, learned the next town and nearest campground were 20 miles away, and got an earful of local gossip.

Clark and I continued to hide from the heat under the expansive tree. We talked idly about life in a small town. It felt peaceful, safe, and romantic.

Two boys, doing daring tricks on bikes, stopped to investigate us. Though they were both the same age, their sizes and personalities were dramatically different—one, gangly and awkward; the other, small, round, and a chatterbox. After their curiosity was satisfied, we asked how they liked living in New Underwood.

"It's kinda boring," one of them said. "Not a lot to do until you can drive."

"Yeah ... but, Steve's place is alright, I guess," the shy kid piped in.

"Steve's place?" Clark perked up, "What's that?"

"You don't know about Steve's place?" the chubby one asked, naively amazed we were so out of the loop.

"It has everything!"

Apparently, that was all we needed to know. Every question from then on had the same answer. Hotel? Steve's place. Good food? Steve's place. Cold drinks? Steve's place. He has the coldest sodas in town!

Of course, we had to see for ourselves.

With the kids leading the way, we were at Steve's in no time. The boys raced off to new adventures; we checked in and took a nap.

~

Dinner was at Steve's place, of course. A band played rocking country music for a big crowd in the parking lot, and it was a packed house inside. There was no place to sit, but an older couple invited us to join them at their booth after noticing us searching unsuccessfully for seats.

We scooted in and exchanged introductions. The pair appeared to be in their late 70s but exuded a youthful happiness. The wife looked at her mate adoringly, hanging on his every word as if on a first date.

The husband was an amusing storyteller. It wasn't so much what he said, but *how* he said it, his words punctuated with long pauses, raised eyebrows, and dramatic facial expressions. He'd lean in and talk sort of low, like he was sharing a family secret, even though all he said was something innocuous like his dad was a farmer.

Turns out he was also an engaged listener, asking us questions beyond the generic ones most people quizzed us on. The couple wanted to know how we kept our spirits up and our relationship on track being together 24 hours a day.

As we sipped beer and discussed life loudly over the din of the bar, a friend of theirs stopped by the table. Without a word, the man slipped into the booth and seamlessly joined the conversation.

"I'm headin' out in the morning for my favorite pastime—killin' rattlesnakes! Want to join me?" he asked with a wink in my direction.

After a burst of laughter and a few elbows to the ribs, he said, "I need a beer!"

Our little group joined the growing party in the parking lot. Everyone seemed to know everyone else. Raucous greetings between neighbors multiplied and morphed. Our new friends soon got sucked into the mob of people and disappeared.

Simultaneously, we got hit with the homesick blues. Watching this familiar camaraderie as outsiders made us miss our own family and friends. Though surrounded by this happy mass of humanity, loneliness set in.

We tried to dance, but felt awkward and out of place. Clark and I were in the same mental space, yet being together didn't make the sadness go away. Instead, standing in the middle of the animated crowd, we felt isolated and alone.

Back in our room, we listened in darkness to the muffled music thumping outside. We snuggled, but didn't really connect, adrift in our own thoughts.

Floating on Water

Day 52: Friday, July 25
Weather: Hot and humid
Distance: 41 miles
Route: New Underwood, South Dakota, to Wall, South Dakota

Lonely feelings still lingered in the morning, but dissipated quickly. Today was a new day. We felt another scorcher coming on and packed quickly. South Dakota is one of the windiest places in the country, and bicyclists know well its strong headwinds. We learned, firsthand, the challenge of pedaling into the wind. Strong gusts kept us cool, but soon slowed our pace to 11 miles an hour. As the day wore on, our speed dropped to 6 mph. We struggled to move forward at all.

Nearing Wall, our destination, we took a back road through farmland which gave us a break from the interstate. We welcomed the change of pace, even though the half gravel/half dirt road had nasty potholes and uneven ground.

Deep in farm country, grasshoppers inundated us, and soon after a plague-like swarm of mosquitoes zeroed in like tiny kamikaze pilots, humming and buzzing with a vengeance. The hoppers sounded like a high-voltage electrical transformer on steroids. One-handedly, we slapped at body parts within reach. Buzz–hum–bzzt–slap! Repeat. Together, we sounded like an off-kilter musical group, with us playing percussion.

So many mosquitoes landed on my bare legs it looked as if I was wearing stockings—black, *moving* stockings. Horrifying.

I stopped and made a fast grab for insect repellent, spraying it so heavily, some mosquitoes drowned on my legs in the process. To my amazement, a few still managed to dig their stingers into my flesh.

As Clark rode up, I drenched him in repellent before he had time to stop. All for naught. It didn't faze the mosquitoes, so we pedaled as fast as we could to escape. Eventually, we lost them and wondered why the insects concentrated in that area. Did we ride through a fertile breeding ground? Was the land cursed? We had no idea.

~

We stopped to watch a group of free-roaming horses clomping slowly along the road. They wandered from one patch of grass to the next, allowing us to stand among them as if we were part of the herd. One especially beautiful mare ambled close and looked me in the eye, chewing and studying my face at the same time. I felt powerfully connected to her, animal to animal. I reached out a hand. She lightly touched it with her soft muzzle and then pulled away. The moment was over.

~

A truck drove up, slowed and idled next to us. A young guy poked his head out the window and asked where we were off to.

"Wall," Clark told him.

"You're going the wrong way," he said. "You missed the turn—it's a few miles back."

"Thanks ...," we called out as he drove off in a flurry of dust.

We turned around and prepared to face Mosquito Hell, *again*.

~

For a little town, Wall was abuzz with tourists. The main attraction is the famous Wall Drug Store. A hopeful, young pharmacist and his wife built the store in 1931, just after the Great Depression. The town was populated by 326 people. In order to make a go of it, the couple came up with a brilliant marketing idea. In a burst of inspiration, they posted a series of billboards, spaced miles apart, to lure travelers from the interstate. "Get a Soda ... Get a Root Beer ... Turn Next Corner ... Free Ice Water ... Wall Drug." Their idea hit it big. Weary, thirsty travelers came in droves.

The free ice water is still offered today, but now the signs hawk "Homemade Pie," "75 Miles to Wall Drug," "Have You Dug Wall Drug?," and "4 Blocks to Wall Drug." Over two million people visit the 76,000-square-foot store annually.

We took turns watching the bikes and investigating the store. I was mesmerized by the sheer volume of stuff. T-shirts, hats, bumper stickers, bobble heads, magnets, rocks, arrowheads, state spoons, knives, glass, sculptures, pottery, Native American items, an enormous selection of cowboy boot spurs, and jackalopes of all configurations and sizes. I bought a postcard.

~

We found a campground nearby and pitched our tent in a sea of motorhomes. Not our preference, but the place was clean, had a laundromat, swimming pool, and store. When the camp manager spotted our tent among all the vehicles, he offered us a better site slightly away from the others, on a grassy patch under a tree.

~

After re-pitching the tent and taking deliciously long showers, we went in search of dinner and found a hopping place. One of the cooks, an exceptionally large woman with thick black hair and a raucous laugh, came in to refill her own beer. The bartender pointed us out as "some crazy bikers." On her way back to the kitchen, the cook came over to say hello.

She commanded the room with her massive energy. After a few words and a frank recommendation on what to order, the woman looked at Clark, pointed at me, and said, "Looks like *she* doesn't miss too many meals!"

Then she snorted out a long, low belly laugh and said, "I should know!" and slapped me on the back. I didn't know whether to laugh or cry.

> Being overweight was always on my mind during the trip. I especially worried about stopping to see old friends who had last seen me when I was a ski bum and in great shape. Looking back, I know they wouldn't care. After all, I love my friends heavy or not—but it feels different when it's about you.

How come I had to ride across the country to get in shape? Don't other people just start an exercise program and stick with it?

It was a hot, muggy night so we took the tent tarp off to allow evening breezes to flow through while still keeping insects at bay. The tent's netted windows allowed ventilation, and our tarp provided extra cover when needed. The tarp kept in the warmth on chilly evenings, but on hot evenings it caused us to swelter.

In the middle of the night, we woke to drops of rain sprinkling our faces. Thunder and lightning penetrated the darkness in the distance. We flew into action after a brief moment of confusion, asking ourselves, "What the hell?" We unzipped the tent, put the tarp back on, tied it down tightly, ripped the clean clothing off the clothes line, put the pack covers on our bike bags, and dove back into the tent. And, we did all this stark naked.

We giggled uncontrollably after realizing we hadn't been out there alone. So focused on our own affairs, we didn't notice others switching their RV lights on and whirling about their campsites battening down the hatches. All around us we could hear the sounds of hurried campers slamming doors and shouting directions. Belongings banged and crashed as they were hurled inside vehicles. Our naked bodies must have been perfectly silhouetted in the beams of light for all to admire.

The human-made noises died down as the sound of rain drumming on the tent grew louder. First it was a slow, steady rhythm, but then turned into a frenzied pounding, echoing off the RVs. Thunder and lightning closed in. The wind blew so hard we were thankful our heavy bodies kept the tent firmly on the ground.

We laid there for the next hour, eyes wide, swallowing back fears of the tent blowing over, falling apart, or being struck by lightning and bursting into a ball of flames. There wasn't a thing we could do except wait for the storm to stop.

Soon, the sides and corners of the tent were soaking wet. We squashed our bodies together in an effort to stay toward the middle and comfortably on top of our thin sleeping pads.

Finally the storm died down and we dozed off. Briefly. A crash of thunder and bolt of lightning hit nearby at exactly the same time. Then the rain started again. As we rolled over to exchange a reassuring hug, our arms sunk into a sea of water. Our mattresses were floating, like a waterbed, but without the heater.

Water dripped in continuously, the tent providing little protection. Everything was saturated. It was a losing battle. I grabbed my front pack, which held my wallet, address book, passport, tape recorder, and camera, trying to safeguard everything by lying on my back with the pack atop my belly.

A lightning bolt struck close. You could hear an evil sizzle ripple across the ground. Rain followed with explosive force. The sea inside our tent grew larger and deeper. Outside, the water bubbled and churned around us. There was no hope of sleep—only a long wait until dawn.

Liza McQuade

Mosquito Merengue

Day 53:   Saturday, July 26
Weather: Hot and humid with strong winds
Distance: 36 miles
Route: Wall, South Dakota, to Philip, South Dakota

Morning eventually arrived. We "swam" out of the tent to assess the damage. Beyond our wet belongings, garbage, a few chairs, and stray clothing were strewn across the campground. Leaves and tree branches littered the area. Mud and dirty water as far as the eye could see.

We waded through deep puddles in search of an open restaurant. On our way, we watched as a tall, thin man ran toward us. He balanced a pizza box while flailing his arms as if to fly and moved in dizzying circles. Had the rain driven him insane? When our paths crossed, everything made sense. Mosquitoes!

After last night's rain, they were out in force and started to come after us. So, we made a run for it and joined the dance, flapping our hands and snapping our sweatshirts hoping to avoid their nasty bites. Now, we looked like crazy people trying to fly.

I shouted to the man as we ran past, dancing and swatting, "Pizza for breakfast … that looks good."

He replied, "There ain't gonna be nothin' left for breakfast if these little bastards don't get away from me."

Then we moved on, continuing the mosquito jig.

After a long breakfast, we returned to an odd welcome. A dozen campers rushed toward us.

"Did you know lightning struck the meadow next to you?" one young woman said, with deep concern.

"We sure had a sleepless night," her husband added. "How 'bout you?"

The dark circles under our eyes served as the answer. But more questions came:

"Did you get wet?"

"Is your tent in one piece?"

"Were you scared?"

"Do you need any help?"

"Did I really see you naked last night?"

After everyone laughed and exchanged stories, it was time to work.

We wrung out our clothes, poured water from our extra shoes, and turned the tent upside down to drip. The good news: the sun reappeared.

Long lines formed in the laundry room, so once again we flung our belongings over picnic tables, garbage cans, BBQ grills, a swing set, teeter-totter, and any place else in direct sun. Then we shook and rotated the gear, tending to it steadily, like you'd turn sausages to cook them just right.

With the sun on our side, most things dried in an hour. Time to ride. We took a road paralleling I-90—Highway 14 toward Cottonwood, Midland, and Haynes. The wind immediately picked up, making it hard to pedal. With several small towns ahead, we planned to stop often. Quinn, only 4 miles from Wall, was our first hope for a break from the heat and wind, but it was so tiny we rode through town before realizing we'd passed it.

Not wanting to snack again on GORP (good old raisins and peanuts), we brightened after spotting a restaurant ahead. Sadly, it was closed.

Cottonwood was the next town. We fought the wind for 11 miles. Foiled again. Population 9. Nothing there.

With each passing mile, the day got hotter, drier, and windier. We grew increasingly tired and cranky. Philip was 15 miles away. Because it appeared in bigger, darker letters on the map, we assumed that meant a larger town and more possibilities for a place to eat. About halfway there, we stopped on the roadside for a rest and an infusion of sugar. We were hungry and tired of fighting the wind. Limited sleep made matters worse. We must have looked drained because a couple in an old Dodge Dart stopped to ask if we were OK.

"Just tired," Clark said. "It was a long, stormy night and the wind is brutal today."

"That's what South Dakota is known for," the driver said. "Blows all the undesirables out of our area," he added with a booming laugh. "I'm Big John and this is my wife Sandra," the man said as he stuck out his hand for a shake.

The couple owned a Harley and said they felt like kindred spirits with cyclists. The conversation flowed so easily, an hour passed before any of us realized it.

"Hey, we're staying at my brother's place a few miles outside of Philip," Big John said. "He's out of town right now, but I'm sure he wouldn't mind if you spent the night in his camper. That is, if you're ready to quit for the night."

"We could be talked into that," Clark agreed with a big smile.

John gave us directions and drove off with Sandra, who waved wildly out the window.

We were so happy to have an excuse to stop riding that we managed to tap new energy and arrived in good time. The old motorhome felt like a luxury hotel after our wet night. We tossed our gear inside, accepted the cold beer they offered, and resumed our conversation.

Soon talk drifted to accolades of South Dakota. John and Sandra grew up there and loved every corner of it.

"It's so flat," John noted. "You can see for miles and miles. No one can sneak up on you out here."

"And there's nothing more beautiful than when the wheat turns that golden color in late summer. America at its finest!" Sandra said proudly.

"Yeah, you know the National Anthem?" John joined in. "Where do you think Francis Scott Key saw those amber waves of grain? In South Dakota, sure as I'm standing here."

As we talked, Big John threw some big steaks on the grill while Sandra whipped up a couple of salads: potato and green. Then we switched from beer to wine, ate our fill, and continued talking long into the night.

> When we told people we were biking across the country, they often assumed we meant on a motorcycle. When they discovered we were on bicycles, their expressions turned to shock, especially after giving our bodies a once over.

WEEK 9

Free Camping

    Day 54:   Sunday, July 27
    Weather: Sunny and warm
    Distance: 83 miles
    Route: Philip, South Dakota, to Pierre, South Dakota

Sandra fixed us a breakfast of ham, eggs, hash browns, toast, juice, and coffee and then packed us a lunch for the road. A feeling of sadness was in the air when we said good-bye. It's funny how connected we felt to people we only knew for one night.

    Clark and I rode together, but didn't talk much, lost in our own thoughts. It was a good day, though; the ride was easy, the temperature cooler, and wind calm.

> Traveling across the plains, Clark thought about Native Americans hunting great herds of buffalo and early pioneers making their way west in covered wagons across the wide-open landscape. It took him back to boyhood memories, pretending to be a soldier, outlaw, or Indian chief. His play-acting scenarios included sneak attacks on Mom, where he'd rope her and take her hostage. She'd untangle herself just enough to shuffle off to the kitchen to finish making lunch. Clark would soon return as a hero to unrope and rescue her, setting her free to be captured again.

We crossed into a new time zone on a bridge in the middle of the Missouri River, just before we hit the capital city of Pierre (pronounced "peer"). This was significant progress; we were now two hours ahead of Portland time and officially on Central Standard Time.

Sandra and Big John suggested we stay at a city park in Pierre along the shoreline of the Missouri River. The camping was free, and, although there were no showers, it had clean bathrooms and tasty drinking water. John told us South Dakota has more free campgrounds than any other state. We were good with that. After setting up camp and relaxing awhile, we locked our bikes to the picnic table and headed to dinner.

I was always nervous about leaving the gear, especially in such an accessible spot. It would have been easy for someone to drive up, grab all our belongings, and dash off before anyone noticed. I mitigated some of the worry by taking my front pack and all my valuables with me. Then I forced myself to trust and enjoy the evening.

~

Happily, our bikes and campsite were untouched. We crawled in the tent and I read aloud until Clark drifted off to sleep. A lone mosquito kept me awake, buzzing my ear and attacking when I wasn't looking. I swatted and missed, swatted and missed—eventually burrowing deep in my sleeping bag so the annoying pest couldn't find anything to bite. I was safe until I got too hot and had to expose a body part to cool off. I played this game all night long.

Clark managed to sleep through the whole thing. Mosquitos never bothered him much. My blonde locks and fair skin always trumped his dark hair and complexion, at least in Bug World. Mosquitos must prefer blondes.

Hospital Breakfast

> Day 55:   Monday, July 28
> Weather: Sunny, warm and windy
> Distance: 73 miles
> Route: Pierre, South Dakota, to Miller, South Dakota

We woke unusually early. Clark had a unique, inexpensive idea for breakfast. Rather than walk two miles back to the main street in Pierre, he suggested we try the hospital cafeteria. It was only a few blocks up the hill, overlooking the park. We selected things that didn't require cooking: cereal, milk, juice, coffee, and a couple low-fat muffins. Plus, we had a bird's-eye view of the beautiful Missouri River and surrounding bluffs.

~

As we packed up, Clark noticed his cycling gloves were missing. While tearing everything apart in search of them, he flashed back to taking the gloves off at a rest stop, just over the river in Fort Pierre, and didn't remember putting them back on. We sat on the picnic table, gear scattered everywhere, contemplating the dilemma. Pedal back an hour one way? What if they weren't there? Or, travel on? Riding without gloves is hard on your hands, and gloves are expensive. We debated back and forth.

At some point during our indecision, a man in his late 50s drove up in a spotlessly clean minivan.

"Where you going with all that gear?" he asked.

"Portland, Maine," Clark answered, in a monotone voice, still distracted by our quandary.

"Oh, yeah?" he laughed, "You've got a ways to go."

Like we didn't know.

"We're almost half way there," I said. "Started in Portland, Oregon."

"No kidding," he said, letting out a long whistle. "How far you heading today?"

That's when we explained about the gloves.

He paused for a moment, sizing us up better, then said, "Hop in. I'll drive you across the river and back."

"That solves our problem," Clark laughed, accepting the kind offer.

We gathered our belongings quickly, then gingerly placed our bikes in the back of his van. Mark, our knight in shining armor, was traveling home after helping a cousin repair a tractor.

"Always had a knack for fixing stuff," he said. "Good thing, because harvest time is almost here."

Then he talked, not surprisingly, about how much he loved South Dakota.

"People take for granted what we have here," he said, looking out the window. "It's pretty special."

We smiled and nodded.

Clark spotted his gloves, lying on a table, as soon as we pulled into the rest stop. He jumped out, grabbed them, and took his seat back in the van.

"Been to the dam?" Mark asked.

Clark shook his head no.

"Well, you can't leave Pierre without seeing the Oahe Dam. I'll take you there, if you have the time," he said.

"We'd love to see it!" I responded.

Along the way, Mark drove by several scenic overlooks, pointing out the Missouri River views and best fishing spots. The Oahe Dam loomed ahead, 245 feet tall. Mark knew lots of facts. The dam created Lake Oahe, making it the fourth largest manmade reservoir in the United States. "I saw President John F. Kennedy dedicate the dam in 1962. I was just a kid back then, but I'll never forget it."

On the drive back, Mark sounded wistful, talking about life in a farming community and lamenting how the lifestyle was disappearing.

"Almost doesn't pay to spend your life working the land anymore. Kids aren't choosing to farm. It's a tough way to make a buck," he said, drifting off into his memories.

~

After Mark dropped us off, we took a long look at the map and calculated we had about three weeks before we hit Wisconsin. And we expected to cross from South Dakota into Minnesota in less than a week. We didn't have a schedule but hoped to reach the White Mountains of Vermont before the snow put a stop to our travels.

Of course, this trip was not about schedules and timetables, but rather about exploring, learning, and adventure. As a good friend told me when we started the ride, "Remember, life's about the journey, not the destination."

A steep hill outside Pierre posed little difficulty, but wind picked up at the summit. We had to push hard against its hefty force, and 24 miles later, in Blunt, we were more than ready for a break. In sync and without any discussion, we dismounted, went inside a cafe, and ordered lunch. By this point in the ride, we could read each other's minds.

> Dust storms were plentiful on windy days across the plains. Dry dirt and debris are whipped up into a vortex and spin across the land like brown tornadoes. At one point, after counting 15 of these whirling vortexes dancing in the distance, I worried we might get sucked in and disappear forever.

Back on the road, progress slowed. More wind. We stopped often to rest and started conversations with whoever was willing so we could justify a longer break. In Highmore, hungry again, we stopped for a bite to eat. We were tired and looked forward to a hot shower and comfortable bed.

"Hey! Where's the best place to stay around here?" Clark suddenly asked the whole restaurant.

A rancher with a commanding personality spoke up first and *told* us to go to Miller.

"A great town!" he boomed. "There's a nice campground. Won't cost you a cent. Go there. It's only a few miles."

"Maybe we will," I said smiling sweetly, yet secretly conspiring to stop at the first motel we saw.

"No reason to stay anywhere else," he commanded.

He was the type of guy you didn't want to argue with. Big in personality and size, confident, and made no bones about owning one of the most successful ranches in the area. He picked up our tab and gave us a pep talk. We allowed ourselves to be talked into moving on.

Of course, we didn't check the map before leaving. If we had, we would have seen that "a few miles" meant 23. We felt compelled to follow his plan, probably because he drove behind us until we were well outside of town. Even Clark felt strangely obligated to do what he said. We gave him a falsely sincere thumbs up when he finally passed us, waving and beeping his approval.

"Wanna go back?" I said, once he was out of sight.

"No, let's go for it," Clark encouraged. "Another free night will be good. Let's camp while we can."

"OK," I agreed, reluctantly.

It took us three hours in heavy wind, but we managed to roll into town with plenty of daylight left. The campground, as the bossy man described, was beautiful, a secluded city park on the edge of town. No showers, but it was free. Day number three without a shower.

We pitched the tent and followed our routine—Clark heading into town for a few beers, while I relaxed at the campsite. Alone time is important.

Not long after Clark left, a suntanned cowboy drove by in a rusty pick-up and shouted out the window, "Have you seen my black calf?"

"Your black cat?" I shouted back.

"No, *CALF!*" he said, emphasizing the "F."

"She hasn't been through here, but I'll keep my eyes open."

"Thanks," he said. "If you see her, let them know at the café, would you?"

"No problem," I said, not remembering to ask which café, where it was, or his name. Only on a trip like this would I encounter such a conversation.

~

Clark was away longer than usual, so I walked into town to find him. I passed the café and saw Clark sitting there jawing with a group of cowhands. He'd been invited to go fishing the next day. The wealthy rancher was right; Miller is a friendly place.

We fell asleep to a light breeze and the rhythmic hooting of a lone owl.

The Kindness of Others

Day 56: Tuesday, July 29
Weather: Sunny and warm
Distance: 32 miles
Route: Miller, South Dakota, to Wolsey, South Dakota

We walked to the café for breakfast, well rested and feeling good. The warm welcome we received made us linger longer, sipping coffee and talking with folks. Another plus to a leisurely breakfast—it gave our tent time to dry from excessive morning dew.

~

Signs warned of road closures from Miller to Wessington. Motorists were being rerouted and delayed, but cyclists were given leeway. Lucked out again. Cars were sent far out of the way, while we were waved through. No she-devils here.

Loose gravel covered the 16-mile stretch, making it slippery. We took it in stride, traveling side-by-side and talking non-stop.

Just outside of Wessington, on a starkly quiet stretch of road, Clark stopped to adjust his bike. Out of the blue, a young mother and three kids appeared, thrilled to talk to two "interesting travelers." They'd spotted us from their front window and ran to see where we were going. We often forgot how unusual our loaded-down bikes looked.

The woman seemed deeply lonely. Her husband worked long hours and took the car, leaving her alone without much money and only the kids for company. We may have been her single diversion for the week. I sensed a longing for adult companionship and a change in routine. My thoughts were interrupted by the kids excitedly inviting us for lemonade.

"Of course. That's a great idea," she said, as the children ran off to fetch the drinks.

We walked our bikes along the road, answering questions about our journey and life in Portland. The woman hung on every word, as if cataloging it to share with her husband later.

The kids burst out of the front door with a yellow plastic pitcher and matching glasses. They spilled more lemonade than they poured but were proud of their efforts. In return, we gave them a big bag of our GORP, which they started to devour before we mounted our bikes to leave.

~

Back on the road, we reveled in the quiet beauty of our surroundings: a landscape covered in earthtones and variegated greens, some plants still bright from an especially wet winter. The fresh smell of summer lingered in the air; we paused several times to take a deep breath and appreciate the peace. An expansive blue sky dappled with puffy white clouds complemented the picture-perfectness.

A little farther on, we came to a small gas station with one rusty pump. Intrigued by its retro appeal, we pulled in for a break. A tiny, wrinkled couple, in their 90s, sat outside on a rickety bench watching the day pass by.

"Well, howdy-do!" the little lady greeted our arrival, "What do you need this fine day?"

Her husband sat silent as a stone, studying us with an air of unsettling intensity.

"Come on in. Need something cold to drink?" she said, easing herself up with the help of a cane. The husband remained immobile, moving only his eyes as we followed her inside the store. They'd owned the place for decades, she told us, but didn't have much business anymore.

Everything was tidy, but old as the hills, as if time stood still. A graying poster with a picture of a lost dog, dated five years earlier, hung amidst dozens of other aged announcements. Most were written by hand and selling things like used tires, baby chicks, taxidermy, and miscellaneous housewares.

I asked the woman if she'd lived in the area all her life.

"Oh, no-o-o-o," she said, almost offended.

"Where are you from?" I asked, curious about her demeanor.

"Well," she huffed. "I'm from *Wolsey*."

"Oh, how nice," I said, giving Clark a secret smile.

From her point of view, Wolsey was far, far away, but in actuality it was 12 miles from her store.

"Where are you going on those bikes?" she asked.

"From Portland, Oregon, to Portland, Maine," Clark answered.

She stared at us blankly, one eyebrow in a raised "V."

Dead silence.

Breaking the awkward moment, Clark said, "We're getting hungry. Where should we eat—here in Wessington or move on to Wolsey?"

"Depends how hungry you are!" the old man interrupted in a loud, raspy grandpa voice.

We hadn't heard him shuffle in. Startled, we spun around toward the sound. Still deadpan, the man turned stiffly on arthritic knees and ambled back out.

We opted for chips from the gas station, then lunch in Wolsey. It was a fast 15 miles. Clark headed to the local tavern for a beer before lunch. I went to the post office to mail a postcard and was immediately surrounded.

"Oh, you're the ones riding the bikes full of stuff, huh?" one woman commented.

"Your husband's waiting for you in the tavern," another one said, laughing. "You do the errands, while he drinks a beer! It's the same everywhere," she teased.

Before I could answer, she added, "What cha doin'?"

"Riding across the country, I'm told," said a man who just walked in and caught the last part of the conversation.

I was surprised the word spread so fast. We'd only been in town 10 minutes.

Meanwhile, back at the near-empty tavern, Clark hit it off with the bartender and was deep in conversation about the virtues of small-town living. The barkeep was also fascinated with the details of our trip and left a phone message for his boss to see if we could spend the night in her vacant trailer. When she called back, he handed me the phone.

"Love to have you stay," a voice on the other line said before I could introduce myself.

"Thank you," I said to the stranger on the phone. "Are you sure it's OK?"

"I wouldn't say yes if it wasn't OK. The place is pretty basic, though."

"Oh, we don't mind," I responded, "Just nice to have a shower and a roof over our heads. How much do you want for a night?"

"I wouldn't charge you anything!" she answered with simple Midwest generosity.

Another free night in South Dakota. How could we pass that up?

The barkeep asked a customer to watch the bar so he could show us to the trailer. He led the way in his pick-up while Clark and I followed on our bikes, staying long enough to get us set up before going back to work.

The empty trailer had more than we needed: two bedrooms, living/dining room, good-sized kitchen, a bathroom, screened porch, and nice yard.

Minutes later, the owner arrived with pillows, blankets, and toilet paper in hand. We wondered if South Dakotans were the friendliest people on earth.

"Is there anything else I can get you?" she asked.

Not a thing.

Before leaving, she invited us for Steak Night at the bar. Going out of the way for strangers seemed to be a statewide pastime.

We spread our sleeping bags underneath the fan, atop the thick living room carpeting, then raced for the shower. After four days of heat, dirt, and sweat, nothing felt better than being clean again.

Clark "admired" me while I primped a bit more—that is, I put on a little make up, my skirt, and a pair of earrings.

The bartender let out a wolf whistle when we walked into the tavern.

"Wow, you guys sure look different!"

"Funny the difference a shower makes," Clark said, pulling me close.

The first drink of the night was on the house. And, as it happened, we never paid for a single drink, nor did we pay for our steak dinner. Kind locals took care of the entire tab. To a person, every patron made a point to meet us and wish us well.

As alcohol fueled the camaraderie, the decibel level went up and personal filters went down. One fellow gave me the lowdown, sharing who was who, which families were feuding, and who was doing what with whom. I was fully up on town gossip in no time.

Another man came over, leaned in between us, and slurred, "You guys are nice. Ni-i-i-i-ce. I could tell the second you walked in that you were really, really ni-i-i-i-i-ce!"

"OK, honey. Celebrating's over. Time to go home," the guy's wife said as she rooted around in his pocket for the car keys.

At closing time, it was sad to say goodbye to everyone. We felt honored to be included in the local fabric of life. We needed it, being so many miles from home.

~

Clark fell asleep immediately. I was awake, energized from all the people, high on life. I stretched out on the floor of the screened porch, listening to the sounds of nature, trying to quiet my mind. Before drifting into slumberland, I peeled myself off the floor and walked toward the bathroom on autopilot.

It was a quick visit with catastrophic results. I flushed and *whoosh*— the bowl overflowed. And it wasn't just a little bit. Water gushed out, covering the bathroom floor. It moved quickly across the room and soaked into the hallway carpet. Then it leaked into the bathroom vents. I could hear it dripping. It was coming so fast and furious. No matter how hard I jiggled the handle, I couldn't get the water to stop.

I ran to the kitchen, found a small plastic cup and tried to frantically bail water, but couldn't keep up. The gushing continued, as I splashed around in the bathroom, thoughts of icky bacteria swimming through my head.

Finally, the logical solution dawned on me. I removed the lid from the back of the toilet, then pulled and pushed the internal mechanism until the water stopped.

The bathroom was a mess. I grabbed a medium-sized plastic bag from my bike pack, slid it on my hand, reached into the bowl, and snatched the toilet paper. I wrung it out, inverted the bag and closed it tight (like when you pick up dog poo).

After bailing duty, I mopped the floor with a dirty towel found under the sink. Because no one was living in the trailer, there were no mops, buckets, sponges, or other items on hand to deal with this kind of a thing. I threw the towel down, soaked up the water, wrung it out and repeated the process again and again. It was a slow, sloppy, dirty job and took well over an hour to finish.

I washed up in the bathtub, feeling terrible about the incident, but don't think one tiny wad of T.P. caused it. This just happened to be the lucky flush.

Huron In

Day 57: Wednesday, July 30
Weather: Rainy and cold
Distance: 18 miles
Route: Wolsey, South Dakota, to Huron, South Dakota

I felt awful about the toilet incident and wrote a sincere thank you/apology note that I hoped would somehow suffice. It was still early and we had no idea how to reach the trailer's owner. So we reluctantly packed up and left.

As we pedaled off, rain settled in. We stopped, threw on protective gear, and went for it. Our goal for the day was to get to De Smet, about 60 miles east. We were still on Highway 14 and expected to stay on it until well into Minnesota. The rain pounded hard, and after 15 miles of soggy travel we stopped for lunch at a Mexican restaurant in Huron.

We were so cold our teeth chattered. Clark went into the bathroom, peeled off his soaking sweatshirt, and put on a dry tee. I followed suit.

The waiter was kind enough to seat us near a heating vent. We dove into a warm bowl of tortilla chips and homemade salsa and washed it down with hot coffee. Next up, a big plate of fajitas and four margaritas.

"Hell with it," Clark said, "Riding is supposed to be fun and today I'm not having fun. We can do whatever we want. I'm not leaving!"

No argument from me.

The waiter called a friend who owned a motel nearby and got us a good price. We checked in, showered, and took a long afternoon nap. That's what this kind of a day was made for.

~

Reaching Huron was significant because we considered it the halfway point. So we coined the phrase "From Huron In" which meant from here on in we'd ride faster, farther, better; eat less; spend less; and weigh less. Everything would improve. It was a phrase that stuck with us the rest of the trip, but nothing really changed.

~

On the two-mile walk to dinner, we passed a couple riding a tandem bike with an attached baby carriage. Inside: a baby and a beagle. The dog sat quietly, looking peaceful but attentive, while the baby pawed at him and giggled. He would give her an occasional kiss, covering her entire face with his tongue, which prompted the little girl to hug him tightly and kiss him back.

> I caught a full view of myself in the bathroom mirror and was disappointed I wasn't any thinner. Clark said he noticed my body reshaping itself, but if that was true I didn't see it.
>
> One observation: When we started this trip, I'd consistently get grease on my calf from the bicycle chain. My chubby calves bumped and rubbed against the chain, and I had to make a conscious effort by arching out my legs to avoid getting a daily dose of grease. Later in the trip, that didn't happen. Clark, on the other hand looked thinner, especially by the time we reached South Dakota. Why do men lose weight faster than women? Not fair.

Magnet Lady

Day 58: Thursday, July 31
Weather: Heavy rain
Distance: 40 miles
Route: Huron, South Dakota, to De Smet, South Dakota

It was raining again, so we took our time getting ready. We brewed motel tea, nibbled on fruit and nuts, and studied the map. The radio alternated from country music to hits from the '60s. We alternated from slow dancing to full-on rock out. That entertained us until check-out time. Our delay tactic worked; the streets were full of deep puddles but at least it wasn't raining as we set off.

Farmland spread out before us. A sea of corn rippled in a soft breeze like the peaceful lull of an ocean and the earth smelled freshly washed.

~

In Cavour, a convenience store parking lot was filled with a long row of Harleys. The motorcycle gang, taking a break inside, made everyone uncomfortable. They talked obnoxiously of drunken escapades, bragging about conquests over alcohol and women.

One guy, with questionable face tattoos and battle scars arrogantly announced, "If I want to give people a good scare, all I have to do is take off my shirt!"

"Or, open your mouth," I whispered to Clark.

The gang whooped, snorting and knocking each other around as they dared their buddy to display his inked skin. The loudmouth tugged his shirt up, baring his devil-covered, hairy beer belly and grinned, showing a full mouth of tobacco-stained teeth.

We tried not to catch his eye.

The men strutted and postured, amping up the level of hostility, trying to outdo each other with loud farts and lewd comments. It looked like there might be trouble when the leader spontaneously stood up, looming large. As he rose, the pack simultaneously snapped to attention and marched out behind him.

Engines revved in a thunderous, deafening roar. Those of us left behind breathed a collective sigh of relief.

~

We were ravenous. A small, homey-looking restaurant in Iroquois had a handwritten sign touting the day's special: beef stroganoff. Our sweet, young waitress raved about it. The dish sounded warming and delicious. We followed her advice. Bad idea. The sauce was runny and flavorless, the noodles were cold, and the meat tasted peculiar. The meal easily won the "Worst Lunch of the Trip" award. I didn't eat more than a few bites and Clark stopped after ingesting a third of his food. The waitress seemed surprised, knowing our hunger level. Clark claimed we weren't as famished as we thought.

~

Liza - A Wet Ride - DeSmet, SD

The rain started to fall, hitting us from all sides with an icy force. This weather made Clark's recurring knee problem act up, so we stopped frequently to give his joint a rest. With 15 miles left to reach De Smet, we were so wet, tired, and achy that nothing mattered anymore. Water pooled in our coat pockets and anywhere else there was a nook or cranny, including our eardrums. Wet streams poured down our faces, and water worked its way underneath our clothes. The rain gear covered us but was useless. It was as wet on the inside as it was on the outside.

Along the way, we took a much-needed rest at a café. My attention was immediately drawn to an odd-looking woman I guessed to be fiftyish. Her thin, brown hair was ratted in the back like she hadn't combed it for a month. A child's Easter hat sat at an odd angle on her head, secured by dozens of black bobby pins. The short orange woolen skirt contrasted with a tight blue blouse that plunged almost to her navel. My eyes wandered down her legs to a pair of clunky green pumps. A bizarre outfit, especially for this time of day. Or any day.

Laying eyes on Clark, she zeroed in like a laser beam.

"Hi-i-i-i …," she purred seductively, sashaying toward him.

Immediately putting both her arms around Clark, she rested her robust ta-tas on his shoulder. The woman attempted to be alluring but fell short. I was apparently invisible to her. Clark locked eyes with mine, pleading "help me."

The only other person in the café fled.

As Miss Inappropriate continued to snuggle my man, I studied her makeup-caked face, waiting for the punch line. But none came. She was stone-cold crazy. She vanished into a backroom abruptly. Clark and I blinked at each other in disbelief, wondering if she was gone for good. Nope.

Her next move? She brought out a big set of magnets, claiming they helped energy flow more efficiently throughout a body. This might have been an interesting discussion, but she got a little too personal with Clark, rubbing the magnets up and down his back and trying to drop them in his shoes. He looked at me in exhausted desperation.

"Interesting," I said, trying to help. "Can I see one of those?"

She ignored me, honing in more intently on Clark.

"Buy sssssommmmmme," she said, trying to beguile. "You'll feeeeeel so much betterrrrrr."

Clark's patience finally gave way, and he asked her politely to leave him alone. She responded by rubbing his legs with the magnets so vigorously it hurt. He asked her again to step back, but she only talked louder and got closer. I tried several times to interrupt, to no avail. The inexplicable behavior became so intolerable, Clark stood up, squared off, and said, in no uncertain terms, "Get away from me. Not interested … in any of it!"

She let out a shrill, diabolical laugh that echoed off the walls. Her eyes turned icy black, and the energy in the room felt stifling.

Clark grabbed my hand and steered me toward the door. He stood for a moment, giving her a don't-even-think-about-coming-near-me-again stare. She took a step back and we were free.

We agreed at the start of the trip that if either of us ever felt threatened or unsafe the other wouldn't question that feeling; we'd simply give a sign and move on. In this case, we were on the same page. Staying one more moment near the crazy magnet woman sounded far worse than facing a torrential downpour on bicycles.

I'm not sure how it was possible, but it rained harder than ever. Our shoes and gloves squeaked as we pedaled; we couldn't see much and didn't feel stable on the slippery pavement. The wind blew in sharp gusts and dark clouds had completely blanketed the sky. Insult to injury.

What a relief to see the "Welcome to De Smet" sign. We checked into the nearest motel. The owner took pity on our bedraggled appearance by giving us a discount and two thick terrycloth robes. He also threw our saturated clothing in his heavy-duty dryer.

Liza Takes Another Header

Day 59: Friday, August 1
Weather: Hot and humid
Distance: 58 miles
Route: De Smet, South Dakota, to Brookings, South Dakota

Clark stopped for a haircut at the barbershop. I sat in an old leather chair that smelled of horse hair. Clark smiled at me from the reflection in the mirror as the barber trimmed away. We got an education on writer and hometown hero Laura Ingalls Wilder, the author of the classic *Little House* children's novels. The beloved books were based on her childhood in a pioneer family that spawned one of the most popular TV series of all time—*Little House on the Prairie*.

> Clark loved to get his hair cut in small towns and odd places at home and around the world. When he traveled, he'd spontaneously stop at a barbershop that caught his eye—one that was down a tiny alleyway or tucked in the basement of an industrial building ... places that wouldn't draw most tourists in. These forays gave him a chance to talk with a diversity of people on their own turf. He visited shops all over the world, including Turkey, Japan, Greece, the Canary Islands, Mexico, Germany, Canada, Spain, Argentina, and Iceland, as well as in nearly every state in the US.
>
> When he got a new "do" in Saipan, he found himself surrounded by four large women who fussed and adjusted his locks. They spoke mostly *Chamorro*, a Malayo-Polynesian language that few today still speak. The ladies addressed Clark in English, but giggled and bantered with each other in their native tongue. After all the primping, they took a group photo that still hangs in the shop.
>
> Clark had beautiful hair, and, no matter who did the cutting, it always looked good. I, on the other hand, have been going to the same hairdresser for over two decades and wouldn't dream of going elsewhere—it would feel like cheating!

As the morning slipped by, we grew anxious to travel. It would be an easy day. The terrain was flat, and the longest distance between towns only 10 miles. The first stop, Lake Preston, had a miniscule main street. As we rolled into town, craning our necks back and forth to check things out, I got caught between Clark and a parked car. I wasn't paying attention when he accidentally swerved toward me. I put the brakes on, overcorrected, and crashed. I hit the cement hard and slid for a few feet, scraping my knees and elbows. Serious road rash.

Hurt and embarrassed, I stood up and brushed myself off, then turned and saw a small crowd gathering. They looked concerned and someone offered me a hand. I thanked him, mumbled something about being OK and limped, bleeding and sore, into the nearest restaurant to hide. After cleaning, patching, and licking my wounds, a piece of homemade apple pie made everything look brighter.

We were back on the road soon. I was happy and oblivious to the world, except for the quiet whir of wheels on pavement. Suddenly, without warning, I was jerked from my reverie by what sounded like approaching thunder. I looked back where the road curved and saw seven massive combine harvesters heading toward us. One behind the next, these monster farm machines and their enormous wheels took up the entire highway, including the shoulders. I beelined for the nearest driveway, fearing I'd be crushed.

Only then did I realize Clark was a quarter mile back. I sensed determination as his legs spun urgently, trying to outrun danger. The metal beasts seemed to have a mind of their own—not under human control—as they bore down. When Clark breathlessly reached the safe turnout, seconds ahead of the combines, we watched them rumble past, drivers never taking their eyes from the road.

After the giant machines were out of sight and Clark's breathing returned to normal, we readied ourselves to set out again. Just before pushing off, we glanced back to check the traffic. Surprise! Surprise! The coast was still not clear. This time, a two-story house was coming at us. We laughed so hard we had to lay our bikes down to hold our stomachs. The semi-driver took his hat off and waved it as he passed with his wide load.

The road was surprisingly busy the last 18 miles into Brookings. It had turned into a divided highway with a gravel shoulder. Traffic whizzed by and drivers made no effort to slow when they saw us, if they saw us at all.

An old bike trail was the next unexpected thing. It was a bit hidden and hadn't been maintained for a long while. There were healthy bushes growing between the cracks in the pavement so we weaved our way between the branches. Periodically, the trail would disappear under water, forcing us back on the main road for a time. The puddles attracted tiny bugs (as small as no-see-ums or gnats) that attacked so viciously they drew blood. Then, to add another challenge, there were random manmade barricades crossing the trail at sporadic intervals. They were too difficult to go around so we had to lift our heavily laden bikes up and over the cement structures. It was slow going, but a decidedly better choice than dodging cars on the freeway.

~

Brookings was hopping. The youthful energy attracted plenty of hip restaurants and shops to the heart of the university district. We checked into a motel, cleaned up, and headed into town, trying to blend in with the students. For a moment, we were young again.

Beige Edna

Day 60:   Saturday, August 2
Weather: Very hot and humid
Distance: 46 miles
Route: Brookings, South Dakota, to Lake Benton, Minnesota

We woke up slowly, cuddling and giggling in bed until almost 9 a.m. It didn't matter. We had an easy day ahead—cross the border into Minnesota and spend the night in Lake Benton, about 30 flat miles away.

Clark's bike needed a few repairs. After dropping it off, we stopped for hot caramel rolls and a two big glasses of milk. We joked with the waitress while tearing off gooey pieces of sugary goodness. After each bite, I'd lick the sweetness from my fingertips.

"Want more napkins?" she asked, with a laugh.

"Nope, don't want to miss a morsel," I answered.

> We noticed beverages tasted different as we crossed the country. Interestingly, milk tasted better as we got closer to the center part of the U.S. I figured it was because we were that much closer to Wisconsin, the Dairy State. The water was starting to taste better to my palate, too. In the past few weeks, it had tasted kind of "tinny," like a tin can … a rusty tin can. We often bought bottled water to avoid that metallic flavor.

The temperature had risen to 95°, and the humidity almost as high. That muggy, sticky-wet Midwest summer weather I remembered so well. We even wished for rain, just to get a reprieve.

On top of the heat, construction on Highway 14 forced us to take a detour. It quickly became apparent there are many ways to navigate back roads. Unfortunately, no one seemed to know the best directions. The first person sent us east, another west. They were both wrong, and we got lost. Or, maybe it was us? We went in circles for what seemed like forever and wondered if we would ever leave the state. Even Clark, the phenomenal navigator, was baffled. After much to-ing and fro-ing, a young delivery driver finally pointed us in the right direction, much to our sweaty relief.

Somewhere near the Minnesota border, we were nearly delusional from the heat. There'd been no sign of civilization for miles. In fact, we thought it was a mirage when we came across the town of Elkton. And dead ahead was paradise—an air-conditioned gas station/snack bar where we could escape the sultry weather. We stumbled inside the store. Finding a place at the small counter, we utilized grunts for communication and guzzled three huge glasses of water, one after the other, pushing the empties silently forward for each refill. We sat nearly comatose at the counter until our gaze fell upon giant-sized, chilled sodas. Once again we mutely pointed toward the objects of our desire and downed them as quickly as we had the water.

With our thirst quenched, our minds started to clear. I realized all eyes in the store were upon us, staring in disbelief. They looked like figures in a wax museum frozen in their poses. Then, it dawned on us how strange and antisocial we must have appeared. Our sudden burst of laughter made people gawk more.

When we recovered from our laughing fit, we explained ourselves to those who stuck around. As our story unfolded, the remaining customers drew near, wanting more details. I noticed the questions changed focus as we headed further east. Still the most popular question remained: Where are you going and where are you coming from? But, now people seemed more concerned about how we were getting home since we'd traveled so far.

We *had* traveled far. Even if we quit right then and there, most would have been impressed by the distance. That felt good.

After reviving ourselves, we headed back into the heat. Confusion set in for a second time that day. I was convinced our brains were melting. Again, we asked several people for directions before making our way to the right road. It felt like we pedaled forever, yet stayed in one place—South Dakota. At every turn, we expected to see a "Welcome to Minnesota" sign.

"We must have crossed the state line by now!"

"Seems like we've been riding for hours. Did we miss the sign?"

It was right around the corner, we'd assure ourselves. And when it wasn't the conversation started over again. Eventually, we flagged a car down to ask if we were in Minnesota yet. The response was, "Oh, yes! For quite a while now!"

~

At the edge of Lake Benton, we came to a flat, grassy campground, but a spot-check of the place revealed gross bathrooms, so we rode into town to check our options. The downtown looked deserted. The heat was keeping people off the streets. As we stood quietly, taking stock of our surroundings, a man in an ancient tan pick-up drove by and leaned out his window.

"Can I help you?" he asked.

"We're looking for a place to stay the night," Clark answered.

"Where ya goin' with all that stuff?" he questioned.

"To Portland, Maine, from Portland, Oregon," Clark said, rotely familiar with the question.

This caused the man to burst into laughter. When he realized we weren't kidding, he said, "My name's Clarence. Hop in, son. I'll show you around."

It was apparent the offer was for Clark only.

"What about Liza?" Clark asked, giving me an "uh-oh" look.

"She can watch the bikes," he said.

After doing a mental calculation, Clark decided it was safe to take Clarence up on the offer.

"It's all right. Go see what you can find," I grinned.

Clark hopped in the truck, waving goodbye as they rumbled off to tour the town. It was a short trip.

"That was quick," I said.

"It's a small town," Clarence said. "Doesn't take long to cover. But, I just remembered one more place."

And they were off again with a stinky belch of exhaust.

When they returned, the two were yucking it up like long-lost friends. Plans were already in place to meet for a beer later. As far as where to stay? There weren't many options. So, back to the campground it was. Dirty bathrooms and all.

Clarence returned for Clark right after we finished pitching the tent. He was clearly a man's man who enjoyed male companionship—and maybe a break from his other half. Alone again, I decided to brave the shower, sliding sandals on to protect me from cooties. I made it a fast one.

While showering, I noticed some large bruises on my body. The big one from the last crash was fresh, but there were numerous other purple-blue splotches left from various falls, stumbles, and bumbles along the way. Although it wasn't something I was anxious to show off, it was interesting to trace our journey by the marks on my body.

~

"He's an eccentric character," Clark told me later, sharing a story about Clarence's penchant for sniffing out free meals. He had a habit of driving through campgrounds and asking random picnickers when the hamburgers were going to be ready. Surprisingly, the tactic often worked.

Clark also mentioned Clarence would be back to give us a lift to "the best dinner place in town," only a couple miles away.

During the short ride he *instructed* us to eat in the bar.

"It's cheaper and has the same food as the dining room. You don't get the frills—tablecloths or candles—but it's the only way to go."

He would know, being the free-food-scorin' guy.

Then he abruptly added, "I'll be back in an hour to pick you up."

"Oh, that's not necessary," I protested, "We can walk home. You've done enough."

"He wants to," Clark whispered. "Just let him, he's nice."

For a moment I wondered if Clark had been brainwashed.

~

The meal was pleasant, but most fascinating were the conversations around us. Clark and I became aural voyeurs—people who purposely listen to what others nearby are saying. It's amazing what some folks blurt out in public. In the Midwest, conversations seem louder; even if you're not interested, overhearing is nearly impossible to avoid.

On one side of us a woman told off her boyfriend. She called him names loud enough for the entire bar to hear. Apparently, he was a philanderer. Then, there was a man with a cartoonishly strong accent sitting behind us. This big boy weighed in at 400+ pounds. He sported fresh-from-the-farm overalls and a day-glow orange baseball cap tilted slightly askew on his massive head. When he placed his order, his already-loud voice grew louder.

The waitress asked, "Would you like a baked potato with your steak?"

"No, I'm on a diet!" he thundered, "I'll have the hash browns with sour cream. She's not on a diet though," he added, pointing to his plump wife, "She'll have the baked potato."

~

When Clarence returned, he took us on a short side trip, to the summit of a hill just outside town. We caught a spectacular orange-pink-purple summer sunset—at that singular moment when it was most brilliant.

Then, Clarence decided it was time to meet "the little woman."

Edna, the Mrs., was beige. Beige hair, beige skin, beige clothes, beige personality. She almost disappeared into the beige recliner in the beige sitting room. She was nice, but the kind of person you might know for a lifetime, yet not know at all.

We talked for a while; well, technically Clarence addressed most of the conversation to Clark which gave me time to take in the setting. The room was neat and tidy, simply furnished with one nondescript sofa, Edna's recliner, a matching one for Clarence, and a boring coffee table. Nothing remarkable and nothing that offered the eye any respite from the beigeness.

Clarence announced he and Clark were going to the garage to look at some tools and, I suspect, get away from the girls. Alone with Edna, I beamed a toothy grin her way, stalling for time so I could think of something to say. She responded with a jumble-toothed smile. Edna sat there innocuous to the world, hands crossed modestly, wearing a light-brown shift, sensible shoes (beige, of course) and coiffed with what can only be described as helmet hair. Oh, how I longed for a breeze to see if it would move.

When I have nothing in common with a person, I talk about the immediate surroundings, something I learned from a girlhood book fabulously titled *How to Get a Teen-Age Boy and What to Do with Him When You Get Him*. So, I discussed the safe and generic topics of family photos (my, what beige grandchildren you have), the standard "where did you and your husband meet" (grade school), and the weather (yup, it's hot out there).

The guys reappeared just in time. I had run out of politely neutral questions and was at risk of inquiring about their sex life. Thankfully, it was time for Clarence to give us a ride back to the campground.

Clarence and Clark talked about fishing, while I contemplated my encounter with Edna. She seemed comfortable with her orderly, beige life. And I was grateful to be on our bicycle journey. We were both content with our lives. Maybe we had something in common after all.

~

We got to see Clarence in action at the campground as the truck bounced to a stop in front of a flaming grill. A woman, preparing dinner for her family, stood in front of a nice fire. Clarence called out, "That doesn't look like a hamburger fire, it's more of a hotdog fire." He had a hankering for something grilled, and sure enough ... his ploy worked.

~

Before bed, we started a campfire and watched lightning flash in the distance. We speculated if and when the storm would reach us. Our guess: half an hour. We were right. When the temperature dropped we jumped into action.

"Time to batten down the hatches," I said, as we quickly gathered our things. In record time and expert fashion, we tightened the rain covers on our bike bags, secured the tent stakes, and stowed the next day's clothes inside our sleeping bags. We dove into the tent and zipped the doors shut, just as the rain started to fall.

WEEK 10

Iron Horse Connection

    Day 61:   Sunday, August 3
    Weather: Extremely hot and humid
    Distance: 59 miles
    Route: Lake Benton, Minnesota, to
                 Lamberton, Minnesota

It rained hard throughout the night, but morning brought dry, warm weather. We packed our belongings and cycled to town for breakfast. Too early, nothing open, so we rode eight miles to Tyler. No luck. Tyler was also buttoned up. We pressed our noses against a few windows, looking for movement.

After a few more miles, insistent tummy rumblings compelled us to stop at a convenience store. Day-old donuts, bitter coffee, and a limp egg burrito served as breakfast.

Thirsty, we stopped in Ballantine, just seven miles down the road. As we sat sipping our sodas in a 1950s-themed coffee shop, who should walk in but Clarence and Beige Edna! They realized few places around Lake Benton were open for breakfast on Sunday mornings and came looking for us—packed lunch in hand. When we acknowledged their thoughtfulness, Clarence simply said, "No trouble at t'all. We ain't got nothin' else to do today."

~

The sun blazed and our speed slowed over the next 20 miles. We were sunburned and sweaty by the time we reached Walnut Grove. Time for another round of cool drinks. A group of bikers dressed in new leathers pulled into the convenience store. They were heading west to Sturgis, South Dakota, for the big motorcycle rally. The celebration began in 1938, and today several hundred thousand bikers swarm upon the small South Dakota town each year. The parties are infamous, choppers iconic, and tattoos impressive.

"Hey, you two are headed the wrong way. Sturgis is the other direction," one of the bikers said, checking out our set up. They were nice guys. A mix of people with jobs in trucking, medicine, law, and insurance who, once a year, get their buddies together for a crazy road trip. One of the guys nudged Clark's shoulder and said, "It's all about the bikini bike washes for me. By the time I reach Sturgis, my bike is *reeeeal* dirty."

Their whole group laughed. I laughed, too. The comment was clearly said in good fun.

> Motorcyclists seemed to like us better than they liked car travelers. We were all out in the elements on our respective "iron horses." Riders always waved, beeped their horns, or did the head bob men use to acknowledge one another. Whatever form of "hello," it made us feel connected.

By the time we hit Lamberton, the heat spiked another 5 degrees, so we headed for the cool comfort of a motel. We bartered the price and checked into a big room with all the amenities we needed: air conditioning and a shower. The only problem was—not a shocker—nothing nearby was open for dinner. Yup, Sunday + Small Town = Tough Luck.

Clark, who'd spent the day dreaming of roast pork, was frustrated and asked aloud, to no one in particular, "Doesn't anyone eat dinner out on Sunday?"

I empathized but knew there wasn't a thing we could do, short of hitchhiking to Minneapolis, which we momentarily considered. Instead, I walked across the street to a convenience store and microwaved a pizza.

Son of Monster Face

Day 62: Monday, August 4
Weather: Sunny and hot (cooler than yesterday), but windy
Distance: 51 miles
Route: Lamberton, Minnesota, to New Ulm, Minnesota

The morning ran smoothly. We gathered our grungy clothes and found a laundromat a couple blocks away. Our timing was perfect. No one was there. We loaded two washers, had breakfast, then threw the clothes in the dryer and went back to the motel to pack up. On the way out of town, we picked up our fresh clothes and hit the road. Voila!

This was the easiest clothes-washing day on record. Depending on proximity to a laundromat, weather, and quantity of sweat-soaked clothing, schlepping big bags of dirty clothes could be challenging. Then, there was the issue of what to wear while in progress, as everything we owned was gross by the time we contemplated practical matters. We'd wear the cleanest of the dirty clothes or, if near a pool, hop into our swimsuits. More than once we donned our rain gear, naked underneath.

The clean clothes smelled heavenly as we folded and packed them tightly into our bags. Another of life's simple pleasures you learn to appreciate when on the road.

~

Our next designated stop: New Ulm. When Clark saw the city's name on the map, it conjured happy childhood memories of sausages and schnitzel. The Germanic name implied there'd be good food ahead. Anticipation of dinner motivated Clark. He jumped on his bike with energetic enthusiasm and was down the road before I could say "clipless pedal." At this rate, we'd cover the 51 miles to New Ulm in record time.

~

Chinese food for lunch in Springfield. Ooh, an international food day. The restaurant had an unusual smell—a mix of exotic spices and feet. A sullen, gaunt teenager took our order. She was scarecrow-like in her one-size-fits-all waitress uniform. The girl virtually ignored us until she presented our bill with a fake smile.

The food tasted like it was born from a can. This was the day I clearly understood the concept of eating to live versus living to eat.

~

Our wind-swept hair and overloaded bikes made us an unusual sight at the small-town, middle-of-nowhere gas station when we stopped to fill our tires. We garnered celebrity status once again. The same questions, from a new audience, helped confirm why we were on the trip and what kept us going. Their excitement reignited ours.

At our next rest stop, in Cobden, we found a sign designating the town but little else. This was not unusual, as the little dots on the map sometimes turned out to be a crossroad and nothing more. We moved on to a bigger dot, Sleepy Eye, and slammed on the brakes in front of a Dairy Queen.

Sleepy Eye was quiet as the name implied, and we might have spent the night, except Clark was fixated on getting to New Ulm, the German food he imagined beckoning seductively. So, we pushed onward. My passion for this fare is not the same as Clark's was. If we were zeroing in on chocolate cake, it would be a different story.

Clark was a half mile ahead when a mystery bug made a stealth attack and stung me in the corner of my eye. It was surprisingly painful and momentarily blinding. I weaved across the road, frantically pawing my face to make sure it was gone. Fortunately, the driver behind me was paying close attention and slowed while I swerved.

"You OK?" he called out the window.

I nodded, smiled, and waved him on. My eye swelled shut shortly after—not a good sign.

Clark was waiting for me at a stop sign.

"What the hell happened to your eye?" he asked with concern. I explained and he kissed the edge of the welt gently. "It should go down in a little bit," he said, after inspecting the bite closer.

As we pedaled through the neighborhoods of New Ulm, Clark asked everyone he saw for a restaurant recommendation. Most suggestions were in the city center, so we checked into a small motel near the one that sounded best. Clark was so excited to be in New Ulm that he bolted out the door to review the menu and get a pre-dinner beer. German, of course. I chose to relax in the room, flat on my back, with a cool, damp cloth on my swollen eye.

When Clark returned, he was beside himself with enthusiasm for our upcoming meal. We walked to the restaurant quickly and were seated right away. Clark grinned over the menu at me, his eyes twinkling with excitement.

I chose the beef *rouladen* and, after some consideration, Clark picked the *wiener schnitzel*, a house specialty. Then he waited anxiously for his meal to arrive. He was all smiles until … the plate hit the table.

Noooooooo. Another huge food disappointment. Instead of luscious, flavorful schnitzel, he got a scrawny, pressed, deep-fried veal patty. Clark looked heartbroken, staring down in boyish disappointment at the almost-inedible mess. He likened the experience to ordering a prime steak and getting a greasy, gristly mystery burger. My entrée was not much better.

When the shock subsided and Clark came back from wherever foodies go when they are horribly discouraged, he finished his beer, ate a few more bites, and shoved his meal aside.

"Well, I'm glad that's over," he said as we walked back to our room.

Psycho Killer?

Day 63: Tuesday, August 5
Weather: Sunny and warm
Distance: 39 miles
Route: New Ulm, Minnesota, to Mankato, Minnesota

It was a restless night's sleep. Clark woke me four times—twice because I yelled for help, trying to escape whatever awful monsters were chasing me, and twice because of his own nightmares about the tasteless schnitzel. One good thing, the swelling on my face had calmed down.

Dragging our exhausted bodies from bed, we walked up the street for breakfast. We each ordered the "Half Breakfast"—half a waffle, one piece of sausage, and a small juice. We ate that quickly, stared at each other, and called the waitress over to order the other halves.

~

We stopped at a bike shop on the way out of town so we could get our cycles tuned up. The mom-and-pop shop's owners told us about a picturesque trail from Mankato to Faribault, heading northeast toward Minneapolis along the Great River Road. It meant we'd have to ride farther south only to go north again, but a bike trail is usually worth the trade-off.

When it was time to go, they refused to take any money.

"A gift from fellow cyclists," the man said, winking at his wife. "May your journey be enjoyable and safe."

~

While we ran a final errand, we heard about the *great* German restaurant in town—the one where people travel from far and wide to enjoy the traditional fare. Apparently, we went to the wrong place. No kidding!

~

Ten miles in, we stopped for a quick beverage break in Courtland. Several cocky teenaged kids circled our bikes and asked what we were "doing."

"It's taken you *this* long to get *here*?" one snotty teen criticized after we told them about our journey, sarcasm dripping from his voice.

"I could be there and back by now!" his pimple-face girlfriend bragged.

"You're slow as shit!" another said caustically.

They spiraled around us, poking at our bikes, even trying to flip our bags open. In the heat of hassling, one big girl caught me off guard by jumping on the back of my bike, landing so hard, she bent the pannier rack out of shape.

Clark stepped in and took charge.

"Get off the bike NOW," he barked at the girl in drill sergeant fashion. Turning toward the others, he snarled, "You have five seconds to get outta here!"

The group scattered, brazen enough to mutter a few parting shots from a distance.

~

Once we turned south toward Mankato, the hilly ride was a joy, and the surly teens became but a fleeting memory. After one hearty climb, we soared along a high ridge, on top of the world. Vast stretches of fields swayed rhythmically as a breeze played across the countryside. We were alone on our lofty pinnacle; so peaceful and perfect, we started to sing.

The descent down the ridge was pure pleasure. Cyclists love the glacier-smoothed hills of the Midwest where you can ride with abandon and glide freely at a sane pace. In mountainous terrain, you have to ride your brakes, the road can be dangerously curvy, and you can't always see what lies ahead.

~

Eight miles outside of Mankato, a neatly groomed gentleman smiled and waved as he motored by. After passing, he pulled over and waited. The man said he was curious about us and, of course, that set off a lengthy discussion. His name was George, and he was an avid cyclist himself. He directed us to a campground, said goodbye, and drove off. But, when we rounded the next corner, there he was again.

"I have a better idea. Why not pitch your tent in our backyard and have dinner with us?"

We agreed. Then the deal got even sweeter.

"We just bought a new house and haven't moved in yet. You're welcome to stay there."

Clark and I exchanged glances, then jumped at the opportunity.

George gave us directions to a crossroad ahead where he would meet us on his bike, then guide us to his new home. He rolled up just as we did, excited to be riding. George took the lead and soon we were standing in front of his gorgeous new home. He gave us the grand tour, talking of plans for each room. It was going to be a showplace when they settled in.

George departed so we could get cleaned up. There was running water and electricity, but no shower curtains or furniture. We bathed carefully to avoid splashing water on the marble floors and dried off with our camping towels. Once the sleeping bags were rolled out on the plushly carpeted living room floor, we stretched out for a rest. I felt grateful for people like George who were willing to take in perfect strangers. These gestures made the trip memorable.

~

We walked the short distant to George's house for dinner. All greenery was neatly trimmed, like his beard. Hedges formed perfect rectangles, not a branch out of place. The grass, like a weed-free golf green, set off a lavish carpet of colorful flowers. The house was impeccable and symmetrical, with identical windows across each side.

Suzanne, George's wife, was a vision of 50+ perfection. Freshly manicured fingers fiddled with a long string of pearls as she told us the plan for the evening had changed to dinner at a supper club.

I ordered walleye, Suzanne picked at a salad, and the boys got steaks. After a couple glasses of wine, the conversation flowed easily. Later, the couple gave us a tour of Mankato. We saw stunning homes with beautiful sunset views and liked the city so much, we added it to our growing list of "Where to Live If We End Up Leaving Portland."

George took us "home" at the reasonable hour of 10.

Beautiful as the house was, we barely slept that night. The emptiness made it feel creepy, with eerie creaks and cracks and spooky sounds haunted houses make in movies. Letting our imaginations run wild, we contemplated the fact that we didn't know these exceptionally friendly people at all. What if they were members of some weird cult that captured people and sacrificed them? Or, ax murderers who seamlessly blend in with everyone else? ("They seemed like such nice, quiet people," the neighbors always report.)

Clark amused himself further by teasing me mercilessly, "I think George is a closet psycho killer. He'll probably sneak back in a few hours when he thinks we're asleep and chop-chop-chop."

"Yeah, right," I responded flatly, trying not to play the game.

"Seriously, who would ever know?" Clark said ominously, "Maybe the whole neighborhood's in on it."

I tried to ignore him.

"Hear that?" he whispered in my ear. "I think it's him standing outside waiting for us to fall asleep."

Clark thought it was funny, but the place had me wide-eyed and set my heart racing. Just as I was nodding off, I heard Clark quietly whisper, "He'll probably wait to kill us in the morning when our guard is down."

Bastard.

Speckled Hands

Day 64: Wednesday, August 6
Weather: Sunny and warm
Distance: 48 miles
Route: Mankato, Minnesota, to Faribault, Minnesota

Imagine my horror when George came bounding through the door in the morning as I was getting dressed. Out of shock, I dropped my clothes when I saw him coming and stood there in just my underwear. Fortunately, I didn't scream, but he must have seen the stunned expression on my face and assumed it was modesty issues. In gentlemanly fashion, he averted his eyes, said "Hi," then turned away to talk with Clark.

He'd come to ask us to stop at his house and sign their guest book. Hmmm … guest book … maybe it's the last thing victims do before the bloodbath!

"I bet the guest book is in the basement, with all the dead bodies," Clark speculated as we pedaled toward our doom.

"Stop it!" I told him.

When we arrived at George and Suzanne's they were as warm and friendly as they'd been the night before. We left a gracious note in their guest book, thanked them profusely (for not killing us), and cycled off.

The experience was hilarious—but only days later, when we were miles away from these lovely people and their beautiful Mankato home.

~

We only made it to the end of the block when a big family shouted from their porch, "Hey, where are you going? Who are you? Take me with you!"

We stopped to answer and moments later six kids and a boisterous crowd of neighbors came running toward the street to meet us. We were surrounded. I took off my gloves to shake hands. People fired questions at us fast and furious. Soon, other neighbors joined the throng. It was crazy!

"When did you start?"

"When will you finish?"

"How will you get home?"

"How long did you train?"

"Why are you doing this?"

"What kind of bike do you have?"

"What are you doing in Mankato?"

"Where will you go today?"

It wasn't long until someone noticed my speckled hands. Biking gloves are partially made of an open mesh fabric. Over time, the sun tanned my flesh, creating a leopard-like pattern. This sparked unusual interest and people wanted to get up close to see the dappled skin. The kids argued over who could touch me next.

"It's my turn to touch her hands," each child begged, as if stroking my hand gave them special powers.

"Good thing I have two of them," I said, trying to keep the peace and answer questions at the same time.

"You should write a book," somebody suggested.

"I am."

~

The Sakatah Singing Hills State Trail is a 39-mile "Rails-to-Trails" path that parallels Highway 60 from Mankato to Faribault, Minnesota. These paths are created when old railroad tracks get covered or removed to create public biking, walking, cross-country skiing, and running trails.

The trail was mostly flat, like you might expect for train travel, and when the path took us uphill, the incline was graded so gently it was barely noticeable. We stopped at scenic spots and bridges to take pictures, and when we were hungry or thirsty there were small towns convenient to the trail.

~

At trail's end, in Faribault, we called our friend Sue to come get us for a few days' rest in Minneapolis. She was there in no time. Flawless skin, perfect body, and dark, shiny hair. Sue looked the same as when I saw her nearly a decade before. How come some people don't seem to age?

Sue is also one of those people who always seems to know what she wants, then goes for it. On the flipside, I'm still wondering what I want to be when I grow up.

We crammed the bikes and gear into her SUV and drove off, giggling and gossiping as if no time had passed. When we pulled into the driveway, Sue and I jumped out of the van, and I ran to her husband, Chuck, for a big bear hug. We exchanged the usual high-energy, catch-up greetings friends do when they've not seen each other for a while. When I turned to introduce Clark, he was nowhere in sight.

Then we noticed him … still in the van, red faced from laughter, a fist melodramatically pounding on the window. Clark was imprisoned, his mouth moving vigorously, yet we could hear only muffled cries. The childproof locks had done their job well.

Darts with the Boy Next Door

Day 65-67: Thursday to Saturday, August 7–9

Weather: Hot and humid, with lots of mosquitoes
Distance: Rest days
Route: Stayed in Minneapolis, Minnesota

After a day of relaxing, we set out by bus for downtown Minneapolis. A nice change of pace from our small-town adventures. We wandered through the Nicollet Mall, a gigantic pedestrian oasis, taking in the positive energy and exploring the shops, bars, restaurants, and other diversions.

Later, we met long-time friends, Tom and Sheryl, for dinner. The directions to get there were, "Go through Loring Park and follow the people with purple hair." It worked. The eclectic café was one of those wonderfully funky places where all paths cross in harmony.

Tom was the boy next door, literally. We grew up together, playing flashlight tag, kickball, and 50 scatter with neighborhood kids during long summer nights. Our street was so quiet the sewer cap in the middle of the street was the game's goal. I remember being "It" and counting to 50 in the center of road with my eyes closed. I was an expert hider in flashlight tag, not afraid to climb up trees or crawl into spider-filled places to conceal myself.

After dinner, we went for a nightcap at a rowdy bar on Lake Minnetonka. While others gyrated on the dance floor, flirting and teasing each other, we played a rousing game of darts. Clark got the prize for most creative technique. He danced up to the line and executed his throw by spinning, diving, and twisting along with the music. Everyone played a reasonable facsimile of the game, except me. I randomly chucked the feathered stingers in the general direction of the dartboard, often missing it altogether.

Imagine their surprise when I accidently won by hitting a bull's-eye.

"YOU won?" the others repeated, shock in their voice. "How could that be? Is that even possible?"

Yup. Winner.

Tom drove us home at 3 a.m. As we pulled into the darkened driveway, neither Clark nor I recognized the house. The address was right, but everything looked foreign. We walked up to the front door and decided we were at the wrong house, so scurried back into the car and spent another half hour driving around the neighborhood until we ended up back at the same place.

This time we tried the key. It worked. We giggled like teenagers sneaking into our parents' home after hours.

~

On our last evening, old college pals, Chris and her husband "Beaver," joined us at Sue and Chuck's house. Gin and tonics, followed by appetizers. Then wine, dinner, dessert, and nightcaps. Conversation topics ranged from the absurd to the sublime. We looked for answers to questions about success, happiness, love, and finding the balance between work and play. Laughter filled the house as we took turns telling stories from the past. Clark fit in perfectly, tossing in jokes and old tales of his own with impeccable timing.

> Clark and I often wished we'd met earlier in our lives so we could have shared all our "young-and-free" experiences together. But in that alternate reality, fate and circumstance might have taken us down paths unknown. So, the here and now, in all its relative imperfection, couldn't have been more perfect.

WEEK 11

Synchronized Mowers

>Day 68: Sunday, August 10
>Weather: Hot and humid, lots of mosquitoes
>Distance: 40 miles
>Route: Red Wing, Minnesota, to an island on the Mississippi River in Hager City, Wisconsin

Before packing up, Clark and I sat outside on the front deck enjoying a cup of coffee and the suburban tranquility. Suddenly, neighbors to the right, left, and across the street raced outside and started their lawnmowers at exactly the same time. It was as if a secret alarm had alerted everyone: "It's time—mow now!"

We watched the synchronized mowers begin their carefully orchestrated lawn ballet.

"Huh…," Clark said after a few moments of stunned silence.

"Yeah, huh," I repeated.

As we sat motionless, all three mowing teams headed straight for us—expressionless, blades spinning, engines roaring—aiming right at the very deck we were sitting on. It was surreal.

Fortunately, their predetermined choreography and legally defined property boundaries prevented them from getting any closer. They turned, in flawless coordination, giving us the chance to escape back inside.

~

It was hard to say goodbye, but we were on the verge of overstaying our welcome. Chuck gave us a ride to the edge of the city to avoid congested traffic. Reluctantly, we forced ourselves out of the car and waved a sad farewell.

We rode to Red Wing and cheered ourselves by stopping for an early lunch. I ordered the fettuccini with 12 green-lipped mussels fresh from New Zealand. Clark selected fish and chips. A minute later, the chef came out to apologize and tell me the menu listing was incorrect. Apparently, my order came with six mussels, not a dozen.

The restaurant was still quiet, so the chef stayed and talked. It wasn't long before he learned Clark was a savvy diner and former instructor at a culinary institute. The foodies compared notes on their specialties, and Clark soon had the chef metaphorically eating out of his hands.

After disappearing into the kitchen for a while, the chef himself arrived at our table with the food.

"I decided you deserve all 12 mussels," he said, placing a big plate in the center of the table.

Clark's eyes lit up.

As much as I wanted to hoard all the little gems for myself, I assured him I'd share.

"Well, maybe just one," Clark said, as he put half the mussels on his plate.

"So, how were your meals?" the chef asked later, facetiously, noting our clean plates. After showering appropriate praise, Clark reached for his wallet and we prepared to leave.

"Hey, I have an idea. You're welcome to stay at my place tonight," the chef offered, then quickly changed his mind. "No, wait! I forgot, it's SEX night!"

He had a friend with benefits—trading meals for back rubs, etc. Understandably, he didn't want to lose out on that.

~

Our long lunch took away all motivation to ride. We needed a place to stay and spent the next hour and nearly eight miles riding around town looking for a cheap motel. Prices were higher than we wanted to pay, so we headed for a campground and found one in Hager City, Wisconsin, on a Mississippi River island. We set up our tent near the water and two big picnic tables. Extra tables were always a coup. They were multipurpose—used for dining, of course, but also for spreading out gear.

Though we were tired enough to hit the hay, it was too early for bed and too late for a nap, so we walked to a country bar nearby. After a few rousing rounds of Crazy Eights, a second wind blew in. We started ordering rum drinks and stayed for hours, talking, dancing, and listening to old music.

Back at the campsite, a good night's sleep was not in the cards. First, it was really cold. I managed to sausage myself into sweats, without exiting my sleeping bag. Second, and especially annoying, was the factory across the river. A noisy hum emanated from it, all night long. Third, trains chugged past constantly, blowing their loud, low whistles. Fourth, and still train-related, the conductors regularly stopped to connect additional train cars, resulting in a thunderous crash that echoed across the water. And, finally, the mosquitoes were out in force.

> I don't like bugs much. Never did. The ones that sting are particularly unappealing. My mom loves to tell the story of the first time I saw snow as a young child. Apparently, I pointed outside, saying, "Bug, bugs, bugs!" with tears streaming down my face. I thought the tiny flakes were insects.

Clark doesn't mind them as much and was only mildly annoyed when a monster-sized bug bounced off his nose. I guess that's the epitome of the adage "Cyclists have smiles on their faces and bugs in their teeth."

Hysterical Markers

Day 69: Monday, August 11
Weather: Warm and pleasant
Distance: 35 miles
Route: Hager City, Wisconsin, to Pepin, Wisconsin

I woke to the sweet sound of someone singing. It was Clark. Despite the short night, he was in great spirits. We packed, anxious for the ride along the great Mississippi River—and, of course, just as anxious for breakfast.

The six miles to Bay City flew by quickly. Nope. Nothing open for breakfast. In another six miles, a sandwich shop in Maiden Rock looked promising. Our hunger was at arm-gnawing stage. If the café hadn't been open, we might have broken in to scavenge for food. Fortunately, it was. The consumption of a steaming bowl of potato soup and a hearty BLT prevented the loss of any limbs.

~

We spent the afternoon inspecting every historical marker along the way, which made me feel variously patriotic, proud, amused, and stupid. We promptly dubbed them "hysterical markers." Poet, journalist, and long-time editor of the *New York Post,* William Cullen Bryant (1794–1878) said Lake Pepin "ought to be visited in the summer by every poet and painter in the land."

As the sun shifted lower in the sky, we set up camp at a mini RV park in Pepin. There were no official campsites for tents, just a stretch of lawn next to the park host's house. By 6 p.m., we were cleaned up and ready for good food, wine, and relaxation. Swedish meatballs called my name and didn't let me down. Clark ordered what turned out to be the biggest, thickest pork chops he'd ever seen. Hog heaven.

Our meal was memorable for reasons beyond the cuisine: the harbor view, a musician softly strumming a classical guitar, the laughter and whispers of other guests, and melancholy woooo-woooos of distant trains passing in the night.

We strolled out to the harbor after dinner. The boats, all lined up precisely in their slips, rocked hypnotically. Walking arm in arm, we talked of love, life, and the pursuit of happiness, nodding to other lovers doing the same thing. Waves quietly splashed along the shore and a watercolor sunset painted the sky pink and purple. I was supremely happy to be on a lake again—it made me feel at home.

~

In the wee hours of the morning, the camp host, who must have forgotten we were outside, shoved a heavy window open and blasted reruns of the 1960s TV show *Green Acres*. We cringed at the bad jokes, giggled at his loud guffaws, and sang along to the theme song. He closed the window when it started raining; the soft, rhythmic pattering soon lulled us back to sleep.

Haunted House

Day 70: Tuesday, August 12
Weather: Rain
Distance: 37 miles
Route: Pepin to Fountain City, Wisconsin

Rain, rain, rain. We didn't want to get up, so stayed snuggled in. There was a short break in the clouds around 9 a.m., so we hurried to pack, rolling the tent up wet.

The sky looked ominous, threatening another downpour. We dressed in our wet-weather gear and ventured on. The ride was magnificent. A storm hovered but never returned. Rain-soaked vegetation glistened with a thousand hues of emerald. Mist-shrouded river bluffs and far-off landscapes created natural works of art no painter could ever capture.

~

Breakfast in the village of Nelson included a hummingbird show, thanks to feeders strategically located outside the restaurant windows. The tiny creatures hovered silently, sipping sweet nectar from one feeder, then darting to the next. Weightless wings flapped invisibly; iridescent bodies floating in midair making the near-impossible look easy.

~

Eleven miles later we rolled into the river town of Alma. The historic buildings and quaint streets fascinated us so much we decided to stay. One imposing, pre-turn-of-the-century inn advertised "great rates."

We knocked and rang, but no one answered. That seemed odd. We rang again, more insistently, and still nothing. On a whim, I palmed the ornate doorknob, giving it a firm turn. The heavy door creaked open.

We stood stock-still, somewhat embarrassed for our intrusion yet intrigued by what we saw beyond the threshold. The antique-filled, heavily draped parlor appeared frozen in another time. Ornate wooden pedestals flanked deeply tufted mahogany settees. Gilded vases adorned marble-topped tables lavishly spilling a bounty of flowers. A bronze lamp with bead fringe stood sentry on an old piano. Needlepoint, velvet, braid, and swag. Everything in perfect, overly elaborate order, as the master of this mansion would have expected. A grand staircase with an intricately carved banister was the obvious focal point. I imagined Victorian ladies sashaying down those stairs when a gentleman came a-calling. Were we on the edge of "The Twilight Zone"?

"Hello?" we called.

No answer.

We stepped into the Zone.

"Hellooooo?" louder this time.

Dead silence.

Our eyes adjusted to the dim light. A sign instructed us that if no one was home to "pick the room you want, leave the key in the door and money on the table when you go." Okaaaaaay. Trust so rare I wanted to stay for that reason alone.

We tentatively explored a bit further, heading upstairs. The guest rooms were quaint, yet formal. Too formal for us rough riders. The bath was down the hall which meant sharing. Not a big deal for seasoned campers. But the house was creepy, and I had the willies.

"I bet there's a ghost in here," Clark commented, echoing my thoughts.

Everything smelled old and musty. It reminded me of the mildewy scent that lingers a few days after you open a lake cabin for the first time in summer. But this was different. The place felt uncomfortable, like maybe we weren't really alone. I not so discreetly checked the paintings for eye holes.

"I'd be scared if you went for a beer and left me alone here," I said subtly hinting that wouldn't be an option.

Still, we were intrigued and continued walking along the narrow hall, opening and closing doors, peeking into every room. One door looked slightly smaller than the others. Without thinking, I opened it. A blast of cold, stale air slammed us in the face. The attic. Oh, crap. I had a strong feeling we shouldn't be there. Clark banged the door shut with so much force the sound reverberated up and down the hall.

"Let's get outta here," he said, looking over his shoulder back toward the door.

What started as a trot, turned into a sprint. We flew down the stairs and were on our bikes before you could say "Boo!" We pedaled like crazy until the inn and Alma were well out of sight. Kind of silly for two grown adults.

~

We crossed the Chippewa River in a gloomy drizzle and continued along Highway 35, paralleling the great Mississippi River. As we passed through the tiny town of Cochrane, Clark spotted an old-fashioned ice cream parlor and uncharacteristically pushed to go in—odd, because I was usually the ice cream person.

The owner was larger than life and charismatic. She zoomed around the shop, straightening chairs, wiping tables, and adjusting napkin holders in a blur of activity. As she whirled up our chocolate malt (one shake, two straws) we naturally started to chat about our cross-country trip. The blender ground to a halt. She incredulously slapped her knee and shrieked, "Really? Get outta here!"

As we shared the thick shake, others filtered in looking for their own ice cream fix. The owner notified each new arrival about our trip. She enhanced her personal version of our story with broad arm gestures and spectacular facial contortions, almost dancing as she dressed the tops of ice cream. So entertaining in her own right that no one noticed when we quietly slipped out the door.

~

We took an old farming road paralleling Highway 35 for the remaining nine-mile trip to Fountain City. We pedaled by miles of cornfields, their perfectly straight rows causing an optical illusion that made us dizzy if we turned our heads to look. The landscape eventually changed to grassy fields, stands of trees, and ponds—our equilibrium once again restored.

Then the honking started. I knew the sound well. It was the loud, unmistakable call of Canada geese. There were thousands of birds. The sky darkened as they flew in tight formation for their landing, swooping by so close we could almost touch their wings. The deafening noise and flap-flapping were exhilarating. We slowed our bikes, stopping to watch the geese glide across the water. It was a magical experience, one that even the misty weather couldn't dampen.

~

Fountain City was named for the nearby freshwater springs. The local landmark Eagle Bluff rises 550 feet above the river, making it the highest point in the Upper Mississippi. The city is located at a forested bend along the river and has the distinction of being the oldest settlement in the county. Some areas in Fountain City are only two houses wide because the river flows to the base of the bluffs.

Long ago, Native American Sioux and Chippewa tribes populated the area. Those with eagle eyes still find arrowheads and pot shards around the bluffs.

We were fortunate the little town had a bike shop. Clark was having trouble with his spokes again; the wheels needed to be balanced, and the bike required a general tune-up. We dropped it off and checked into a motel.

A waterfront restaurant known for its catfish lured us in. But, feeling a twinge of guilt for our big motel splurge, we opted for hamburgers. Platter after platter of delectable catfish trailed heavenly aromas by our table as we dejectedly munched our boring burgers. We hoped we had room for an order of catfish. Nope, not even we could manage a double dinner that night.

Duped by a Dalmatian

Day 71: Wednesday, August 13
Weather: A perfect riding day; sunny and warm with no wind and no mosquitoes!
Distance: 55 miles + 5 miles to dinner
Route: Fountain City, Wisconsin, to West Salem, Wisconsin

It was a gorgeous morning. Clark popped over to the bike shop and discovered the repairs totaled only $10. Not quite as good as our freebie in New Ulm, but close. Already a good day.

We loaded up and hit the road by mid-morning. Rolling green hills outside Fountain City took our breath away. I'd forgotten how beautiful Wisconsin is, especially in the summer. After a few miles, we turned onto the "Great River State Trail." This bike path starts about 10 miles south of Fountain City and heads toward Onalaska, where it connects to the "Sparta to Elroy Trail" and continues farther south.

It was a bit challenging to find the trailhead, as it commenced in a wildlife refuge. The dirt road had a lot of potholes, but our bikes could handle the rough terrain.

Clark is a purist. He had a mountain bike. Mine was a hybrid—half mountain and half road bike. Clark's bike could handle gravel and dirt a little better than mine, but I could go faster on the pavement. I figure I got the best of both worlds.

The trail was so far from the main road you couldn't hear traffic, like hiking in the backcountry. We passed marshes, streams, and ponds and stopped along the way to view wildlife from under a dense canopy of trees. There were all kinds of birds, including heron, ducks, and storks, as well as minks and turtles. Frogs, still as statues, sat upon lily pads. I felt at home and in tune with nature.

We peeked through telescopes set up at strategic viewpoints, zooming in for close-ups of our animal friends and sweeping views of the panorama.

Clark - Corn Off The Stalk - Outside Trempeleau, WI

In time, the trail transitioned to a mix of compact gravel and dirt, making the ride easier. Clark stopped at a cornfield that spread out on both sides of the road. He dismounted and headed toward the towering stalks. With a quick swipe, he tore off an ear for himself and then one for me. After peeling the tender husks back, rows of plump kernels revealed themselves. Clark took the first bite. His expression said it all. Even without cooking the corn was fresh and sweet.

Trempeleau seemed a perfect town: tidy homes, all lawns meticulously manicured. I wondered if they performed synchronized mowing here. We spotted a quiet, eerily motionless Dalmatian. He seemed to be studying us intently. I was happy to see he was tied to a porch. There was something really strange about this dog. I couldn't quite put my finger on it.

We got off our bikes and squinted in its direction—no movement. We inched forward. The animal stayed stock still, never flinching. I was hoping it wouldn't go nuts and break its leash. Yet, the strangeness was intriguing. We continued slowly toward the Dalmatian.

"Hey, buddy … you're OK. You're alright," I said.

No response.

No surprise.

Closer inspection revealed it wasn't a dog at all—rather, a strikingly realistic replica. Similar to the plastic garden ornaments, like pink flamingos and little trolls, that adorn certain yards. The leash had thrown us for a loop. The people who set up this joke—if it was one—got us good!

~

We rode on, away from the tiny Utopia, passing through Onalaska and skirting the corners of La Crosse. Traveling east along the trail, we cycled under a railroad trestle, across an expanse of wildflowers, and found ourselves at a well-tended campground. We almost missed the place because it was hidden among a clump of trees.

The camp was sparsely occupied, so plenty of premium space was available. We found a sunny spot near the meadow along the banks of the La Crosse River and set up camp. The gear hadn't been unloaded since the rain in Pepin, so things were still damp. Fortunately, late afternoon sun baked everything bone dry well before nightfall.

~

Dinner choices: get back on our bikes and ride several miles into West Salem or purchase a frozen-then-microwaved pizza from the camp store. We opted to ride. In the past, the thought of pedaling one more minute had been out of the question. Wow. We'd come far. The ride was well worth it. Comfort food. Homemade chicken potpie with warm deliciousness inside and a crispy crust outside. This, plus a salad, glass of wine, and plenty of fresh-baked bread made us happy.

On the way back to camp, we complimented ourselves, "We rock." At home, there was no way we'd ever ride bikes to and from dinner. Like nearly everyone else, the car would be the mode of transportation. But that night we pedaled into the fading sunset, strong, proud, and victorious. And, we still had energy left. The campground provided free firewood a quarter mile down a dirt road. We hoofed it together the first trip, then I went back and forth several more times while Clark worked on building the campfire.

We sat around the fire talking for hours, watching dense fog creep slowly over the meadow, swallowing everything in its path, coming closer and closer, eventually shrouding us in a mysterious and beautiful cocoon. We couldn't see a thing, so focused on the sounds around us. Animals scampered close by; then scurried away. The fire crackled, caving in on itself; burning down to glowing embers. We unconsciously kept our voices low, not wanting to spoil the magical moment.

Town Scandals

Day 72: Thursday, August 14
Weather: Rain
Distance: 20 miles
Route: West Salem, Wisconsin, to Sparta, Wisconsin

By morning's light the rain reappeared, the sun only making a brief showing. Real wetness came from the heavy dew. Again, the tent was rolled up wet. The fog that entertained us the night before brought misery that morning. The air was so cold we kept moving in an effort to get our blood flowing.

Delayed by a group of campers interested in our trip, we talked with them while hopping up and down to stay warm. Finally, I couldn't stand it anymore and risked rudeness by blurting, "Let's hit the road."

We pedaled quickly back to West Salem for breakfast, lingering an extra-long time to enjoy hot tea and local gossip. Through eavesdropping, we figured out the pretty waitress was having an affair with one of her customers, who was wearing a wedding ring. Our ears perked up more when another guy talked loudly about being in love with her. She noticed us listening and gave us a secret smile.

We finally pulled ourselves away from the real-life soap opera and cycled out into the gray–black day. The air felt thick and depressing. Passing cars slowed and people called out warnings.

"Be careful out there. A bad storm's on its way," one woman cautioned.

"Head for cover tonight! There's a big one comin'," a young guy hollered.

"Ride fast!" we were advised by other drivers.

We pedaled with a deep feeling of doom.

Things got worse when my bike started to drag. Air was leaking from the tire, and pumping it didn't last long. Soon, it went completely flat. I filled the tire again, this time at a gas station. But in minutes it was pancaked. Flat tire number seven—on the rear. An ideal excuse to get a motel room and sit out the impending storm.

Our timing was impeccable. The rain started in earnest the moment we checked in. The apocalypse was upon us. We closed the curtains, took long baths, watched movies, and napped the day away. Tra-la-la.

The storm conveniently cleared up in time for dinner, giving us the perfect window to walk to an Italian restaurant and scarf a big bowl of spaghetti, a loaf of garlic bread, and a bottle of wine. We waddled back home through a light mist, hitting our room just when another round of heavy rain blew into town. The water pounded outside all night, but we were content, vindicated in our decision to stop.

We're Not Leavin' Till We're Heavin'

Day 73: Friday, August 15
Weather: Sunny and humid
Distance: 42 miles
Route: Sparta, Wisconsin, to Elroy, Wisconsin

The morning brought more rain. Should we stay or should we go? Days like this were often misleading. If we stayed, it could clear up and turn beautiful. If we left, it might rain all day. Whatever decision we made, Murphy's Law usually ruled.

Our attention turned toward fixing the tire. We'd procrastinated. When Clark took the tube out to patch it, he found two punctures instead of one. This explained the speed of air loss. By the time he finished, the sky had cleared, making the decision to move on easy. Sometimes putting things off worked in our favor.

We rode along the Elroy-Sparta State Trail, America's first Rails-to-Trails project. Built on the former main line of the Chicago and North Western Railway, the trail opened in 1967. It is one of the nation's most popular trails, with three 100+-year-old rock tunnels along the 32-mile route. The path winds through hidden valleys and connects to 101 miles of additional trails used by hikers, bicyclists, and snowmobilers.

The first tunnel was pitch black and nearly three-quarters mile long, making it necessary to walk the bikes. Our lights didn't punch much of a hole in the darkness, and only seeing a few inches ahead was disorienting. I felt a bit claustrophobic. The limestone walls dripped with water and kept the temperature low. We heard voices echoing far ahead in the inky obscurity. Pushing the bikes and heavy gear such a long distance, feeling almost blind, left the impression of time standing still.

I was relieved to finally see daylight ahead. Exiting the tunnel into the brightness jarred my senses. I squinted toward the sun, peeling off my damp sweatshirt and letting the rays warm my skin.

"Ahhh, that was refreshing," Clark said, putting his sunglasses back on as he mounted his bike.

We glided along smoothly, bantering with other cyclists about our trip and theirs. We were traveling the longest distance of anyone, which led to the usual questions. However, new on the list: how many days have you gone without a shower? Our record was three days. Some long-distance riders were proud to admit that they could outdo us, declaring such records as five and even six days, like it was a badge of honor, albeit a reeking, malodorous badge.

The ride took us through rolling hills and lime-green pastures spotted with cows and Queen Anne's lace. Tunnel #2 had massive 20-foot wooden doors flung wide open, beckoning us inside. At a third of a mile long, it was a less daunting challenge, even though we still had to walk our bikes. The last tunnel, also one-third-mile long, was so straight we could see a pinprick of brightness in the distance—the proverbial light at the end of the tunnel.

~

Elroy was our destination. The crabby proprietor of the motel said "No way" when we politely asked for a price break, even though only one other room was taken. His wife, who was more congenial and a better businessperson, offered us a 10% discount.

The first-floor room was dingy and old, but at least we could lock up our stuff. As we settled in, the grouchy geezer mowed the lawn, taking the opportunity to glare at us every time he roared past the window. The man spent a lot of time going back and forth. The grass must have been higher in our section. I shut the window to avoid the gas fumes and his ugly stares. Disturbing.

~

We walked a mile into town and ventured into a small bar. A wall of smoke hit our faces when we pushed the door open. As our eyes adjusted to the darkness, I spotted racy girlie posters on the walls. The scantily clad women were draped over cars holding rifles.

Despite the early hour, the place was already hopping. It seemed an ordinary evening at a little watering hole. Some average-looking guys with beer bellies laughed and talked loudly. A few heavily tattooed people sat circled around a table. A pair of overweight women leaned on the bar nursing beers, one cheek apiece on the stools. A busty woman played video games wearing a T-shirt that read "We're not leavin' till we're heavin'."

We took a seat at the bar, responsibly putting both cheeks on the stools. A man with droopy, bloodshot eyes and bulbous honker sat down next to Clark. Soon a conversation about food started up, which led to a discussion about bratwurst. Clark mentioned he was looking forward to sampling one of the famous Wisconsin German sausages. The man said he had a "brat" (correctly pronounced like "bra" with a "t" on the end) for lunch.

"Dems are go-o-o-o-o-d," he said, slurping inward through his gums, ending with a mostly toothless, drooly smile.

That single moment in time was one of the most disgusting, yet fascinating food descriptions I've ever heard. And, to this day, I still think of him whenever I bite into a brat.

Look at the Legs on That Girl!

Day 74: Saturday, August 16
Weather: Heavy rain
Distance: 60 miles
Route: Elroy, Wisconsin, to Montello, Wisconsin

The sky looked ominous, but we weren't going to stay another night at the Grouchy Man Motel. We packed up and went for breakfast—another café where people watching was at its finest. We observed the happenings from our corner table. One man spoke at full volume, his voice booming through the restaurant and probably out into the street. His conversation was impossible to block. The guy was one of those people, like the ones on trains, planes, and public places, who argue with their mates and divulge intimate details about their lives, oblivious that they are airing dirty laundry to everyone within earshot.

The restaurant filled up with more loud people. It was a loud people convention. We were intrigued. The noise level rose to an undecipherable din. When I aimed my attention toward a nearby booth I could make out a few words: underwear, pissed, kids, a-hole, and toenails. I turned my head to another booth and got an earful: sleazebag, carburetor, left the scene, and beat the shit out of ....

Next, our attention shifted to the door. A rotund woman, dressed head to toe in pink spandex, had arrived and knew everyone. She moved from table to table, sharing the news. Loudly, of course. Everyone stopped to listen. Her 16-year-old daughter had been knocked up by a local bum. Her no-good, jackwad of a husband had left her for a cousin (not sure if she meant his or hers), and she'd just lost her job.

One elderly woman put her head in her hands and said, "Ohhh," as if to say, "Her problems overwhelm me." The whole restaurant nodded in agreement. Including us. I had unconsciously stopped eating, staring so intently my mouth flapped open in awe at the scene before us. Clark noticed my stupor and focused his own stare on me. When I realized it, we laughed hysterically until we noticed our voices were the only ones echoing through the room. Everyone's attention was on us. No one moved. Only their eyes darted back and forth. They had finally noticed the interlopers!

The sky had grown darker, and although we weren't too anxious to head out into the imminent storm we needed to leave the cafe before we embarrassed ourselves any further.

Following a tip from some locals the night before, we started our ride on a beautiful back road, heading toward the town of Mauston. We encountered a San Francisco-steep hill a few miles later. Although we were huffing and puffing, we got to the top quickly. On hills like this, I created my own switchbacks, riding in serpentine fashion, back and forth. This allowed me to pedal up steep slopes without falling off my bike from going too slowly.

Unfortunately, the quick victory to the top was overshadowed by the weather taking a turn. Thunder cracked, and the clouds grew darker. The sky opened up and moments later we were soaked to the bone and still had 10 miles to the nearest town. Our efforts turned to pedaling as fast as we could. Arriving in Mauston, we settled our dripping bikes under an awning of the first tavern we saw and ducked inside for potato-cheese soup and a few beers.

After lunch, the waitress, a big Germanic woman, loud but friendly, struck up a conversation using a flat Midwestern cadence like in the movie *Fargo*.

"Well, where ya goin'?" she asked, putting a strong accent on the "o."

"Portland, Maine," I responded.

"Oh, yaaaaaahh? Well, where ya comin' from den?" she continued.

"Portland, Oregon," I said.

"Oh, yaaaaah? How's that goin' for ya?"

~

I noticed my own Wisconsin/Midwest inflection gaining strength as we traveled farther east into the state. It came naturally, as if I'd never left. Clark noticed the change in my speech pattern, too, and loved listening to me interact with people from the "homeland." He enjoyed the subtle linguistic changes and accents we encountered all across the country. Dialectic transitions also proved another way to mark our progress from west to east.

~

Things got worse when we hit Highway 82. The traffic was as heavy as the rain. Imagine rush hour combined with a Category 3 storm.

We crossed the Wisconsin River in a deluge and struggled to see the road. It seemed the rain would never stop. But it did. Nearly 15 miles later in Oxford, the sun peeked through the clouds. The warmth felt good on our backs, and, despite being tired, wet, muddy, hungry, and thirsty, we'd covered a lot of miles. A bench in the town center called our names. It felt good to stretch and soak up the sun.

Benches have always held special meaning for us. Early in our courtship, on a sunny afternoon, we took a spot on a park bench talking, laughing, and staring into each other's eyes—like lovers do. Clark hugged me close and gave me a playful peck on the cheek. I smiled and looked directly in his eyes, and without thinking we got lost in a kiss. We were oblivious to everything but ourselves, until … we literally fell off the bench.

Hitting the ground jolted us back to reality. Oh, yeah. We're in public, acting like silly teenagers. Splayed on the grass, in hysterics. After collecting ourselves and repositioning on the bench, the laughing started again when we discovered a middle-aged couple had seen the whole thing.

~

The traffic grew heavier and the drivers more rude. They sped past, barely leaving us room to ride. A trucker zoomed by, forcing us off the shoulder and into the bumpy grass. Another truck's wheels spit pellets of dirt and stones in our faces, and the trailer careened dangerously close to our bikes.

That's what scared me the most—trucks kicking up rocks and taking out an eye, or worse. We were lucky we didn't suffer any serious damage during the trip.

~

At long last, Montello was ours. What a relief. We decided to play our favorite game, "Divide and Conquer." We set off in two different directions and scoured the town for a room but had no luck. Everything was booked for "Father Marquette Days." He was a French missionary and explorer, one-half of the historic Marquette–Joliet expedition team, and best known as the first European to see and map the northern portion of the Mississippi River.

Change of plans. Eat first, then figure out where to sleep. Clark had a hankering for dinner. No argument from me. We made friends with a bartender who graciously checked a few accommodations for us. Even the campgrounds were full. We hinted about staying at his house, but that idea fell on deaf ears. A waitress soon took his attention away, and we were left to solve our own problems.

"Well, you said you wanted an adventure," Clark said calmly, "Here it is."

He was right. I was the one who talked about the wonders of adventure, how it keeps you young and your life interesting. So, there it was—a travel adventure (or opportunity, as I like to think of it) staring us in the face.

Our outlook changed.

"Hey," Clark suddenly remembered. "I think I saw a campground sign just outside of town. Should we check that out first?"

~

The campground was larger than expected and teemed with activity. Best of all, they had room for us. Kids ran wild, loud music boomed, and parents let loose, socializing, drinking, and laughing.

We set up camp, spread our belongings to dry, and rode around to get the lay of the land. As we explored, a young man shouted, "Hey, bike people, where are you going?"

I stopped politely and pulled over, ready to answer him from the road. To my absolute horror, he screamed and pointed, "Wow! Look at the legs on this girl!"

And, it didn't stop there. The commentary got louder, drawing more people near to get a gander at my exposed flesh.

"How did you get legs like that?"

"Can you believe those things…?"

"She's got the thickest legs I've ever seen!"

"You're like Super Woman!"

It's entirely possible the whole state heard him.

My face went beyond red. I think the young man may have been trying to say my legs were muscular, because I didn't pick up any animosity. But, his intentions didn't really matter. Every eye zoned straight in on my calves and thighs. There was nowhere to hide, and I couldn't melt into the crowd. All I could do was stand there feeling humiliated.

And where was Clark during this debacle? He had cycled ahead to the camp store before he realized I'd stopped; he'd missed the entire embarrassing experience.

I retreated to the tent to read, soon getting lost in my book. Clark went for a beer, returning just after dark. Before long, we were sleeping blissfully, even though the rowdiness outside the tent continued into the wee hours. It was a comforting mix of sounds, almost like white noise. We slept better there than anywhere else during the trip.

WEEK 12

How to Dislodge a Cockroach from a Human Ear

  Day 75: Sunday, August 17
  Weather: Cold and heavy rain
  Distance: 15 miles
  Route: Montello, Wisconsin, to Princeton, Wisconsin

A quiet, cold drizzle tapped on the tent. The campground was so silent we almost forgot where we were.

  At breakfast, a pair of Germans, also riding the trails of Wisconsin, invited us to sit with them. A lively conversation ensued. I said very little, as I don't speak German, but enjoyed the sound of the language and watching them connect so fluidly. Clark's ability to communicate in other tongues was astonishing.

~

  The temperature dropped 10 degrees. A hard rain made matters worse, and Highway 23 almost certainly would be packed on a busy summer Sunday. A challenging 10 miles to Princeton lay ahead. The ride was horrendous—slippery and harrowing. I was happy to make it to town in one piece. Clark filled our tires at the gas station. I wondered aloud if we should spend the night. The man on the other side of the air pump popped his head around and said, "Excuse me for sounding nosy, but my neighbor owns a B&B and they might have room. Should I call him for you?"

"Sure, that would be great," Clark said with startled excitement.

It was a pricey place, but he justified spending the money this way: "It includes breakfast, so that's actually a savings."

"Good point," I concurred, not needing any more convincing.

We were treated like royalty from the moment the owners opened the door. They invited us to park our bikes in their garage and throw our wet clothes in the wash, then showed us to a lovely room. After rinsing mud and crud off in the shower, Clark went to explore the town and get a beer. I took a much-needed bath and spent quiet time reading.

To our surprise, the B&B hosts invited us to join them for dinner. Clark was so thrilled he headed downstairs to socialize before me. I guess he was ecstatic about a home-cooked meal. Funny, breaking the ice is usually my department. I appeared downstairs a few minutes later and found Clark entrenched in conversation. The host offered red or white wine. I chose red, because I always do. On the menu: salad, cheddar bacon burgers, green beans, potatoes, and the best sugar cookies I've ever eaten. And more wine.

The four of us got along well, with the conversation veering from the important facts of life to the best way to dislodge a cockroach from the human ear: If the bug is alive, pour a tiny amount of vegetable oil into the ear to suffocate it. If the bug is dead, flush it out with warm water. Never stick tweezers, cotton swabs, or other pointy objects into the ear, because (gross) they can push the bug further toward the eardrum, which could cause injury and hearing loss.

We all agreed that men fall asleep faster than women.

As Clark and I snuggled in to bed for the night, we congratulated ourselves for staying. Even though we only covered 15 miles, the cost of the B&B was far less than we originally figured since it included dinner, breakfast, laundry, early check-in, and new friends.

We talked until sleep overtook us—him before me, of course.

You Can Go PP If You Want

>Day 76:   Monday, August 18
>Weather: Overcast, but cool and pleasant
>Distance: 43 miles
>Route: Princeton, Wisconsin, to Fond du Lac, Wisconsin

Breakfast at the B&B was delicious, but we had to sit with an extremely dull couple and their two annoying, whiny, twitchy kids. The parents barely spoke, preferring to grunt and point with their forks when they wanted us to pass food in their direction. No thanks when we did. The family gorged then left without a word.

We longed for our host-friends to sit down and join us for a chat, but they were too busy tending to other guests. The hostess remembered us yearning for sweet corn and specially prepared some for us. We gobbled down a couple ears apiece and sat there extra long sucking the sweetness from the cobs. Not your conventional breakfast fare, but we loved it.

Thinking the local paper would be interested in our trip, the hosts set up an interview. After breakfast, the reporter paid us a visit. The questions were the same as those asked all across the country. We'd had a lot of practice, so the Q&A went smoothly. The reporter even let me hide my legs behind my bike before taking photos.

~

We traveled back roads to avoid a repeat of the previous day's busy route. Highways D, K, A, and KK took us around Green Lake, the deepest inland lake in Wisconsin. At one point during our scenic ride, the urge to pee hit us. We stopped and waited for a gap between cars before diving into thinly veiled bushes to do our business. We managed it without getting busted, but 30 seconds after getting back on our bikes we passed a big, clean public restroom with a wonderful view of the lake. Another classic case of "Murphy's Law."

~

Many rural Wisconsin roads are designated with letters instead of numbers. At a junction, we asked a young woman which way to go. She innocently recommended a shortcut, "You can go PP if you want."

Clark responded, "Ooh, oui oui!"

The girl stared at Clark a moment and then we all burst out laughing.

~

Clark clocked us at 28 mph, a good clip for us. The speed likely influenced by our food deprivation. Motivation always came down to food.

We stopped in Rosendale, a tiny dot of a town with a population under 1,000. The village is known for its strict enforcement of the speed limit. We heard people sell T-shirts declaring "Rosendale: That's the ticket!"

~

A new record: 43 miles in less than three hours, including stops, and we were in Fond du Lac. Visions of bratwurst danced in our heads, but first we had to find accommodations.

~

A man with a thick beard and commanding voice shouted out his car window, "Hey, where are you going?"

We answered. He screeched to a halt. Flattered by his interest in our trip, we talked for over an hour. It's amazing how riding bikes opened up easy friendships and lines of communication that never seemed to happen when traveling by car.

The lure of brats was powerful. I think we could smell them in the air. No kidding. We settled on a motel in close proximity to the brats, and then it was time for our much-anticipated bratwurst dinner, a delicacy I enjoyed often growing up. Clark was salivating. He was a Wisconsin brat virgin.

The restaurant was dark inside, which enhanced its interpretation of Old World interior design. The waitstaff wore what appeared to be Halloween costumes to match the era. All good fun. The place was packed with families and friends out on the town, but it didn't take long to be seated.

Heavenly, meaty scents wafted in the air. We eyeballed thick prime rib sandwiches and lusted after cheese-draped bowls of French onion soup. Sensory overload. We must have said "Mmmmmm…" a dozen times.

When our brats arrived we savored them with our eyes first, then sniffed in deeply. I watched as Clark raised the sausage mouthward. Our eyes met briefly as he bit into the brat. Juice squirted from two sides, just as brats do. A smile spread across Clark's face. It was a good day.

The Green, Green Grass of Home

Day 77: Tuesday, August 19
Weather: Gray skies with light sprinkles
Distance: 54 miles
Route: Fond du Lac, Wisconsin, to Dad's house in Sheboygan, Wisconsin

Clark awoke in a philosophical mood, asking the age-old questions: What's really important in life? And how do you achieve it? Answers are easy to contemplate since "thinking time" is plentiful when you're on a bike all day.

"It's about freedom and peace," Clark said seriously. "That's what brings happiness for me. Not battling for a better job, more money, or power. Our trip is ultimate freedom. We can go anywhere we want and change directions on a whim. We stay where we want, eat what we want, and spend our days the way we want. We determine the route, the miles, when to start, and when to stop."

"Freedom is priceless," I agreed. "But, we couldn't have done this trip without first earning the money. The only way to buy a few months of freedom, if you're not born into wealth or win the lottery, is to work and save."

We were quiet a moment, Clark drifting off in his own thoughts, me envisioning the balance of life.

It had always been one end of the spectrum or the other for us. Time or money: Free time with just enough to get by or working under mountains of pressure, earning well but having minimal downtime.

"I want peace in my life. Fewer possessions and obligations," Clark said, breaking the silence.

I agreed. His philosophy made sense as a way to stay sane while moving toward a simpler existence. The details of exactly how to get there were still TBD.

> The people we spoke with during our trip used the word "freedom" with a sense of personal yearning. They wanted what we had. Many in the world lack freedom—freedom to be who they really are and do what they want most. Our trip allowed us to be free spirits. We hoped others would follow suit to find their personal freedom, whatever their journey may be. If you really want to do something, no matter what it is, it's worth the effort to find a way to make it happen. It's part of what gives life meaning.

We tried to follow the map out of the city, but the many twists, turns, and name changes made it a challenge. Even Clark, the human GPS, was confused. As we stopped to consult our map for the umpteenth time, a 50-ish guy noticed our confusion and offered to help. It was hard to concentrate on what he was saying due to his expansive handlebar mustache. The waxed curlicues stuck out four inches on each side and bobbed up and down with every word he spoke.

"Three blocks down … (twitch, twitch, twitch)."

I was mesmerized and repelled. I wanted to grab my scissors and snip off his silly 'stache.

Clark thought it was cool. But, I couldn't help thinking if he was my husband I'd get him drunk and cut that thing off as soon as he fell asleep. In the morning, I'd claim he'd done it himself while under the influence.

How odd that I can take something so unimportant and weave a diabolical plot for correcting it. Clark should watch himself.

Mustache Man had no sense of my evil plans and invited us to stay at his home that evening. Fortunately for him, I was almost home.

~

The ride was exhilarating! Everything was summer green, green, green. Rolling hills, long stretches of crops, big red barns, clear blue lakes, and lots of dairy cows. Some people find the smell of farm fields a bit unpleasant. Not me. I think of it as earthy and life giving. Of course, I didn't actually grow up on a farm, but lots of my friends did. So, through osmosis, it's in my blood.

We pedaled slowly through a teeny-tiny village one street long and had a moment of Zen when church bells chimed. The booming clangs reverberated against our bodies as the late-morning hour was marked one rapturous "bong-g-g-g-g-g" at a time.

~

To provide Clark with a uniquely Wisconsin experience, I insisted we stop at a cheese factory I knew lay directly in our path. The term "factory" is a misnomer in this instance. Yes, there are some machines used, but traditional cheese making is a very hands-on craft proudly passed from generation to generation.

We stopped where cheese had been the family business for four generations. Clark's engaging personality and knowledge of food once again resulted in special treatment. While giving us a tour, the owner shared company history, introduced us around, and took us through the cheese-making process. Along the way, the patriarch cut chunks of aging cheddar from a big block for us to sample.

Clark described the cheese as, "Firm, sharp, and slightly earthy."

Muffled giggles erupted from two of the younger kids.

Watching the family working together in harmony was inspiring. No doubt the work is hard and hours long.

"This is our heritage," the man explained. "We don't think of it as a series of dreadful chores. We hope what we're doing today is nurtured and continued for all generations that follow."

~

We took Old Plank Road Trail east, paralleling Highway 23. The 17-mile trail was created for bicyclists, runners, walkers, horseback riders, skaters, moped riders, cross-country skiers, and snowmobilers. The western trailhead starts in the Kettle Moraine Forest in Greenbush, a place of fond childhood memories. The picturesque town is home to the historic Old Wade House, one of the earliest stagecoach inns in Wisconsin; it also features a blacksmith shop, carriage museum, and sawmill. It's a fascinating step back into time.

While pedaling through Plymouth, I told Clark about "Antoinette." She lives there year-round, is 20 feet tall, and weighs 1,000 pounds. Antoinette is a giant metal cow erected during the city's centennial celebration in 1977 to honor the local dairy industry. More specifically, she's a black and white Holstein with fabulous udders. It would have been fun to make that detour, but we were anxious to see my Dad.

Pedal. Pedal. Pedal.

Kohler—as in *the* Kohler Company, the plumbing fixture, furniture, tile, stone, hospitality, and world-class golf destination giant—is one town away from home. The Village of Kohler (note the capital "V") was incorporated in 1912, by the son of the Kohler Company founder and developed as a planned garden/industrial community. Frederick Law Olmsted, the renowned landscape architect who designed New York's Central Park and the Biltmore Estate's grounds, helped with the 50-year master plan. Over 100 years later, there is a continuing emphasis on natural and historic preservation. Sometimes holding onto the past is a good thing.

~

The ride on Old Plank Trail was nothing short of perfection—truly one of the nicest routes on the trip, and not just because I was back in my old stomping grounds. We encountered a variety of gentle ups and downs, twists and turns, and a view clear and open for miles.

A nostalgic daze swept over me when we finally rolled into Sheboygan. Giddy anticipation suddenly transformed into disorientation. We were on a road I'd traveled many times as a kid, but it looked different. Gone were the open fields, now replaced by two-story apartment buildings and new businesses. Coming in from the west on a bike was a lot different than arriving from the south (Milwaukee airport) in a car.

Everything looked smaller than I remembered. Houses, streets, schools, and stores seemed tiny in comparison to my memories. I felt like a giant returning home to Lilliput. I stopped to get my bearings. Clark pulled up beside me.

Just as I opened my mouth to discuss Lilliput, a man about my age pulled his car over and asked if we needed help or directions.

"No. We're alright," I answered. "Just taking in the changes."

He smiled, turning his gaze toward our bikes inquisitively. That was all it took to knock me back from the past to the present. Suddenly, I felt the urge to blurt out the whole trip story to this stranger. And I did, not pausing for a good 10 minutes. I rambled on, talking non-stop about traveling cross country, growing up in Sheboygan, the fact that my Dad still lived in town, and we were on our way there now. That was it. Everything was out and I abruptly stopped talking.

Clark and the man stared at me intently without saying a word, processing the apparent ravings of a lunatic. They were either trying to digest the last bits of my lengthy monolog or politely waiting for me to get a second wind and start babbling again.

A look of amused recognition crossed the stranger's face.

"I know who you are and your Dad, too," he said with a grin.

Uh, oh. This might be awkward. I searched his face, imagining him as a pimply faced teen, but nothing rang a bell.

Had we dated? I didn't think so. Did I say something unforgivably mean to him in junior high? Not my style. Maybe he knew me from my perky little cheerleader days. Where did THAT girl go?

I decided to lie. Shame on me.

"Oh, yeah," I said brightly. "You look familiar."

This seemed to please the stranger, so he mentioned his name.

"Of course!" I responded, lying my ass off. "It's so good to see you again."

Terrified my deception would soon be discovered, I concocted another fib that we were running late and needed to shove off.

I waved furiously as my "old friend" drove away.

"Bye!" I called out. "Take care … see ya … whoever you are… ."

Clark was flabbergasted when I confessed my sin. Guess I'm a better fibber than I thought.

I realized Dad and his wife Mary wouldn't be home yet, so we had some time to kill. The perfect place for a cold brew was an old tavern hangout, where the beer was always 25 cents. Unfortunately, it was gone. That felt weird. It had been there forever. My favorite burger joint was gone, too. They served a mean butter burger in the days before we all worried about gluten and cholesterol. I tried not to show my disappointment as we pedaled along in search of a back-up bar.

We settled on a typical Midwestern corner bar, one that sits in the middle of a residential neighborhood. There were a few old-timers sitting on brown vinyl barstools shooting the breeze, engrossed in a card game. They didn't look up when we came in. The bartender acknowledged us with a slight nod. Some 1950s girl group tune was blaring from the Wurlitzer jukebox and a now-vintage Hamm's Beer clock glowed from the back wall. It looked exactly like all the other corner bars I'd seen. The smell was even the same.

We slid into a curved booth, our legs gluing themselves to the plastic seat. There was no menu, but we could see the taps from our position. We yelled our order to the bartender when we realized he wasn't going to move from his perch. Old Milwaukee, Blatz, Schlitz, and Leinenkugel (or "Leinie," as the locals call it). I wanted Clark to get the full corner bar experience. This also included an immersion into the famous Wisconsin accent.

We sipped our beer and listened to the codgers communicate in their native habitat. Their voices rising and falling, accents so thick you had to listen carefully to figure out that they were speaking English and not German or some Scandinavian dialect.

When I took a job in radio broadcasting, I'd worked hard to rid myself of the accent, but found the sounds of their voices comforting.

It was time to go home. Mildly sedated by the beer, we took a familiar route up North Avenue, heading east toward Lake Michigan. We passed my junior and senior high schools and made a detour through the gates of the old cemetery. My friends and I walked through that cemetery on our way to school for six years, through rain, sleet, and mounds of snow. We never thought it was scary, simply a time-saving path to school. We rolled by my friend Betty's house, then Ebo's two-story home. Memories came flooding back. A lump formed in my throat. I could see my house.

Dad was waiting in the yard and rushed toward us, arms wide in welcome. We hugged and laughed. He was a huge supporter of the trip and never doubted for a moment we would make it. Dad and

Clark unpacked the bikes while I wandered through the house, going room to room, touching the familiar and noting the new. I sat in my old bedroom, now a guest room, and closed my eyes. Just like earlier impressions, the house seemed smaller than I remembered. No. Cozy. *Cozy* was the right word.

I looked out the open windows. The trees were bigger and vegetation more lush. I could smell flowers, too. Maybe roses. And someone was grilling something meaty. Kids were playing down the street, just as I had. To the right was the blue–gray expanse of Lake Michigan, so large you couldn't see the distant shore even on a clear day. I was home.

My introspective trip down memory lane was sharply interrupted by a burst of laughter. It was Clark and Dad male-bonding in the backyard. I watched them for a few moments, my two favorite guys.

Mary arrived home minutes later. We showered her with hugs and hellos, then shared dinner preparations for a poolside BBQ. Dad fired up the grill and popped a bottle of wine. I shucked corn and set the table. Clark helped Mary skewer chicken kabobs and made a salad. Clark looked relaxed and happy as he entertained everyone with stories from the road. I felt myself relaxing, too.

> Dad's house was one of our designated "friendly outposts." Again, we were shocked by the amount of mail waiting for us from family and friends. It was like Christmas morning! We'd also forgotten about the box we mailed ourselves before starting the trip. It contained vital items, like sundries and fresh clothes.

Memory Lane and Butter Burgers

Day 78-80:   Wednesday to Friday, August 20–22
Weather: Rain off and on, mostly on
Distance: Rest days
Route: Never left Sheboygan

We slept late and woke happy after registering where we were. The next few days were spent enjoying long chats, leisurely meals, poring through photo albums, and exploring the area. I took Clark on several walking tours of the neighborhood, admiring beautiful brick homes and greeting folks along the way. I divulged more childhood history as we hiked the short, wooded trail behind my house to Lake Michigan, then walked a mile to Vollrath Park along the sandy beach.

The park was a kid's vision of paradise when I was growing up, with its big playground full of swings, slides, and merry-go-rounds. Tennis in the summer, ice skating in the winter, a pond brimming with all kinds of fish and birds. There used to be a small zoo, but it's long gone now. I remember feeding the deer and bunnies and watching the bears emerge from their cave to swim in the pool. My favorite creature was named Bonnie. She was a massive buffalo, with big brown eyes and a gentle personality.

Then there's the "bowl," a large, manmade amphitheater of cascading grassy hills created in 1930. In the summertime, we rolled ourselves down the hills, spinning wildly to the bottom, where we ended up in a giggling, dizzy heap. In the dead of winter, we bundled up and whizzed down the slopes on wooden toboggans and silver flying saucers. When it was time to graduate, seniors from both high schools sat in rows of chairs lining the bottom of the bowl while our families cheered from the hills.

~

We had lunch at an old favorite, The Charcoal Inn, which boasts the honor of a favorable mention in *The New York Times*. We had butter burgers on sturdy hard rolls, fries, and vanilla malts made with Wisconsin ice cream. I felt 16 again!

~

I had time alone with my Dad during our stay. This gave me the chance to remind him how much he's loved. The night before we left,

Dad and I took a trip to the grocery store. Because neither of us cooks much, thanks to our mates, we were like two unsupervised kids in the aisles.

"Ooooh, this looks good." Into the cart—plunk.

"How about this?" Plunk.

"A dozen cookies?" Gentle plunk so as to not break them.

"Dad, I haven't had these in years!" Basket!

"I guess we should pick up a couple of these to go along with those." Plunk, plunk.

We came home with five bulging bags of groceries, even though our task was defined by a very small grocery list. Clark and Mary laughed as we hustled all the goodies into the kitchen.

Time to eat.

Brats were prepared Wisconsin style: boiled in onions, butter, and beer before grilling. We had sweet corn, potato salad, lots of seasonal fruits and vegetables, and plenty of wine. As if this wasn't a feast in itself, we continued the gluttony with ice cream and cookies, then justified this behavior by saying we were not only celebrating but also fortifying ourselves for tomorrow's journey.

Turtle Woman

Day 81:	Saturday, August 23
Weather:	Sunny and warm
Distance:	An hour by car, 5 hours by ferry, and 3 or 4 miles around town
Route:	Sheboygan, Wisconsin, to Ludington, Michigan

We spent a busy morning getting ready to leave and prepping the bikes for another month of riding. I had to replace my rear tire because the tread was almost worn off, no doubt due to the weight on the back of the bike—some from the bags and supplies and some from my body weight.

It was also time to emotionally gear up. It's a sad, empty feeling whenever you say goodbye to people you love. It would be a rough day, so I steeled my soul.

Even though Clark wasn't feeling tip-top (must have been that huge dinner), it was time to move on. We had concerns about getting over the Adirondack, White, and Green Mountains to the east. An early, snowy season was predicted, and we didn't want to put chains on our tires to get over the mountains.

We decided to cross Lake Michigan by ferry to avoid the large cities of Milwaukee and Chicago. Dad and Mary drove us to the boat ramp in Manitowoc where we would take the *S.S. Badger* to Ludington, Michigan. We snapped a few final pictures and said teary goodbyes. Then we realized Sheboygan was our last "friendly outpost." We had no more safety nets to look forward to as we pedaled eastward.

~

Cyclists were quickly waved past vehicles and sent to a special area on the ferry. We strapped our bikes to the wall to prevent them from toppling. I was protective of my silver steed and spent extra time making sure it was secure. Clark casually looped a couple straps around his bike and headed upstairs to get a seat. I felt an overwhelming sadness as the ferry chugged away and familiar shores disappeared from view.

Mary had packed us a healthy lunch, so all we had to do was sit back and enjoy the show—people watching, that is. A group of square dancers, dressed in their finest matching husband-and-wife square dancing outfits, paraded around the deck as if royalty. It was a whole lotta crinoline and flounce.

We spotted a 400-pound woman with a little, skinny man. He followed her every action, almost like a child, copying her move for move. She read the paper. He read the paper. She crossed her legs. He crossed his legs. He would watch and mimic, looking for approval after each sequence was complete. It looked like a creepy game of "Mirror Me."

We turned our attention to a traveler we dubbed "Turtle Woman." She was eating her sandwich in a most peculiar way. After taking an enormous bite, with half the food hanging from her face, she would chew from right to left in turtle-like fashion. Stretching her neck as she swallowed the big load helped reinforce the effect.

A couple of French Canadian sisters, on a motorcycle trip, kept us company for a while. We felt a special connection to them because we all traveled on two wheels. Their strong French accents amused us, especially when they mentioned a stop in Yellowstone to see "zee geezers."

A chilly wind whipped up as the evening wore on, and threatening clouds darkened the sky. The excursion took four hours, and somewhere in the middle of Lake Michigan we had crossed into our final time zone: EST. We could see lights dotting the horizon as we came within a few miles of shore.

People milled about, ready to take their leave, gathering belongings, heading back to their cars. They would wait in a line to leave while we effortlessly untethered our bikes, disembarked, and rode west, never to see Turtle Woman, Mirror-Me Boy, or the square dancing troupe again.

It was almost 7 p.m., and the weather looked menacing. Knowing the campground was well out of town, and with Clark still feeling queasy, we chose to stay at a warm, dry hotel. The elderly front desk person was unpleasant. She begrudgingly told us to park our bikes in the secure storage area. We were happy the room was locked, but when we needed to access our bike bags later it was a big damn deal. The old biddy was so rude she even huffed at us. She probably thought we were riff-raff. On any other day, we would have left in disgust. But, we were in no mood for a tussle.

~

We settled into our fabulous (not really) accommodations, then set out in search of dinner. Our initial sour experience turned around when we left the hotel. Despite the weather, downtown Ludington had a vibrant energy. People were out and about, celebrating the weekend. Strains of music filtered through the air and muffled laughter spilled from every doorway.

Clark nosed out a great place for dinner, right on the water. The wait was nearly two hours, but the time flew by when we made some new buddies, Wisconsin natives celebrating a friend's birthday. Coincidentally, they had also come over on the *Badger* and were staying at the same hotel. The conversation started with hilarious comparisons of check-in encounters. We shared a couple rounds of drinks, and eventually the conversation wound its way to our trip. Their enthusiastic interest spurred us on to share the more "interesting" tales, including Beige Edna, Turtle Woman, and Chuckles the Clown.

WEEK 13

At a Crossroads with No Clue

    Day 82:   Sunday, August 24
    Weather: Hard rain in the morning, a misty/sunny afternoon, and rain again at night
    Distance: 35 miles
    Route: Ludington, Michigan, to Manistee, Michigan

Time for a big decision: which route to take? During the trip's early days, we only looked ahead to Wisconsin and stopped studying the map east of Lake Michigan. Maybe we subconsciously thought we'd never make it that far. There'd be plenty of time to figure everything out. Of course, that never happened—so here we were at a major crossroad without a clue.

The Great Lakes region is so large, with so many bodies of water, there's no simple way around them. The most direct route was due east, but that meant traveling through or near Detroit. Too big and busy. The other option was to head north around the Great Lakes, up into Canada and back down into the United States. This route would be significantly longer, but probably safer.

Two cups of coffee later, we chose Canada.

By noon, we had directions for back roads out of town and were sailing along well-paved, gently undulating byways. As if being lulled into a hypnotic trance, we rolled effortlessly up and down the hills and valleys, feeling like babies rocking in a cradle. Our strong legs pumped in unison, while enticing glimpses of the lake blinked through the trees and birds sang us a soothing lullaby. This was the rhythm of the ride.

~

We stopped to eat Mary's leftovers at a tiny, out-of-the-way park near Manistee. The softly sloping hills were brilliant green with breathtaking views of an unusually blue and calm Lake Michigan. The intoxicating combination of the relaxing ride, full tummies, and pleasant break made us lazy.

We rode a few miles into town and decided it was a fine place to spend the night, even though our mile count was only 32. Tomorrow, we promised each other, we'd cover more ground. Our rationalization: the challenge of getting back into the swing of long-haul cycling when we'd been eating, drinking, and partying for days. You have to work up to it slowly.

After settling into our motel, we walked into downtown Manistee. "Delightful" would be a good word to describe our impression. We strolled along the waterfront, admiring the well-preserved buildings, imagining what life was like back in the glory days. We watched a drawbridge cranking its massive arms open wide to let a ship travel through and felt the deep steel-on-steel reverberations. Again, we marveled at how an experience is so much more interesting when you're on foot or on a bike versus speeding by in a vehicle.

~

Dinner was mediocre. Not terrible, not good, just okay. Clark, the consummate foodie, was reminded of a funny line from a Billy Crystal film, and said sarcastically, "Food's brown, hot, and plenty of it!"

> When food is created from scratch—with fresh ingredients and a little love—it can take you all kinds of places. For many, including myself, warm, fuzzy memories of childhood spring forward, conjuring recollections of afternoons sitting in Mom's kitchen and chatting while dinner was cooking. It's easy to summon familiar aromas when pleasurable feelings from the past bubble to the surface.
>
> Most people have fond memories of Grandma's cookies, Dad's fried chicken, neighbor John's special spaghetti sauce, or that one thing at a restaurant you could never recreate at home. I've seen people tear up when they eat good food, reminded of loved ones far away or long since gone. Passing recipes down through the generations is one way of sharing our history and making us feel loved and connected to one another. Yes, eating well is more than filling our stomachs; it's also about family, friends, love, and life.

One Pedal at a Time

Day 83: Monday, August 25
Weather: Partly cloudy, turning into clear skies late in the day
Distance: 36 hilly miles
Route: Manistee, Michigan, to Alberta, Michigan

We slept in later than usual, pulling the covers over our heads, rolling over, trying to ignore the new day—no doubt still in denial about getting back on the road and having to exercise again.

We ran into "real" cyclists once in a while. They were up and on the road early in the morning, excited to start the day. We usually slept in late, ate a big breakfast, and lollygagged as much as possible. We often didn't start riding until late morning and, even then, stopped a lot, chatted with anyone interested, and never missed lunch or an opportunity for a snack.

We were not "by-the-book" cyclists, but then again there must be more than one book. I figure you can live your life, your dream vacation, or your weekend the way you choose. You can create your journey with your own rules, your own way. No right. No wrong. No missed meals. The world is more satisfying when you make your own path, no matter where you're traveling—across country or through life.

~

We started our ride along Highway 110, outside of Manistee, one of the most beautiful roads on the trip. Gently rolling hills, minimal traffic, and a huge shoulder are a cyclist's dream. The road meandered along Lake Michigan, passing many sprawling, well-kept homes. Most appeared to be summer places, where we imagined people dressed in all white, playing croquet and sipping drinks served on silver trays. This, of course, was all fiction, but the thought started us dreaming about retiring there.

The next stop was the small town of Oneckema. We guzzled orange juice and contemplated staying the night, partially because the town was cute, but mostly because we liked the name and the various ways we tried to pronounce it (Oh-Neck-key-ma, Oh-neck-a-ma, Ohney-keyma, to name a few).

The air felt heavy. Rain approaching. We could have talked ourselves into staying but felt strong and in the mood to ride, so we forged ahead. A little farther north, in Arcadia, we had a chance encounter with a long-time sport fisherman. It was hard to determine his age or even guess the decade. His face was deeply crevassed with wrinkles, but brown eyes twinkled under hooded lids. The man's body was strong and sturdy, his leathery hands lined with blue–green veins.

He told stories about fishing all the Great Lakes and the "Big One" that got away. We must have charmed him sufficiently because he offered to take us fishing. Tempting, but we resisted and bid our friend goodbye.

We had a steep climb ahead of us. Sometimes, doomsday types gave us dire warnings about challenging hills to come, spawning doubts about our ability to handle them. Other times, people encouraged us by bringing up the positives—a rewarding (sometimes exaggerated) view at the summit or a great ride back down. For us, ignorance was usually bliss. If we spent time worrying about steep roads, we ran the risk of starting the ride already defeated.

> Our minds are powerful organs, and, as most people understand, much of what we do can be accomplished more effectively by having the right attitude. The success of a trip like this, barring accidents or any serious health issues, is determined between your ears. So, I preferred to start a climb without knowing anything. (Sort of like an ostrich, but different.) That way, you take it as it comes, one pedal at a time.

The climb was indeed a challenge; estimates were an 8% grade or more for the first half mile. Clark chose the fast track and lumbered up the hill steadily. I was behind, as usual, going at a slow, but sure, turtle's pace. When I laboriously rounded the hilltop, Clark and a group of strangers clapped and cheered for those final exhausting pedals. He had already made friends with a group of RV travelers impressed with our journey. One appeared, as if by magic, with two big bowls of strawberry ice cream. The treat didn't last long.

After parting ways, we tackled another climb, this one by foot. Our challenge was a long stairway up to a lookout atop the highest point on Lake Michigan. We raced up the stairs with sugared-up energy. It felt good leaving the bikes behind for a moment. The view was spectacular and well worth the physical effort. The vast lake fringed by trees reminded us of Oregon's coast and brought a touch of homesickness that hit like a blast of cold air. We walked back down in melancholy silence and rode on.

~

The last climb of the day, another grueling upward stretch, didn't feel quite as daunting as when we started the trip. We breathed deep and pushed hard, but not to the point of total exhaustion. What goes up, must come down, and so we did, landing in the little town of Alberta. Our campground was a big, open field with a bunch of decrepit motor homes parked in it. Some looked abandoned. Psychologically and physically, we were ready to stop, so found ourselves an out-of-the-way spot at the edge of the field big enough for a tent.

A warm shower and dinner made a big difference in our mental health. Plus, tucking ourselves into sleeping bags seemed like the best idea in the world.

Snap, Snap, Snap

Day 84: Tuesday, August 26
Weather: Warm and clear
Distance: 55 miles
Route: Alberta, Michigan, to Traverse City, Michigan

We stood outside the restaurant like hungry sentries at 7:45 a.m., a full 15 minutes before the doors opened. That was a first. We gobbled our breakfast fast and furious. Satiated, we returned to camp to pack our gear, which was still wet and heavy with dew. Massive drops dripped from the tent tarp and bike bags. Our clothes and sleeping bags inside the tent were damp. The drying process would slow our departure.

A couple of (nosy) camp neighbors came over to supposedly say "hi" and then proceeded to watch everything we did with an unnerving intensity. Normally, we enjoyed interacting with curious folks, but these strangers invaded our personal space like we hadn't encountered before. They stood close, blocking us as we tried to go about our morning routine. They asked a million questions, didn't wait for answers, and snapped pictures from every angle. People can be very strange.

"Are these your bikes?" *Snap Snap*

"Is that all your gear?"

"How much money do you carry?"

"Is there someone following you in a car?" *Snap Snap*

"What do you do when it rains?" *Snap*

"Do you have a cell phone?" *Snap*

"Is it hard to 'do it' in a sleeping bag?" *(Wow.)*

"How many miles do you go a day?" *Snap Snap Snap*

"Why are you doing this?"

"Are you afraid of serial killers?" *Snap Snap*

"How old are you?!"

"Are you as strong as you look?" *Snap*

"How did you get away for so long?" *Snap Snap*

"Do you get butt rash?" *Snap Snap*

"What do your family and friends think?" *(About the butt rash?!)*

"Are you packing a piece? A knife? Any other weapons?" *Snap Snap*

"Move in closer together, would you?" *Snap*

Geez.

When they were done asking questions, the couple walked backward to their campsite, taking pictures as they went; long shots, I guess. Or, maybe they didn't want to turn their backs on us in case we had lied about packing a piece.

~

It was 10:30 before we hit the road. After a mile, I realized my towel was still drying in a tree. I volunteered to ride back and get it alone. Sure enough, the minute I hopped off my bike the weirdo interrogators spotted me and darted out of their trailer.

"Forgot something, huh?" *Snap Snap*

"Don't wanna share a towel, do ya?" *Snap*

"Can I take a picture of your legs?" *Snap Snap Snap*

Dear God ... I grabbed the towel, trying to hide my thighs with it, then mumbled something about Clark being ahead of me and cycled out of camera range as fast as I could.

~

We traveled a side road from Alberta to Benzonia, then along the riverfront for seven miles, ending in Beulah. From there, we switched to Highway 31 through the tiny town of Honor. Just outside that little burg a young woman directed us to old farming roads that led to Lake Anne. These back ways, like many others, were nowhere to be found on our maps and a pure joy to ride along.

We didn't carry detailed county maps for every place we traveled; rather, we counted on directions from locals to supplement our routes. Hand-drawn directions were some of our favorites.

If all else failed, we could usually count on Clark's good sense of direction. If we followed mine, we'd still be circling our Portland neighborhood. I'm what you might call "directionally impaired."

It was already a 50+ mile day—every inch a piece of cake. With a clear night ahead, we aimed our wheels toward a campground on the outskirts of Traverse City. The most confusing part was finding our way there. When we stopped to consult the map, people suddenly appeared from every direction to offer assistance.

"Are you lost?" a man shouted from across the street.

"Do you need directions?" someone else inquired. "How can we help?"

"Where are you going? Are you OK?"

Friendly behavior was plentiful all across the country, but especially in the Midwest. If so much as a bewildered look crossed our faces, residents screeched to a halt and ran over to help. Pulling out a map is sort of like sending a silent distress signal.

We were directed to a paved bike trail that would take us to the campground. One kind soul called ahead and reserved us a spot. As we set out, two derelict-looking guys with matted hair and ragged clothes came pedaling in our direction. Their old cycles rattled and shook. The duo stopped abruptly, dead center in a secluded section of the trail, and got off their bikes.

"Hey, man. Do you have a spoke wrench?" one asked.

They made me nervous, and Clark looked uncomfortable. Would they crack us over the head with the tool? We silently sized the men up for a few long seconds.

"Here you go," Clark said, as he pulled a small wrench from his bike bag.

The taller of the two took it without a word, then knelt by his bike to make an adjustment. The other one commented on the beautiful day.

A bit startled by the sudden normalcy of the situation, I stammered, "Yes, yes, it's lovely out here."

Clark offered another tool to make the repair easier and received a grateful thank you.

"Are you heading to the campground?" the tall one asked, after finishing his repairs.

"Yes," Clark said. "We heard it's nice."

"It is," they both agreed.

"But, it's hard to find and a lot of people get lost. Follow us."

They jumped on their bikes and pedaled away, glancing back to make sure we were trailing behind. The route was indeed hard to follow. Good thing we had trailblazers. The path twisted and turned, stopping and starting unexpectedly. We were led under an isolated bridge and tensed, mentally mapping escape routes. In tune with each other, we unconsciously separated ourselves, Clark ahead and me behind, so if they bonked us on the head one of us could ride for help. Happily, we didn't need to call in local authorities. The guys guided us safely to where the route was easier to follow.

Shame on us for judging these men only on their appearance.

~

The last four miles to the campsite involved playing a real-life game of human Frogger. We had to traverse several busy roads. Cars whizzed past, never stopping or slowing to let us cross. It made me dizzy. We finally found our break and high-tailed it across the lanes, hearts pounding, too afraid to look right or left.

Eventually we made it to the campground, limbs intact but minds a little worse for wear. After setting up the tent, Clark headed to the showers and I settled in. A ranger drove past and suddenly screeched to a stop in front of our campsite. He hopped off his noisy moped and marched toward me with the authority of a king about to behead an enemy.

"Just exactly which site are you in?" he snapped.

"We're in 36," I replied, trying not to get huffy myself.

"Well, you're not in 36 or 37," he said accusingly. "You're right on the line. Choose. One or the other."

Apparently, one corner of our tent was technically in another site. There were no clear lines of demarcation and hardly anyone else staying in the campground. I bit my tongue, but here's what I wanted to say:

"For God's sake, who cares? No one's here!"

But, instead, I plastered on a sweet face and sugary voice.

"Oh, really?" I said, giving him a wide grin (*blink, blink*). "Thanks for letting me know. I couldn't see the boundary. Which direction do you think would be best to move?"

The game worked. In fact, he was almost taken aback by my calm demeanor. Even his threatening posture softened.

"Well," he said, "There's no one here. (Duhhhhh.) I guess it doesn't really matter. I'll just change the numbers and mark you down as paid." He shuffled his paperwork in matter-of-fact fashion, then abruptly tramped off to his moped. He gave me an odd salute, revved up his machine, and roared off.

Luckily, he didn't see me roll my eyes. Sucker.

I gave Clark the full rundown when he returned.

"I knew it!" he said. "I *knew* that guy was going to be a problem. He gave me a weird look as I headed into the showers."

Clark gestured toward the bathrooms to dramatize his point. All at once his expression changed from indignant to puzzled to hilarity when he realized he'd used the women's instead of the men's.

~

Dinnertime. We took extreme measures for good food that night, including scaling a chain-link fence to gain quick access to the waterfront restaurants. Too lazy to walk the extra blocks, we scurried up the metal fencing like monkeys at the zoo. Food is a powerful draw.

Boaters headed for safe harbor before sunset as we and other romantic couples watched them glide silently into their slips. We sipped gin and tonics, drinking in the soft breezes as day turned to night.

Meeting the Postals

Day 85:   Wednesday, August 27
Weather: A perfect day—crystal clear, sunny, and warm
Distance: 43 miles
Route: Traverse City, Michigan, to Eastport, Michigan

How quickly life changes on the road. Neither of us slept well and awoke to a morning we would later refer to as a "traversty." Freeing as it is, long-distance traveling can be extremely stressful, especially when physically and mentally drained. Clark's knees were throbbing, and I was struggling with a severe case of cramps. Not a good combination. A heated argument ensued about our "trip of a lifetime."

It was hormones, testosterone, and exhaustion talking. I headed for the bathroom to pull myself together. While washing up, I met Becky, another cyclist staying at the campground. She was so enthusiastic and friendly I couldn't help but smile, despite my red, blotchy face and swollen eyes. I mumbled something about getting my period and not feeling well. Thankfully, she didn't notice. I'm either a good actor or she chose to ignore my horrifying appearance.

Becky was a ball of energy and talked enthusiastically about how much fun she and her husband David were having on their nine-day cycling trip around the state. She could hardly control her exhilaration. They loved every moment on the road—the riding, the camping, the fresh air. She exuded happiness and lightened my foul mood.

Meanwhile, back at the campsite, David was talking to Clark with that same infectious energy, bringing my mate out of his funk. Perfect timing. It wasn't long until we were laughing and talking about our journey as if nothing unpleasant had transpired.

It took the four of us a while to pack our respective gear as we wandered back and forth to each other's campsites talking and comparing notes. They told us plans were in the works for a cross-country trip of their own, three years down the road. *Hmmmm ... planners.*

Becky and David worked for a post office in the Midwest and lived on a "farmette," a small residential farm, along the Mississippi River. They were extremely organized and worked well together as a roadie team. It made us laugh; here they were planning more than three years in advance. We represented the opposite extreme—preparing for less than three weeks and spending no time considering whether we were actually capable of physically or emotionally embarking on such a journey.

Likely their method was a wiser, safer way to travel. But, *que sera, sera*. There are many ways to create your own quest; I say do what works best for you: planned or unplanned, organized or winging each day as it comes.

We were almost packed and ready to hit the road when Becky casually mentioned where they planned to camp that night. Of course, they were way ahead of us on that thought process. We said we'd try to meet up and camp together later. They rode off singing and laughing.

We finished packing and discussed *our* morning goal: breakfast. Five miles left on the bike trail—surely there would be a place to eat ahead. We rode forward, effortlessly and congenially.

~

It wasn't long until we were back on the dreaded Highway 31. Nightmarish traffic, potholes, and a tiny gravel shoulder. Rude drivers blasted by at great speed.

A roadside fruit stand selling sweet, dark cherries drew us in. We devoured a whole basket, spitting seeds into the nearby pasture. Cherries were out of season at home this time of year, so it was a nice surprise to find them. I tucked a second basket in my bag for later.

The break from traffic had done us good. We calmed down enough to finally notice the Tuscany-like beauty of the countryside. We were so focused on not getting killed, we hadn't realized we'd been transported to another world. Straddling our bikes to leave, we heard the woman working the cherry booth shout, "Hey, wait a minute! There's a side road through the residential area that'll bring you into Elk Rapids and even save you a mile."

Another priceless tip.

~

We immediately felt at home in Elk Rapids. It's surrounded by water: Lake Michigan and the bay, of course, plus Elk, Birch, Torch, and Bass Lakes. Water everywhere you look. Fruit orchards and beaches punctuated the landscape, adding more allure to the panorama before us. Perfect weather, a chance meeting with kindred spirits, a peaceful side road, the stunning landscapes … we were in the moment, everything fitting together as it should.

We stopped for a bite at a bustling outdoor café. I ordered what turned out to be the best bagel I'd ever eaten. Clark had a small baguette with butter and jam. As we enjoyed the chewy goodness, the energetic Becky and David rode up. They'd fallen in love with Elk Rapids, too. We discussed our camping plans, looking forward to seeing them later that night.

~

The day rated a 10, and no better place to enjoy it than on our bikes. Late in the afternoon, we split back onto the highway and found our way to the campground just outside Eastport. We chose an open space next to our new friends. Becky and David were gone, but we recognized their bikes and gear.

We took a short hike to the lake, then descended a steep set of stairs to the beach. Our friends were relaxing on the sand in the distance, no doubt enjoying what they mentioned was their third anniversary. We pretended not to notice them, assuming they might prefer to be alone, but they shouted our names and seemed happy to see us. So, we decided not to worry about their romance time.

After a swim, we basked in the sun. I was chosen as the day's hero when I offered to run back up the long flight of stairs to get a six-pack cooling at their campsite. David had turned their panniers inside out and filled them with ice. A creative make-shift refrigerator. How clever.

Before dinner, we each took showers in coin-operated stalls. I managed to shower on a quarter, equal to three minutes of water—a record for me.

Our group walked the half mile to a restaurant just outside the campground. We were told they served Guinness Stout and good food, an excellent combination. I ordered perch, while everyone else went for beef. The conversation was easy, spirited, and sometimes downright silly. In honor of their anniversary, Clark and I bought the nightcap.

On the way home, we sang old camp songs and collected wood for a bonfire. Together, we built a roaring blaze. It turned out to be one of my favorite nights in a campground. Friends, new or old, make all the difference.

Later that evening, Clark and I took a walk to the lake. The night sky was magical. Crystal clear, the cosmic expanse filled with brilliant stars. Lying on our backs, we found familiar constellations, counted five shooting stars, and saw the Milky Way distinctly. Amazing and humbling. We gazed up in silence for a long time.

It was also on this night Clark made peace with the death of his father. His dad had passed away the previous Christmas. Seeing the vastness of the universe in such clarity made Clark feel as if he and his dad were somehow connecting.

Philosophically and most sincerely, Clark believed his father had turned into light or pure energy and was now a part of the infinite nighttime sky. There was a strong feeling he was watching over the family saying, "I'm okay, and you will be, too."

I listened quietly, staring into the heavens, Clark sharing feelings from the depth of his soul.

I'd never seen him so at peace.

Fairy Houses and the Land of Million Dollar Sunsets

Day 86: Thursday, August 28
Weather: Gray and overcast
Distance: 50 miles
Route: Eastport, Michigan, to Petoskey, Michigan

We woke feeling refreshed and alive. The morning was dry, not even any dew to dampen our spirits. Sweaty clothes, wet swimsuits, towels, and tent were now bone dry and ready for packing.

Spontaneous Revolutions

Becky and David were up before us, of course. She strolled over with international mocha coffee, a pleasant surprise. Funny thing; I didn't notice my "cup" was a plastic cottage cheese container until I rinsed it out. There's a sign of a seasoned camper!

We were traveling in opposite directions today, sad to leave our companions. That feeling epitomizes the beauty and melancholy of a long trip. You meet people, bond with them, and then they're gone. We snapped lots of pictures before saying goodbye, promising to stay in touch. Becky and David took off ahead of us, their happy laughter drifting back to the campsite. We left minutes later, feeling equally lighthearted.

~

The terrain was hilly again, but we didn't care. The quiet back road afforded views of rolling countryside, green pastures, and cherry orchards spreading out for miles. Even the threatening sky was beautiful with its impressionistic mélange of dark and light clouds on a background of aqua blue. No matter what Mother Nature had in store, she presented it with an unmatchable artistic flair.

Liza - 2,000 Mile Mark - Outside Charlevoix, MI

The odometer turned over to 2,000 miles. We stopped, took a few photos, and congratulated ourselves. Actually, we'd traveled closer to 3,000 miles at that point, but the odometer only worked sporadically and we'd lost the official count. It was probably better that way. The journey, not the physical distance traveled, was the true spirit of the trip.

~

Charlevoix, nestled between Lake Michigan and its namesake Lake Charlevoix, captured our hearts. When we saw the picturesque harbor, quaintly hip downtown, and windswept beaches with grand family mansions and quirky stone cottages, we understood why the town is known as "Charlevoix the Beautiful."

Architect Earl Young created 30 of the stone "Fairy Houses" between 1918 and the 1950s. Their design is pure storybook whimsy: undulating cedar shake rooflines, bumpy stone walls, chimneys decorated like crazy frosted birthday cakes, and rounded windows decked with fairytale window boxes. The early homes were described as "arts and crafts" or "chalet style" and the later homes as "rounded and organic, part Tolkien, part Keebler elf."

I pictured us as cartoon characters pulling into our Hobbit-like garage in our cartoonmobile and planting oversized flowers in a stone fence-ringed yard.

~

We wandered around downtown to take in the ambiance and worked up an appetite. Several people suggested a restaurant with "French onion soup to die for." Learning the place was only a few miles out of town, we hopped on our bikes and sped toward the soup. The road was easy and flat. We were soon at the restaurant's door, just in the nick of time for lunch. The waitresses busied themselves with cleanup tasks and gossip, mostly ignoring our presence. One young lady took pity and placed our order. We sat patiently, anticipating the luscious soup, steaming, rich, and cheesy.

A massive disappointment. The broth was too thick and salty and the cheese unpleasantly burned. Maybe the cook had already gone for the day. Maybe we got the last dregs from the pot. Who knows? So, we turned our attention and compliments to the tasty breadsticks provided with the meal. Two baskets' worth.

We amused ourselves watching two older, well-dressed women who seemed both bothered and fascinated by our presence. They couldn't stop staring and whispering to each other. It was funny to imagine their internal struggle: "Look at the way they're dressed. Does she ever brush her hair? What's that black smear on his leg? What are they up to? Should we talk to *those* people or not?"

Apparently, they couldn't stand the suspense and eventually broke down and came over. The pair grilled us with all the usual questions. Curiosity finally satisfied, the busybodies bustled off.

~

Our next stop was the wealthy community of Bay Shore. The town was incredibly clean, the streets practically polished, and we felt out of place in all our grungy glory. We rode past high-end boutiques, a yacht club, a perfectly groomed golf course, and gigantic mansions. Even the equestrian center looked stately. We pulled over to peek inside. Normally, a place like that would be a little rank with the random pooping, sawdust, and flies, but you could practically eat off the floors at this fancy horse barn.

I got a flat at the edge of town as we were leaving—#8. The back tire. A bigger deal to fix than a front tire. All equipment and bags needed to come off, plus the greasy chain and wheel had to be removed. Thankfully, Clark was becoming an expert at changing tires and managed to do it in record time.

The weather looked menacing, but we still planned to camp in Petoskey. Anxious to set up before the downpour started, we pulled over in a hospital parking lot to get our bearings. One of the administrators was heading home and offered to direct us to the campground. He was so friendly we forgot about the impending threat and talked a long while. The man told us the waterfront town of Petoskey is a popular four-season vacation destination and is called the "Land of the Million Dollar Sunsets." Some people visit and never want to leave. Others pass down family cottages through the generations. As a child, Ernest Hemingway lived there, and many of these memories are woven into his writing.

A distant thunderclap nudged us to move on. The four-mile route was flat, fast, and mostly along a bike path. Everything was going smoothly, until the path split. Now what? Just at that moment, our hospital friend appeared like a knight in shining armor.

"It's this way," he said, hopping out of his car and pointing to one of the forks. He'd worried we might get stuck at this juncture.

"Gotta run, I'm late for dinner," he confessed with a smile. With a few short beeps, he drove down the road out of sight. We never saw him again but will always remember his kindness.

So many people went that extra mile to help us during the trip. Amazing and wonderful. We were shown time and time again the true generosity of the American spirit.

The storm had moved in another direction by the time we reached the lakefront campground. I set up while Clark rode a mile to town to pick up dinner. He returned with a feast of Brie, bread, whitefish, tomatoes, a bottle of Merlot, and dark chocolate. The beautiful, clear night was memorable not only for the sumptuous banquet but also for our romantic exploration of moonlit sand dunes.

> The nature of the trip was starting to morph in a new direction because we were enjoying the camping aspect more. Camping is freeing and makes a long trip more affordable. But, weather has a tremendous impact on how much fun it is. When it's nice, camping's the best. In contrast, when it's raining and cold, the experience can be hellacious. But, we were getting hardier, both mentally and physically.
>
> A shower—who needs one?
>
> Bugs in the teeth—bring 'em on!
>
> Steep hills—we can tackle anything!
>
> Cycle on narrow, winding roads with lots of traffic—we're not afraid!
>
> Cold, sideways-blowing rain—where's my bike … I'm ready to ride!

"Hey, Lady! Nice Equipment!"

Day 87: Friday, August 29
Weather: Chilly and overcast
Distance: 30 miles
Route: Petoskey, Michigan, to Cross Village, Michigan

The morning broke dew free. There was an overall dryness in the air—not totally arid like Nevada but dry for this part of the world. It felt good. The leaves were turning from green to red, gold, and brown, and the days were getting shorter and colder. Fall was definitely on its way. It was also a subtle reminder that time was slipping by and we needed to kick up the pace to reach the Atlantic before the weather stopped us altogether. (And, of course, before we went broke.)

~

We were up and on our way early. Clark sniffed out a suitable breakfast spot, but so had many others. He also saved us an hour of wait time by making friends with an older couple who were already seated. He boldly asked if we could join them. They seemed pleased and more than happy to share their love of the area. After an interesting breakfast, we thanked our tablemates for their hospitality and headed out.

The hill to Road 119 was steep and took us to a bluff overlooking Lake Michigan—a stunning vantage point. According to many, the "Tunnel of Trees" is the most beautiful drive in the state. The twisting road is densely flanked by hardwoods and evergreens, their crowns intertwined into a comforting canopy. The light flickered through the late-summer leaves, creating scattered patterns on the pavement. Up and down the hills we pedaled, rewarded by periodic glimpses of the water below.

~

We came to the town of Good Hart, famous for its historic general store. The small, red building, built in 1936, is a step back in time with its 1901 cash register, glass-front counter bins, and carved oak cooling case.

We indulged in fresh-squeezed lemonade, humongous sandwiches, and brownies before pedaling on. The winding road offered nice views of Bear, Hog, Trout, and Whiskey Islands. The miles melted away.

We saw an old couple toddling slowly down the street in Cross Village. The gentleman looked up when I rode by, waved his cane, and shouted, "Hey, lady! Nice equipment!"

Hilarious. The last time anyone said that to me, they actually meant my body—not my bicycle and gear. Oh, the pain and humor of getting older.

We spotted the Legs Inn, a fun and funky restaurant and cottage complex built of huge boulders, driftwood, chunky logs, and lots of creativity. The temperature was dropping fast and a severe thunderstorm forecasted.

We schmoozed the hotel manager to barter a great rate. Our cabin was four blocks away and close to the lake, but we had to cycle down a steep hill to reach it. The ride felt like that stomach-flipping moment when you plunge down an enormous rollercoaster drop. The scary thrill ride was worth it because the tiny cabin we were expecting turned out to be a roomy house. Palatial compared to the tent.

After chores, we took a short walk to the lake. The panoramic vista allowed us to see for miles in the distance. A thunderhead grew big and billowing on the horizon. The sky darkened and turned sinister, then transformed into wisps of swirly, benign clouds. Moments later, the sun emerged and the heavens cleared.

We had dinner at Legs Inn. The menu is heavily populated with Polish dishes, honoring the heritage of the family who has owned the restaurant for over 90 years. The white borscht, pork with cherry sauce, and dessert cordial were standouts.

We had a strange experience walking back to the cabin. Creepy is a more apt description. We ran into an odd fellow who said he was part of a rescue squad. He kept pacing in a circle and taking his hat off, scratching his head with great gusto, and didn't seem to be rescuing anyone at all.

He told us there was an old man dying from alcoholism inside the house, as he glanced nervously toward a ramshackle cottage. Apparently, the ailing man refused to go to the hospital. A large group of friends and family were hovering outside, singing in low voices, waiting for the man to die. Without saying anything more, the head scratcher walked away and melted into the crowd. It was a "Twilight Zone" moment.

Clark and I moved on, quietly reconciling what we'd just encountered. The incident started a conversation about death and dying. We realized one's outlook on life changes dramatically as people we love start to get old, sick, or die. As a child, the world seems so alive. Parents are typically in good health, friends are young, and even grandparents don't seem that old. Life was good when we were kids, and somehow, back then, we couldn't imagine that ever changing.

As we age, the reality of death hits closer to home. Many people are afraid of dying and the great unknown, others choose not to think about it at all, and some see death as a door opening to the next life and have no fears of what comes next.

Loss is never easy. We all deal with it in our own ways. Some people never let go of pain. Most people eventually find peace with the death of a loved one, just like Clark had with his father.

Hypnotized Zombies and the Toilet Team

Day 88: Saturday, August 30
Weather: Gray and cool, turning to heavy rain later
Distance: 39 miles
Route: Cross Village, Michigan, to St. Ignace, Michigan (Upper Peninsula)

Sleep was elusive. I woke up a lot, uncomfortable much of the night. My Achilles tendon hurt. So did my hips, knees, ankles, and bum. The pain was hard to ignore. Sometimes, nights on the road were like that. Even the nice soft bed didn't help.

My eyes were also a problem. They looked puffy, and I lived in constant fear of "Monster Face" returning. I should explain. "Monster Face" was a mystery allergic reaction that happened to me right before the trip. My eyelids swelled shut, and the skin around my nose and underneath my eyes puffed out so far I looked like a boxer who lost a big fight. More accurately, like a monster.

I'd set up a quick appointment with my doctor, who was concerned about blindness and anaphylactic shock. Although it didn't turn out to be serious (likely a reaction to new soap), I started the trip on a heavy dose of antibiotics. The swelling eventually subsided, but I always worried the monster would reappear.

My eyelids felt heavy when I blinked, and a nasty headache pounded. I hoped it wouldn't get worse. It dawned on me that, the night before, I'd washed my face with products supplied at the cabin and suspected the soap might have one of the same ingredients that made my eyes go "monstery" three months earlier.

I rolled over and slept another hour while Clark walked to the store. He hiked up and back down the steep rollercoaster hill and returned with breakfast ingredients: kielbasa sausage, eggs, milk, juice, bread, and butter. My man whipped up a nice meal.

~

It was after 11 a.m. when we hit the road. Step one out of the gate was to wheel our weighty bikes back up the sharp incline to the main road. There was no way we could shift low enough without going in the opposite direction. So, we grunted our way up. Even though the day was gray and cool, we were sweating and felt rain in the air. We headed north on little back roads traveling around Sturgeon Bay, not sure where we'd end up sleeping that night. That mystery amplified our devil-may-care sense of adventure and made the trip fun.

The ride turned out to be phenomenal. We enjoyed the bounty of nature in all its glory and reveled at the lack of traffic for such a busy travel holiday.

We stopped for a break at a little roadside store. The clerk was so grouchy, we almost felt sorry for her, assuming this was her regular demeanor. How sad to live life in such a mental state. Although it was not like us to support ill-tempered shop owners, we knew our choices were limited. Our purchase? A large soda.

As we sat outside quenching our thirst, Miss Crabbypants whisked out several times, sweeping and bustling about, obviously annoyed by our existence. We chose to ignore her but laughed louder than normal at our own jokes to bust her chops.

Our attitude improved when a nice couple with four kids stopped by the store. Spotting our bikes, the questions started. One of the children reminded us of Clark's son, Ryan. The young boy was stick skinny, red haired, freckle splattered, and very bright, based on his line of questioning. His parents alluded to how much he ate for someone so svelte.

The grandmother owned a vacation home in the area, and they were on their way to it. We laughed when they confided, "She comes up here to get away from us and then we follow her."

I felt pangs of homesickness watching the family enjoy each other's company, especially missing both the kids. I got so lost in sentimental thoughts about Ryan and Taea it took a while to notice the sun had come out and it was now a beautiful day.

The ride went well until downtown Mackinaw City. There, we hit crazy traffic and throngs of tourists. People bumbling and stumbling in every direction, darting about in a shopping frenzy. Trapped in the crowd, we had to dismount and walk our bikes, as it was nearly impossible to maneuver without accidentally knocking people aside.

I shouted to Clark above the din, "This reminds me of the madding hordes in Wall, South Dakota."

"Be careful not to jinx us," he cautioned. "Just saying the word 'Wall' means we're going to get soaked tonight!"

The night in Wall was our wettest to date. We weren't anxious to repeat that episode. Getting away from the current insanity as fast as possible was the immediate goal. The bridge crossing was reportedly a nightmare for cyclists, so we inched our way to the Chamber of Commerce for more information and an alternate route.

Good thing we did. As it turns out, the city does not allow cyclists to cross the Mackinac Bridge, unless you're part of a scheduled ride, one that was previously booked and approved; otherwise, you pay the Mackinac Bridge Authority a small fee for a lift.

We rode a few blocks to the designated rendezvous spot and waited only 10 minutes for the truck. Our driver explained the reasons for the no-bike rule. Part of the danger is from heavy traffic combined with virtually no shoulder. The risk of getting hit is high. The other problem arises from the width of the grating on the bridge. Narrow wheels, like those on bicycles, can easily get stuck in a gap and throw a rider. When there's a planned ride, the city thoughtfully lays down matting to make it easier. According to our driver, problems occur even with those precautions. He told us a woman on an organized ride had recently veered off the matting and got into trouble. Her wheels stuck and she did a header, smashing into a wall and hurting herself quite badly.

We had a great view of Mackinac Island from the bridge. Being in a vehicle allowed us to crane our necks around and safely take a gander at what spread out before us.

I remembered visiting the island as a kid and have fond memories of the horse-drawn carriages. Motorized vehicles have been banned from the island since 1898. You travel there by ferry or small plane, then get around on foot, bicycles, paddle boats, skate boards, saddle horses, and carriages.

Our driver dropped us at the St. Ignace visitor center in the Upper Peninsula, better known as the "U.P." While studying the wall map, a knowledgeable employee showed us a shortcut through the woods.

The "shortcut" took us through deep sand for a quarter mile. We had to push our heavy bikes through that mess. Sand filled our socks and shoes, the wheels kicked grit into our gears, and the coarse granules worked their way to our bike bags, teeth, and hair. So much for the great tip.

As we pulled into the busy campground, grateful to get settled for the night, the "No Vacancy" sign flicked on. Nooooooo! The garish light blinked at us, mocking our bad timing. We had no choice but to move on.

Back on the road, the tourist insanity continued, people streaming everywhere; bumper-to-bumper cars, trucks, and motorhomes all honking their horns; and road construction bottlenecking the whole works even more.

We happened upon a colorful carnival of arts, crafts, and food booths contrasted oddly with random guys selling junk off blankets or just asking for money. People spilled from bars, loud, obnoxious, and aggressive, making lewd remarks at unsuspecting passersby. Rowdy party madness. We were two granola bicyclists completely out of place and imagined ourselves as Jane Goodall, observing primate behavior in the jungle.

Too ludicrous for us. Time to go.

> We were very disappointed when we discovered Clark's favorite pin, the jackalope from Wyoming, had been lost or stolen, along with my South Dakota pin, a personal favorite.

The weather turned cruddy. We were anxious to find a place to sleep before the storm hit. Signs announcing another campground loomed large after a few miles. Reverting to all smiles, anticipating a good night's rest, we approached the front desk. But—surprise, surprise—were told brusquely there was no space left. We innocently inquired if we could pitch a tent in an unused corner of the park, explaining we were cold and tired. The "hostess" turned her back on us, emotionlessly unsympathetic to our dilemma. This was a first. By contrast, most places would happily accommodate backpackers and bicyclists.

Of course, we understood campgrounds fill up quickly during holidays. We didn't expect a prime spot, but her refusal to even pretend she cared left us speechless. We took another gander at their big sign on the way out. "A Good Samaritan Park" it said in large letters. That gave us a laugh.

We continued on, hoping to outrace the clouds now darkening the sky fast and furiously. Deep potholes, no shoulders, and cars spitting rocks and mud at us relentlessly made the ride harrowing.

Yay. A National Forest campground had vacancies. We pitched the tent, changed clothes (no showers there), and left on foot to search for dinner. We slogged a couple miles to a time-worn casino and opened the door into a world of semi-darkness and a bombardment of noise and cigarette smoke. Slot machines created a cacophony of clanging bells and sirens. A crackling loudspeaker emitted incomprehensible babble. Flashing, twirling lights had a dizzying effect. Everything was bathed in an eerie, vibrating glow, illuminating people of every shape and size. We watched as they monotonously plugged quarters into slots, one after another.

The hypnotized zombies made no effort at personal interaction. Their blank stares fixated on the machines. Most had a butt stub clamped between their lips. All intermittently sipped drinks from large plastic cups delivered by robotic waitresses. Clark and I moved slowly through the smoky-blue haze, taking in every detail, almost in a trance ourselves. Our senses hit overload.

The old machines raucously boop-BOOP-booped, every so often emitting a clang-clang-clang-clang before belching out a slew of coins. One zombified player barely reacted when his big win came clinking into the tray. Instead, he automatically plugged the coins back into the hungry beast.

Strange as it was, this alien world held our attention. One woman gave her machine a swift kick before limply shifting over to the next one. Another guy sat stone still, except for his little arm moving up and down feeding the slot. He reminded us of those creepy mannequins where just one body part is animated, repeating a stiff movement every few seconds.

We were convinced the machines had control, stealing money and human souls.

A man at a blackjack table caught our eye—he was very confident in his bets. Thin and well dressed, but with too much product in his jet-black dyed hair, the player's chalky complexion paled in comparison to his nicotine-stained teeth. He was wound up tight, fingers drumming the green felt, while his foot jittered restlessly under the table.

He noticed us watching, stopping the game for a moment to take us in with dark, deep-set eyes. His chest puffed as he refocused attention on the table. "Hit me!" he said, glancing back at us to make sure we saw his smooth move.

He won.

His tablemates groaned and walked away to find their fortune elsewhere.

"Are you in or do you just watch?" he asked us.

"Watchers," Clark answered.

A new dealer was getting ready to take the table, which gave us a minute to talk. He learned we were riding bikes. We learned – at age 54 – he was a professional gambler, making a decent living at it for years. Divorced five times, he only stayed in a town while his hands felt "hot." Once they cooled, he'd move to the next casino, traveling cross-country and back again in search of the big win.

He talked about sleeping all day, then rising at 4 p.m. to eat and "go to work." He bragged, a little too loudly, that from cards to craps he was the Casino King! We nodded in unison like a pair of stunned bobbleheads and moved stealthily away when he turned his attention back to the table.

We escaped across the street to an all-you-can-eat buffet to cleanse our brains by filling our bellies. For two hours, we indulged in cracked crab, gobbled roast beef, and crafted gargantuan salads, filling our plates with every round. A weary cyclist's dream. We topped our feast off with dessert heaven, relishing a double helping of cherry pie, cookies, and nut-filled brownies.

It was fun while it lasted. Like stuffed pigs, we waddled slowly to the door, leaning on each other for support. It was pouring outside and our rain gear was back at camp, so waited it out in hopes the storm would pass.

We hovered outside the restaurant, hiding under the awning, burping and farting. When the deluge eased, we wobbled down the block to a gas station and ducked inside for warmth, pretending to shop and stalling for time. Clark bought a cigar and we continued browsing until the station attendant gave us the "are-they-riff-raff" stare. We left to avoid an unnecessary confrontation but didn't go far.

While under the store's protective canopy, a friendly couple filled up on gas and gave us a wave.

"Are you folks heading (burp, excuse me) north by any chance?" I said as cheerfully as I could.

"Yes," they said, suspiciously. "Why? Is something wrong?"

"We're on our bikes," Clark blurted, barely attempting to hold back a disgusting belch.

I quickly covered the sound by spitting out a flurry of explanation, "But they're back at the campground … we have to walk there … cold and wet … cross-country bike trip … couldn't the rain wait until we were back in our tent? I mean … could we get a ride to the campground?" I finally stammered.

They paused for a long moment, earnestly studying our faces.

I thought I heard Clark pass a little gas.

"Well, I suppose we could," the man said, probably not wanting to help, but not wanting to turn us down either.

"Great, thanks!" we said, practically pushing them aside to get into the warm car.

After a few awkward moments, we fell into an interesting conversation about our respective lives. It didn't take long to get to the campsite. We sat and talked in their toasty car until 6:30 p.m. before saying good-bye and diving into our tent for cover. Inside for only seconds, we realized water was seeping in.

A long, wet evening loomed. Clark warned me not to jinx us earlier. I never should have mentioned Wall, South Dakota. The storm raged on. Water dumped on us from what felt like giant buckets helicopters use to douse forest fires. We felt trapped. Too early to sleep, too full to be romantic, and too wet to do anything else. The playing cards were inside my bike bag, away from the tent, and I already read the only book I carried.

We were lazy and antsy. I passed time by recording the sound of rain hitting the tent and trying to direct water puddles away from the sleeping bags. We played our favorite game of "What would we do if we won the lottery?" That amused us for about an hour. Then the nightmare began.

Diarrhea.

This noxious and painful bout was undoubtedly due to gluttony. It hit me hard and fast. I raced out of the tent, getting drenched during my dash to the outhouse, where I sat in a cold, dark stall until the attack was over.

I hobbled back to the tent, exhausted from the vile disgorging, cursing myself for overeating. I was blazing a path back to the outhouse 20 minutes later. And three or four times more during the night, all in the pelting rain.

Each time I made a mad sprint to and from, I couldn't help but track in mud, water, and bugs, getting the mess all over us and the gear. I was too sick to care. Sleeping was out of the question for either of us. Every time the runs hit, I had to crawl over Clark (or, more honestly, step on him) in my rush. Then had to throw on pants, coat, and shoes and finally grab a flashlight for the bathroom ensemble to be complete.

Upon each return, I thought the worst was over. Because I didn't want to sleep in wet clothes, I disrobed every time, which made sense for a while—but I still had a few trips to make.

At one point, I considered speeding to the bathroom completely naked because I didn't care anymore.

I might have been inclined to wait out my purgatory if the one-hole outhouse had been nicer and featured decent lights or a place to sit other than the single, unisex toilet.

Clark was compassionate about the experience, staying positive and supportive. He helped me dress and undress, ignored my feet in his face and body crushing his and even helped get the door zipped up and down, handing me a flashlight on the way out each time. We got into a rhythm and worked well together as a "toilet team."

By dawn I'd exorcised my demons, the rain had disappeared, and all was right with the world again.

WEEK 14

Nothing Works Better for a Tummy Ache than Donuts

    Day 89:   Sunday, August 31
    Weather: Off and on sun and darkness, misting and dry
    Distance: 52 miles
    Route: St. Ignace, Michigan, to Sault
                  Ste. Marie, Michigan

The morning was a welcome sight, and neither of us whispered a complaint at having to roll up our tent and supplies, still dripping from last night's downpour. Nor did we say a word when we found the "waterproof" pack covers did a lousy job keeping the wet out of our clothes and gear. And we didn't whine when the mist grew heavy and foreboding. We were just anxious to move on and forget last night ever happened.

    The first 25 miles carried us along the Mackinac Trail, paralleling I-75. Mother Nature seemed schizophrenic, making it hard to decide what to wear at any given moment. When it's misting, rain gear keeps you dry but also makes you hot and sweaty. And, because sweat makes you wet anyway, it usually feels better to get some air and be wet from the rain instead.

    The traffic, like the weather, changed regularly. At first, cars sped past, spitting water and dirt as they blasted by. Not long after, the heavy traffic thinned. But just when we got comfortable having the road to ourselves, it would ramp up, preventing us from enjoying the peace.

We stopped at a party store around the 14-mile mark and ordered coffee and donuts to officially start the day—because nothing goes better with a sore stomach than donuts. The storeowner was a crotchety old coot, but somehow likeable and entertaining. He complained about tourists flooding the area during summer and fall.

"It's too crowded," he griped, screwing his face up like a dried apple head doll. "I like the fact that nothing happens here. Today's as crowded as I ever want it to be," he announced, eyeing us and the only other customer in the store distrustfully. "Any more than this makes me crazy."

We suspected he already was.

~

The next stop was the "mythical" Rudyard. Mythical only because of how people talked about it when we asked about the dot on the map.

"Oh … Rudyard? Nothing there. Nothing there at all!"

"Rudyard? Hmm … I don't think there's even a town there."

"You won't find a thing in Rudyard. Stock up on supplies before then."

We expected to find a ghost town, complete with tumbleweeds and boarded-up storefronts. Instead, we discovered Rudyard had a motel, several restaurants, a gas station, tidy modest homes, and a nice post office.

It's all about perspective. We'd been traveling through some of the country's smallest towns so, to us, Rudyard looked like a metropolis.

~

Kinross, five miles down the road, was another small town mostly ignored by auto traffic but appreciated by cyclists. It had all the amenities of Rudyard, though we didn't take advantage of them. We should have.

Just outside town, Clark developed a bad case of hypoglycemia. He stopped in the middle of the road, weak and shaky, wordlessly rifling through his bag for sugar. He downed a candy bar, Rice Krispies Treat, apple, and bag of walnuts in minutes, barely chewing. No doubt last night's gorging, sleep deprivation, and donut breakfast contributed to his erratic blood sugar. Clark finally perked up enough to ride on.

Shortly after, a road sign indicated Sault Ste. Marie, Michigan, was 20 miles ahead. The sign also noted that Sault Ste. Marie, Canada, was just a few miles further: twin Sault Ste. Maries, in two different countries, separated only by a narrow expanse of Great Lakes water. I wondered if borders had changed at some point.

Though exhausted, we covered the entire U.P. that day. An impressive effort considering our lack of sleep.

We stayed on U.S. soil that night and found a decent motel, on the main road, and negotiated a good rate. The room was perfect for two tired cyclists: clean and bright, a big bath, extra floor space, and a large TV. We looked forward to a night of pure relaxation. And to staying dry.

The lack of sleep finally caught up with us. A light dinner, then lights out.

> Along the road, we saw a sign that read "Senior Citizens Center" with an arrow pointing toward a very specific direction. When we looked that way, all we could see was a cemetery. I hope it was a joke.

Liza McQuade

A Leisurely Labor Day

Day 90: Monday, September 1 (Labor Day)
Weather: Sunny and pleasant
Distance: Rest day
Route: Sault Ste. Marie, Michigan (U.P.)

Clark couldn't sleep and kept me awake because of it. He nudged me often until I woke up, saying he wanted to talk—nothing important, just chitchat. I tried to join him in conversation but was mostly incoherent. When it became clear a true discussion wasn't going to happen, he kept me awake tossing and turning.

Since sleep was elusive, we got up early for breakfast. After a satisfying meal of blueberry pancakes, we were still groggy and sluggish. It was Labor Day, a perfect excuse not to go anywhere.

This turned out to be a good decision. We took a nap and read the paper, then completed some much-needed chores at a leisurely pace. In the afternoon, we pulled up lawn chairs and sunned ourselves in the backyard while munching on fresh fruit and contemplating life.

Clark smoked a cigar, puffing circles of smoke and watching them rise and disappear. A peaceful look spread across his face. He was totally relaxed and in tune with the world. I watched him quietly as he trailed a butterfly's flight from flower to flower. Catching my gaze, Clark reached for my hand and gave it a gentle kiss. It was perfect moments like this that made the trip, and all its challenges, worthwhile.

~

Around midnight, a thunderstorm moved in. Huge bursts of lightning hung in the sky, creating patterns across the walls and over the bedspread. Loud cracks of thunder rumbled and shook the world. I counted the seconds between flash and boom, listening as the storm moved away. Quiet rain lingered, tapping the windows rhythmically, finally lulling us to sleep.

Loonies and Toonies, Eh?

Day 91: Tuesday, September 2
Weather: Windy, gray, and cold
Distance: 53 miles
Route: Sault Ste. Marie, Michigan (U.P.), to Bruce Mines, Ontario, Canada

Rested and ready to ride. Atypical of our usual *modus operandi*, we knew exactly how to get to the bridge that would take us to Canada. For both weather and safety reasons, we donned our bright-yellow rain gear before venturing across. The journey was longer than expected, nearly three miles. Clark's personal dislike of bridges was amplified by the impending bad weather. We pedaled fast, soon realizing our worries were unnecessary. There weren't many motorists out at this time of day, and those on the road seemed patient and drove slowly around us. The crossing was easy—one of the nicest. We paid a small toll, friendly officials took a look at our passports, and there we were, on the other side of the lake and in another country.

We stopped in the welcome center first thing to exchange some money and get maps, directions, and fresh water. We learned Sault Ste. Marie is one of the oldest settlements in North America. The area has been inhabited for at least 2,000 years. The first people to settle were Native Americans—the Ojibwa, also known as Chippewa. Jesuit missionaries, traders, explorers, voyageurs, soldiers, and artists have also lived along the area's St. Mary's River.

> Canadians call their money "loonies" and "toonies." The "loonie" is $1 coin and has a picture of a loon on it (the bird) and a "toonie" is the $2 coin. We first discovered this when we heard a women say, "Could I have change for a five? I'll take two toonies and a loonie!"

The Canadian Sault Ste. Marie was busier and harder to negotiate than the American counterpart. The road was bad and the cement choppy, with big potholes, and there was a lot of traffic. After logging 3,000 miles, we were more assertive riders, now confidently integrating with traffic and no longer intimidated to claim our space on the road.

Road signs guided us in both French and English, making us feel like world travelers even though we were only a few miles from the U.S. border. Canadians use kilometers instead of miles, so we had to mentally adjust to that. Since 1.24 miles equals 2 kilometers, it gave us a psychological boost because it felt like we were covering more turf than we actually were.

A few miles outside the city, the road changed to a four-lane highway with a wide shoulder, almost a half lane's worth. The potholes seemed to disappear and the grade was moderate—a little up and little down, just enough to make it interesting. Before we knew it, we were in Echo Bay.

We satisfied ourselves with junk food: chips, sodas, and candy bars. The store owner chatted with us as we crunched on our snacks. She was the first person we heard use the famous Canadian "eh?" after every sentence.

"Need some road fuel, eh?"

"How long have you been ridin', eh?"

~

Once we got to Bruce Mines, located on the shore of Lake Huron, we stopped to study the map. The choice: ride a long distance to the next town or stay put. It's like that sometimes because cities aren't equally spaced. We learned to stay in tune with our map to avoid being in the middle of nowhere at the end of a long day or forced to ride in the dark until dangerously exhausted. Spending the night in Bruce Mines made sense since we'd already passed our 50-mile daily goal.

We cut through alleys and side streets and found an inexpensive place to stay. The room was nice: clean, with two double beds, a shower, and space enough to put our bikes inside.

After quick showers, an exhilarating walk to the lake put us in good spirits. We walked briskly, greeting people along the way, and counted four more "eh's?"

~

We were awed by the horseshoe-shaped harbor's natural beauty. Nearby, an empty wrought-iron bench beckoned us to sit. We took the opportunity to steal a kiss.

In the distance, a lighthouse stood guard on rocky shores, creating an idyllic backdrop for the marina. Boats bobbed silently, snugged safely in their berths. Gulls floated on an updraft, squawking as they effortlessly dipped into waves for fish. A lone sailboat, far off shore, caught our attention. We watched as its mainsail puffed plump and full of wind. The boat veered smoothly around a tip of land and disappeared from sight.

I've always loved boats; something about them is peaceful and romantic.

Caught up in the moment, I turned to Clark and said, "I could stay on the road for a year. I wish we could keep riding. Maybe we should ride our bikes home, too. What do you think?"

Without waiting for an answer, I rambled on. "You know what I've always wanted to do? Ride my bike around Turkey … hike the dolomites in Italy … what was that trail in Spain? Oh, and walk along the wall in China. And Africa. A safari! Kangaroos in Australia!"

"One trip at a time," Clark said, interrupting my oration. Pulling me close, he kissed my forehead, bringing me back to the present. "Let's just enjoy where we are right now."

~

Clark was excited to find a German restaurant. He ordered fork-tender veal schnitzel adorned with a creamy mushroom sauce that pooled seductively over the entire plate. This was accompanied by red sauerkraut, piled high and arranged perfectly, plus a side plate of white asparagus.

I couldn't resist a filet mignon with sautéed mushrooms and hearty baked potato loaded with everything. Clark savored a fine Riesling and I chose a full-bodied Cabernet. We capped the meal off with a Canadian apple pie and a tawny 20-year port.

Before falling asleep in each other's arms, Clark whispered how much he loved me. I snuggled closer and said, "I love you, too." We were really good together.

> I caught myself in the mirror and realized I wasn't wearing makeup. Surprisingly, it felt OK. For most of the trip I didn't wear cosmetics, the first time in years I allowed myself to appear publicly without it. It's a girl thing. I'd packed mascara and blush for special occasions, but didn't bother with it much. Obviously, a make-up-free face hadn't hampered my strength to ride or my enthusiasm to talk with strangers. Clark even commented I looked nice without make-up. Of course, having a tan helped.
>
> Never in a million years would I have previously sauntered in to a restaurant looking like I did most of the trip. There were times I had sweaty helmet hair, feeling dirty and stinky after a ride. But somehow it was okay. If I smiled and was pleasant, people didn't seem to notice. Riding *sans* make-up, *au naturel*, made me feel free.

The Ride-and-Dive Method

> Day 92:   Wednesday, September 3
> Weather: Crystal clear but very windy
> Distance: 63 cycling (+20 riding in the safety of a car)
> Route: Bruce Mines, Ontario, Canada, to
>   Espanola, Ontario, Canada

Heavy road construction hit within blocks. Not to be deterred, we put our heads down and used an effective system devised during our travels. The traffic flaggers would let us go first and we'd ride as fast as we could until the cars behind caught up and got impatient. Then, we'd pull over and let a stream of vehicles go by. After the last car, we'd ride like the wind again while the flagger let the opposing traffic move forward. We called it our "sprint-and-wait" technique.

New tar had just been laid along one stretch of road. We worried the sticky substance would get on our wheels, be pulled up through the chain, ruin our bikes, and turn our legs pitch black. The sound of our tires traveling across the freshly tarred road was eerie, an irritating, muted whine that changed pitch according to our speed. Fortunately, we made it through that section unscathed and tar free.

After 10 kilometers of construction and another 10 of "regular" heavy traffic, we sidetracked on the business route, shortly rolling into Thessalon. A river ran through the town's center. Many vehicles towed fishing boats or campers. Some had metal canoes strapped to their roofs. Forested mountains surrounding the city looked like an outdoor adventurer's paradise.

We found our way to a restaurant that overlooked a beautiful bay, located on the North Channel of Lake Huron. We stepped inside for a breather and ordered pie and a cup of coffee, using that as an excuse to stay awhile. The dining room was quiet, so the manager had the time and inclination to chat.

After the usual small talk and pleasantries, he became quite serious and warned us of the dangers of Highway 17. Extra caution would be needed. He kindly offered to give us a lift to a safer section, but that would mean waiting for hours until he was off work. Disheartened, we considered his thoughtful gesture, ultimately deciding to forge ahead on our own. Farther east, he promised, the road would be nicer.

We were in trouble as soon as we left the city limits of Thessalon but bravely rode on. In only a few miles, we were blown off our bikes, lost our balance, tipped over, or were flung to the ground roughly. This happened a half dozen times. Truckers whizzed by at top speed so close it forced us onto the gravel, where we'd lose traction and struggle to stay upright. At one point, I watched as a big truck whooshed past Clark, creating such a wind that he wavered dangerously close to the vehicle before shooting onto the road's soft shoulder. It looked like he was performing a clown balancing act, which would have been funny if we weren't so scared.

This continued for several hours; we made minimal progress. Sometimes there was a two-inch shoulder, but mostly there was none at all. Our nerves were wearing thin. We worried we'd be dead in another mile. Several drivers flipped us off or gave us wicked stares.

One guy slowed down enough to shout angrily, "What the hell are you doing on this road? Do you have a death wish? Get outta here!"

Good idea, we thought, but how? There was no alternate route for this stretch of the trip. It was going to take forever. Finally, we spotted a sign for a town five miles ahead. This gave us a bit of hope. If we could make it there, we could rest and revisit the map in safety.

After some time, we passed a small store on the opposite side of the road. Thinking this was the town's gateway, we anxiously searched for more signs of civilization. After another mile, we realized that store *was* the town. Retracing our steps seemed more of a hassle than going forward. In any case, going back was not in our nature.

Instead, we devised another creative way to ride. Waiting for a natural slowing in the traffic, we hopped on our bikes and pedaled as fast as we could until we heard cars and trucks closing in on us again. Then we'd carefully head onto the gravel, balance ourselves and time it so we could rev up and get going again when the coast was clear. This was better than being forced off the road. Clark rode in the back and took to yelling "NOW!" when the timing was right.

We high-fived every time we went from one surface to the other and didn't fall. Clark appropriately named this technique the "ride-and-dive" method—a version of our "sprint-and-wait" system used earlier in the day. As an alternative, we tried to ride and walk on the gravel, but the bumpy, slippery rocks made it difficult to go anywhere. Progress was slow and we were harried but managed to make it six long, painful miles in a few hours.

After another hour and a few more miles, a young man in a van braved the gravel and managed to safely pull over just ahead of us.

"Are you nuts?" he shouted. "People die on this road. Get in. I'll give you a lift out of here—this is no way to tour the country!"

He didn't have to tell us twice. Once safely in the van and out of jeopardy, we realized how frightened we were and it shook our confidence. When in a dangerous situation, adrenalin takes over and you do what needs to be done. But when you make it to a safety zone and mentally replay what happened, it can make you lose your mojo.

Our driver must have noticed our dazed expressions. "This road is crazy," he said thoughtfully. "You guys would have been dead meat out there."

He paused for a moment to let that fact sink in. "I've rescued other cyclists on this road and they looked pretty much like you do now—pale and shaking."

We laughed at his attempt to cheer us up and knew he was right. At that moment, we gasped and held our breath as a truck nearly sideswiped a car while trying to pass. Tires screeched, the semi's massive horn blasted, and rubbery-smelling smoke swirled from under the truck.

"I rest my case," our driver said.

While cruising along with our roadside protector, he told us his friends bought brand-new, shiny snowmobiles this year, enviously describing their latest bells and whistles. He went on to say his snow machine worked just fine. In fact, he liked it. But then his youthful logic kicked in.

"Yeah, that means I have to get one, too, eh?" he grumbled.

When we asked why, he replied, "To keep up with my buddies, eh?"

Clark grinned and offered mature words of wisdom, "I have a better idea—just get new friends, eh?"

The gentleman chauffeured us to Espanola, where we bought ferry tickets for the Georgian Bay crossing we'd make in a couple days. It was a rare circumstance when we actually planned ahead.

We still had 70 miles to reach the ferry crossing but were ready to call it a day. We pedaled through Espanola looking for a motel, but nothing was available. One of the big manufacturing plants in the area was closing its doors. Scores of workers were there to help shut it down and had booked every motel room for miles.

Luckily, we had an option. One motelier owned property nearby and offered to let us camp for free. It turned out to be a nice place—private, in the trees and away from the din of traffic. It felt safe and was relatively flat, making it easy to find a spot to pitch the tent.

We set up camp quickly and walked a couple miles back to town for dinner, heading for the nearest Italian restaurant. We recovered from the day's stresses with a liter of good wine. We split big orders of lasagna and creamy fettuccine Alfredo, telling ourselves we deserved it. We ate and imbibed for several hours, thankful to be alive after our horrendous day on the road.

Lumbering back to the campsite, we passed a fruit stand that was open late and bought a small basket of peaches for morning. Once inside the tent, we were warm and toasty, wrapped together, buried in our bags, ready for sleep. Predictions pointed to a freeze, with temperatures expected to plummet to 3°C (37°F). Brrrr....

> At long last, I had conquered those damn clipless pedals and fallen for the last time. No more skinned elbows, bruised knees, or embarrassing tumbles. I was now Master of My Bike, skilled at safely popping out of my pedals when I had to stop unexpectedly. Triumph was mine.

Babble ... Chew ... Babble ... Chew ... Tilt

Day 93: Thursday, September 4
Weather: Windy and cold (strong headwinds)
Distance: 56 miles
Route: Espanola, Ontario, Canada, to Manitowaning, Ontario, Canada

The buzz on the street: Last night was the chilliest of the season. Thanks to our wine-filled evening, total exhaustion from the crazy ride, and combined body heat, we'd barely noticed. When the occasional leg, arm, or butt cheek would get uncovered, we'd adjust our position and fall right back to sleep, staying comfortable all night.

We dressed quickly and dragged ourselves from the tent's snug confines at 7:45 a.m. (not exactly the crack of dawn). After hiking to town, we visited Tim Hortons. The coffee aroma was heavenly, and the rich, steaming brew warmed our bellies. We supplemented two decadent cinnamon rolls with a couple of peaches.

Refueled and satisfied, we headed back to our campsite to break down the tent. The owner stopped by with a small menagerie of animals in tow (two cats and a dog) to see how we fared through the brisk night.

The dog was an old boy, his face and muzzle white with age. The woman mentioned he was hard of hearing, nearly blind and arthritic, which caused him to periodically lose his balance, trip over unseen objects, and sometimes not know what was going on around him. He seemed very protective of the cats who lovingly rubbed up against him. Although he enjoyed having his fur stroked, the old grouch wouldn't let us touch his feline friends. When we got close, he'd jealously muscle in between and prevent us from petting either one.

The dog also had a tendency to forget where he was. He seemed to drift off, then suddenly realize we were there and bark like we'd just arrived on the scene. We laughed so hard it prompted a story from his master.

Yesterday, the ancient canine had been outside barking at traffic when a stranger walked across the property. He sauntered right behind the dog to the front door and knocked. The gentleman talked with the woman on the porch for a good 10 minutes, then left, crossing behind the pooch again. The old geezer never noticed the intruder.

~

What a beautiful morning to cycle. We enjoyed the ride despite the hilly terrain and crisp temperatures. After 20 energizing miles, lunch at Whitefish Falls seemed like a good idea. We headed straight to a bar unanimously recommended by locals and found a spot on the deck, out of the wind, overlooking the river. The horizon was striking even though the sky was gray and overcast. We felt grateful to be on this wondrous journey—living in the moment with each other, the landscape, and life itself.

~

There was a strong headwind as we set out on one of the windiest afternoons since South Dakota. We got a good workout straining to fight the weather but managed to clock eight miles an hour all the way into Little Current. A brief break at the visitor center allowed us to hide from the wind, snack on leftover peaches, and get oriented. We didn't rest long because we were focused on making tomorrow's ferry. The wind got stronger with every mile, the temperature fell further, and ominous clouds moved in.

Out of sheer determination, we stayed positive and pedaled on. At Sheguiandah, on a bay of the same name, we successfully outran the impending storm. The day's goal was Manitowaning. If we made it that far, we'd have less than 30 miles to catch the ferry in the morning.

It was late, and we were tired when we rolled into Manitowaning. Neither of us saw the sign or realized the campground was three miles back. Probably because our heads were down low, aerodynamically slicing through the wind. No way were we getting back on our bikes. Thirty minutes of bantering and bartering with a motel manager resulted in a tough conquest. We finagled the price down substantially. This parlay entertained us all.

We were ready to strip out of our clothes and get cleaned up. Per normal routine, Clark showered first so he could go to town and quaff a beer before dinner. This was fine, as it gave me more girl time. The shower felt extra good. Clark walked eight blocks to a burger and fries joint. I joined him an hour later. The draining ride eventually caught up with us. Elbows on the table, chin cupped in my palms, I struggled to stay upright. Clark leaned sluggishly at a 45-degree angle. By the time the meal arrived, we were so exhausted it was tough to keep our eyes open, much less carry on a coherent conversation. Babble ... chew ... babble ... chew ... *tilt*.

Clark's Nose Knows

Day 94: Friday, September 5
Weather: Sunny and windy in the morning, calm later in the day
Distance: 32 miles
Route: Manitowaning, Ontario, Canada, to Tobermory, Ontario, Canada

Once in our saddles after a groggy start, we pedaled fast, pumping hard up the hills and against the wind, making every effort not to stop. We arrived an hour ahead of the ferry's departure. I had time to change out of my unflattering bicycling shorts.

After boarding, we ran for the highest point on the boat so we could watch the launch from the best vantage point. We were relieved to be passengers and not actively involved in moving any kind of transportation forward ourselves. Seagulls circled the boat—augk, augk, augk—swooping and pooping. They caught the wind and sailed along with us effortlessly. I envied the ability to fly.

The gulls were crafty, scoring food from people perched on the deck. Tourists, with arms outstretched, waved tasty tidbits of bread to entice them in closer. The clever birds knew exactly what to do to keep everyone entertained.

During the ferry ride, we met two other sets of long-distance cyclists. We hadn't encountered many others along our route. The first pair on the ferry was an older couple who matched; everything was identical right down to their bikes, panniers, helmets, gloves, and clothes. Even their hand gestures, head movements, and darting eyes seemed in sync. Their slender, athletic bodies were replicas. If you saw them from behind, you'd be hard pressed to tell the two of them apart.

They boasted about their trip—a week-long tour of the area, covering lots of predetermined miles, and nights spent in high-end B&Bs booked months in advance. They plastered themselves close together, but stood a few feet back, purposely creating a void between us.

I suspect our mismatched appearance turned them off. As we attempted further conversation (which we thought was interesting, light, and amusing), they acted bored and standoffish—until they learned we were traveling cross country. With that, their faces turned crimson (simultaneously, of course), and I sensed signs of jealously. The pair abruptly said goodbye, turned, and marched off in unison, leaving us scratching our heads.

Our next encounter with another cycling team was much different. We bonded right away. The two guys, in their late twenties, were educated, articulate, fun, and fascinated by our journey. They were experienced cyclists who appreciated our stamina and *joie de vivre*.

The pair invited us to join them for a beer. They were well-traveled cyclists, spending every vacation riding. Their tales included broken bones, frozen nights, eight flat tires in as many hours, and a five-day stint in a Mexican jail for peeing in the street and then refusing to pay the fine.

The coordinated couple we met earlier wandered by, suspiciously interested in eavesdropping on our animated conversion. We waved them over, but they pretended not to see. Curious as they were, they couldn't bring themselves to join us.

When the ferry docked, we continued our party with the young guys over lunch in downtown Tobermory. Over several rounds of beer and hardy appetizers, we kicked back in the warm sun and compared notes on bumpy roads, heavy traffic, beautiful places, friendly people, and the freedom we felt on the road.

The hours felt like minutes. We were sad to say goodbye to our buddies, but they were ready to rock and roll. The camaraderie, libations, and carb-loading motivated them to ride and us to search for a comfy place to rest a while. Ahh, youth …

We found a perfect cabin motel on a quiet side street, close to the heart of town. Our room was small so we rearranged the furniture to fit our bikes inside. This meant we had to hop over them to reach the bathroom, but at least they were safe and dry indoors.

~

Tobermory was active and alive. We moseyed around the streets and boardwalk, holding hands, shopping, exploring, and watching boats come and go.

The town is situated on the Bruce Peninsula where Lake Huron meets the Georgian Bay. It's a beautiful place, and not at all surprising that it's a haven for hikers, kayakers, photographers, world travelers, golfers, and anyone who loves the great outdoors. The area is also the freshwater scuba-diving capital of the world, with over 20 shipwrecks resting in the surrounding waters.

The Niagara Escarpment, formed over 400 million years ago, extends nearly 465 miles from eastern Wisconsin through Michigan's Upper Peninsula, across Ontario, and on past New York's Niagara Falls. In Tobermory, you can see the escarpment's sharp 200-foot cliffs plunging into the Georgian Bay. Stunning.

~

As night fell, Clark used his exceptional culinary talents to choose a fine dining restaurant for dinner. He ran reconnaissance by reading menus, poking his head into dining rooms, eyeballing plates of food as they whizzed by, sniffing the air, and discreetly peeking into restaurant windows.

Clark struck gold. The minute we walked into the restaurant it felt right. We were immediately acknowledged by the maître d' and led to a window table where we could watch the ebb and flow of activity outside.

Our waiter recommended the house special martini for me, a fruity concoction that I thoroughly enjoyed. Clark ordered a classic martini with extra olives. We toasted to the good life and stole a kiss before the bread basket arrived.

Dinner was extraordinary. Creamy bowls of chowder laden with plump clams, micro-green salads with heirloom tomatoes and goat cheese, and delicate, caught-that-morning whitefish, all complemented by a crisp Chenin Blanc. After dinner, in true European style, we indulged in an assortment of delicious cheeses and chutneys.

On our way out, Clark circled his arm around my waist, looked back at the restaurant, triumphant in his choice, and said, "Now *that* was good."

Sometimes Food is Funny

Day 95: Saturday, September 6
Weather: Strong winds
Distance: 38 miles
Route: Tobermory, Ontario, Canada, to Lion's Head, Ontario, Canada

We rose at first light and went for an early morning walk through Tobermory. So peaceful. We found ourselves daydreaming about moving there. After breathing in the fresh morning air, we craved a good breakfast. Well, maybe it was actually the luscious aromas wafting from a bakery that did it. We were lured in and lingered over baseball-sized blueberry muffins with crunchy brown sugar topping.

We didn't want to leave but knew the weather would inevitably change and Portland, Maine, was still a long way off. While reluctantly packing our bikes, I noticed the metal support rod on my seat had broken off on one side. I'm not sure how the damage happened but deduced it occurred during one of my many tumbles. How dangerous was it to ride this way? Would my seat snap off?

We made a judgment call the seat would be okay, at least for a while. (The damaged seat caused no mishap for the rest of the trip, except to make me nervous when I thought about it.)

Before leaving, a neighbor from the motel stopped to say hello. Roy, a Wisconsin native, slapped me on the back when he learned I am, too. Quite a talker, candid and open. Our kinda guy. He endeared himself by talking about Wisconsin. Top on his list were "Packer Mania" and beer. He claimed "There's a bar on every corner in the state." I let him spin his yarns without interruption, although having grown up there I knew "every corner" wasn't exactly true … well, maybe every other.

~

Barely out of town, we spotted a store touting "Smoked White Fish." We'd heard it was a local favorite and simultaneously screeched to a halt and ran in to purchase some for the road. The owner suggested we try it with cheese bread. Mmm, that sounded good. But, sadly, he didn't sell it, which prompted a quest to find some.

We checked every store within a few-mile radius, zigzagging from place to place with no luck. We were bound and determined, on a jag. Here's the irony: We routinely refused to ride two minutes out of our way when traffic might potentially kill us but had no problem cycling four or five miles to look for something tasty, like cheese bread. It's all about priorities.

The cheese bread search was futile but not the day's only frustration. Pedaling was a challenge with a strong headwind. When it wasn't pushing us backward, it hit hard from the side, blowing us into traffic. We pedaled five times harder and went only half as fast and as far. All of that work with no cheese bread payoff—I'm not sure how we managed.

Clark was not in the mood to ride any more. "Sore buns," he said. I think he was already missing Tobermory and questioning our decision to leave. We could have spent the day sitting in a cozy café enjoying the local charm. But, never knowing what a new dawn will bring, we had forged ahead.

The wind shifted again, this time in our favor. A tailwind accelerated our journey into Lion's Head. We circled around a few blocks, pondering where to stay.

A man, busy working on his house, told us about local accommodations. As it turned out, he also owned a cabin a few blocks away and agreed to rent it to us for the same price it would cost to camp. We jumped at the offer.

The place was pretty rustic. An overwhelming smell of mildew permeated the filthy two-room cabin. I'm allergic to mold and mildew and was sneezing in minutes. The bathroom had no toilet paper or hot water, and a lone dirty hand towel hung from a nail hook. The raw wooden walls were devoid of any decoration except for one of those animatronic fish plaques. I had visions of it whispering my name in the middle of the night: Lizaaaaaaa, Lizaaaaaaaaa … (glub, glub, glub).

The only saving grace was a small fridge to stow our carefully wrapped smoked fish. Oddly, we still had delusions of finding cheese bread.

~

We discovered a restaurant a few blocks away with a lot of cars parked outside. A good sign. Clark ordered ribs while I chose a healthy vegetarian stew with feta cheese, olives, and sun-dried tomatoes over rice.

Clark's plate arrived first, loaded with juicy, succulent ribs and a bounty of French fries. His eyes lit up with anticipation, but he politely waited for my food to arrive. Moments later, we spotted the waitress bustling through the restaurant, making a beeline to our table. My stomach growled anxiously, but that came to an abrupt halt when I gazed down upon the bowl of blandness that appeared before me.

It was some kind of unappealing brown concoction with an odor I can't describe—in fact, so unappetizing Clark immediately handed me two ribs without speaking a word.

Disheartening as it was, the food gave me the giggles. The more I tried to control myself the harder I laughed. I'd almost get it together, then glance up at Clark and start again. Meanwhile, he was trying to keep his own amusement in check. Our laughter was the kind that comes from deep down—ridiculous and unstoppable. We completely lost it.

Of course, the people at the next table noticed and couldn't resist asking, "What's so funny? Are you laughing at your meal? What's in it? We want the same thing!"

"No, you don't," I said, trying to sound composed. "I wouldn't recommend it."

This prompted them to look in my bowl. Although they were too polite to say anything, their faces were a dead giveaway: What the *&^%!*? There's no way we're ordering THAT!

This incited us to laugh harder. No doubt we were creating a scene. Customers across the room stared, and the waitstaff started eyeballing us. Ultimately, we were "asked" to move into the bar so others could enjoy a quieter ambiance while dining. Three rowdy women held court in the center of the lounge and waved us over to join their little party.

They'd noticed our laughing fit from their perches and thought we'd make good company. We took turns buying rounds and whiled away the hours. The group of long-time friends, now in their 50s, gathered annually to hike a new section of the nearby Bruce Trail, which is similar to the famous Appalachian Trail in the eastern United States.

They only walk the first day of each four-day get-together. Then they party hardy, nurse sore muscles, and make plans to do it again the next year.

Their conversations were peppered with "eh's."

"Pretty nice day, eh?"

"The dinner was good, eh?"

"You're having a good time, eh?"

We teased them until the craziest of the gals brought up a good point.

"It's better than saying 'huh?'! Pretty nice day, huh? That's what you say in the U.S."

She was right. "Huh" doesn't sound any better, so Clark jumped in with a compelling thought.

"What if you lived on the border? Then you might say, 'Pretty nice day, eh, huh?'"

One of the ladies fell off her stool laughing.

We dreaded going back to the love shack when the night came to an end, especially since it was pouring. The trio offered us a ride, but we chose to dash the two short blocks. Even though it was an old, ratty place, we were grateful to have a roof over our heads and enough medicinal alcohol in us to keep any germs at bay.

WEEK 15

The Ketchup and Mustard Map

    Day 96:   Sunday, September 7
    Weather: Windy and cold
    Distance: 59 miles
    Route: Lion's Head, Ontario, Canada, to
                  Owen Sound, Ontario Canada

After a round of "Rock, Paper, Scissors," I won first dibs on the bathroom. I hadn't noticed the distinctive rust stain and filthy lime ring in the toilet bowl. During the night, a monstrous cockroach must have taken a swim and met a watery death. A hairy leg suddenly appeared to move. I hit the flush handle with my elbow instinctively and he swirled out of sight.

    Anxious to clean up and get on our way, I turned the shower on to let the water warm up. The pipes banged and clanked. I pulled the moose-themed curtain back and stepped in, but regretted the decision the moment my feet touched the stall floor. It was covered in a gross, slippery slime. Something grayish-green sprouted in the corner. A petrified washcloth lay clumped in the soap dish; no soap in sight. Ewww. I jumped back out, stark naked and dripping wet, racing by a notably interested Clark. My mission: to find soap and two plastic bags to craft into protective footwear so I could finish bathing.

In the end, Clark bypassed the shower all together.

~

While chaining our bikes to a bench outside a diner, we heard familiar laughter. Our friends from last night were seated at the circular horseshoe counter—the kind where you order right from the cook. Once again, their light-hearted demeanor made them the center of attention. One gal pointed with her fork toward two empty seats next to them.

There was never a lull in conversation. It flowed naturally. Even the cook and regulars joined in the spirited banter. As we paid our bill, one of the locals volunteered to give us directions to Owen Sound, our next destination. She drew a detailed map on her napkin, using ketchup and mustard from squeeze bottles to highlight the roads and points of interest.

The back road was smooth, quiet, and ketchup free. Horse farms dotted the countryside. Mares and their foals trotted with us behind fences. They'd whinny and curiously watch us ride away, as if they wanted to tag along.

At the 21-mile mark, we came to Wiarton and stopped for soda and a double-scoop of ice cream. Wasps instantly swarmed us! They were relentless, diving into the soda cans and fearlessly flying into our faces, buzzing around our heads like they were searching for a way in.

Clark took it in stride, casually swatting them with a map so he could get a drink of soda without one riding the can into his mouth. In contrast, I ran around wildly flailing my arms, in serious jeopardy of losing a scoop. While thrashing about, one of the little bastards became embedded in my ice cream. Game over. I threw the cone to the ground and ran for cover inside the store.

Meanwhile, outside, Clark seemed unaffected by the galaxy of wasps orbiting around him. Inside, I watched my ice cream melt into a gooey, insect-covered puddle. No appetite for another cone.

Clark finally waved me out and protectively helped me on my bike. The wasps didn't sting either of us, but they didn't go away either. The torment continued as they circled our bikes and crawled into our front packs. They continued to dive bomb from all directions as we sped out of town. Thankfully, a strong wind moved in and blew them away.

We stopped down the road for a second shot at a wasp-free beverage. The country store was tiny but had enough room for a little bakery in the back. The aromas wafting in the air were heavenly. Our eyes scanned the shelves and there it was. The infamous cheese bread!

We cracked open the smoked white fish and fresh plums we had stashed in our bags and had ourselves a feast on a picnic table outside the store. The cheese bread lived up to all the hype. We ate every last crumb.

~

Traveling along, we rolled up and down gentle hills, passed idyllic farmland, and glimpsed views of the sound. Out of nowhere, a Great Blue Heron swooped overhead. We stopped in time to see it grab a snake in the brush nearby and start to devour it. The bird arched his head back, spastically gulping the snake down, inch by inch. We stood frozen as we observed this up-close spectacle of nature.

~

Owen Sound is in a lush valley, surrounded by ravines and hills punctuated by a harbor and bay. We walked our bikes through the center of town to give our legs a rest.

In one block, we skirted around some degenerate types knocking back something out of a bag. The mostly toothless men ogled my behind, winking and nudging each other. A few young women, who looked older than their probable ages, leaned on signposts or dozed in abandoned building doorways.

Moving on, we mounted our bikes and headed out of the city center to a find a place to stay. "Up" was the only option to get out of the valley. This meant ascending a steep hill about six blocks long. It was a tough one, the kind where first gear feels like 10th. Our exertion paid off. We found a reasonably priced motel at the crest of the hill. We paid up and moved in.

The room was simple but felt like a palace when compared to the previous night's less-than-appealing accommodations, with its big bed and all-important clean sheets, sparkling shower, and hot water. We ordered Chinese take-out, ate our fill, then collapsed in front of the TV.

Rottie Man

Day 97: Monday, September 8
Weather: Constantly changing between sunny and cloudy, windy and still
Distance: 90 miles
Route: Owen Sound, Ontario, Canada, to Cookstown, Ontario, Canada

Another hill. What?! We thought we were already at the top, but a short, very steep climb awaited us. It only took seconds to get the blood flowing and the sweat dripping as we started humping up the hill. The traffic picked up, and the dangerously slim shoulder eventually disappeared. After a few harrowing miles, we pulled over to consider our options.

A young man, stopped on the opposite side of the road, shouted, "Hey, are you guys alright?"

"Yeah, there's just more traffic than we expected," Clark shouted back.

"I know, the road here sucks," he said, as he dashed across the street to join us.

His name was Kirk. He was a chef at a high-end restaurant and had a sense of humor that wouldn't quit. Clark and Kirk immediately bonded over their food connection and dry wit. Unexpectedly, an oversized truck screeched up next to us and slammed to a halt that rocked the vehicle. We could hear metal junk slam around in the beat-up jalopy. A red-faced man with a balding head and long, scraggly ponytail glowered at us from the open window. His eyes bulged with some deep, unknown rage.

"Get out of here now," he threatened. "You're on my property and if my Rottie breaks his chain, you're in trouble. This is your only warning!"

We were stunned. What had we done? No greeting, no questions, no introductions. He was so out of control we just stared at him. (There went my theory that men with ponytails are cool.)

We looked around, trying to figure out how we could possibly be on his property. It was enclosed with a prison-grade chain-link fence and those spikey things on top. We were definitely outside that boundary.

I finally managed to spit out a few words, "We were just talking and…"

He cut me off by screaming, "I saw you standing here! I *saw* you standing here! You have no business standing here. It's not your property and I have a crazy-mean Rottie!"

He was out of control, pounding on the side of his truck for emphasis. I winced every time, imaging that meaty fist hitting me. His nostrils flared like a bull ready to charge.

"We're not touching your property, man. We're leaving in a minute," Kirk said calmly, "I was just trying to help these riders. Relax."

"I got a Rottie," he repeated loudly. "And he don't like strangers much."

With that he barreled away, the over-sized tires pelting us with gravel. What a bizarre encounter. The guys started laughing as they brushed dust off themselves, apparently undisturbed by the man's behavior. I was concerned the nutjob might turn around and mow us down.

"Ooooooh, the Rottie Man!" Kirk mocked. "The dude probably has a meth lab or grows pot in his basement," he speculated. "Welcome to Canada. We're not all lunatics like that, eh?"

"Good to know," Clark replied, shaking his head.

"Let's move before he does another drive-by," I said nervously, as we waved goodbye to Kirk.

We wheeled our bikes a few blocks to an obviously public spot to check the map and reconnoiter. As expected, Rottie Man drove by. His menacing glare sent chills down my spine. Clark just huffed and went back to the map. The second time "R.M." passed, we pretended not to notice.

~

We put our heads down and pedaled for 40 miles without stopping, then picked up a new map in Collingwood. The next section of road was confusing, even for Clark and his stellar sense of direction. We cycled to Wasaga Beach on what looked like a tiny back road on the map. Unfortunately, we ran into terrible truck traffic. One driver plowed by so fast and close that we purposely tumbled off our bikes onto a grassy bank rather than risk turning into pancakes.

We laid there breathless for a moment. But, we were troupers, so we gritted our teeth and pushed on for another 20 miles. Clark was disheartened. Our map was so misleading he couldn't tell where we were or how far we had to go. I tried to keep him calm. Almost magically, a young couple driving in the opposite direction spotted our frustrated faces and turned around to see if we needed help.

They assured us the town of Angus was only five miles away, then cheered us up further with homemade chocolate chip cookies. The beauty of our trip was, again, encapsulated in small moments like this. We took a break in Angus, had a cold drink, and stopped at a bank to replenish our cash. After exploring a bit and relaxing our muscles, we took off.

We stopped in Baxter for lunch. After a chance to rest and revive, we headed east. Our challenge was to find the best route around Lake Simcoe. It seemed we were always trying to get around something: a mountain, freeway, big city, lake or other body of water.

Just outside Thornton, a huge white dog came tearing out of nowhere and chased me down the street. He circled my bike barking wildly and tried to jump up at me. I wasn't sure if he was friend or foe. My latest dog-whispering technique was to slow down and talk with a soothing voice, "Good boy, you're all right, you're okay, don't bite my leg off, I'm a friend."

He "ruffed" at me a few more times, calmed by my tone, his circle widening away from my bike. He started to run back across the street to his yard when suddenly a car came out of nowhere and almost hit him. The driver swerved violently to avoid the dog but nearly killed me in doing so. Our eyes met for a terrifying second. He was paralyzed in fear, gripping the steering wheel, eyes registering shock at my sudden appearance. I'm not sure whose heart was beating faster at that moment. I missed a deadly collision by a hair.

He kept driving without so much as tapping the brakes, probably so panicked at the thought of nearly taking two lives that he just wanted to get the hell out of there. Clark was riding ahead and missed the whole thing. The adrenalin kicked in. I raced to catch up and found him pacing around on the side of the road. He was ranting about a speeding driver nearly knocking him off his bike. What a coincidence.

~

Cookstown was a bust. No place to stay, so we continued on. Five miles later, we almost knocked each other over as we hurriedly turned into a KOA Campground. The large flat field had room for lots of RVs, but no trees or greenery. Very sterile and empty. While pitching our tent, we heard a happy whistle as the campground host came strolling toward us.

"I couldn't help noticing you guys drinking grape soda when you checked in," he teased us with a grin. "That doesn't seem right. You deserve something a little more adult for all your hard work."

With that he handed us two ice-cold beers.

"On the house," he said. "This is from my private stash. Enjoy!" And with a cheery wave he left as quickly as he had come.

In one brief moment, everything got brighter. Now we saw things differently. Instead of feeling stark, the campground seemed clean. Instead of lonely, it was peaceful and all around us was nature, even if it wasn't lush. We finished setting up camp, happy and content.

We were starving and started the hunt for dinner. First, a dash across the busy interstate, then a mile-long trudge on its shoulder—the promise of a good meal motivating us.

The restaurant we came across looked busy and we hoped no reservation was needed. A waif-thin woman, with a bun pulled so tight she looked alien, greeted us with an icy stare. Straightening her neatly pressed jacket and squaring her shoulders, she assessed us with displeasure. Her lips pinched as she considered whether to allow us inside. No words were passed. The silence was deafening. Her judgmental rudeness was too much for Clark.

"Apparently, two cyclists traveling across country don't meet with your approval. Never mind, you don't meet with mine."

We were out of sight before she figured out what hit her.

At this point, our only choice was fast-food chicken at a nearby mall. Surprisingly, the meal was delicious. The juicy meat was roasted rather than deep-fried, accompanied by creamy coleslaw, a loaded baked potato, and a bottomless glass of iced tea. It was a paper-plate, plastic-fork, thin-napkin kind of place. But, it would have been easy to fool hoity-toity diners if the same food was served on fancy china in a candlelit setting.

We walked leisurely back to our campsite. I read while Clark smoked a cigar and observed the night sky. It was going to be a cold night so we bundled up and snuggled in together. The long day had its share of disappointments and frustrations, but we managed to travel 90 miles without realizing it. Before drifting off to sleep, we agreed to pedal hard the next day and get to the shores of Lake Ontario, a challenging 100+ miles away.

> I could barely zip the sleeping bag over my body when we started the trip. The undertaking was like stuffing a sausage into a tight casing. Now, I enjoyed zipping up my bag with ease and still had space to roll over and breathe comfortably.
>
> Ahhhh, the simple pleasures.

Lunatics Outside the Door

Day 98: Tuesday, September 9
Weather: Sunny and warm
Distance: 120 miles
Route: Cookstown, Ontario, Canada, to Port Hope, Ontario, Canada

The morning dew covered our gear, leaving it sopping wet. We didn't want to deal with it, so walked to the mall for breakfast. Fog like the proverbial pea soup was so heavy we could barely see two feet in front of us. We lost sight of the KOA office just steps outside the gates and couldn't discern the well-lit McDonald's right across the street. We walked the eight blocks in near-blindness. Crossing the freeway was a scary guessing game. Two steps forward, three steps back. Once safely across, and seated in a 24-hour diner, our ragged nerves calmed.

Fortified by strong coffee and cheese Danish, we were ready to face the freeway again. The fog had lifted by the time we got back to the campsite, replaced by bright sun and clear skies. An unusually warm September day awaited.

We cycled with renewed energy and resolved to sleep on the shores of Lake Ontario that night. It was slow going. We traveled 2 miles east, then 3 miles south, 1 mile east again, then curved around in what seemed like a circle. The confusing twists and turns made it feel as if we'd made no progress at all. This went on for hours and caused some bickering, until we realized the road wasn't our design. The plan was to go as far south as we could while avoiding the metropolis of Toronto.

We had a brief respite from traffic near Mt. Albert, but traffic on Highway 30 unnerved us again. A massive lumber truck forced me off the road, pitching me face down in the gravel. I was scratched, scared, and humiliated. My mood turned dark and fed into Clark's negative state of mind. Feeding off each other's energy often exacerbated a stressful situation, much to my distress. I could feel it happening.

Things lightened a bit when we hit Highway 8. We managed not to get killed … or kill each other. It was one of those pissy days. One moment, everything was fabulous; the next, not so much. We were moving forward, but the zigzag riding was slow and disconcerting. Nevertheless, we continued our mission: Get to the water by day's end.

Trying to decipher the map led to more frustration. At one baffling juncture, Clark thought we were in one place but I was convinced we were farther along. He said north. I said south. The crabbiness quotient cranked up a notch. He was usually right about directions, and I rarely questioned his map-reading expertise, but this time I knew I was right. Clark refused to listen, intent on studying the map and ignoring me.

In the heat of our stand-off, a woman mending a fence nearby guessed what was happening and offered to help. What courage she had to jump in the middle. Maybe she was oblivious, maybe she understood, or maybe she was some sort of angel. In no time, we had clear directions to Port Hope, right where we wanted to be. And, just for the record, I was right.

Twenty miles to go on that arduous day. We plodded to Highway 28, then rested in front of a house with (guess what?) another Rottweiler. The pooch practically popped a vein barking at us. We were so tired it was easy to ignore him. Eventually, he barked himself into exhaustion and moved on to other interests. The dog's owner flopped across a dilapidated couch on the porch, a cig hanging from his bottom lip. He looked oddly like Rottie Man, even had the ponytail and beer gut going. Clark quietly joked about them being cousins. Rottie Man 2 didn't say a word, but never took his eyes off of us. Wonder what he was thinking? His fixed stare was disturbing, and it was getting dark.

Eight miles outside Port Hope, we pulled over to rest again. A nearby farm field looked like a good place to pitch a tent. We eyeballed it for a moment, but the thought of a good dinner kept us going. I later likened this day to "Alice in Wonderland's" journey—the one where she ran and ran but stayed in one place.

At the "Welcome to Port Hope" sign we paused for a forgiving kiss. A stop at the closest gas station to inquire about the cheapest motel foreshadowed what was to come. The young attendant seemed uneasy making a recommendation and tried to steer us toward more pricey digs. We insisted on cut-rate accommodations.

"Okaaaaay, this is a cheap one and not too far away," he said, looking worried, eyes shifting back and forth uncomfortably.

Vaguely registering but dismissing his nervous demeanor, we were on our way. It was almost 8 p.m., cold and dark. Because we were overly tired, it took a while to find the place. Our exhaustion and the dimly lit parking lot hid many truths. We chuckled a bit at the "Bate's

Motel" appearance and walked inside. The check-in experience was ... interesting. The clerk barely looked at us and only grunted a few words. His dead, bloodshot eyes gazed occasionally toward the door, as if he was waiting for something to happen. Then he stared at the floor for extended periods while we waited for our next instructions. Drunk? Drugged? We could have been wielding bloody swords and he wouldn't have batted an eye. But this wasn't a four-star joint. Hand over your money; I'll give you the key. Get out.

We walked stiffly to the room. It was a dive, but we were so tired the condition of the place didn't really register. We pulled our bikes inside and headed out to eat, stumbling inside the first restaurant we saw. It never felt so good to sit down. After wolfing down something non-descript we headed back to the motel slowly.

A tall, gaunt man staggered toward us, followed by a sloppy-drunk woman traipsing behind him a few steps. She was yelling incoherently, "John, you ... *ot me ayoun* never." Or something.

As he passed, he veered threateningly into my path. Clark pulled me quickly out of harm's way. I got a good look at the guy. A knit cap covered the crazy's straggly hair. Even in the dark, his wild eyes hinted at trouble. The stench of beer and cigarettes wafted and lingered in the air. The woman took off her hooker heels and chased after him, pounding on his back for attention.

Back in the relative safety of our room, we fell into the lumpy bed for a well-deserved sleep.

~

At bar closing time, a loud pounding on the door shook us from a deep slumber. A woman outside was screaming for someone.

"John, lemme in! Lemme in NOW, John. Come on, John. I know you're in there. Lemme in!" She rattled the doorknob and banged on the windows so hard I was afraid they'd break.

The entire neighborhood must have heard the commotion, although I'm not convinced there was another soul staying at the motel or anywhere nearby.

Clark flew out of bed and shouted toward the door, "Get the hell out of here! You're drunk and you have the wrong room."

That quieted the woman for a moment, then the pounding started again.

Clark flung the drapes open and was surprised to see the same bar hag we'd encountered earlier that night. Still shoeless, her black pantyhose were striped with runs. She was having trouble standing, leaning on the door for support. Clark shut the drapes and came back to bed. She mumbled a bit, then stopped.

It was nearly impossible to fall back asleep after having our senses so rudely assaulted, but we finally drifted off. The moment we were back in REM mode, the phone jolted us awake. I answered, but no one was there, so hung up. The phone rang several more times. No one said a word, but I heard muffled breathing.

When the calls stopped, the drunken woman came back. Clark peeked through the drapes and saw she was accompanied by the same guy she had chased down the street earlier. We could hear them trying to fit a key in *our* door.

Clark yanked the drapes back and bellowed, "Get the hell away from here." He used his most menacing expression to accentuate his displeasure.

She boldly flipped him off, which infuriated Clark, setting off a three-way screaming match through the door. No managers appeared, no neighbors shouted "Shut up!," and, most importantly, no cops swarmed in. This confirmed our suspicions that no one else was around.

They were loaded and confused. Clark moved to my side of the bed, closer to the door, and with heightened senses we waited for the light of day. But, there was more to come. This time we heard whispered voices outside our room, then someone playing with the lock, rattling the door loudly to get in. Clark jumped out of bed just as our drunken "friend" entered the room. She had a key!

Clark moved faster than I'd ever seen him move. He ripped the key out of the woman's hand, shoved her back outside, slammed the door, and locked it before she knew what hit her.

Silence. Then, we heard, "You're a dead man."

The satanic tone shot chills through my body.

She was at the window again. We locked eyes. The look on her face was pure evil. We were afraid she was more than a drunk—maybe an escapee from jail or a mental hospital. What next? Would she spray bullets through our room? Would she come back with more friends and break down the flimsy door? Would they wait until morning and stalk us on the road?

We tried calling the front office and police, but just like a bad horror film the phone was dead. I seriously questioned our decision not to bring a cell phone. Strange that she could call in, but we couldn't call out. We wondered if she'd cut the phone wire. And how did she get a key to our room? Was there demonic control going on?

We talked about one or both of us going for help. Was it safer to be trapped in the room with lunatics targeting us or be outside with no protection? Dawn wasn't far off, so we moved a chair by the door and kept a steady eye out the window.

The anonymous phone calls continued until daybreak and then stopped. Maybe they were vampires.

Between our real and imagined fears, it was the scariest night of the trip. We waited nervously and listened in silence as the wind picked up. An odd, desolate bump-bumping of a cardboard box tumbling around in the empty parking lot sounded menacing, like a premonition of impending doom.

A Few Miles, a New World

> Day 99: Wednesday, September 10
> Weather: Windy and raining
> Distance: 10 miles
> Route: Port Hope, Ontario, Canada, to
> Cobourg, Ontario Canada

We tentatively opened the door, making sure the coast was clear. The streets outside proved other humans existed. A truck rumbled by as we walked to the office. The real world was waking up. The motel manager's face remained hard and immobile as we enlightened her about our horrifying experience and demanded our money back.

She pretended not to understand, shrugging her shoulders, feigning ignorance. Clark gave her his wordless death stare. It was intimidating to be on the receiving end of that. But the woman's harsh façade remained in place, probably accustomed to the complaints of unsuspecting travelers.

"What do you expect when you stay in a place like this?" she snapped.

I was incredulous and tried to match Clark's death stare, but she didn't notice me. Her gaze remained fixed on Clark. She was so nonchalant I wondered if she was in on the break-in.

Clark changed tactics and persisted. Instead of getting angry, he used psychology, inserting words that put fear in shady hearts: police, authorities, report, arrest, and shut you down.

I was impressed with his calm, assertive insistence.

"I'll give you half back," she finally relented.

"No. A full refund," Clark responded calmly. "Unless you want me to call the cops."

He slid the two keys toward her—our key and the mystery key—and then yanked them back quickly.

"I want to know how a stranger got our key and why we couldn't call for help," Clark demanded. He was seething.

She had no answers and grudgingly handed over the full refund. Clark counted the money, making sure there was no insult added to injury, and we left.

The harsh light of day brought a new perspective on what a hellhole we'd stayed in. A door hung off a hinge, dirty boot prints leaving evidence of an unknown assailant kicking it in. Broken windows and jagged glass. A red stiletto soaked up dirty water in a puddle. Garbage overflowed the dumpster. Everything in disrepair, like people had just given up.

There was no sign of our intruders and no movement from any of the rooms. Our business was done. We packed quickly, anxious to slip out of the motel and leave town. Fearing the crazies might spot us, we walked our bikes quietly from the parking lot and up the road, using hand signals to communicate.

We wanted to distance ourselves from the motel. Cobourg was 10 miles away, far enough to feel safe and a place to rest and regroup. A light, misty rain turned to a heavy drizzle as the wind picked up. We pedaled as fast as our tired bodies (and minds) could go.

A few miles can make a big difference. We let go of the night's turmoil and embraced our new surroundings as the sun poked through the clouds. Cobourg was beautiful with its perfectly restored buildings, reminiscent of Old World Europe. Quaintness reigned. Colorful flowers spilled from pots placed in nooks and crannies. Interesting shops lined the streets. Restaurants featured diverse menus with food sourced from local farms.

Cobourg is nicknamed "Ontario's Feel Good Town." It, indeed, felt good.

An enticing German restaurant caught our attention. We dismounted our bikes to take a closer look at the menu. The owner abruptly appeared, annoyed we had leaned our handlebars against his window, reprimanding us in a thick German accent. Clark smiled, responding in perfect German. He offered our apologies and asked the gentleman if we needed dinner reservations. Our indiscretion was quickly forgiven and the reservation confirmed.

I listened as the two conversed jovially, trying to pick up what they were discussing. It turns out Clark inquired about a place to stay. The man steered us toward a motel hidden away in a lovely lakeside neighborhood. We bid him *Auf Wiedersehen* and were off to check-in.

The motel manager knew we were coming and was outside to greet us. The reception area was cheerful, and fresh-baked cookies awaited, still warm from the oven. To sweeten the deal further, he gave us a special rate, without any prompting.

Our room was newly painted, everything white, clean, and welcoming. The bed looked deliciously comfortable, sheets, blanket, and spread tucked in neatly and wrinkle free. Lace curtains created dappled shadows on the walls. A combination of spa-like beauty and tranquility.

A storm rolled in, but we were getting hungry. We donned our rain gear and found our way to Victoria Park Beach. The slight detour was invigorating and cool air hitting my face felt good. We strolled out to the lighthouse, listening to falling drops pelt the water and watching waves crash over the jetty. It reminded me of growing up on Lake Michigan. I'd spent hours observing winter waves and ice pummel the shore, changing the landscape over the years.

~

Two big, cheesy bowls of French onion soup and hot bread took the chill out of the cold, wet day. Satiated, we went back to the room for a nap. The weather intensified, and the storm raged outside; rain pounded our deck, wind gusted, and branches rapped on the window.

After dark, we headed to the heart of town and discovered it was transformed by thousands of beautiful, soft lights dotting the buildings and trees. Everything bathed in a candlelight glow. The street was bustling. We strolled along, hand-in-hand, glancing into restaurants and shops, watching the merriment within.

We quickened our pace, eagerly anticipating an authentic German meal. The host smiled and checked our reservation, motioning to a waitress to seat us by the window. We sipped a velvety, red *Spätburgunder* and watched the parade of people pass by outside. As the wine warmed our spirits, Clark suggested I order for us.

I chose *Kartoffelsuppe* to start, then Hasenpfeffer and *Schlachtplatte*. Translation: bacon and potato soup, rabbit stew, and mixed sausages with sauerkraut. Peach cobbler (a la mode, of course) for dessert, with a nightcap of Obstler, a classic German fruit Schnapps. I loved it when Clark ordered a nightcap, because it meant more dessert for me.

Clark leaned back with a satisfied expression, "That was the best German meal I've had since living in Europe."

That was it. We deserved to spend another day in Cobourg; it was simply too wonderful to leave.

Liza McQuade

The Way to a Man's Heart

    Day 100:   Thursday, September 11
    Weather: Heavy rain
    Distance: Rest day
    Route: Enjoyed Cobourg, Ontario, Canada, on foot

Rain was coming down hard as we started to stir. A peaceful night's sleep in our little hideaway refreshed us at last. Feeling lazy, we sipped coffee in bed and fantasized about winning the lottery.

The weather cleared as we lingered over breakfast. Then, a few practical matters were at hand. First up, laundry. We carried our clothes to the nearest laundromat. I loaded them up while Clark took his bike to a repair shop.

These two simple chores worked up a hunger that a spinach salad, pasta, and escargot quelled quite nicely. So did the liter of Reisling.

The rain moved back in, and by the time the check was paid it turned into a downpour. So off we ran, racing from doorway to doorway, ducking for cover under trees until we were home. We stripped off our wet things and dove into bed for an afternoon of lovemaking, napping, reading, and resting. I'm not sure we could have scripted a nicer day.

~

The waiters recognized us the moment we stepped back into the German restaurant. No complaint from me on having a repeat performance. Clark whet his whistle with a Hefeweizen beer. We ordered broccoli and mushroom soup and indulged in the *schnitzel* and *spaetzle* paired with a crisp and savory Grüner Veltliner wine. Black Forest cake crowned another exceptional meal.

Clark whispered "I love you" as we walked back to our sanctuary. I giggled, silently acknowledging the truth: the way to a man's heart is through his stomach.

Bartering Gone Bad

Day 101: Friday, September 12
Weather: Clear and sunny
Distance: 63 miles
Route: Cobourg, Ontario, Canada, to Picton, Ontario Canada

We woke to heavy fog, gray skies, and the threat of rain, a bit disheartening since it's not as enticing to ride in inclement weather.

On the walk along the beach to town for breakfast, we met an odd but friendly old man who'd lived in Cobourg forever. He had cartoon caricature features: a monstrous head, pointy nose, and fleshy cheeks. He walked hunched over with a gait like Quasimodo.

I wrongly assumed he might be a bit crazy, but it turned out he was articulate and knowledgeable. He shared highlights of Cobourg's history, brightening as he passed along anecdotes of a bygone era. There were ghost stories, encounters with famous travelers, and reminiscences about his love life—a woman who stole his heart and died long ago. He dabbed tears from his eyes with a wrinkled handkerchief, apologizing for going on so long.

We were both touched. Clark squeezed my hand gently and let go. Instinctively, I moved closer and gave the old man a hug.

"Thank you," he said warmly as he hugged back for a long moment. The gentleman regained his composure, straightened up, and tucked the hankie back in a pocket. We could tell he still wanted to talk.

"You're here at the right time. It's quieter now."

In the summer, Cobourg is packed with tourists. He estimated a diverse mix of 1,200 to 1,500 people a day might share this little stretch of beach. During daily walks along the water, he observed clusters of people, their territories defined by the boundaries of their beach towels.

The Italians picnicked with platters of antipasto, crusty bread, and wine discreetly hidden in paper bags. The Greeks drank Ouzo, disguised in paper sacks, and dined on stuffed grape leaves, lamb wrapped in pita, and baklava. The Russian crowd opted for vodka cloaked in the same fashion and ate hearty kebabs and tiny smoked sardines. Canadians and Americans munched on cold chicken, chips, cheese, and crackers while drinking beer camouflaged in brown paper wrap.

Since drinking on the beach is technically illegal, the man said concealing the evidence was the best way for tourists and locals to hide it from the obviously tolerant authorities.

With all the talk of food, we were getting hungry. I took the opportunity for a final hug. Clark shook the man's hand, gave him a bear hug, and said, "Thank you, sir. What a pleasure to meet you."

~

Breakfast was an exercise in frustration. The restaurant offered a package deal: an entree, coffee, and toast for one reasonable price. But, when I simply asked to substitute juice for coffee, the "waitron" seemed confused, staring at the order pad blankly. Pen hovering over paper, she wandered off without a word. At her next appearance, she brought me another person's order, which looked tasty but wasn't mine. She snagged it off the table without apology and trundled back toward the kitchen, then made a beeline to another table of diners. After plunking the plate down robotically, she disappeared behind the swinging doors for a long while.

The toast was missing the next time she showed her face. Clark received scrambled eggs instead of fried, and coffee rather than tea. No juice in sight. We looked at our plates, then back at her, then back at the plates. She picked them up silently and walked away. We sat there stunned. Apparently, asking for a slight change in menu was completely discombobulating. That was the last we saw of her.

Another waitress eventually brought us breakfast. Not what we ordered, but breakfast nonetheless. We dug in without complaint.

~

The sun was finally shining—a beautiful day for a ride. We coasted happily on a side road that took us along the water's edge. The route transitioned away from the lake into a heavily wooded forest. The canopy of leaves was speckled with yellow and orange, a preview of autumn's glory.

Life was good. A day like this reminded me of what's important. I looked at Clark and smiled. His face lit up, just like it always did when I smiled that way. He could tell I was happy and in love. We both were.

~

We picked up the pace and pedaled at what we thought was record speed. Without warning, two young men on bikes appeared from behind, barely winded—their packs small and bicycles sleek. Traffic was light, so they slowed to ride parallel with us.

"You look like a mule train moving along with all that baggage. Where are you going?" one of the guys inquired.

We gave them the condensed version.

They were on a weekend adventure, covering several hundred miles. Soon, they left us in the dust, waving and out of sight in the blink an eye.

It was after 2 p.m. when we stopped for lunch in Brighton. The cook, who also waited tables, told a story about a disappointing trip to "The States."

"I went to Tennessee to see movie stars," she explained with complete sincerity. "I spent the whole week looking and didn't see a single one!"

We smiled, engaged by her sweet personality and infectious giggle.

She confessed returning home upset but vowed to give Tennessee another try.

We suggested L.A.

The other diners chuckled quietly. Even the grumpy-looking guy in the corner couldn't help but crack a smile.

~

The miles clicked by effortlessly until we had to slow down behind a loaded hay truck. Clark grinned and said, "Well, this is new. I'm not sure quite what to do. Follow or pass?"

As soon as there were no other cars in sight, we jacked our pace up to 28 mph and passed the truck with ease. I glanced at the driver as we zoomed by. The farmer sported a dusty John Deere cap and clenched a short stogie between his lips. He looked bothered by our maneuver.

I swear he sped up. We could almost feel the heat of the engine on our hinders. For nearly 7 miles, our hearts and legs pumped hard. The truck turned left into a driveway just as we were losing momentum. We stopped to check our pulses and, once satisfied we weren't going to keel over, pedaled on.

~

A dog barked aggressively, but unseen, in the distance. The incessant sound grew louder and closer. A broad-chested, thick-legged canine came into view. Its head was gigantic. He wasn't leashed and paid no attention to the commands of his master. The black beast shot toward me, growling and snapping at my heels. Adrenalin kicked in. I humped along as fast as I could. Dogs love a chase. He barreled along next to me, snarling and trying to nip my ankles. The master did nothing.

Unconsciously, I veered into the middle of the highway, then traversed to the other side of the road, screaming for the dog to stop. I careened out of control, hit the gravel, and tumbled down a hill. After coming to a rest, I looked for the animal. He was sitting there, smugly staring at me from above. He won.

The master peered down at me for a moment and walked away without a word. The dog turned tail and followed.

My heart thumped wildly. I stayed frozen on the ground for some time. It occurred to me that Clark was riding ahead and had missed the whole incident. I brushed myself off, collected my scattered belongings, and dragged my bike back up to the road. When I caught up to Clark I was still visibly shaken and white as a sheet. He held me close until my composure was regained. I'm not sure what scared me more: the possibility of an insane dog ripping my leg off or the fact that I'd veered into the middle of a highway without realizing it. I was lucky nothing more serious happened.

The day was winding down. Time to think about lodging. We turned into a small motel, parked our bikes, and headed for the office. A man with a white, neatly trimmed beard scowled at us from behind the counter. He was tall and thin, almost emaciated. Hearing aids nestled in each ear. A plaid shirt, tucked tightly into high-water pants, accentuated his narrow frame. I fixated on his belt buckle. It was an absurdly large 3D eagle crafted of a brass-like metal. Mesmerizing.

An awkward amount of silence passed before Clark broke the ice loudly.

"Good afternoon!"

The man took a startled step back. His sourpuss face gave away an immediate distaste for our presence. I inquired politely about the price of accommodations. When the owner stated the rate, Clark asked if he would take $10 less.

A distinctly throbbing vein pulsated on the man's forehead. He growled his refusal in a rough German accent, spewing us with spittle. He was clearly offended by our innocent attempt at bartering.

I tried to ease the tension: "Oh, you don't feel like bartering today?"

His face turned darker crimson. He scanned us back and forth, up and down.

"You wouldn't ask a restaurant for a discount would you? Would you barter at Kmart? Or the grocery store? How come you try to barter here?"

Clark seemed stunned and stood up taller, testosterone flowing through his body. Sensing a possible "issue," I tried a softer approach and smiled.

"We barter everywhere. Most people are happy to fill a vacancy, so it's usually a win/win ...," my voice trailing off as I saw he was unbudgeable.

His frown furrowed deeper and his nose flared and twitched.

Clark took over again. In fluent German, he said, "I was born in Munich. Where in Germany did you grow up?"

Something snapped inside the man.

"What does *that* have to do with anything?" he spat in English. "Where I'm from has nothing to do with whether you'll be allowed to stay here or not!"

OK. Things weren't going well.

"I didn't mean to offend you," Clark said sincerely. "I speak German and always look for a chance to practice."

"I'm Dutch."

We were striking out on every turn, wondering which foot to put in our mouths next.

"I think you should find another place to stay."

Good idea. We bumbled into each other trying to get out the door at the same time.

~

We found another motel half a block down—light years away. Undeterred by our last encounter, I tried to barter. I just couldn't help myself. Clark gave me "The Look."

The clerk peered at me curiously for a moment then said, "How does 20% sound?"

I gave Clark a sideways glance, pleased that I hadn't lost my touch, and put the credit card down with a smile.

Celebrity Status and Then the Fall from Grace

Day 102: Saturday, September 13
Weather: Sunny and clear
Distance: 59 miles
Route: Picton, Ontario, Canada, to Wolfe Island, Ontario Canada

I ordered an English muffin and fruit for breakfast. A safe, yet uninspiring choice. Clark went straight for eggs benedict. He tortured me by circling a forkful of rich goodness past my face. My eyes hungrily devoured it as he scooped the luscious chunk into his mouth. He won the menu-decision contest. This time.

Following breakfast, we pushed aside our plates and plotted the day's route. A few cups of coffee later, lost in our maps and engrossed in our dreams, we had planned the remainder of our trip without realizing it. As much as this plan was down on paper, we knew things could and would change again.

We walked along the river holding hands, pleased with ourselves for actually planning ahead. Birds dipped and dove for their morning meal, and suntanned fishermen trolled for a catch, their little motors buzzing along.

~

It was only 10 kilometers from Picton to the Glenora Ferry landing. Although purely accidental, our timing for a boat ride was perfect. We pedaled right up onto the vessel and minutes later were chugging across the short stretch of river to the other side.

~

We wandered quietly among crumbling gravestones in an old Adolphustown cemetery. Americans loyal to England's crown fled to Adolphustown to avoid the prejudice they felt at home. In 1784, shortly after the first Loyalists landed in Ontario, one of their children died. The cemetery was established as the first Loyalist burial ground.

The setting was so powerfully serene, I contemplated what it must have been like to live and die there so long ago. We laid down on the grass, taking in the gentle breeze, watching the branches sway to and fro, drifting off in our own meditative thoughts.

Melodious humming shook us from our reverie. A woman approached, her arms laden with flowers. She smiled and waved, stopping to set the vase down near a large gravestone.

"There's an historic church up the way, if you're interested. Church of St. Alban the Martyr," she told us. "It's closed today, but I'll be happy to make a call and see if someone can meet you for a tour. Would you like that?"

How could we refuse? In minutes, we were standing in front of the church, admiring the Gothic architecture and large, round stained-glass window. We saw a plump, bespectacled woman racing toward us, waving so enthusiastically her whole body undulated like a dog wagging its tail. She was out of breath by the time she reached us. Beads of sweat glistened on her round face. She patted disheveled hair back in place and straightened her drab brown dress.

"Welcome to St. Albans!" she said with a slight bow, greeting us like English royalty.

We started the tour, exploring every corner of the church, every inch of the property. Whatever question we had, she knew the answer—effortlessly. Construction on the church started in 1884, 100 years after the Loyalists arrived. The first service was held in 1890. The building was meticulously crafted of local stone, replacing an earlier wooden structure on the site. A unique bell tower housed a bell believed to be the oldest in Canada. Our guide was fascinating, passionate and made history exciting.

~

A few miles later, we found another reason to stop. Fresh cider and apples, just-picked from the tree. The vendor cut a chunk of apple for each of us to sample and offered a little taste of cider. The ploy worked. We bought a dozen apples and a two-liter jug of juice, gulping the sweet-tart liquid straight from the container. I poured the extra into our water bottles and packed the fruit for a treat later in the day.

The traffic was so light, we almost had the road to ourselves. Amherst, Wolfe, and a scattering of smaller islands dotted the vista. We wheeled along the water, stopping often to eat apples and enjoy the views. During one intermission, New York was visible in the distance.

The Kingston Ferry was 25 miles ahead, then one more ferry after that, and we'd be back in the good ole U.S.A.

~

Loyalist flags hung in the harbor town of Bath, where a strong allegiance to the town's history still exists. There was a Loyalist bookstore, Loyalist Gardens, and a Loyalist Golf and Country Club. The European influence evident everywhere.

We were hungry. No time to be picky, so popped into the closest place still serving lunch. A bell dinged above our heads when we opened the door, signaling our arrival. Diners glanced up momentarily then went back to eating. A waiter smiled and pointed to a spot near the window. We surveyed our surroundings and noticed everything was clean, but old and worn. Many meals had been enjoyed there.

Flowered plastic cloths covered small, creaky tables. Ours was a little too wobbly, so Clark wedged a sugar pack under one leg to give it more stability. The silverware, wrapped in a paper napkin, sat next to a small basket of jams and a tiny vase sprouting plastic flowers.

Varying shades of green paint decked the walls—grayed from years of smoke and oil produced during cooking. The windows looked as though they hadn't been opened in a while, painted shut without much thought to fresh air. A long, deep crack ran from floor to ceiling, with patterned fissures snaking out in every direction like tiny tentacles.

An exceptional meal was delivered to our table. Giant-sized BLTs adorned with four thick strips of smoky bacon, a generous slather of mayo, heirloom tomatoes, and baby lettuce. Our minestrone soup was loaded with handmade pasta, vegetables picked from an organic garden and topped with freshly grated Parmesan cheese. It was 3 p.m. when we swallowed our last tasty bite and pushed our chairs back with happy hearts.

~

We pedaled leisurely toward Kingston. Outside the city center, we passed a grand brick building that looked like an historic castle. The bright red roof had matching turrets, looming from each side of the entry. An expansive lawn, divided by a long row of red and white flowers, led directly to the door. Welcome to Collins Bay Institution, a medium-security penitentiary built in 1930 and the oldest operational federal prison in Ontario—nicknamed "Disneyland" by locals.

~

We flew through heavy traffic, weaving expertly between vehicles and around pedestrians, as if we were born to ride. Rocketing into downtown, spirits soaring, we were high on life and feeling strong.

Downtown Kingston seemed to be celebrating our arrival. Rowdy packs of university students spilled into the streets. Hormones and testosterone filled the air. The night was young, but we could already feel the energy surging. Long, noisy lines formed at restaurant doors. Bands blasted their music, the crazy cacophony thumping and echoing off buildings.

Someone shouted, "Yeaaaaa, cyclists! Go, go, go!"

The crowd chanted in unison, "Go, go, go!"

We gave the masses a "Wooohoooo!" in reply and they went wild. We fully expected the paparazzi to pop out, but pedaled faster, propelled by the gusto of the crowd.

No time to soak in our celebrity status. We were on a mission. A mission to board the ferry. Behind us, the festive throng gave a few final cheers, then melded back into itself and moved on to other shiny objects.

~

Again, our timing was perfect. The Wolfe Island ferry was loading as we arrived. We strapped our bikes safely to the wall, bolted up the steps, and found seats as the ferry left the dock. We were a little sad to see the lights and frivolity of Kingston disappearing behind us, but happy to see Wolfe Island and the potential of new adventures ahead.

As usual, once on the other side, cyclists and "walk-ons" were allowed to go ashore first. While walking our bikes down the ramp, we asked a pair of locals for lodging and restaurant recommendations.

~

The hotel was built in 1832, the room basic with no special amenities. The upside was the waterfront setting and having the bikes locked safely on a protected porch just outside the door.

After bathing and putting on our freshest set of clothes, we walked to the restaurant that had been recommended. The 30-minute wait was painless. Clark enjoyed a couple cold beers as I sipped a daiquiri on the outside deck. A well-dressed waiter ushered us to a table located in a far corner, near the kitchen. We felt uncomfortable at once, extremely underdressed for the formal setting. The food looked incredible, so we ignored the stares.

Once seated and forgotten by the other patrons, we were in for a treat; our meals were every bit as good as we imagined. Medium-rare tournedos of beef with a light, flavorful sauce and a hint of rosemary for me. Clark went with one of his favorite dishes—rack of lamb. Everything was expertly prepared; the broccoli rabe was cooked al dente and potatoes done to perfection. We selected an excellent Malbec to go with our meal and savored every sip. It was the perfect ending to our adventure in Canada.

Well, except for one thing: Clark found a piece of hard plastic mixed in his Caesar salad. He called the waiter over. Pointing to the plastic piece he said in a low voice, "I found this in my salad. I thought you might want to know."

When there was no reaction, he added, "Someone could easily break a tooth or choke. The kitchen might want to check the rest of the salads, in case there's more."

The waiter barely apologized. We saw him consult the manager, who glanced at us suspiciously but didn't bother to come over to our table. Apparently, they assumed we were lying, probably trying to scam a free meal. Had we been well-dressed customers, apologies would have flowed and drinks been comped. We weren't happy with this treatment but didn't bother explaining our circumstances. They were obviously biased and we thought it better to reflect our feelings in the tip and by leaving a note.

~

Back at the hotel, we sat on our deck overlooking the Saint Lawrence River, grateful for the clear sky and warm weather. We gazed at the twinkling stars, watched the lights of Kingston in the distance and the ferry traveling back and forth carrying the evening revelers.

Clark lit a cigar and observed how far we'd come: from our first days of aching body parts and no knowledge of long-distance cycling to now. Simply by taking it one pedal at a time and tossing in a bit of luck and learning, we were now several thousand miles toward our goal.

WEEK 16

It's Hard to Argue with Sore Buns

    Day 103:   Sunday, September 14
    Weather: Sunny and beautiful
    Distance: 27 miles
    Route: Wolfe Island, Ontario, Canada, to Clayton, New York

Terrific food is almost a drug for us. This explains why we chose to venture back to the pretentious restaurant for breakfast. The dining room was closed, but the bar was open. A new day, new wait staff—friendly and welcoming. We ordered a couple three-shot lattes, eggs Benedict and split a lavish platter of mixed fruits. Even though the place was humming with activity, the bartender took the time to shoot the breeze with us.

    We took a final walk to the water for a quick goodbye to the Saint Lawrence, quietly enjoying the silence and breathing in the morning air. Suddenly, a honking V-formation of Canada geese appeared overhead. We strained our necks to watch the spectacle. There were thousands of them, winging their way south for the winter. The noisy gaggle left formation and landed all around us. They're much bigger than they appear in the air and were a little intimidating due to their number and vocal prowess.

We stood very still and they allowed us to be part of their pack, mostly ignoring our presence.

Clark whispered, "Did you know they mate for life?" looking at me with love eyes. He still took my breath away after all these years.

~

It was about 10 kilometers across the island to catch the ferry to the states. The ride was effortless. We floated along the smooth, empty road, gliding up and down the gently rolling hills. Beatles songs burst from our lungs ("Blackbird singing in the dead of night ..."). Small island birds erupted from their perches and fluttered around sporadically as we pedaled by, disrupted in waves that matched our pace. They quickly settled back onto their branches to discuss our visit, as if they were saying, "Cheerio and top of the morning. Hope your stay in Canada was pleasant."

~

The ferry was small and open, with room for only eight cars. We boarded, strapped the bikes to a railing, and found a prime place to enjoy the scenery. I felt a little melancholy when I realized we'd be on the road only three more weeks. In the beginning, we focused on getting to the finish line and how many miles we'd traveled each day—or didn't. Now, it was all about the journey, the life experiences, the people we met, and how this adventure had deepened the unbreakable bond between us. I stared into the crystal-clear water, lost in my thoughts, lulled by the ferry's gentle rocking.

~

Home again, back in the U.S.A. Our trip through customs in Cape Vincent, New York, was simple and efficient. We pedaled away minutes later and found a place to exchange our Canadian money for U.S. currency. We were treated to outstanding previews of the "1000 Islands"—all shapes and sizes scattered where the Saint Lawrence River meets Lake Ontario. Pirates and bootleggers once patrolled the area now cruised by vacationers and those lucky enough to have a cottage in the land of near-endless shoreline.

"I don't feel like riding anymore. I'm tired and have sore buns!" Clark blurted out suddenly.

I countered with a suggestion for a lunch break instead. Truthfully, I wanted to keep traveling and cover more ground because it was such a beautiful day. Ultimately, Clark got his way. It was hard to argue with sore buns.

We checked into a small motel and—first things first—went in search of authentic "New Yawk" pizza. And found it. The crust was thin and crispy, covered in fresh mozzarella, light on sauce, and perfectly charred around the edges. Clark plucked off bits of fresh basil and popped them into his mouth before expertly folding a large slice in half. I followed suit.

The rest of the day called for some serious relaxing. After dinner, we cracked open a copy of Jack London's "Sea Wolf" I'd picked up along the way. We read to each other late into the evening and fell asleep dreaming about our next trip—sailing around the world.

Three Dog Day

Day 104: Monday, September 15
Weather: Windy and overcast then sunny and warm, a perfect fall day!
Distance: 46 miles
Route: Clayton, New York, to Gouverneur, New York

Before setting out, we went to the post office and mailed a stack of postcards, a box of receipts, lightweight summer clothes, and journal tapes home. All things we wanted to keep but didn't need to carry. Every extra ounce counted.

A stop at the Antique Boat Museum was fascinating. We were enthralled with a story about twin brothers who sailed across the ocean following Christopher Columbus' path. The boat was so tiny we wondered if the brothers despised each other after being together in such close quarters for weeks. Hope they got along well.

We felt an affinity with adventure travelers like them, inspired by their bravery and arduous undertaking.

~

A beautiful back road into the hamlet of La Fargeville hinted at fall, with trees just starting to show their autumn colors. The last of the corn had been harvested from now-brittle stalks. Pumpkins grew fat in fields.

We pedaled into beautiful farmland, breathing in the crisp scents of fall, rolling through tiny dots on the map. Small, scarcely populated towns sprinkled with antiquated buildings and faded remnants of original signage. History unfolded as we quietly cycled through one community that had seen better days. A sign, scrawled on a window in white paint said it all, "Sorry. Closed."

~

We dubbed this our "three-dog day," choosing the name because every time we passed a farmhouse it seemed a minimum of three dogs would race out to chase us. Many of them were only curious, wanting a whiff of our strange contraptions. Other pooches wanted to play and run along just for fun.

Some canines, though, weren't at all happy with our presence, growling and snapping as they tried to nip our tires. Others played tricks by darting toward us then stopping just short of our wheels. Some took a stealth approach, sneaking up from behind trees and surprising us by popping out in random places to snuffle at our bikes.

At one point, six dogs surrounded Clark, all barking, yipping, and circling with aggressive intention. He had no choice but to stop and hope they didn't tear him to pieces. This is how he discovered the most effective system yet: Just say, "NO!"

Pointing directly at the dogs and shouting firmly "NO! GO HOME!" worked well. In unison, the dogs stopped, turned away from him, and obeyed.

Later, a particularly big, ugly, unkempt dog came charging after him. Clark employed his most authoritative tone and commanded "NO! GO HOME!" The matted beast stopped in his tracks and turned his attention to me. Being a fast learner, I roared "NO!" adding a scary Maori grimace face for added intensity.

Holy shit! It worked. The animal stopped, looked at me quizzically, tipping his head back and forth as if to say, "Well, okay. Be that way." He turned his butt toward me and sauntered back home.

We continued along back roads, the Indian summer sun warming our backs. No traffic and gently undulating terrain made for perfect cycling. Our pace somehow melded. Early on, I'd fly down hills willy-nilly and typically had better stamina. Clark was more cautious about his downhill clip and couldn't ride as long without a break. But he'd ride faster uphill, beating me by quite a distance.

Now, we were well matched and traveled at a similar pace, riding close together, talking and laughing as we rolled along. Honestly, there was nowhere else we'd rather be. It just couldn't get any better.

> Our days were always full. To the outside world, the day-to-day plodding along may have seemed uneventful.
>
> It was the small things that mattered most. Fresh air on my skin sometimes felt soft, like warm velvet; sometimes sharp, when it was cold.
>
> The aroma of rain even had different scents, depending on temperature, terrain, and time of day. Dew-dappled flowers filled the air with sweetness, while a heavy rain accentuated the pungent scent of manure in farm fields.
>
> The quality of light fascinated me: the luminous, lavender clouds of dawn; the deep, dark black of night, illuminated only by a sliver of moon; and the bright, reflective light that shimmers on a body of water.
> Mother Nature filled us with an array of sensory experiences, both intriguing and surprising at times. In fact, she put us more in tune with each other, amplifying the natural instincts that develop between couples who've shared a long history together.

In Gouverneur, after traveling 46 miles in 3 hours, 7 minutes, and 13 seconds, we stopped for the night.

"Another Full Moon and I'm Still in Love with You"

Day 105: Tuesday, September 16
Weather: Another sunny, pleasant day
Distance: 45 miles
Route: Gouverneur, New York, to Cranberry Lake, New York

On our way to find breakfast, we spotted a billboard-sized, 3-D roll of Pep O Mint Life Savers erected on the village green. We learned the candy was created as a sweet treat that could withstand summer heat better than melty chocolate. Pep O Mint was the first flavor. Local entrepreneur Edward John Noble purchased the rights from the inventor for $2,900 in 1916. Noble changed the original cardboard packaging to a tinfoil and paper wrap, which kept the Life Savers fresh longer. The rest is history.

~

We like to support mom-and-pop restaurants whenever possible. The food is usually better than fast food and often created from fresh, local ingredients. The experience was sometimes more colorful, too. This day was no exception. Our waitress wore heavy orange make-up and false eyelashes, her hair teased way out of proportion to her height. She was shouting to someone out of sight at the top of her lungs, "Go ahead and fire me then! Oh, my *gawd*."

Knowing we heard her but clearly not caring, she showed us to a booth and said without batting a heavy eyelash, "*Youse* want *cawfee*?"

We nodded affirmatively, stifling laughter.

"Welcome to New *Yawk*," Clark whispered in my ear.

We ate breakfast and continued ordering coffee, just to stay and watch the show. She'd disappear behind swinging doors and we'd hear a muffled argument or a pan crashing to the floor. Moments later, the door would fly open, the waitress' arms piled high with trays and plates, acting as if nothing unusual was occurring.

As the world turns.

~

We followed the Oswegatchie River most of the day, contentedly moving closer to the spectacular Adirondack Mountains. In the town of Fine, we stopped for a snack and rested on an outdoor bench, taking in the quiet pace of life. Neighborhood dogs and cats wandered lazily from yard to yard in search of the best spot for another nap. We started feeling lazy ourselves, finding it hard not to join them in their repose. The lawns looked especially inviting, like soft, green comforters.

Clark was the first to get a move on. He pulled me up, gave me a quick peck, and said, "Time to saddle up. It's now or never."

We turned onto a tiny back road and were unexpectedly transported to Utopia. Sunlight illuminated the bright reds, yellows, and oranges of the changing leaves, creating a heavenly canopy of color above our heads. In this otherworldly cocoon, we were rendered speechless by our glorious wrapping. This dreamland transitioned to a glittering lake, magically throwing sparkles everywhere. We literally got off our bikes and gave the environment a long round of applause.

Energized by our enchanted respite, we cycled on and encountered an especially steep hill. So steep that, despite being in the lowest gear, we had to stand on our pedals to propel ourselves forward. It was a struggle all the way. Good thing it was short. Something didn't feel right when we reached the top. Had we gone the wrong way? We rang the doorbell at a nearby house to ask directions. The door opened almost immediately to a dewy-faced young mom with a baby on her hip.

"You shouldn't have come up this hill," she told us, smiling slightly at our disappointed expressions. "You missed your turn and need to go back down to pick up the right road."

We laughed out loud, still breathing heavily from the climb. The baby giggled with us and waved bye-bye. The ride was more fun going downhill. We easily found our turnoff and got back on track.

~

A coyote paced back and forth across the road ahead of us. Nose in the air, he intently searched for the direction of some tantalizing scent. The animal was so engrossed in whiffing he didn't notice us glide up only yards away. We watched silently for 10 minutes as he tried to target his prey. Eventually, unable to catch a scent, the creature sauntered off into the woods without a glance in our direction.

~

"How far is it to Cranberry Lake?" I asked a grocery store clerk.

A broad grin spread across his face. "No distance at all—this is it," he said.

The miscalculation reminded me of a time in my 20s, when I'd just moved to Jackson Hole, Wyoming, to be a ski bum. My new friend Karen took me hiking and promised we'd stop for a drink in the town of Moose. Our trek through the majestic landscape was outstanding and made me thirsty. As she pulled up to a lone general store in the middle of nowhere, I asked, "Aren't we going to Moose for a drink?"

"We're here," she answered, "Welcome to Wyoming."

~

A cold, clear night was forecasted. We set up camp quickly and walked a long block toward downtown Cranberry Lake. Hand in hand, we played the day over out loud: *cawfee*, Pep O Mint Life Savers, napping kitties, Adirondack mountains, the tunnel of love, Mother Nature, the baby waving, an oblivious coyote, sweet memories, feeling strong and healthy … the flow of the day had been perfect. Everything fell in place, reminding us how lucky and in love we were.

After a romantic dinner overlooking the lake, we noticed something baffling. Plastic deer positioned on the grass disrupted the idyllic view. Their immovable postures and blank stares were hardly realistic. In fact, quite creepy.

We noticed a lot of plastic lawn ornaments in the front yards of homes in small towns starting somewhere in the Midwest. Synthetic flamingos, garishly painted mushrooms, gigantic turtles, rigid little girls holding faux-wicker baskets, and platoons of gnomes and fishing trolls graced many yards. The lawn ornament business was booming.

~

The temperature dropped drastically at sunset. Although we were cold, it was a beautiful, cloudless night. We found a spot near the lake to watch the moon rise.

Snuggling together, Clark touched his head to mine and again said, "Another full moon and I'm still in love with you."

The Butterfly Whisperer

Day 106: Wednesday, September 17
Weather: Sunny with a slight wind
Distance: 50 miles
Route: Cranberry Lake, New York, to Saranac Lake, New York

We woke up well before 6 a.m. refreshed, happy, and ready for some hot coffee. A brisk walk a block away carried us a few decades back in time. The restaurant's walls were plastered with signs saying things like "Manager Special: Buy one hamburger at regular price and get the second one for the same price." And "Answers $1.00. Answers which require thought $2.00. Correct Answers $4.00, but dumb looks are still free." Every available space was taken up with such wisdom.

We read aloud, seeing who could find the most ridiculous adage. Without realizing it, we got a little carried away. But everyone loves a laugh, and before long a man with a neat mustache, potbelly, and rosy cheeks made his way to our table and joined in. When we ran out of comedic fodder, he sat down next to me, grinned, and asked, "Your name Clark?"

"Yup."

"Me, too," the man said, sliding further into our booth. "Not a lot of us out there."

"Where you from?"

With that, our story unfolded. And an hour later the two Clarks were fast friends.

As it turns out, it wasn't only the name, beer bellies, and mustaches they had in common. Both had a love of motorcycles, hunting mushrooms, poetry, and fishing. It was a treat to watch the Clarks having so much fun and an intriguing glimpse into the way men bond and communicate. I listened to the jokes, anecdotes, and competitive banter about how to be the best as each interest came forward. The two bear-hugged and pounded on each other's backs, like guys do, in their instinctual goodbye ritual.

~

We scattered our belongings, still wet from the morning dew, across the children's empty playground. Towels, tent pieces, sleeping bags, clothes, and shoes were strewn on the swing set, slide, teeter-totter, play horse and stretched across the sandbox to dry.

As the sun and light breeze worked their magic, a fellow camper stopped by to say hello. He was a handsome man in his late 60s with a kind face and engaging smile. His wife had sent him over because they were worried about us sleeping another night in the cold.

People are amazing. They looked out for us, wherever we were.

~

We were in the foothills of the Adirondacks and rewarded with spectacular views at every pedal stroke. The weather was clear, but the wind picked up as the day wore on. Occasionally, heavy gusts swept through the mountains, creating a low whistle in the distance and causing tree tops to bend over sharply. During one of those high-wind moments, we stopped for a break. As we stood catching our breath, we spotted a monarch butterfly struggling against the wind.

Clark, who loved the colorful creatures, extended his hand toward it.

"I'll see if I can get her to come to me—watch."

He pursed his lips and made quiet kissing sounds, like when coaxing a kitten out of a tight spot.

"Come on—you can do it, you're alright, come here," he said in a soothing voice while holding his finger high in the air.

Clark continued for several minutes and, even though the wind was strong and the butterfly had to struggle against it, she was heading his way. I was utterly amazed.

After a few more minutes, she landed on his hand perch, flapping her wings slowly as she came to rest. Maybe living things, no matter what species, respond to kindness and know when and where it's safe. Or, maybe Clark had a deeper connection with the butterfly. Whatever it was, she sat for a long time resting while Clark talked quietly to her. It wasn't until I moved in to take a picture that she flew off. Clark kept his hand up high and tried coaxing her back. For a moment it looked as if she was trying to return, but several big gusts of wind followed by three fast-moving trucks blew her off path. Soon she was out of sight.

I'm not sure I would believe the story had I not seen it with my own eyes.

~

We'd made good time, traveling from Cranberry Lake to Childwold and on to Piercefield, then into the town of Tupper Lake, all before noon. It was hunger rather than exhaustion that forced us to stop for lunch. Hungarian goulash, one of our favorites, was on the menu.

Our waitress, a girl in her late teens, was sweet and welcoming. "The food is fantastic! You'll love it," she gushed. Adorable and convincing, the young lady reminded us of Clark's daughter Taea.

We ordered in hopes of a good meal but were disappointed when a plate of overcooked macaroni noodles with canned tomato sauce and a blop of cheese arrived. It was bland and lukewarm, but we scarfed it up anyway knowing it was the fuel we needed to continue our ride.

Neither of us wanted to disappoint our lovely waitress with the truth when she asked how we enjoyed our lunch.

"It was memorable. Thank you," I said. Clark added, "And the service was excellent." We followed that with toothy smiles and made a fast move for the door.

Just before mounting our bikes, a muumuu-clad woman in a floppy sunhat came up and timidly asked to take our picture. We agreed, and she fished into her oversized purse for a camera. After digging deeper and deeper into the bag with no luck, she gave up and dumped the contents onto the sidewalk. Not one, but two, cameras came tumbling out, along with several sets of keys, a pack of cigs, three lighters, gum, lipstick, lots of paper, glasses, a bag of candy, a can of dog food, a pair of scissors, a lone curler, and something she snatched up so quickly we didn't see it.

We struck a pose and held it until we were both uncomfortable, smile muscles twitching. She tried to snap a shot for a full 10 minutes on one camera and then on the other, but couldn't make either work. We held our stance like statues while passersby started to gather. Our photographer was getting flustered, almost in tears. Someone in the crowd volunteered to help and reached for the camera. The woman wanted no part of a stranger touching her equipment. She yanked herself backward, violently shoved the camera into her bag, and stormed off down the street. This startling behavior created an awkward silence, until somebody asked to take our picture. The crowd went wild and everyone who had a camera or cell phone whipped 'em out.

~

Clark looked longingly at a beautiful motel on the lakefront. We talked about stopping, but I pushed to move on. I knew there was a steep climb leaving town and preferred to get the hard work over first. As we discussed our options, I used a ridiculous technique that often helped to motivate us.

When we were trying to hurry each other along, we talked in a nasal tone often used by cartoon characters and TV nerds who are anal and overly organized.

"You're laaaaazy and not very organiiiiized," one of us would drone.

"I'm waaaaay more organiiiiized than you. I'm ready to riiiiiiide and yoooooou're noooot," the other would retort.

"I can paaaaaack my baaaaaag more efficiently than yooooou," as we continued on and on, trying to outdo each other.

Just as we were employing the nerd-talking method, a car pulled up, and the female passenger leaned out the window and asked in the very same nasal voice, "Are yoooooou on an orgaaaaaniiiized tooooour?"

I thought I was going to die.

Fortunately, Clark was closer to the car and forced to respond. I stepped behind him to hide the laughter ready to erupt. I fought back the urge to double over with giggles by holding my breath, which led to embarrassing snorting, making me laugh harder.

Poor Clark. He was solemnly explaining our trip to the carload of people while I convulsed in the background. Every time the woman asked a nasally question, I'd set off on another fit.

When it became too obvious to ignore me, Clark explained, "She's in a silly mood today." The people in the car probably thought I had some kind of mental disorder and felt sorry for Clark but seemed oddly unfazed by my behavior.

I waved in acknowledgment but couldn't speak as I neared hysteria and tried to quell it by thinking sad thoughts. But that didn't work. Nothing was going to work.

"Have a gooood triiiiiip," the woman waved as they drove off.

Clark was finally free to let loose. We laughed until our stomachs had knotted cramps. This crazy incident and ensuing hilarity gave us the energy needed to keep riding.

~

At Saranac Lake, we called it a day and checked into a quiet motel with a view of neighboring Lake Flower. A grassy walkway stretched for several miles in each direction. In the distance we could see the Adirondack Mountains, in the heart of the High Peaks Region.

After cleaning up, we started the dinner hunt by asking for recommendations at a nearby store. The owner didn't hesitate, a Mexican place, several miles outside of town, was his enthusiastic reply. It sounded perfect and we were anxious for a good meal, but hesitated over the distance. We've learned when someone says "a couple of miles" it could mean anything from two miles to 12. In a motorized vehicle, most people don't pay close attention to mile markers.

But the store owner was in tune with our concern and added, "Are you going there right now?"

"Yes," we said, We're always ready to eat!"

"I'm heading that way. I'll give you a lift."

That was all the encouragement we needed, not worrying one bit about how to get home later. He locked the shop and off we went. Only minutes later, he dropped us at the restaurant door. Surprisingly, even though it was early, the place was packed.

We started on thirst-quenching margaritas, setting the stage for the night. The food was *delicioso* and the place a raucous fiesta of fun-loving folks. We ordered another margarita round and then another, and I got uncharacteristically intoxicated.

My overindulgence made our walk home a bit challenging. Had Clark not been holding onto me, I could have ended up in the lake. Or was it the other way around? In any case, we stumbled along singing, laughing, and trying not to fall down. The distance remained a mystery, but we made it back to the room safe and happy.

Olympic Dreams

Day 107: Thursday, September 18
Weather: A sunny, crisp fall day
Distance: Rest day
Route: Played in Saranac Lake and visited Lake Placid, New York

Our day off gave us the perfect chance to see Lake Placid, home of the 1932 and 1980 Olympic Games. A 10-mile bus trip got us there in no time. The route was a preview for the next day's ride. Although it was interesting to see the path ahead, sometimes it's better not to know, especially with the number of hills awaiting us.

The beauty of taking alternate transportation is that we didn't have to worry about the bikes while being tourists. Usually, it was a hassle figuring out which of us would be on duty first to watch the gear while the other explored a store, art gallery, or other attraction.

We visited the Olympic Center at the Lake Placid Olympic Museum and saw the famous Olympic flags and the spot where the opening ceremonies took place. Many of the biggest names in skating train there. A few athletes practiced diligently at the skating pavilion, twirling, gliding, and jumping seamlessly over the ice. We were mesmerized by their grace and strength.

Misconceptions and Liars

Day 108: Friday, September 19
Weather: Cloudy, turning to afternoon sun
Distance: 38 miles
Route: Saranac Lake, New York, to Elizabethtown, New York

We slept in late and lingered over breakfast, sipping our morning brew and calculating how many miles we had till we hit the Atlantic Ocean. Our goal was to create a timeline in which to do it, and our main concern continued to be the possibility of inclement weather, especially early-season snowstorms in the mountains. Despite worrying about getting caught in bad weather, we still regularly journeyed off our path to play and explore. Some of our best adventures happened that way.

With a plan in place, we pushed on and covered the hilly terrain we'd seen from the bus the day before. Around a tight bend in the road, we came upon the recent aftermath of a terrible accident. The damage looked horrendous and deadly. Long black skid marks streaked the pavement and a trail of gravel sprayed out several hundred yards. The front end of the old car was completely smashed, headlights dangling from wires and grill missing. It leaned at an odd angle due to the blown-out tires.

The victims and emergency vehicles were gone, the tow truck not yet there. Only the crumpled car remained as evidence that something horrible happened. We were inexplicably drawn to look inside. Broken glass littered the seats and floors, congealing blood spattered the gray leather interior, deflated airbags hung like dead balloons—one from a steering wheel twisted into an unrecognizable shape. Contents from the glove box had spilled out: random papers, pens, and a family photo. It felt like ghosts of passengers lingered nearby.

How profoundly heartbreaking to imagine someone probably took their last breath here. I felt queasy and sad and quietly said a prayer. Clark seemed to be doing the same; head down, eyes shut. I gave him a moment of reverie, then took his hand. We held each other tightly, no words needed.

~

The ride was somber, but our spirits slowly brightened as we neared Lake Placid. Though we weren't particularly hungry, it was time to refuel to conquer the steep climbs ahead.

We parked our bikes near the windows of a huge restaurant. An impeccably dressed hostess with giant Chiclet teeth blocked our path, then refused to seat us. This made no sense. The place was empty. Chiclet Chick claimed they were expecting a large group for lunch and couldn't accommodate us.

Something about how she pursed her lips as she gave us the once-over made me doubt her sincerity. She probably assumed we were transients based on our attire—me, especially, in my stretched-out legwarmers and old sweatshirt. This attitude left a bitter taste in our mouths. She was a terrible community ambassador, so we left town without eating—or spending another dime.

~

Our stomachs were rumbling by the time we reached Keene. Deckside seats at a more welcoming restaurant gave us stunning views of the Adirondacks. We devoured triple-decker Italian sandwiches, steaming bowls of minestrone soup, split a side of fries, and washed it down with three Arnold Palmers each.

Someone left a brochure on the table next to ours that described Keene and the surrounding area in great detail. All of Keene is located in Adirondack Park, the largest state park in the nation. Breathtaking.

~

We'd already covered 25 miles and discussed spending the night (swayed by the scenic distraction) but voted against it. Logging a few more miles would make it possible for us to cross into Vermont in the morning.

The old parable "what goes up must come down" seemed illusive. The next 12 miles out of the Keene Valley were all uphill. We geared down and pushed on. The steepness eventually mellowed, and as if on cue, a sunbeam broke the clouds and illuminated the summit before us. Hallelujah!

> I came to truly respect early explorers as we made our way across the country. Imagine what they must have experienced blazing a trail into new frontiers without decent maps, restaurants, or the option to stay in a motel. Even the most rudimentary amenities and creature comforts were not available. And here I was thinking we were roughing it by traveling unplugged.
>
> What incredible challenges those first pioneers faced: harsh weather, limited food and water, no communications, loneliness, and the constant threat of illness, injury, or attack. There's much to admire and learn from their fortitude.

A basic but clean-looking motel in the heart of Elizabethtown caught our eye. The manager happened to be outside. He scrutinized us intently, guarding his fort, already assessing us as "bums on bikes." The hard-boiled old coot gave us a frosty reception, punctuating his disdain by dredging up a glob of spit and discharging it on the ground. Marking his turf.

"I just booked my last room."

Liar.

"Doesn't look like anyone's here," Clark responded.

"I'm booked," the man snapped back sharply.

A stare-down ensued.

"There's a motel outside of town that will suit you better," he said sarcastically. With that, he turned heel, marched back inside, and slammed the door.

For the second time in a day, we were treated as "unfit." Most times, the response was interest, admiration, and respect. You could never tell what was coming at you.

We found another a motel a mile outside town. Unfortunately, the room was small and dirty; the water only ran cold, the TV knobs kept falling off, and the curtains didn't close properly. The bedframe cracked, and mattress swayed erratically when we sat on it.

No time or energy to change accommodations. We were tired and the air felt heavy like a storm was brewing outside. We decided to stay put.

~

We dined at the Deer's Head Inn Restaurant, the site of the Adirondacks' oldest inn. The original structure was built in 1808, but fire, time, and changing vacation patterns altered the name and buildings over time. According to local lore, one proprietor hid booze under the porch during prohibition. He retrieved the hooch through a secret door by using a long-handled pole. When the porch was replaced in 1991, the old bottles were found—all of them empty.

We lingered after a gratifying meal and bottle of Bordeaux, then strolled charming streets with seasonal visitors, postponing the inevitable return to our unsavory digs. On the way back, we stopped at a liquor store to pick up a few mini bottles of Bailey's to numb ourselves.

A park bench served as our hideaway while we clandestinely sipped the creamy liqueur. By the time the last drop was drunk, we were both sufficiently anesthetized.

The Plastic Tempest and Cyclone Woman

> Day 109:   Saturday, September 20
> Weather: Heavy rain and cold wind
> Distance: 10 miles
> Route: Elizabethtown, New York, to
>   Westport, New York

Hard rain pounded all night, and despite the leaning, lumpy bed we were glad to be inside. Cuddling to the music of water on the roof, we woke up, limbs asleep, still wrapped in each other's arms—the cheery song of birds our alarm clock.

Time to check out of our sorry motel and move on. Light rain soon turned to thick, heavy drops, splashing high as they hit the pavement. Falling harder and harder, the deluge drenched us.

Our bright yellow, hooded rain ponchos didn't offer much protection. Water seeped in everywhere, finding its way through every nook and cranny, pockets included. The tires kicked up mud from puddles while the wind whipped the raingear into billowing capes, making us look like superheroes. The Plastic Tempest and Cyclone Woman we dubbed ourselves.

I struggled to see through my mud-splattered glasses, so we ducked under an overpass, the concrete shield offering protection. But it was cold. The rain hammered on and the temperature dropped further.

The distant lights of a gas station beckoned, so we made a beeline for it. Now fully waterlogged, Clark shook himself off like a big dog before going inside. When the proprietor of the little place gave us the cliché line "Wet enough for ya?" I shivered and shook my head in agreement, too cold to verbally respond.

A cup of coffee warmed our bones. When would the rain let up? It went on and on. Every so often the weather hinted at clearing. We'd ready ourselves to ride, then the clouds would let loose again. Back and forth, back and forth.

We'd buy another coffee and continue the wait. To kill time, I perused the two aisles. Canned goods, fishing supplies, chew, sunglasses, Styrofoam coolers, chips, beef jerky, keychains, dangly car air fresheners, and three shelves of sweet treats. Jackpot! I mulled over purchasing a Ding Dong or Twinkie ... then bought both.

Other travelers filtered in and out, buying gas, sodas, and cigarettes. The topic of the day continued to be the weather. And us. Our disheveled appearance made it obvious we were the owners of the dripping bikes parked outside. Everyone wondered where we were going. We told our story over and over.

One couple was especially intrigued. The wife called us an inspiration, saying our trip underscored how desperately they needed a break from long hours and family pressures. We overheard them happily tossing about vacation destinations as they headed out the door. It was nice to know we made a small difference in someone's life, at least for that moment.

After they left we felt energized and tried again to ride. But as soon as we stepped outside the skies opened and wind blew so hard the station windows shook. We dove back inside. After two hours, Clark spotted clearing in the distance—our chance to take off. But less than a mile down the road, the rain came back in torrents. There was nothing left to do but power on into the nearest city, Westport. We pedaled as fast as we could through sheets of water, ignoring our chattering teeth and sopping shoes.

My fingers felt frozen in place and my face stung from the hard strikes of the icy drops. Wet clothes were heavy on my body and felt rigid from the cold. To make matters worse, visibility was only a few feet ahead. We rode close together, but in silence.

I told myself, like I always do when the situation is grim, "Thankfully you're strong and healthy. This will be over soon and then it'll make a good story."

At the Westport city limits, we stopped at the first motel in sight, our bodies so frosty it took extra effort to get off the bikes. Clark knocked on the office door. Silence. Then we walked back and forth in front of the windows trying to spot someone. Anyone. No one was there. Shivering in place and not wanting to ride another minute, we wondered what to do next.

A young couple, who'd been watching us through their motel window, ventured outside.

"The owner left just as you were coming down the hill," one of them told us sympathetically. "I happened to notice you because, well, you're not a typical vision in this kind of weather."

"Yeah, I'm sure we're quite a sight to behold," I said laughing outwardly, but panicking inwardly.

"It's been a helluva day," Clark added.

Would it ever end?

Maybe the couple noticed our *oh-shit* expressions or maybe they were just curious. Nonetheless, we were distracted from our situation, standing under the dripping hotel awning, answering questions about our journey. I wished they'd noticed me staring longingly toward the door and invite us in. No such luck.

The owner returned a long, cold half hour later. This time we didn't barter. The door to our room was barely closed when we stripped off our saturated garb and headed for a hot shower.

The closest restaurant was a hilly mile away. The heavy rain had finally given way to a light sprinkling, so the trek was manageable. We caught glimpses of Lake Champlain, beautiful even in the misty gray. The restaurant was packed with others seeking refuge from the weather. We found a small table tucked away in the back of the noisy room and ordered warming chicken soup, BLTs, and onion rings.

The adolescent waiter only showed interest in a couple tables, regulars who returned his witty repartee. Waiter Boy appeared to have no recognition of anyone else in the room. He doted on his friends, dramatically laughing and flamboyantly waving his arms as he talked while making plenty sure *they* had everything *they* needed. When it came to other customers (oh, like us), he plunked down the food then quickly rejoined his pals … until it was time to drop off a check.

We watched with disturbed amusement as one middle-aged couple tried to get the waiter's attention throughout their meal. They flailed their arms to no avail and then resorted to finger snapping. Nothing worked. A brief conversation with the manager also got them nowhere. So frustrated, the pair stood up mid-meal, slammed money down on the table, and walked out.

This momentarily caught the waiter's attention. He smirked and rolled his eyes sarcastically, then went back to his important conversation. We weren't the only ones watching. Following the last display, two outdoorsy-looking men sitting next to us made eye contact and we all burst out laughing.

"Quite the attentive service," one of them said facetiously.

"Amazing, isn't it?" Clark concurred.

"We'd heard stories about some New Englanders having trouble accepting new people," the other man added. "If it's true, that waiter is their poster child."

We guffawed and moved on to other subjects. The guys, Gary and Doug, had rented a home with their wives and two other couples. Like any great vacation, the group spent most of it eating, drinking, and playing on the water. Today, they'd come across the lake in a speed boat, determined to have a good time, despite the weather.

Doug asked what we were doing in New York, so we launched into our story. Before long, we had another invitation.

"Come stay at the vacation house with us for a couple days," Gary said. "There's an extra room."

This was a tempting offer, especially when Doug mentioned the next day's forecast was warm and dry.

With super-hero powers, the waiter overheard this comment and spewed obnoxiously from across the room, "Tomorrow is supposed to be exactly the same as today."

Doug trumped him by declaring, "He speaks!"

The customers around us broke into laughter. Point for our side.

WEEK 17

Humpty Dumpty Falls Again

    Day 110: Sunday, September 21
    Weather: Cold and windy, but clear
    Distance: 55 miles
    Route: Westport, New York, to Middlebury, Vermont

I could've stayed in bed all day but felt Clark stirring. He was in especially good spirits, energetic and ready to ride.

    At the city limits of Port Henry, the terrain changed to a steep uphill challenge, without much warning. I shifted gears quickly; the chain stuck and pedals froze, which brought my bike to an abrupt halt and sent me face first onto the cement. My right foot released from the pedal, but the left one got jammed, trapping me under my bike at an abnormal angle. While I struggled to get up, a stream of cars passed inches from my twisted body—they slowed to look, but no one offered help. I was sprawled on the asphalt, flopping and thrashing, struggling to get free.

    Clark didn't know I fell until a passerby shouted from his car, "Biker down in back."

    Clark ran down the hill to help, looking pale and worried. By the time he arrived, I'd managed to contort my body into a strange inverted pretzel shape. He freed my limbs and I wobbled to a standing position, trying not to cry. I hurt and limped up the hill while Clark wheeled the bike alongside. (The bruises from this crash lasted until the end of the trip.)

At the summit, Clark gave me a long, sympathetic hug. We stood together taking in the view: the historic town of Port Henry below and spectacular Lake Champlain in the distance. The diversion helped ease the pain of my embarrassing fall.

"Is my little Humpty Dumpty ready for breakfast?" Clark humorously inquired.

We pulled our bikes up to an old red caboose that had been converted into a diner. Metal steps at the back lead to a landing—the type where, in the old days, a politician waved during a whistle-stop tour. The narrow restaurant was packed, but our waitress seated us right away and served everyone efficiently, all while being charming.

We sat with a retired postman who talked about close calls with neighborhood dogs. He showed off deep scars from the four times he'd been bitten on his daily route. The worst wound was inflicted by a mixed breed. Every day, the mongrel seemed to know the mailman was coming, barking uncontrollably and lunging against the door. This day, the door wasn't shut tightly. In a split second, devil dog managed to escape and take a chunk out of the man's calf before the owner could intervene.

The postman convalesced for several months, then took an early retirement. He'd had his fill of dangerous canine liaisons. We came away with a greater appreciation that all of our "doggie encounters" resulted in little more than close calls and fast heartbeats.

~

It was time to cross over Lake Champlain and into Vermont. We'd considered cycling south to catch the ferry at Ticonderoga, but were told the Chimney Point Bridge was faster and the views more beautiful. This route was also hillier, as is often the case with gorgeous scenery. We were not disappointed. A breathtaking stop at Chimney Point opened up a wide expanse of the extraordinary lake and farmland beyond.

Stories still prevail about a Lake Champlain "monster," much like the one in Scotland's Loch Ness, known as "Nessie." It's said that when Frenchman Samuel de Champlain explored the area in 1609 he reported encountering a "lake monster, thick as a man's thigh and five feet long with silver-gray scales that a dagger could not penetrate." Native American lore puts the size of the monster closer to eight or 10 feet, with a snout over two feet long. We kept our eagle eyes peeled, scanning the lake for any sign of the big beast, but he didn't show his scaly self.

We crossed the bridge and entered Vermont, putting one more state under our belts. This was a major milestone, an important psychological marker, like the rush of breaking through the wall in a marathon.

~

Our first stop in Vermont was the tiny town of Bridport. We had a snack and restocked our saddle bags with fresh fruit, candy, nuts, and cheese. The day finally warmed enough to remove extra clothes. I pulled off my sweatshirt and sat down to discreetly slip off my tight black legwarmers. As I did this, I caught two teenage boys staring at me from across the parking lot. Maybe they were hoping for a full striptease.

I looked down and was mortified to see my lily-white thunder thighs exposed to the light of day. The lower half of my legs were deeply tanned, which only emphasized my pasty thighs. They bulged out over the spandex bike shorts like a burst sausage.

Clark hadn't been paying much attention to my disrobing. When he noticed the boys ogling me, he gave them a "don't-even-think-about-it" look and stepped in front of me protectively.

I hurried to finish changing and make my escape, grateful for Clark's intervention. The boys slunk off.

~

Middlebury was our next stop. Founded just after the Revolutionary War, history permeated every corner of town. Charming buildings along the main street punctuated a long prosperity. Pristine gardens and lawns flanked cobblestone walkways. Imposing white clapboard homes had been lovingly cared for by generations of families. The idyllic village was exactly as I imagined New England might look.

Middlebury College added a youthful energy to the town. A scholastic year had just started and you could feel excitement in the air. Students gathered 'round tables at coffee shops, sipping exotic java and snacking on pastries. They strolled the streets, deeply engrossed in important conversations, oblivious to anyone around them.

The many Victorian B&Bs were out of our price range and camping wasn't an option. We reluctantly cycled on, settling on a small, nondescript motel outside Middlebury proper.

Stopping for the day allowed us to contemplate our course. We spent the afternoon debating whether to ride up and over the mountains or find an easier route. The mountains would be more scenic but presented narrow, curvy roads with heavy traffic. Wanting to avoid danger (and exertion), we made a more prudent plan—heading south to Rutland, then hitting the Atlantic coast at Kennebunkport, Maine. I borrowed a highlighter from the motel clerk and set about tracing the rest of the trip so the map would be easy to follow from atop a bike.

We expected to get to the Atlantic Ocean in a week and relax a few days before heading home. Exactly how to do that was to be determined. All that mapping made us hungry. In just under a mile, we nosed out a family diner serving "homemade comfort food." Big piles of stringy roast pork appeared at our table along with huge servings of real mashed potatoes and plenty of fresh gravy. We ordered apple pie for dessert and a carafe of rosé. The chef and owner, a grandmother of eight, came out from the kitchen to say hello and joined us for a glass of wine after we raved about her delicious food.

By the time we left, the temperature had dropped significantly, which made for a cold walk home. I was dressed in pants, sweatshirt, and a jacket. Clark, wearing only a T-shirt, shorts, and sandals, held me close to stay warm. Nice chance for me to reciprocate as a useful partner.

The Grim Reaper

>Day 111:   Monday, September 22
>Weather: Changed constantly
>Distance: 35 miles
>Route: Middlebury, Vermont, to Rutland, Vermont

Our day started along Highway 7, a joy to ride with wide shoulders, minimal traffic, and big sections of smooth, freshly paved road. The route took us around Lake Dunmore. Beautiful in the morning mist. We cycled past huge white homes with picket fences and screened-in porches, reminding me of childhood. In between the houses, we'd catch glimpses of the Green Mountains, which looked steeper and wilder than expected. It was quiet and peaceful, but no doubt the summer crowds swelled with good weather. By mid-morning the sun was strong, warming us and sending glittering reflections off the water. We held hands and pedaled together.

"This is the life!" I shouted.

"We LOVE Vermont!" Clark said euphorically.

With that we broke into song.

~

The route around Lake Dunmore ended too quickly. We wanted to hang onto our seventh heaven moment, so stopped to soak in the beauty. Simple things gave us pause: fish jumping for insects and waterfowl paddling silently over the water. When perceived danger approached, they flapped into action: honking, signaling their mates, and complaining loudly at whatever threatened their peace.

Our discussion turned naturally to how well matched and happy we were together. Among the sea of people we'd met over the years, somehow we found each other.

We'd had our challenges, like most couples do, but bottom line: We were soulmates who loved and respected one another. We had also become ideal cycling partners, our touring style and speed similar. Adventure travel has its frustrations, no matter who you're with. But the two of us made the trip work. At that moment, we wouldn't have traded lives with anyone for any reason—and we vowed to remember it.

~

When dark clouds moved in and the temperature plummeted, we mounted our bikes, pedaling fast to keep warm. I was amazed at how quickly the weather could change, especially in the mountains. It's safe to say weather patterns are predictably unpredictable all across the United States.

Some 20 miles past Forestdale, we saw a white wooden cross and memorial under a big tree. Flowers, mementos, balloons, teddy bears, and pictures of a teenaged boy commemorated his short life.

The young man was around the age of Clark's son, a poignant realization that stabbed our hearts. The grief of losing a child must be unbearable. As we stood quietly, a man pulled over and joined us. I broke the silence after a few moments.

"How sad. He barely had time to enjoy his life."

The man, a pastor, said he felt compelled to stop and say a prayer, even though he didn't know the boy. He lowered his head and spoke solemnly. After a few moving words, we talked in earnest, our bikes once again being the conversation starter. He had been a bicycle racer in his youth and admired us for taking this journey.

"It's important to make time to do things that are meaningful. People need to stop and appreciate what they have—spend time together and love each other. You look very happy, so you must already know this."

The depth of his statement made tears well in my eyes. He was right.

We stood by that small memorial sharing our deepest feelings. Clark talked about the pain of losing his father. The pastor listened thoughtfully then rested his hand on Clark's arm.

"My dad died not long ago. There were months of serious grieving before I could even start to heal," he said soothingly. "As you know, it's a slow process. Hits you and you break down. Then you're numb and sadness comes back to hit you again—sometimes even harder. Ultimately, the pain starts to subside, though you never forget your loved one."

As the man opened his heart, Clark felt comfortable enough to talk about his experience in Vietnam. Something he rarely shared. He spoke of the horrors and pain of the battlefield, admitting the memories were overwhelming at times. Clark was still deeply haunted. He was grateful to have the strength and luck to make it through the war, but with guilt, questioned why he survived and others didn't.

The minister listened intently, nodding and expressing his understanding with minimal words. A master at this kind of thing.

When the timing was right, he left us with a final bit of wisdom.

"Life is short; never postpone happiness. It does my heart good to see you taking the time to enjoy life's simple pleasures. I'll pray for a safe and fulfilling journey."

Meeting the pastor didn't feel like an accident. Sometimes people step into our lives at the perfect moment and say the perfect thing. Whatever the case, this serendipitous roadside encounter made a meaningful impact on our journey, and lives, long after the return home.

~

The rough pavement of the truck route was riddled with cracks and potholes. We made a game of weaving around the hazards and entertained ourselves doing so until an 18-wheeler forced us off the road. That put a stop to our playful mood.

As we stood on the roadside gravel, psyching up to ride again, a woman came marching toward us. She was dressed for farm work: dirty boots, jeans, no make-up, and hair pulled back tight.

"You should move on," she warned. "My husband's expected home soon and he hates cyclists."

I couldn't imagine where she was going with that thought.

"Farmers have to maneuver big machinery around the 'damned slow bicycles,'" she said, repeating her husband's words.

The cycle-loathing hubby was belly-aching just that morning about autumn, "when riders show up in god-damned droves."

Clark glared, but remained silent.

"Um, okaaaaay. Thanks," I said, trying not to let confusion cross my face.

As we started to make our escape, she softened and told us about a back way into Rutland.

"It's a pretty road and my husband *NEVER* travels that way."

We headed straight for it—neither of us anxious to meet him or his big, bad equipment.

~

The route was strenuous, but rewarding, with scenic views of the mountains. The last few miles were especially slow. Clark had bike troubles and needed to stop frequently. Spoke problems. We could hear them breaking, snapping, popping, and binging out of the rim, hitting the pavement. Yikes. Was the bicycle self-destructing?

Losing a wheel on a downhill run was a real possibility. We continued cautiously, up and down the hills, trying to enjoy the view while listening for breaking spokes.

Suddenly, my bike was airborne! I'd hit a huge hole in a clogged metal grate and smashed down hard. My upper body rammed the handlebars, wrenching my shoulders and slamming my teeth together. Jaw muscles popped, shooting pain into my ears, immediately producing a pounding headache. Another one for the record books.

After arriving safely in town, Clark headed in one direction to ask around for a place to stay, and I in the other. We circled back with the same answer: a small motel on Main Street.

The motel was a bit of a dive, but we bartered the price down and settled in. A shower felt extra good on our road-weary bones.

Clark inspected his bike closer and noticed several big cracks in the rim of his back wheel. The cycle shop was closed for night, so nothing left to do but eat.

We walked into town and hit gold by discovering a restaurant that served a half-chicken, salad, green vegetable, mashed potatoes, gravy, sweet potatoes, dessert, and coffee—all for $9.99. The food was good, especially the sweet potatoes, or "candied yams," as the menu stated. Anything with the word "candy" in it gets a thumbs-up from me.

Clark jolted upright mid-meal with something stuck in his throat. Coughing uncontrollably, wheezing, and sweating profusely. Red-faced, he couldn't speak, so raised an index finger in the "give-me-a-minute" signal, then raced to the men's room. I heard muffled hacks, gaks, and other throat-clearing sounds from where I sat. Then it went quiet. I asked the waiter to check on him. The young man returned from his reconnaissance mission, gave me an "I dunno" shrug and went about his business.

Other diners looked alarmed, too. Ready to call for help, I suddenly spotted Clark walking around outside, still trying to clear his throat. Thankfully, he didn't appear to be in serious danger—just uncomfortable.

I paid our tab and we went back to the room. Clark recuperated while I thought about the day's close calls with the Grim Reaper: death by truck, death by crazy farmer, death by broken wheel, death by Humpty Dumpty, and death by choking.

Hello, Neighbor

Day 112: Tuesday, September 23
Weather: Cloudy and rainy
Distance: 0 miles
Route: Rest day in Rutland, Vermont

No problem convincing ourselves we needed a recuperation day. The broken bike. My sore jaw from the previous day's airborne act. Predictions of a big storm heading our way. Plus, Clark's achy muscles and sore throat, probably caused by his hack attack. Enough said.

Clark took a hot bath while I flipped TV stations idly from news to talk shows, cartoons, music, and back again. Outside, the storm clouds gathered. It was mid-morning before we ventured out for breakfast.

While I finished my last sips of coffee, Clark paid the bill.

A woman in line to pay noticed his Oregon t-shirt and asked, "Are you from Oregon?"

"Yeah," Clark smiled. "Portland."

"Really? What part?"

I joined the conversation, followed quickly by the woman's husband. We soon discovered we were former neighbors living only a few blocks apart. Boston was their current home, but plans to move back to Oregon were already under way. What a small world.

Back at the motel, we set about doing chores. Clark took his bike to the shop while I gathered laundry. I hiked the heavy load a mile downhill to the nearest laundromat, two bulging plastic bags of dirty clothing. As our garb spun through the wash cycle I shopped: yogurt, fruit, juice, cheese, chips, and throat lozenges. Then I waited out the drying cycle by reading trashy magazines, which were amazingly entertaining. After the clothes were dried and folded, I trudged the mile back uphill, juggling the laundry and my purchases.

It started to drizzle less than a block into my trek. At block two it was a full downpour. I became Cyclone Woman again, schlepping our stuff strongly and swiftly uphill. All went well until I tried to cross the street.

Relentless traffic was tearing down the road showing no signs of slowing. I stood, heavily burdened, wondering how to get to the other side safely. It took 10 minutes of false starts before I randomly chose a moment to make a run for it. Fortunately, the traffic slowed to let me cross. Or, maybe the rain enhanced Cyclone Woman's special talents.

I was soaking wet and exhausted by the time I got back, my arms ready to fall off and my super powers evaporated.

Meanwhile, Clark learned his tire was a goner. It had ripped from the sidewalls and had gashes in several places; the rims were twisted and bent and all the spokes destroyed. Even the surrounding metal was severely stressed.

He needed a whole new wheel, replacing it for the second time during our journey. Maybe the first repair was done incorrectly, maybe his gear too heavy or the roads too rough. Whatever the reason, we were glad the problem was getting fixed before a serious accident occurred.

We spent the afternoon napping and listening to rain pound on the roof. Just before 5 p.m., we jogged two miles to the bike shop before it closed. Mother Nature accommodated us, stopping the rain while we finished this final chore. Clark cycled back, testing his new wheel, while I walked, enjoying the earthy, clean smell of fresh-washed streets.

~

We arrived at our dinner destination just as three busloads of senior citizens were leaving, some shuffling along with walkers, some just shuffling. The restaurant staff looked frazzled. Every table was splayed with dirty dishes and glassware, and the floors were covered with gummy footprints, crumpled napkins, and stray silverware. A lone dinner roll lay flattened near the cash register, and a carved wooden cane leaned against a wall.

The hostess and waiters had plopped down on chairs to take a post-frenzy rest. The cooks, their billowy white hats askew, were even seated. As the only patrons in the place, we received great service, but I suspected the crew would have preferred to close the doors and go home.

Twin Lobsters

Day 113: Wednesday, September 24
Weather: Early fog, then sunny and clear
Distance: 55 miles
Route: Rutland, Vermont, to Claremont, New Hampshire

We woke to heavy fog and wagered whether it would clear up or rain in the next few hours. I bet on clearing, but it was one of those days it could easily go either way. The sun came out after breakfast, making me the winner of our 50¢ bet.

After 25 miles of lazy rolling hills, we arrived in Ludlow, a charming ski town just outside the Green Mountain National Forest. We pedaled slowly, breathing in the crisp fall air. Too bad it was so early. On another day, we would have found a reason to spend the night.

The Black River follows and crosses Main Street. The inky waterway lived up to its name except where sunlight bounced off stones in the shallow sections, turning the water momentarily brilliant blue.

My ski bum heart beat faster when I spotted Okemo Mountain, in the distance. The summit is over 3,300 feet, Vermont's highest vertical drop. Outlines of the now-quiet trails were etched into the mountainside and chairlifts hung idly, waiting for the winter's round of skiers to arrive.

Along Scenic Route 131, we saw our first Vermont covered bridge, one of just over a hundred in the state. It was built in authentic truss framework fashion and looked like a romantic tunnel of love. Not long after, we made an easy bridge crossing over the Connecticut River and wheeled into New Hampshire. Another state line and another day closer to the end of our journey.

Claremont was settled along the Sugar River in 1762. The water power generated by the river made the town prosperous during the Industrial Revolution. Large textile mills, machine works, and paper manufacturers sprouted up along the Sugar's banks. The newly wealthy built fine Victorian homes, stately mansions, and an Italian Renaissance Revival opera house.

For us, the most interesting history was that surrounding the "Cornish Colony." From 1885, for several decades, Claremont was home to a group of artists, writers, sculptors, poets, musicians, and journalists who joined sculptor Augustus Saint-Gaudens to live and work in the inspiring setting. Saint-Gaudens is best known for his Chicago sculpture of Abraham Lincoln, Boston's Shaw Memorial, and the General Sherman statue in front of the Plaza Hotel in New York City.

~

We asked the motel clerk for a dinner recommendation.

"Mmmmm ... If you're looking for seafood, I know just the place," he said.

We hiked nearly two miles to the edge of town, habitually willing to do what it took for a good meal. A long line of customers snaked around the outside of the restaurant—always a good sign. It was Twin Lobster Night, meaning you got two for the price of one. It felt decadent, and even though we said we wouldn't indulge until reaching Maine (a self-imposed motivator), this was too much to resist.

Clark studied the crowd once we were seated, hoping to learn the nuances of how to best eat the local specialty. Though he knew how to crack one open to get to the luscious meat, everyone has their own particular method. As a chef, Clark was always inspired to advance his culinary knowledge. He zoned in on a rugged-looking man, with a deeply tanned face, who had an easy confidence while handling his crustacean.

The man felt us gawking. His initial expression was quizzical, but a smile appeared when he learned of Clark's intentions. "Jerry" adapted to his teaching role with satisfied diligence, showing off his effortless cracking and sucking skills. Clark followed suit, taking on his student role with the same flourish. Customers at surrounding tables watched with interest and clapped when Clark raised a big chunk of lobster high in the air, then popped it in his mouth with pomp and circumstance.

> We observed the culinary world change as we crossed the country and encountered menus peppered with enticing local specialties. Seafood on the West Coast slowly turned from ocean fish to steak, buffalo, elk, venison, and lake fish as we traveled east. The Midwest offered the addition of pork, sausages, and brats. Then, in the East, we started seeing fresh seafood drift back into focus. Locally grown and produced fruits, vegetables, cheeses, nuts, and wines complemented the menus, transitioning along the entire trip.

An Unexpected Invitation

Day 114: Thursday, September 25
Weather: Back and forth from sunny and clear to cold, overcast, and cloudy
Distance: 33 miles
Route: Claremont, New Hampshire, to New London, New Hampshire

The new day brought new opportunities and a chance to eat again. We found a promising breakfast diner a block away. The moment we stepped inside the small-town restaurant, attention turned our way. We were newcomers, dressed in bicycling gear. The patrons were curious and friendly. They immediately bombarded us with questions, then spread news of our trip to their friends and neighbors, who soon arrived at the diner to meet us. Instant celebrities. Before long there was a crowd around our table, everyone talking at once. We answered questions shot from every direction as fast as we could.

"No, we didn't train before we left."

"Yes, we still love each other, but make alone-time every day."

"Yes, we get REALLY wet sometimes."

"… and really hot or cold."

"No, we don't carry a cell phone. Yes, that was a conscious decision."

"Actually, our hands are more sore than our butts."

We enjoyed our momentary celeb status and nudged each other playfully when we heard our favorite colloquialisms: "Get outta here," "Cut it oooouuuut!" and "Yer killin' me!"

The staff enjoyed our visit, too. We overheard the waitress on her phone: "Yeah, that's what I said—Portland to Portland. Yes, on bicycles. Can you believe it? How crazy is that?!"

After wrapping up her call, the waitress brought out samples of scrapple for us. It looked a little scary. And chunky. Scrapple is cornmeal mush mixed with chopped "scraps" of cooked pork, broth, and various seasonings. This mixture is cooked, packed into loaf pans, cooled, then sliced and fried in butter. Often, cooks add their personal touch by throwing other leftovers in. That's part of the fun. To me, this concoction tasted greasy and gross. But with all eyes on us, anxious for a reaction, Clark smacked his lips and said "Mmmmm mmmm." He liked it!

> Clark's knowledge of the culinary arts often led to free food samples. Chefs, waiters, waitresses, restaurateurs, bartenders, home cooks, and all-around foodies recognized his expertise and went out of their way to offer up tasty bites. They seemed instinctually drawn to him. I loved the way Clark's face lit up when he learned new culinary tricks and techniques or tried new foods. Since it was apparent he knew good quality, we were typically bestowed the best of everything. Lucky me to be traveling—and sampling—alongside him.

In Newport, 10 miles away, we stopped to rest, meandering through town, pressing our noses against store windows, and chatting with anyone who wanted to talk. What a fun surprise when we saw a line-up of colorful woolen blankets from Pendleton, Oregon. We spotted the familiar striped designs, as well as those featuring Native American story-telling patterns. The heavy blankets have been produced for over a century, warming and comforting generations of families. Seeing the iconic Pendletons made us feel proud … and a little homesick.

Time to forge ahead.

A massive tree, rooted solo next to a busy road, struck a stunning pose against the city backdrop. The silhouette brought us to a full stop, as if it was reaching out for attention, displaying fall colors like a proud peacock. The sun glistened off the leaves, highlighting a range of hues that glowed with inner beauty. We stood under its immense canopy to admire the splendor up close.

When the sky turned gray and temperature plummeted, we rode quickly in an effort to warm up. Not long after, the sun returned, and we found ourselves on a back road traveling along the shores of Sunapee Lake and Little Sunapee Lake in beautiful rolling terrain.

Then, we couldn't figure out where we were. The map was confusing. Nothing made sense. We looked from road signs to store windows and back again, but still no concrete clues, so we pulled into a strip mall parking lot to get a closer look at the map. We must have seemed notably disoriented because a woman spotted us from across the parking lot and shouted out her car window as she drove toward us, "Can I help you find something?"

"Where are we?" Clark asked.

"New London, New Hampshire," she said with great enthusiasm.

"Wow," I said. "We're much farther than I thought."

"Is there a liquor store near here?" Clark quickly added.

She laughed long and hard, amused two long-haul cyclists would ask for booze instead of a tofu burger or protein shake. She moved her car closer so we could talk without shouting. Her name was Carla. She was fun, easygoing, and smart. After talking 20 minutes, we asked about a reasonably priced motel.

She let out a guffaw and said no place in town was affordable.

"How about staying at my house?"

Carla didn't have to ask twice—we accepted right away.

From there she took charge. She pointed to a nearby restaurant and told us what to order and to wait there while she ran a few errands. We did as we were told, ordering the clam chowder and warm bread. Delicious. Maybe the best we'd ever had. We scraped every bit of lusciousness from our bowls, holding ourselves back from licking them clean.

In less than an hour, Carla was back at the restaurant with a friend and a detailed map to her house. Patsy, who had cycled across the country with her husband a few years back, was bubbling with energy. She was thrilled to talk to fellow cyclists and pulled Carla into the booth with us. We settled into animated conversation, instantly connecting.

The waitress buzzed back and forth, half eavesdropping and half keeping up with our beverage needs. Carla suggested we stop to meet her husband David on the way to their house. We were in high spirits as we pulled into his workplace.

"Is David here?" Clark asked confidently.

"Yeah, that's me."

"Oh, hi. We're staying with you tonight and wanted to say hello."

"I guess you met my wife!" he said, with sweet sarcasm.

We talked a few minutes and continued on our way. A few blocks from their place, a neighborhood dog joined us, happily racing alongside with a big stick in his mouth. We put our bikes inside the garage, as Carla had instructed, and then found the key exactly where she told us it would be. We let ourselves in and navigated the way to "our" bedroom—the back one on the left. It was a lovely space. We cleaned up and relaxed a while.

Soon after, Carla and David arrived home, followed by a neighbor, more friends, two dogs, and a slew of kids. We worked together to make dinner and laughed the entire night. Long into the evening, after the others went home, we theorized about life: its meaning, keeping relationships together, and finding true happiness. It felt as if we'd known each other all our lives.

> Carla told us a year later that her daughter had been upset with her for inviting strangers to spend the night. It was one thing to talk with "unknowns" in a parking lot or ask new people to stay for dinner, but giving them a key to your home before you get there is altogether different.
>
> "What if they rob us, Mom?"
>
> "I don't think they will," Carla said, offering reassurance. "I have a good sense about people. Besides, what could they carry off on bikes?"
>
> Children warning their parents to be careful—what a role reversal!

An Unfortunate Accident and Über Peepers

Day 115 & 116:	Friday and Saturday, September 26 and 27
Weather:	Sunny skies and crisp air
Distance:	0 miles
Route:	Rest days in New London, New Hampshire

We slept soundly and late; it was 8:30 before we rousted ourselves from bed. David and Carla had already gone to work but left breakfast warming in the oven. A note invited us to make ourselves at home. The note also included an invitation from Patsy and husband Greg to have dinner and spend the night at their house. We pondered the offer but, not wanting to be a burden, felt we should ride on. I called Patsy to give our regrets. She sounded disappointed, but understood.

However, when I called Carla to tell her we were leaving, she protested. "Oh no, you *have* to stay with them! Why hurry? Like you said, what's your adventure all about? Living in the moment, right?"

The next thing Clark heard me say was "Good point, that's all the convincing I need."

Clark was an easy pushover when I shared the conversation. "Let's do it!"

I called Patsy and we were back on.

~

Carla and David's "bed and breakfast" included the use of a car. They suggested we leave our bikes and gear at their house, then drive downtown, explore, and make our way to Patsy and Greg's after. I packed an overnight bag, while Clark went out to familiarize himself with the car. Just as I was stepping out the door to join him, I tripped over my own two feet, wrenched my ankle, and did a header. I could hear a pop and felt my ankle twist beyond its normal range of motion. I fell with a hard thump and laid there in pain, afraid to move.

Clark came bounding over to help me and immediately slipped into medic mode, inspecting my injury to gauge its seriousness. I was uncharacteristically silent; it hurt too much to talk. After determining it wasn't broken, we both breathed a sigh of relief.

I picked myself up and limped to the car using Clark as a support. He ran back inside to get a bag of ice for the swelling. The injury put a damper on the day, and we wondered if this was the end of the trip. How would I ride with a badly twisted ankle? We were so close to the finish line—would we have to stop? If I couldn't ride, would Clark continue without me?

Not a chance.

I was determined to make it to the end, so did my best to remain positive. "I'm sure it will be fine in a little while. Good thing we already have a rest day planned," I said, with self-doubt swirling in my head.

Later, my ankle swelled to twice its normal size. The pain was intense and walking was out of the question. It even hurt sitting in the car. This is where we hit a defining moment in the trip and in our relationship. I struggled to remain positive, but Clark was really down.

"It will be 10 days or more until your ankle heals," he said sadly. "We won't be able to complete the trip …."

I ignored my throbbing ankle and summoned the emotional will to interrupt his negative thoughts.

"Of course we'll finish," I replied, trying to sound optimistic.

"No. These things take time."

Clark stared off into the distance, while I silently cursed my clumsiness and hoped I'd be able to continue. The landscape blurred past as I quietly gathered my thoughts. Mind over matter. I needed to finish the trip.

"Look," I said with conviction. "I'm worried, too. Really worried. But, I promise, I WILL make it to Portland. If I have to crawl to the end and haul my bike after me, I WILL do it."

Clark looked at me with full concentration and slight amusement. I continued.

"I refuse to quit. I'm equally disappointed AND in pain. I'm doing everything I can to stay positive. I would appreciate it if you'd do the same because your negativity is not helping. We'll find a way to make this work."

Clark let out a long sigh and gave me a hug.

"Sorry, baby. You're right. We'll get there … together."

~

Patsy and Greg's house was a beautiful place with a big yard and lots of privacy. We settled into our room, which didn't take long, since we only brought one change of clothes and a few toiletries. Patsy noticed me limping and provided a new bag of ice and a couple ibuprofen. She asked if we wanted to ride along while she ran errands in Hanover, the home of Dartmouth College.

The 40-minute drive made me sleepy. Patsy's voice was soft and soothing, like a meditation recording. The pain progressed to my knee. I wanted to lie down and struggled to participate in the conversation. I rambled absentmindedly, closing my eyes and trying to sleep and talk simultaneously.

Patsy parked on campus and headed toward a bookstore.

"I'll meet you back here in an hour," she called out over her shoulder, "Explore the campus and enjoy the sun."

The fresh air felt good, but I was only able to hobble half a block to a bench.

"I'll sit here and wait for you to get back."

Clark looked concerned but wandered off, glancing back twice before disappearing around the corner. I studied my ankle, now swollen to an unrecognizable state, and forced back tears. I closed my eyes and let the sun bathe my face in warmth, grateful for a moment alone to wallow in my pain and exhaustion.

A bit too soon, we piled back into the car. Me, more gingerly. Patsy, knowing how much pain I was in, kept things upbeat by sharing tidbits of local history and lore as she drove home.

First things first. She opened a bottle of "medicinal" wine and replenished my ice bag, just as Greg arrived.

"Who's hungry?!" he said, making the perfect introduction.

Greg's enthusiasm for cooking was infectious. He and Clark bonded quickly. It wasn't long until tantalizing scents and animated conversation filled the kitchen. Being with this couple was easy and natural. We went through three bottles of wine, devoured an excellent four-course meal, and covered myriad thought-provoking subjects. It was past 2 a.m. by the time Clark and I hit the sack. Happily, the wine had eased my pain and we both slept soundly.

~

Clark was the first to rouse in the morning. I know this because I was awakened by his fingers inspecting my tender ankle. He suggested I needed another day to recuperate.

"No, no, no. I'll be fine," I assured him.

We padded toward the kitchen in search of coffee. Greg and Patsy were right behind us. Carla knocked on the door and joined the party. Greg donned an apron and whipped up a fabulous breakfast.

I've always loved "the morning after." People seem more real. Everyone in their PJs, hair out of place, too groggy to worry about what others might think. People are simply more themselves. This morning was no exception. We sat around the table laughing, talking, and making plans to get together in Oregon the following year. I had no doubt we'd see each other again.

We gathered our few belongings and started saying goodbye at noon.

As we headed outside, Carla studied my limp and said, "I think you sprained your ankle for a reason—you were meant to stay longer."

What an angel! Done deal.

Carla lent us her car for another day so we could become leaf peepers, the nickname for people who visit New England in fall to enjoy autumn's splendor.

Highway 11 took us toward Franklin and Tilton, then 93 led straight to the mountains. At Lincoln, we branched off onto Highway 112, rounded a sharp curve, and WOW. Clark and I were like kids watching fireworks.

"Ooooooh! Ahhhh!" he'd exclaim over each leafy color palette.

"Wow, wow, wow!" I added.

"Yesssss!" Clark continued, craning his neck and peering into the rearview mirror for a better peep as we drove along.

We were now "Über" Peepers.

~

When we got back, Carla and David were entertaining. Neighbors, kids, and friends sprawled on the floor to watch a movie. The house was a happy gathering place. I propped my leg up on an ottoman and we joined in. The happiness level in the room was sky high.

> While we were leaf peeping, we came across a man selling special "foliage viewing glasses." Curious, we pulled over. The vendor swore the red-tinted glasses made the leaf colors brighter. We were skeptical because a small sign stated the only way to try the glasses' special powers was to purchase them, no refunds. I elbowed Clark and pointed discreetly to the sign. I'm not sure how the leaves could look more spectacular than what we saw with our naked eyes. No enhancement needed.

WEEK 18

Hard to Leave, But Time to Go

    Day 116:   Sunday, September 28
    Weather: Sunny and pleasant—a beautiful fall day
    Distance: 40 miles
    Route: New London, New Hampshire, to
                 Meredith, New Hampshire

The soft bed was difficult to leave, and though we felt so at home with Carla and David we didn't want to overstay our welcome. They fixed a hearty breakfast and we fell into another energizing conversation. Before we knew it, the morning was gone.

They invited us to stay another night, but it was time to ride. We didn't expect to cover a lot of miles, but moving, even a little, would help regain the traveling spirit and might actually support the ankle-healing process.

I was comfortable with the up-and-down motion of standard pedaling, but worried about snapping out of the clipless pedals when I had to stop. Releasing from them required turning my foot sideways, which would be painful.

"I'll adjust your pedals so you can get out of them with less pressure on your ankle," Clark said.

Carla gave me an ace bandage for my ankle and packed a big lunch for nutritional support. Their generosity never seemed to end. Everyone hugged goodbye with genuine sadness, but we looked forward to repaying their kindness the following year in Oregon.

Before long, we were coasting on wooded back roads leading away from our friends but heading toward new adventures and the Eastern Seaboard. So far so good; the ankle brace was doing its job. Soon, we were moving fast, smiling big and enjoying the ride. I was having so much fun zooming down a smooth hill ahead of Clark, I missed a turn. Wheeeeeee! Only when I heard his voice in the distance, did I realize my mistake.

"Liiiiiiizaaaa! Come back. You overshot the turn-off," Clark shouted.

I circled back, grinning as I sped by, taking the lead again. Clark sprang back on his bike for the race. Adrenaline flowed as unadulterated joy took over my body. Clark's winded laughter behind me confirmed he was experiencing the thrill, too. So engrossed in the moment, I didn't notice when the pavement abruptly turned to loose gravel.

In a split second, I slid across the rocks and slammed to the ground. Again.

A woman saw my fall from her front yard.

"Are you okay?" she called, while running toward me, peeling off her gardening gloves on the way.

"Yes, I think so. Just a skinned knee," I said, lying prone under my bike. "Thanks for asking."

She put out a hand and circled an arm around my back to help get me upright, just as Clark arrived on the scene.

"Oh, no. Not again," Clark playfully chided, once he knew I was okay.

The woman laughed softly, "I'm just glad you weren't hurt."

Judith was fit and strong, with graying hair pulled back in a ponytail; she exuded a kind of beauty that radiates from within. I guessed she was in her 60s, but could have been older.

"How about some lemonade and a bandage?" she offered, nodding toward the house.

Stacks of leaves were raked into neat piles. A cobblestone walkway led to her beautiful white home, black shutters flanking the windows. A pinecone-shaped brass knocker adorned the crimson front door. Completing this idyllic scene, a gray kitten snuggled with its mother on a wicker chair.

"I'll be right back with drinks and cookies," Judith said, as she disappeared into the house.

Clark and I made friends with the cats. The kitten entertained us by hanging upside down off the wicker and zipping back and forth like a kid jacked up on sugar. Judith knocked the door open with her hip and set a heavy tray of lemonade and goodies down. Her homemade peanut butter and chocolate chip cookies smelled, and tasted, like heaven.

We talked for an hour, reveling in the kindness of strangers.

~

The ride took us north toward Highway 4 and Lake Winnipesaukee and, in 10 short miles, we arrived in Danbury. Autumn's colors were at their peak. Even tiny orange and yellow blossoms poked through the cracks in a rock walkway.

I broke out Carla's lunch and we picnicked on a grassy spot in the town center. Sun warmed our backs as a chipmunk hopped and pranced around looking for scraps. Clark was the first to stretch out for a nap. I followed suit, happy to rest my ankle for a while.

~

As we settled into a comfortable pace, I heard the screech of tires, then watched in horror as a driver careened down the road. He passed four cars at a time—in a no-passing zone—and sped directly toward me. It was evident the guy wasn't moving back into his lane, so I veered onto the narrow shoulder. The crazy driver laid on his horn, glaring psychotically as he barreled by. A whoosh of air, followed by a blast of nauseating exhaust fumes, fueled anger and fear.

Another car, maybe drinking buddies of the last driver, slowed and passed dangerously close to Clark. A young guy in the backseat swore loudly and sent a bottle hurtling. Clark saw it coming and ducked but felt the tip of the container graze his ear before it smashed to bits close by. He veered sharply, lost control, and landed head first in the gravel. Cruel laughter and taunting came from inside the vehicle as the car peeled away, a rooster tail of dirt left in its wake.

Clark was picking little pieces of gravel from his cheek and right knee as I rode up to check on him.

"Assholes," Clark muttered.

Yep.

~

We made it to Bristol with our nerves intact and scoured the city hoping to stop for the night. No-vacancy signs permeated the place. We resigned ourselves to riding nearly 20 more miles into Meredith when our luck turned. On the way out of town, we found a small motel, with a steakhouse right next door. What a relief.

Liza McQuade

Off Again, On Again

Day 117:	Monday, September 29
Weather:	Heavy rain
Distance:	23 miles
Route:	Bristol, New Hampshire, to Moultonborough, New Hampshire

Pounding rain prompted us to roll over and snuggle in for a few more Zs. Leftover fruit, nuts, and TV talk shows filled the time until check out. We enjoyed being lazy. By late morning the rain lifted, so we suited up to ride. I checked my ankle and noticed it was turning colors: black, blue, red, and yellow—almost matching the leaves outside. It was still sore but seemed to be healing.

The day consisted of taking clothes off and putting them back on, getting wet and drying off, getting wet again. We traveled only short distances at a time. Just when we thought the weather was clear, it rained again. And when we stopped to dry out somewhere inside, the sun came out, shining brightly until we were back on our bikes and away from shelter. We guessed wrong all day.

In Moultonborough, after 23 miles of on-again, off-again rain—and inside-outside retreats—we gave up and checked into a motel. According to the front desk staff, the best restaurant in town was right next door. Before making ourselves presentable for dinner, we wrung out our sopping belongings and spread them around the spacious room to dry. It looked like the aftermath of a hurricane.

~

The rich, buttery scents from the intimate French restaurant smelled enticing, making us *trés* hungry. Only one other couple was seated when we arrived for early dinner. Monday in a small town.

The restaurant owner came over to greet the "new faces in town," listening with great interest when he learned of our cross-country ride. Apparently impressed, he comped us an escargot appetizer with a crispy crumb topping. The meaty mollusks were presented in their shells, bathed in a pool of luscious lemon-herb-garlic sauce. We mopped up every last bit of succulent juice with chunks of warm baguette.

Clark moved on to a herbed rack of lamb and creamed spinach. I ordered Cornish game hen with brandied butter sauce and green beans al dente, plus au gratin potatoes to share. An eight-year-old bottle of pinot noir perfectly complemented our selections. Après dinner, the pleasure continued with a fine, old port for me and Courvoisier for Clark.

We later bid *adieu* to one of the nicest dining experiences of our adventure and strolled back to the room hand-in-hand.

Laughing Fever

Day 118: Tuesday, September 30
Weather: Overcast
Distance: A grand total of 6.5 miles
Route: Moultonborough, New Hampshire, to Wolfeboro, New Hampshire

The day started with a walk to the post office, where we encountered a drive-up window. That was new to us. We didn't see a door to the refurbished bank building, so I spoke confidently into the microphone.

"Do you have an inside?"

There was a long pause, then a roar of laughter.

"No, I'm completely empty," a disembodied voice answered.

After realizing what I'd said, Clark and I cracked up.

Everyone inside the post office heard us through the speaker and caught the laughing fever. Soon, all we could do was hold our stomachs and grunt out single syllable words. Using this primitive form of communication, we were directed to the entrance at the back of the building.

A round of applause broke out as we walked through the door. Then another communal laughing fit ensued. We were in the post office over an hour. Four minutes to complete our mailing needs and 56+ minutes in a gabfest. Our tanned faces and biking clothes gave us away, so we launched into our now well-rehearsed cycling saga. The employees had entertaining stories of their own about small-town life. Bursts of laughter echoed off the old bank walls.

There's no better way to connect than to share a good belly laugh.

> Post offices are a social hub for most little communities. The pace is relaxed and folks are friendly in this harmonious network. People come and go all day, running into friends and neighbors, often catching up on local news or sharing tidbits from their personal lives.
>
> I felt at home watching the ebb and flow of the interactions; these simple moments reminding me of my own small-town childhood.

We picked up Route 109 outside Moultonborough, which soon fed into 171. Great riding: easy up-and-down roads and lots of fall colors. I was full of zip and zeal, and then—boom—flat tire #9.

Clark - Fixing A Flat - Outside Moultonborough, NH

A flat didn't faze us anymore, and we jumped into action. I wheeled over to a safe spot and stripped the bike bags off the rear wheel, while Clark found the repair kit and set up shop. He changed the tire quickly. Neither of us complained, and our mission ran like clockwork. That is, until Clark spotted a tiny hole in the sidewall of my tire. Something that could cause problems down the road.

Before we could weigh our options, a woman driving past noticed our travails and stopped to offer help.

"Are you alright?" she asked pulling her yellow Honda up close. "Do you need anything?"

"I think I've got it," Clark answered positively. "But thanks for stopping."

"I'm driving back this way in a few minutes, so I'll check again," she said, giving us a cheery wave as she drove off.

We turned our attention back to the bike.

When an old pick-up truck came along shortly after, I flagged the driver down. The senior couple inside seemed a bit wary at first but obliged and stopped.

"Do you know where the closest bike shop is?" I asked, standing back some to help them feel more at ease.

"Not sure," the driver said. "Let me think a minute."

At that moment, our friend in the yellow Honda returned, pulled over, and popped out of the car.

"You're looking for a bike shop, right? There's one in Wolfeboro," she said assuredly. "Maybe these folks could give you a ride," nodding in the couple's direction, as their eyes widened a bit. "I'd give you a ride if my car were bigger," she continued, with a sweet smile.

She was so persuasive that the couple, Jake and Sarah, agreed to be our taxi. We hoisted our bikes in the back of the old beater. Clark was directed to sit in the bed of the truck with the bikes and some boxes, while I squeezed into the front seat between Jake and Sarah. Awkward. I tried to suck everything in so none of my body parts were touching theirs. It was impossible. We were squished in so tight, we had to become friends.

They kept me entertained by talking at the same time, Jake telling one story and Sarah another, both becoming incrementally louder in order to get their individual points across. Then, somehow their voices would coalesce into one story, with slightly different details and moments of arguing. Soon, they would launch off again on separate stories, one in my right ear, the other in my left. Maybe they were slightly deaf or had been married so long they didn't notice the discrepancy.

Jake drove erratically, stomping the clutch and shifting gears roughly. We lurched forward in fits and starts, weaving back and forth, occasionally crossing the center line. Jake should have hung up his keys a while ago. I clung to the dashboard for dear life.

Poor Clark. I heard disturbing clunking sounds of bikes and body tossing about in the back, as Jake sped around curves and randomly slammed on the brakes. In the rearview mirror, I caught brief glimpses of Clark's head bobbing around. He was banging back and forth like a load of loose lumber.

At one point, Jake careened off the road into an orchard. I thought he'd lost control of the truck. Or, perhaps he was an axe murderer driving somewhere desolate to hack us to bits. It terrified me until I realized he was only trying to show us a nice view of something we couldn't see through the thick branches. We raved about the beauty anyway.

"Do you mind if we stop at our cottage to unload the boxes?" he asked.

"Not at all," I replied.

He pulled onto a dirt road, nearly hidden by dense woods and heavy underbrush. We bumped along about a quarter mile until reaching a clearing with a small log cabin and large garden. Rustic, but inviting. Blankets and sheets flapped gently from a clothesline. Fishing gear propped up on the front porch railing completed the scene. Were we in a Norman Rockwell painting?

Jake unloaded the boxes and Sarah invited us inside for a tour. It took my eyes a moment to adjust. The front room was comfortably dark. The scent of old pine, woodfire, and breakfast permeated the air. Comfy chairs faced an old, boxy TV in a corner, and yellowed paperbacks lined a tall shelf. A low, round coffee table rested on a braided rug in front of the fireplace.

In another corner, a huge, old organ sat ominously. It felt spooky. The size dwarfed the space. Pipes of varying lengths reached toward the ceiling. Some of the ivory had chipped from the keys, revealing the wood beneath, looking like a wide gap-toothed smile.

Jake had followed my gaze.

"It belonged to my parents. They had a big place on the coast. Didn't have the heart to get rid of it when they passed."

I saw a hint of sadness creep in around Jake's eyes. Sarah put a gentle hand on his back and shuttled us all into the bright kitchen. The mood immediately lightened when Sarah offered us freshly brewed iced tea and homemade gingersnap cookies.

Looking around, the retro mix of styles somehow made sense. Checkered curtains, a Formica-topped table surrounded by vinyl-covered chairs, a fridge from the 1960s, and a deep porcelain sink.

Their small bedroom was cozy and had a feminine touch, with a chintz bedspread and eyelet lace curtains. A claw-foot tub dominated the bathroom, and a clunky, avocado-green toilet and matching sink flanked the opposite wall. Must have been in vogue many decades ago.

~

We waved to Sarah from the truck as Jake backed up and swung around toward the main road to Wolfeboro. After a quick trip, Jake dropped us off in front of the bike shop. He waited to make sure the tire we needed was in stock and, I suspect, was ready to drive us to the next town, if necessary.

Clark gave Jake the thumbs-up about the tire and waved until the truck rumbled down the street out of sight. The shop had everything we needed. When the bike tech learned of our cross-country trip, he did everything he could to help us.

To make repairs more affordable, he let Clark use store tools to do the work himself, but stood by giving him tips and advice. I also stood by and kept the conversation going. That was my special purpose.

The tech determined that my rear brake pad was adjusted wrong, which likely caused the hole. He also showed Clark a few other alterations that made our bikes ride better. Too bad we didn't learn these things sooner.

We spotted a couple, around our age and with bikes loaded like ours, walking toward us. Kindred spirits. Their eyes brightened when they saw us, too.

"Hallo!" they said lightheartedly, with an accent I couldn't detect from just one word.

"Hello!" we responded with matching enthusiasm.

We stopped tire-to-tire, taking up the entire sidewalk.

They were visiting from Holland, on a 3-week bike trip through Vermont and New Hampshire. We clicked right away, compared notes, laughed at coincidences, then planned to camp together that night.

The four of us rode to the one-and-only campground. Unfortunately, it was closed for the season. They were disappointed, but we were secretly elated (a good excuse to stay in a motel again).

We found a modest place and checked in to our rooms. The Dutch couple chose to eat dinner from leftovers stashed in their bike bags while we enjoyed a hardy restaurant meal and a nightcap or two. Their lights were out by the time we returned. Guess we didn't have so much in common after all.

Liza McQuade

Glam Girl and the Chorus

Day 119:   Wednesday, October 1
Weather: Mixed and cold
Distance: 58 miles
Route: Wolfeboro, New Hampshire, to
           Old Orchard Beach, Maine

The morning's weather was a mix of clouds, a bit of sun, sprinkles on and off, and gusts of wind. The only consistency was a chill in the air. We could smell Old Man Winter right around the corner, even though it was only October 1. Summer had passed so quickly, and our adventure about to end. We packed quietly, deep in our own thoughts.

The ride was fun. Light traffic, smooth pavement, and a route bordered by trees painted with brilliant autumn colors. We would soon enter the last state of our trip. I had mixed emotions about that milestone—sad to know the adventure was coming to an end but joyful about the notion that we would make it to Portland. I knew Clark was reflecting on the same thoughts.

In Wakefield, a few miles west of Maine's border, we stopped to enjoy breakfast and say farewell to New Hampshire. As we leaned our bikes on a prime spot outside the restaurant window, a man sprinted toward us. He looked to be in his mid-50s, handsome and fit with a full head of silvery-gray hair. We could feel storytelling time coming on and gave him an abbreviated version.

"Hold on a minute!" the gentleman said, as he raced toward his car.

He was back in a flash with a map in hand.

"I can show you the best way to get to Biddeford, Maine."

He opened the large map and pressed it against the restaurant window, pointing at roads, trailing his finger along the interwoven lines.

When he was satisfied we understood the route, he efficiently folded the map back into a small rectangle.

"I'd like to chat more, but I'm off to a golf game and don't want to keep my buddies waiting. Time is of essence when you're 79!"

With that he dashed to his car, threw us a final wave, beeped his horn, and jetted off.

We stood staring after him, mouths agape.

"I hope I look that good when I'm his age," Clark said.

Me, too.

~

One step inside the diner carried us into the past. A U-shaped counter, with old-fashioned, red-padded swivel stools, took up half the space. The two corners contained mismatched tables with chipped Formica, each topped with a mini jukebox loaded with songs from bygone days. Faded posters of Elvis, the Rolling Stones, Beach Boys, and Dave Clark Five lined the walls. An immense soda fountain, straight out of the '50s, was the centerpiece.

Our entrance didn't go unnoticed. Heads simultaneously turned in our direction. A middle-aged couple, a waitress, and a dishwasher were the only ones in the place. They had an easy camaraderie and waved us over in their direction.

The waitress parked us at the next table over, handed out menus, and described the "blue plate special." After the usual small talk, we were telling our story—once again. The small group listened eagerly and the audience grew as new customers filled the diner. We had to start the story over and over. Those who heard the repeats seemed to enjoy hearing them again and again. In fact, they helped explain to others by chiming in and finishing for us.

"We're on a long-distance bike ride," I would begin.

"Yes, from Portland to Portland," the chorus said.

"And they didn't train," someone added. "Can you imagine?"

"It was hard at first …," Clark began, then got interrupted.

"It took a month to get out of Oregon," one man said, as if he had been on the trip with us.

"Tell about the rainstorm in Wall, South Dakota," another prodded.

"And Chuckles the Clown!" a chorus member piped up.

After several hours sharing tales, we'd barely picked at our meal. For once, food was not a priority. It was hard to leave such ardent admirers, but we didn't want another day to slip past. We said goodbye and left with the crowd cheering us on. Clark flipped them the peace sign and I did my best queenly elbow–elbow–wrist–wrist wave.

Before long, the Welcome to Maine sign came into view. Exhilarated, we flew off our bikes, high-fived, and kissed in New Hampshire—then ran across the state line and did it again in Maine. We whooped and hollered and congratulated ourselves. We had reached Maine intact.

~

We rode on, passing the towns of Acton, Springvale, and Alfred, covering ground fast, enjoying the crisp fall breeze. We cycled quickly through Biddeford, a good-sized city too far from the coast for a view. At a stoplight, we asked a passerby for directions to Saco. The directions also came with a warning.

"This is one way to get there," the young woman told us, pointing forward with a skinny, manicured finger. "But there's a huge hill ahead—you'll never make it. Go across the bridge instead," she said condescendingly, as she scanned our bodies, back and forth, up and down.

She paused, then continued to inspect us, simultaneously looking at herself in the car mirror and describing an alternative, "less-exerting" route. We both stopped listening and caught each other's eye. I could feel Clark contemplating a smart remark, but he saw me smile and let it go.

With her "rescue mission" complete, the woman popped on glamorous sunglasses, flipped her hair like a runway model, and sped off in her little convertible.

"Really?" Clark said sarcastically.

No way we'd take her advice. We rode confidently toward what was, indeed, a steep hill, but compared to what inclines we'd ridden in the past, it wasn't much of a threat. Nanny, nanny, boom, boom!

We took a breath, geared down, and pedaled up quickly. It was steep, but certainly not worth a reroute. After all those miles, we were once again reminded to never change plans based on other people's perceptions of us.

~

All of a sudden, there it was—the Atlantic Ocean. Not our final destination of Portland, but close. I was speechless, filled with mixed emotions.

We stood hand-in-hand for a long time, silently taking in the magical moment. The world was still. No one in sight, no sounds distracting us, not even a wisp of wind. Absolutely tranquil.

A cold breeze picked up, we shivered and our trance was broken. Growling stomachs further convinced us it was time to move on.

We rode into Camp Ellis and a short time later were having lunch at an ocean-view table. Huge bowls of rich lobster stew quieted our bellies. We communicated via exaggerated nods of approval and discreet slurping sounds.

Inspired by the big chunks of lobster, we set a new goal and committed to eating lobster in every possible form before returning to Oregon.

~

We headed north a few miles along the coast toward Old Orchard Beach, a now-quiet summer tourist destination. There were a few people in stores, but the streets seemed deserted. Family vacations had come to an end and kids were back in school.

A man raked leaves with great gusto outside a motel. A large "Closed" sign was posted on the front lawn. He smiled and waved, so we stopped to ask where we might find an inexpensive place to spend the night. He pointed toward the heart of town, then paused to study us more closely.

"You can stay here if you want," he offered. "I just closed for the season, but I'd open back up, if you like."

"Perfect," Clark said, then bartered a terrific rate.

"The name's Stan, by the way."

"Liza, Clark," I added, pointing to each of us as appropriate.

Check-in was a breeze. We clacked down an empty hallway in our bike shoes, wheeling our cycles toward the room. We dropped our belongings and headed straight for the ocean. The wide sand beach stretched for over 7 miles, not another person in sight.

After several hours of lounging, we went for a long walk through town. A sign, hand-lettered in gold, advertised "Fresh Lobster."

"Sit anywhere you like" was all we needed to hear from a waitress who popped her head out the door. Of course, we chose the best table with the best view. I ordered my lobster sautéed in a light tomato sauce with seasonal vegetables. Clark ordered his steamed with a side of lobster bisque. A Spanish Tempranillo perfectly suited our shared mussel appetizer.

As we clinked glasses, the waitress asked what we were celebrating. After a brief overview, she was off sharing her new knowledge with other patrons. One couple timidly approached and inquired why we'd do such a thing. Although it seemed incomprehensible to us, not everyone would choose this kind of adventure. We were amused by their concerned looks as they pondered what was wrong with us. Our incredible summer of fun and adventure obviously sounded like pure madness to them.

The Trip-and-Fall Café

Day 120: Thursday, October 2
Weather: Sunny and warm
Distance: Rest day
Route: From motel to beach and back again, and again, and again

I slept long and deep, waking to bright, sunny skies and Clark kissing me on the cheek.

"You're beautiful," he whispered in my ear. "Do you know how much I love you?"

"I love you, too. Always and forever," I whispered back.

Clark's smile melted my heart. "You're the love of my life. Let's stay another day," he said as he pulled me closer.

~

It was settled. Another day on a sunny beach, a comfortable room, and all the lobster we could eat. What could be better? Well, maybe breakfast, for now.

Along a side street, we discovered a hidden eatery, tucked beneath an office building, a real locals' place. A small sign, posted at an odd angle, warned customers to step down. Unfortunately, Clark didn't see the sign. He did that stumble-flailing-acrobat dance, but managed to recover and land on his feet at the last second.

"Whoa, Nelly. Careful!" a waitress shouted as she sprinted toward Clark.

We learned three people had fallen there. One woman tumbled down the steps and crashed into the glass pastry case. She was bruised and scratched up pretty badly. Another broke her leg; the third, her arm.

"A new sign is coming next week," the waitress offered meekly. "Glad you're okay."

"Me, too. That'll wake you up in the morning!" Clark said as he dissolved into laughter.

After breakfast, we headed for the beach. The Indian summer warmed our bodies as we basked in the sun for several hours.

"Well, hello!" a cheery voice called out as we walked past the office back to our room. "You must be our bicyclers."

Noting our puzzlement, Stan's wife introduced herself.

"My husband doesn't re-open the motel for just anyone," she laughed.

This started a relaxed round of conversation.

She had thoughtfully clipped two-for-one lobster dinner coupons for us. But, there was a catch: We'd have to bike three miles uphill and

Spontaneous Revolutions

back again. We thanked her and headed to the room to discuss logistics. According to Clark, the best place to contemplate what to do for dinner was over lunch. We loaded up on wine, cheese, crackers, and fresh shrimp at a little store and walked back to the water for a picnic.

Stan was touching-up paint on a door when we arrived back at the motel.

"How 'bout a lift to the restaurant tonight? 6:30?" he offered, as if psychic.

Our faces said it all.

~

There was a waiting list by the time Stan dropped us at the door, but customers got seated quickly and we were ordering in no time. Going all out, we took full advantage of the coupons and chose the four-lobster special (that's four lobsters for each of us).

Here's the secret to putting away that many: avoid the extras. No bread, vegetables, desserts, or sides of any kind. Wine doesn't count.

The couple at the next table sized us up, and the man commented sarcastically on our voracious appetites.

"Are you celebrating something?" the wife quickly interjected.

The husband's sarcasm ratcheted down significantly after we mentioned we'd just bicycled cross-country from Portland, Oregon.

"Wow! OK, then. Eat up," he said, as if we needed his approval.

We straightened our bibs and dug back in. Before leaving, he snapped a picture as evidence of their encounter with people who could put away four lobsters in one sitting.

Stan arrived just as we waddled out the front door—bellies first.

Liza McQuade

Portland to Portland in 122 Days

Day 121:   Friday, October 3
Weather: Partly cloudy
Distance: 28 miles
Route: Old Orchard Beach, Maine, to Portland, Maine

We were close to the finish line, our adventure nearing an end. The reality weighed heavily on us. Clark's somber mood matched mine as we packed. Gazing out the window, I reasoned silently that the cool, gray morning would make leaving our oceanside paradise a little easier.

After breakfast at the trip-and-fall café, we strolled back along the beach and mounted our bikes for the final leg of our journey. We pushed off without saying a word.

The coastal road was beautiful and deserted. We only stopped once, to admire a lone tree still in full fall regalia—brilliant colors created a striking contrast against the leaden sky. Pedaling along, breathing in the ocean air, our attitudes brightened. We reviewed our incredible summer, laughing about the horrors and highlights encountered.

Eventually, we turned onto Highway 1, a well-traveled road with motorists hurrying to get to the city. The pace too fast, at a crossroads, we chose a quieter path with rolling hills that snaked along the ocean. Lovely marshlands, brilliant fall colors, and gorgeous homes complemented the setting.

Clark & Liza - We Made It! The Atlantic Ocean.

We wheeled the bikes through the sand at Cape Elizabeth for a photo of our front tires in the Atlantic Ocean. Proof of victory! Our bikes finally wet their wheels in water of both coasts, just as we'd hoped. I took off my shoes and stood in the cool surf, enjoying the sensation of sand squishing through my toes.

While we were basking in our success, a young couple walked up the beach toward us, each trailing a tiny horse on a leash. The animals were only a little larger than our dog and seemed shy and sweet. I stroked their adorable mini pony heads as we talked with the owners. They were excited to know they had just witnessed us ceremoniously dipping our tires into the ocean.

The horses decided it was time to move on, nudging the couple gently with their soft muzzles. We watched as they all ran along the beach, kicking up sprays of sand in their wake.

My heart beat faster as we approached our final destination. This was it; we'd made it to the other side of the country. Portland to Portland in 122 days. With tears welling, I dismounted my bike. Words escaped us. We hugged for a long time, then parted.

Clark gazed at the ocean with the most magical expression.

He tipped my face up toward his, looked deep into my eyes and said, "I'm ready to plan our next adventure."

That's my guy.

EPILOGUE

Reflecting back on the trip, we learned many lessons along the way and confirmed many truths we already believed.

Most people are good and kind. They opened their hearts and homes to us freely, offering a place to stay, a cool drink, a hot meal, and a way to share in their lives. Though we never saw most of those wonderful people again, the impression they made on our lives was profound and lasting.

Believe in yourself. Trust your gut and don't let naysayers, doubters, and negative nellies sap your positive energy. The greatest reward is when you take personal pride in your own success and triumphs, especially when you believe in and respect yourself.

Surmounting a challenge is mostly a mind game. Whether you're making an important life decision or scaling a big mountain, don't psych yourself out. Tackle that challenge head on, even if you have to get off your bike and walk up that steep incline. One step at a time. The rewards are plentiful and bragging rights sweet.

Enjoy life—close up. Take the time to savor the minutiae and ignore the big picture for a few moments every day. Immerse yourself in the intricacies of a flower blossom or the silky texture of a baby's cheek. Breathe in life and let it fill your soul.

Life is a journey, not a destination. Ralph Waldo Emerson got that right. On our journey, we lived in the now, staying present and in the moment with our surroundings—traversing the country, taking risks and roads less traveled, celebrating the milestones, and recharging our spirits. Live, love, laugh. We did it all.

Clark and I were great partners. Sure, we had our ups and downs along the way. But, in the end, we knew without a doubt, we were soulmates in this journey called life.

THE RETURN

Now, how to get home! Of course, we never gave that much consideration. Lots of options: fly, bus, bicycle, train, rent a car, hitchhike, or any combination of those. So, in typical Liza/Clark fashion, we decided to celebrate our success first and worry about the return later.

Exploring Portland, Maine, was our top priority. We loved it. Most of our time was spent in the Old Port District, which had a friendly feel, loads of good restaurants, and an active night life. This Portland also had the familiar rain—we were very much at home with the wet.

After a few days of debauchery, we settled in to make our choice. Flying was too fast: After moving at our slow pace for months it would seem shocking to get home so quickly. And bicycling all the way back was unrealistic—out of time and money! We gave serious consideration to hitchhiking … surely there were more wonderful people to meet. Long-haul truckers, for example, might enjoy having a bit of company for a few hundred miles. We could always hop back on our bikes if we got ourselves in a sticky situation or felt like stretching our legs.

Ultimately, the romance of the train called our names. We had to catch a bus from Portland to Boston to pick up the train heading west. We also had the option to get on and off at several locations for the same price. It gave us some flexibility and the chance to check out a few towns along the route. We would get off for 24 hours and then back on when the train came through the following day.

With the travel plan in place, we spent the afternoon boxing up our bikes and stuffing in the tent, sleeping bags, biking shoes, and other gear to send home via UPS. We kept our rear panniers with a change of clothes, books, and a few other travel items. When we finally dropped the bikes off, it felt like saying goodbye to old friends.

The following morning, we hopped a bus to Boston and with only an hour layover got on Amtrak's Lakeshore Limited to Chicago, then switched to the Empire Builder for the rest of the way. We relaxed the moment we boarded and found a place to sit. The train wasn't crowded. We had our own row of seats for most of the ride, plus we enjoyed the dining car, snack bar, and observation deck. The big windows allowed us to see the passing countryside. Amtrak travels along beautiful routes through the woods, paralleling waterways, and over mountains. Small towns went rolling past, and the seasons were marked by the greenery of summer turning into the many shades of fall.

We were lucky to travel past some of the very same places we biked through a few months earlier. Clark spotted the bike path in Sparta, Wisconsin, where we remembered racing the train on a sunny day. We also passed a campground where we spent a magical evening watching the fog roll in. We held hands and traveled backward in time as the memories came flooding forward.

Some of our happiest moments were listening to the clickety-clack sound of the train's movement and the whistle that followed us on our journey—both on the bicycle trip and in life.

Inside the train, the whistle sounded distant and muffled. The sound felt like a metaphor. Our wonderful summer together was getting further away and already seemed a bit like a dream. Train whistles carried us back to the days when we first met and were newly in love. We'd lie in bed, gazing at the moon and listening to the distant sound of trains passing in the night.

Over the next five days, we played and replayed the bike journey in our heads as we watched the scenery and memories of our trip float past.

We got off the train twice—in Wynona, Minnesota, and in Whitefish, Montana—to get our legs back on solid ground and a good night's sleep. Whitefish made the list of places we considered moving to.

On the last leg of our journey, through Glacier National Park, we pressed our noses against the windows and enjoyed the spectacular scenery. Snow gathering on the mountains reminded us that we finished our trip just in time. The train moved slowly ... cracking, straining, and popping as it pulled up the mountain passes, using all its energy. We looked out the windows, until darkness took the views away.

When the morning light streamed in, we were in the Columbia River Gorge. Almost home. As the sun danced across the water and the walls of the gorge presented themselves, we looked at each other and said, "We could live here." But wait ... we DO!

I guess Dorothy was right ... there really is no place like home.

Our Route - Portland, OR to Portland, ME

THE AUTHOR

Liza McQuade was born in Sheboygan, Wisconsin—a "Leave It to Beaver" type city along the shores of Lake Michigan.

Communication of all forms is her passion. McQuade worked in the radio, TV, and film industries for over 30 years, as a news anchor, reporter, producer, writer, public affairs/service director, senior project manager, and location scout. She received numerous awards, including the California Governor's Commendation for a documentary on illiteracy, and won an Associated Press award for breaking the "Women in the Box" story. She is a trained mediator and led the Oregon Mediation Association as the Executive Director. She loves to share the benefits of talking it out versus duking it out.

McQuade has always been a spontaneous, free-spirit adventurer. Instead of getting a real job out of college, she backpacked the Appalachian Trail with minimal experience as a hiker. She completed the Portland marathon at age 50 (a bucket list item). She didn't win but finished in relatively good shape, except for a monster blister.

She's traveled extensively, including Argentina, Belize, China, Guatemala, Mexico, New Zealand, Russia, all over Europe, Canada, and every corner of the United States.

She makes it a point to stay in local hotels or with families to make the experience richer. She spent a month living with two different families in Russia, shot a five-part television series in New Zealand, and, while in Guatemala, accepted a 50-mile car ride from some locals, joining six other people, two dogs, and three chickens. Out of college, she spent three winters as a ski host in Jackson Hole, Wyoming, moving there on the spur of the moment without knowing anyone, having a job, or a place to live. She contends these last-minute adventures have been some of the best in her life.

As a kid, she lived in Harpenden, Hertfordshire, England, outside of London, for a summer. She stayed with relatives, played with the neighbor kids, and experienced the sting of nettles for the first time. This did not dissuade her from further travel.

McQuade loves people from all walks of life. She's been compared to a black lab, who runs around with a ball meeting new people and seeing who wants to play. At the time of publishing, she has two stepchildren and three grandkids.

McQuade and her late husband, Clark Campbell, trained for their cross-country bike ride by eating in dozens of restaurants, pairing the meals with amazing wine, and discussing how they were going to get in shape … tomorrow! She's currently learning to cook and has finally managed to make a few edible dishes. She resides in Portland, Oregon.

To Reach the Author: lizamcq@yahoo.com

Lightning Source UK Ltd.
Milton Keynes UK
UKHW020615280922
409568UK00007B/615